IN COMMAND

IN COMMAND

Theodore Roosevelt and the American Military

MATTHEW OYOS

Potomac Books

AN IMPRINT OF THE UNIVERSITY OF NEBRASKA PRESS

Library of Congress Control Number: 2017044999

Set in New Baskerville ITC Pro by E. Cuddy.

CONTENTS

Acknowledgments ix

Introduction 1
1. Beginnings 15
2. In the Arena 43
3. The New Hand on the Helm 98
4. Arms and the Men 145
5. The Institutions of Command 188
6. In the Fullness of It All 231
7. Battles without Blood 261
8. Looking beyond the White House 302
9. The Last Crusade 337
Conclusion 364

Notes 373
Bibliography 413
Index 427

ILLUSTRATIONS

Following page 220
1. Theodore Roosevelt at the Naval War College
2. Maj. Gen. William Shafter
3. Roosevelt and the Rough Riders
4. Cdr. William S. Sims
5. Capt. John J. Pershing
6. Theodore Roosevelt on horseback
7. The submarine *Plunger*
8. Orville Wright and the Wright Flyer
9. USS *Louisiana*
10. USS *North Dakota*
11. The world cruise departs Hampton Roads
12. The world cruise returns
13. Theodore Roosevelt and Leonard Wood

ACKNOWLEDGMENTS

I owe a debt of gratitude to the many individuals and institutions that made this project possible. It is appropriate to thank Allan R. Millett first, as he suggested the writing of this book. Peter Maslowski was another mentor who helped to set me on this path, and Richard Kohn applied his critical eye to my work. Over the years friends and colleagues have shared their time and insights, and I would especially like to acknowledge Mark Grimsley, Mark Thompson, and William Prestowitz for their intellectual insights and companionship. Jonathan Mertz warrants a special word of thanks for his hospitality toward an itinerant scholar and his interest in all things Theodore Roosevelt.

The professional archivists and librarians at the Ohio State University Library, the Library of Congress, the National Archives, Harvard University, the University of North Carolina, and Radford University deserve much praise for their expert assistance. At Radford University, the College of Humanities and Behavioral Sciences and the Department of History provided crucial travel support, a semester's sabbatical, and other assistance. Students over the years have served as a sounding board for ideas, but I would particularly like to single out Christopher Smith for his assistance on this project. Tom Swanson, Sabrina Stellrecht, and the other staff at the University of Nebraska Press provided many helpful suggestions in the development of this work.

Finally, I want to thank my family. My parents, Lynwood Oyos and Bedia Shaheen Oyos, instilled in me a love of learning, and family travels exposed me to the rich historical landscapes of North America and Europe. One such journey took me through the North Dakota Badlands and inspired me to learn more about Theodore Roosevelt. The support of my mother-in-law, Mary Lou Wilkey, must be remembered, but I owe the most to my wife, Cindy Wilkey, and my children, Gillian and Hayden. Despite having to share me with Theodore Roosevelt for many years, they offered only love, patience, and encouragement.

Introduction

It was a scene worthy of an artist's brush. The day began cloudless, with palm trees in bold relief against the azure sky. Lofty peaks provided a striking backdrop. It was also a day of battle, 1 July 1898. An American army expeditionary force readied to assault Spanish positions around Santiago de Cuba, where a Spanish naval squadron sheltered. Although unknown to the troops at the time, the attack represented one of the last acts in the war to wrest Cuba from Spanish control. Nothing seemed to go right for the Americans in the hours before the battle. Units had trouble finding their positions, and Spaniards poured deadly fire down from the San Juan Heights, which the Americans had to take if they were to reach Santiago. The tropical temperature grew stifling, as the original jump-off time of 10:00 a.m. passed without orders to charge. Finally, at about 1:00 p.m. the Americans began the attack. Before the day was done, 205 Americans died and 1,180 more were wounded. The Spaniards, the defenders, lost fewer, with 215 killed and 376 more wounded.[1] And on that same day, one man became a national hero.

Theodore Roosevelt lived what he called his "crowded hour" on 1 July 1898.[2] That day Roosevelt led the Rough Riders, or, formally, the First U.S. Volunteer Cavalry Regiment. This unit, composed of rugged westerners and eastern elites, had already captured national attention. Now the man recently elevated to command of the regiment was engaged in a battle that would represent the pivotal moment of his personal and political life.

When the American charge began, Roosevelt rode, the only Rough Rider who was mounted, until he encountered a wire fence, and then he continued to lead his troops on foot. Earlier that day shrapnel from Spanish artillery had bruised his wrist, and during the charge a bullet nicked his elbow, but even as others fell around him, Roosevelt reached the crest of the first height, Kettle Hill, unscathed. Then, after a pause to provide supporting fire for the troops assaulting San Juan Hill, Roosevelt charged again—and nearly alone. In the heat of the action, most of his men did not hear the order, for "after running about a hundred yards I found I had only five men along with me." A furious Roosevelt stormed back to the American lines, rallied his troops, and led them across the valley between Kettle and San Juan Hills. By the time he reached the top of San Juan Hill, most of the Spaniards had fled. Roosevelt claimed he shot one of the remaining defenders with a revolver salvaged from the sunken battleship *Maine*.[3] With that, American forces had swept the heights outside Santiago.

As he recovered from the exertion of battle, Theodore Roosevelt was a happy man. He had just proved many things to himself and, he believed, to others. During much of the 1890s, he had preached "jingo doctrines" about the political, economic, and cultural benefits of war, and when the war with Spain erupted, he proclaimed that "a man's usefulness depends upon his living up to his ideals in so far as he can." He could not "stay comfortably in offices at home and let others carry on the war."[4] Roosevelt had kept his part of the civic bargain by volunteering for the army and, by so doing, insulated himself against charges of hypocrisy. If he survived the conflict, then he would survive with his political standing intact, if not strengthened.

Roosevelt's determination to serve, however, stemmed from something far more profound than merely a wish to advance his political fortunes. He wanted to repay a historical debt, affirm his own sense of moral worth, and supply a legacy for the

Roosevelt family line. Roosevelt's father, Theodore Senior, had failed to fight in the Civil War, even though he was in his physical prime and a strong Lincoln Republican. The elder Roosevelt, "Thee," had married a southerner, Martha Bulloch, and, rather than risk a conflict in the Roosevelt home, had avoided service in the Union army. He instead hired two substitutes to take his place. Theodore Junior lionized Thee—after all, he called his father "the best man I ever knew"—but, although he never admitted it, this blemish on his father's record must have caused him shame.[5] His feverish efforts to get into the fight suggested his determination to erase this memory and prove the fighting qualities of Roosevelt men. He wanted to demonstrate his manliness, and that of his family line, not only to himself but also to a larger public in an era when perceptions of manhood were closely tied to concepts of individual and national vitality.[6] Thus, having withstood heavy fire, Roosevelt was convinced that he had passed the ultimate test in life and showed that he had a moral core made of the sternest stuff. He was a man who could thrive on danger and the gore of warfare. Soon after the fighting, even amid hardship, he boasted, "I am as strong as a bull moose." Perhaps even more gratifying to him as he surveyed the scenery from atop the San Juan Heights was the belief that he had done something that would cause his name to be honored, something like the heroes of classical mythology or medieval legend. He confided to his friend Henry Cabot Lodge that "at least I feel that I have done something which enables me to leave a name to the children of which they can rightly be proud."[7]

The fighting exhilarated Roosevelt and also promised political opportunity. At the crest of the San Juan Heights beckoned both martial glory and high political office. The governorship of New York was the immediate prize, and it lay within reach. Scandals had discredited the current Republican governor, and Roosevelt, as biographer Edmund Morris has described him, was now the "most famous man in America." Roosevelt mustered out of the army and jumped into the gubernatorial race barely over a month after leaving Cuba in August 1898. The race was close. Roosevelt would win by 17,794 votes, but this victory set him on the path to even higher office. First came the vice presidency and then the presidency after anarchist Leon Czolgosz shot William McKinley in September 1901.[8]

If Roosevelt's experience in the war with Spain represented the making moment of his national political career, then it also was decisive in molding his approach to military affairs. Together, Roosevelt's year as assistant secretary of the navy in 1897–98, when he prepared for possible hostilities against Spain, and his time as a Rough Rider formed thereafter the common reference point for his involvement with the military. His exploits during 1897 and 1898 confirmed for him many of his prewar ideas and provided him with the experience—he already possessed the confidence—to become one of the most, if not *the* most, active commanders in chief in the peacetime history of the American republic.

Books about presidents as commanders in chief invariably examine wartime administrations.[9] Roosevelt did not preside over a war with a major power, although he did inherit the pacification campaign in the Philippines. Fought at a distance, the Philippine conflict would primarily test his ability to manage a scandal, after charges of American atrocities against the Filipinos emerged early in his presidency. If war were to come with a great power, Roosevelt felt that he could perform as well, if not better, than some of his predecessors. He certainly believed that he could do better than one of his successors, Woodrow Wilson. He reserved a special venom for the former Princeton University president, especially when Wilson did not address forcefully enough, in his opinion, trouble on the Mexican border or the depredations of German submarines on the high seas. Wilson, he wrote in June 1917, shortly after American entry into World War I, "is merely a rhetorician, vindictive and yet not physically brave; . . . he can not help believing that, in as much as sonorous platitudes in certain crises win vote[s] they can in other crises win battles."[10]

Although Roosevelt did not have a war to conduct like Wilson, he nonetheless left an indelible imprint on the American military establishment. From 1899, when he became governor of New York, to 1909, when he departed the presidency, Roosevelt worked on a long military "to do" list. For the navy, among other things, he expanded the number of ships, reorganized the fleet, promoted submarine development, orchestrated fleet reviews, pushed administrative reform, decided on an international base system, reviewed the role of the Marine Corps, and supported the fundamental redesign of battleships. The army list included the creation of a general staff, new institutions of officer education, an overhaul of the promotion system, militia reform, and aviation experiments. Roosevelt did not accomplish all that he set out to do, but during his presidency he cemented the foundation of a thoroughly modern military establishment.

When it came to things military, Roosevelt seemed to be everywhere. He loved to clamber around warships, hike through the local woods with officers, view gunnery practices, inspect the latest army gear, negotiate with Congress for larger forces, and insert himself into myriad other activities both big and small. This image of Roosevelt lends itself to the iconic view of him, much of it self-created, as a many-sided man, with all cylinders working at top speed. Much truth, however, resided in the imagery. Roosevelt cared passionately about the American military, and not just because the navy and army were crucial to protecting the American homeland and overseas interests. As national institutions, the armed forces represented the vitality of American foreign policy and, in Roosevelt's mind, expressed as well the vigor of the American people as a whole. Still, even in the realm of military affairs, there were limits to Roosevelt's passion. In campaigns to overhaul the administrative machinery of the War and Navy Departments he was notably absent. He also held the Marine Corps in contempt and had little use for the National Guard, the nation's first reserve. Both of those services ran afoul of Roosevelt's deep self-righteous streak and, worse, appeared in his mind to be obstacles to his overall goals for the military and the nation.

Biographers such as Kathleen Dalton and H. W. Brands have portrayed Theodore Roosevelt as a crusader or a romantic figure. Such descriptions relay well the essence of the man and provide an avenue for understanding the complexity of his intellect and his actions. As Dalton writes, he not only saw himself as a heroic figure but also sought to stamp "a whole people with the mark of Galahad."[11] Nowhere in Roosevelt's life was this truer than in military affairs. He was, as Brands writes, obsessed with soldiering, but he wanted to ensure that the same qualities that had inspired him, and that he witnessed among many others in the army and navy, were imprinted on a fast-changing society.[12] Physical hardiness, dedication, public spiritedness, honor, and courage were just some of the attributes that Roosevelt believed—and he was not alone in this belief—had allowed America to become a great nation, bestriding a continent and ready now to leave a larger mark on the world. He feared, however, that in a nation of burgeoning cities, expanding wealth, and a swelling immigrant tide these virtues would be lost. He dreaded an insidious rot that would weaken the nation from within and divert it from an even greater destiny in the twentieth century. Much of his public life represented a crusade to save Americans from their worst instincts, and he saw the military services as prime vehicles for keeping the United States on the noblest of paths. The army and navy would allow the American nation to participate with some safety in imperial struggles, and participation in those contests would help preserve the national moral fiber.

In other words, Roosevelt's definition of national defense stretched beyond the traditional calculus of numbers of troops, training, equipment, and organization. For him a cultural construct was involved that represented a key part of the social contract. The armed forces were more than instruments for maintaining American safety even as the country assumed new international duties; their members were literally to embody the best in civic virtues and serve as inspiring paragons for the rest of the nation. Thus, on a variety of levels, Roosevelt saw the army and navy as vital to the continued greatness of the United States. Roosevelt spelled out this connection between military service and moral living in June 1897 when he instructed naval officers: "The fight well fought, the life honorably lived, the death bravely met—these count for more in building a high and fine type of temper in a nation than any possible success in the stock market."[13] He wanted a nation of heroes led by men, such as himself, who were willing to perform heroic work on and off the field of battle.

This system of thought, in which Roosevelt laced together traditional military matters and foreign policy interests with the intellectual threads and cultural concerns of the late nineteenth century, revealed the complexity of the man's thinking. Indeed, upon entering the presidency, he stood almost uniquely prepared to weave together sometimes disparate elements regarding the national well-being and present them as a coherent system of policies, practices, and intellectual objectives. Although sometimes his contemporaries derided him as insane for his bold pronouncements or bursts of frenetic activity, his mind was first-rate.[14] Coming from a prominent New York City family, he had the benefit—despite a sickly youth—of private tutors, travels abroad, a Harvard College education, and encounters with the leading intellectual, business, and political lights of the day. By the time he was twenty-four, he was a respected author, and by the time he was president he had written ten books. Even as president, Roosevelt was famous for devouring one book, and sometimes two, every evening. He could also speak three foreign languages and had at least reading knowledge of four other tongues.[15] He was, as David Burton has written, one of the learned presidents.[16] That perspective of Roosevelt gets lost in the enduring popular image of the Rough Rider, the cowboy, the hunter, the inspiration for the teddy bear, and the irrepressible president who proclaimed "bully!" and really seemed to be having a wonderful time.

In advancing his agenda for the military, Roosevelt tapped many of the broader currents coursing through America at the turn of the twentieth century. Carl Sandburg's 1914 description of Chicago as the "City of the Big Shoulders" seemed an apt projection on the country at that time. The United States had progressed from a thin strip of barely unified states hugging the Atlantic seaboard in the late eighteenth century to an increasingly muscular colossus ready to make its mark on the world. Theodore Roosevelt's America contained nearly seventy-five million inhabitants in 1900 and could claim over a half million manufacturing establishments of various sizes. Most of the population still made a living from the land, but that reality was changing fast. Urban centers exploded with growth and brought the attendant problems of overcrowding, poverty, crime, and disease. To manage the complexities of far-flung business operations, new bureaucracies and management systems were developed. "Rationalization" became a watchword of the day, as an organizational society emerged. Governmental officials faced increasing difficulty handling local, state, and national affairs, and thus the administrative state came into being.[17] The spirit of reform was abroad in the land as progressive reformers sought not only to make government more responsive and efficient but also to advance other social and political agendas such as city beautification, slum improvements, prohibition of alcohol, and woman suffrage. After all, the progressive movement seemed to be as much about instilling, or preserving, a proper character as it was about installing modern systems of management and government.

Roosevelt's presidency promoted progressive causes, and his reform initiatives addressed a range of issues. He sought to assert governmental authority over business trusts, conserve natural resources, promote efficiency in government, and even reform the American system of spelling. Just as in other parts of American society, this tide of reforms swept into the War and Navy Departments. Proposals included an overhaul of army and navy administrative systems, improvements to military education, and the adoption of merit-based promotions for officers.

Other influences affected Roosevelt's thinking and actions. He reflected some of the main intellectual currents of the day. His concern for the fitness and continued greatness of the American people demonstrated social Darwinian influences, although he put little stock into the idea of competition as the primary engine of societal change.[18] As a gentleman scholar, Roosevelt showed greater interest in the ideas of historian Frederick Jackson Turner. Roosevelt admired Turner's writings on the frontier, for if there was one factor that explained for him what made the American people great, it was the frontier. He wrote to Turner in 1894, after reading Turner's essay, "The Significance of the Frontier in American History," and told him, "you have struck some first class ideas."[19] His studies of the frontier, along with his own experiences in the West, confirmed for him the "frontier virtues" of courage, honor, duty, and physical endurance that he wanted to preserve in the twentieth century within the army and navy officer corps and also in the larger American society. It was, in part, out of concern for the erosion of such virtues with the end of the western frontier that he called for an expansive foreign policy. And these ideas regarding frontier attributes tied directly to his ideas of strenuous manly living.

Roosevelt also reached back further in the nation's past for inspiration. His ideas regarding civic virtue, for example, echoed not just the manly ethic of his own day but also the thinking of the country's founders. Much like the American revolutionaries, he envisioned America as a "Christian Sparta," a land of austere, public-spirited, and heroic people who were not distracted or dissipated by an undue pursuit of wealth.[20] The founders had drunk deeply from the well of classical Greek and Roman experience, and Roosevelt, himself exposed to a classical education, wanted to perpetuate this ideal in the twentieth century.

The impact of the early American republic on his thinking did not end there. His ideas about constitutional prerogatives and governmental powers lay anchored in this period. In a historical sense, Roosevelt injected himself into the dispute between Alexander Hamilton and Thomas Jefferson over the future course of the American government, economy, and society. Hamilton triumphed with him in every way. He embraced Hamilton's vision of a vigorous national government and openly despised Thomas Jefferson's strict-constructionist approach as impractical, inefficient, and counterproductive. In fact, he maintained a nearly bottomless reservoir of contempt for the third president. One 1896 blast contended that "Jefferson's influence upon the United States as a whole was very distinctly evil," in reference to Jefferson's small government attitudes.[21] If good people were going to be able to do good works, then, Roosevelt believed, they had to have the powers to do so. Such thinking was the basis for his vigorous approach to the presidency, as well as many of the other offices that he held. His work on behalf of the military thus represents one expression of his efforts to maximize federal authority as a steward of the American people's best interests.

Among all the influences at work on the twenty-sixth president, especially in his conduct of military affairs, two strains emerge that made Roosevelt the embodiment of the contradictions within progressivism. One part of him stood for modernization, as he pushed projects to give the military services the latest in technology, training, education, and administration. The other part of Roosevelt worked to preserve the values of an older, more traditional America in an increasingly collective and impersonal society. Born in 1858, he was, after all, literally a child of the era right before the industrial revolution reached full throttle. Thus, just like many of his progressive contemporaries, Roosevelt could be pictured as something like the Roman god Janus, with one face looking forward and the other looking back. In military matters, this dualistic perspective worked best for Roosevelt during that crucial period of the late 1890s, when so many of his basic martial conceptions were cemented. The further he got from that crucial period, the quainter some of his ideas for military policy would become.

So how best, then, to think of this complex man and his multifaceted work in military affairs? Like any prominent political figure, he was many things to many people. Some praised him as a force for innovation and reform. Others saw him as an upstart who had not really paid his dues. Yet others recognized his public relations genius as useful for advancing their own projects. Still more found him to be an irritating dilettante. To be sure, Roosevelt stirred up more than one military controversy, sometimes intentionally and sometimes unintentionally. And despite the fact that he was a great friend to the military services, many officers did not like his methods and found him to be an unwelcome, disruptive presence. A measure of truth lay behind all these perceptions. Thus, the problem remains of how to sum up his many levels of involvement. Perhaps the best way is to view him as the man leading the charge, the catalyzer of action. Roosevelt was not particularly innovative himself, but he could recognize innovative ideas and wanted to make things happen. He would promote the ideas of others or, more often, attempt to put spirited, intelligent people in positions of authority so that they could act on their ideas. Roosevelt liked to surround himself with promising individuals, and he used his talent for publicity to push them to the fore. As a result, during his presidency he would advance a number of men to higher commands who later proved their worth during World War I. Not surprisingly, the individuals he pushed forward mirrored himself: younger, active, forceful, and, above all, dedicated to the call of their country. These men bore more than a passing resemblance to those that he had led up the San Juan Heights in 1898.

Somehow imagery of the Rough Rider seems too pat, too simple, and too much of a concession to common culture for assessing Roosevelt's myriad involvements with military matters over a busy lifetime. Indeed, the enduring popular image of Roosevelt the Rough Rider masks the multidimensional nature of the man and his deeds and, in many ways, has made him instead into a brand name. Schools named after the twenty-sixth president invariably field athletic teams named "The Rough Riders." In addition, one product marketed to commemorate the centennial of the teddy bear dressed the furry creation in a cavalry costume and, much less tastefully, a brand of condoms has even used the Rough Rider label.

Yet the hard-charging Rough Rider bears powerful explanatory power when it comes to Roosevelt and the American military. It symbolizes his romanticized conceptions of military life before, during, and after his triumphant moment in 1898. War, after all, frequently affected his life, whether the conflict was the Civil War of his childhood, the Spanish-American War of his prime, or World War I of his declining years. The Rough Rider also represents Roosevelt's ideal of noble service for a higher cause that led him to push so hard for his goals, whether it was an officer's commission in the war with Spain or military reform and modernization when he was president. In addition, the Rough Rider helps explain why Roosevelt would work harder for certain military policies and not others. If a particular proposal, such as a naval general staff or National Guard reform, did not fit into his particular military experience, then it received relatively little attention from him. Finally, within the Rough Rider also lays the tragedy of Theodore Roosevelt. During World War I he hoped to relive the glories of 1898, only to find he was out of step with the military realities of total industrialized war. His martial spirit, however, would inspire his four sons to fight in that war, and, when one died, the death brought home to him the true costs of battle.

The following chapters examine Roosevelt's varied involvements with things military, from his boyhood to his death in January 1919. The study, though, focuses on the period from 1897, when he became assistant secretary of the navy, to 1909, when he departed the presidency. During that time he had the greatest involvement with the American military and made the greatest impact on the armed services. This particular exploration devotes relatively little attention to Roosevelt's use of the military services in support of his diplomacy, except in cases where a deployment had an impact on American military policy itself. Roosevelt's actions in episodes such as the Panamanian revolution or the intervention in Santo Domingo have already received thorough coverage in other works. Rather, this study probes Roosevelt's efforts to reshape the American military establishment itself. Although he never achieved all that he set out to do and experienced setbacks—some of his own making—he accomplished much, and the American military was far different when he left the scene than when he first encountered it. The sum of his labors would make him one of the most important commanders in chief in American history.

1

Beginnings

On 22 September 1901 Theodore Roosevelt spent his first day in the White House after William McKinley's assassination. He worked signing papers that day. Roosevelt, however, did not work alone. He felt the presence of a man long dead, his father, the man for whom he was named, Theodore Roosevelt Sr. The younger Roosevelt, now president of the United States, took comfort from the feeling and confessed that evening to his sisters, "I feel as if my father's hand were on my shoulder, and as if there were a special blessing over the life I am to lead here."[1]

Theodore Roosevelt Sr. had died in 1878 at age forty-six from an intestinal tumor. Alive or dead, he loomed over his son's life. From the elder Roosevelt stemmed many of T.R.'s dominant personality traits and his moral code. In his *Autobiography* Roosevelt praised his father as a man who "combined strength and courage with gentleness, tenderness, and great unselfishness." Theodore Senior, he claimed, refused to tolerate "selfishness or cruelty, idleness, cowardice, or untruthfulness" in his children. He also produced a unique feeling in his son: "He was the only man of whom I was ever really afraid." This paragon was also hardworking in business and a dedicated philanthropist. He aligned himself with the Republican Party and gained a solid reputation as a political reformer. From Theodore Senior, the lines ran directly to his son's elevated sense of righteousness, high moral code, work ethic, devotion to public service, reformist credentials, and Republican partisanship. A physically active man, the elder Roosevelt inspired his son to overcome asthma and other illnesses and embrace strenuous living. Reputedly, when the man whom he idolized told him that he would have to make his body, a young T.R. threw back his head and determined to meet the summons as if it were his first call to arms. Thus, from the name on down, Theodore Roosevelt was his father's son, and his later behavior was, in many ways, a product of his father's example.

Individuals at any given point in their lives represent the sum of many influences. Theodore Roosevelt expressed volumes, sometimes literally, on so many of the intellectual, cultural, political, and racial ideas of the time that he has become a window for scholars to analyze the values of his era.[2] Although understanding the larger forces at work on, or through, a prominent individual can help to make sense of the past, for Roosevelt and the people of his day, the formula was much simpler. They were the heirs of Victorianism, and, for them, character explained people and their behavior. Roosevelt was perceptive enough to recognize that he was the product of the values of his immediate family, and these early personal influences had a profound impact on his later attitudes and actions in military affairs. Such an exploration is useful for comprehending his world as he would have understood it. But the later war hero and commander in chief also embodied, appropriately, a composite of his father's and mother's sides of the family.

Theodore Roosevelt Sr. imparted more than a strict moral code, a devotion to physical activity, and a duty to serve. His work ethic preserved a family fortune made in Manhattan real estate and promised his offspring a comfortable existence and considerable freedom to indulge in leisurely and intellectual pursuits. More important, "Thee" Roosevelt's example through philanthropy taught a lesson that well-intentioned individuals could improve society. The older Roosevelt played significant roles as a financial contributor and advocate in organizations

designed to foster good character. In New York City he promoted the Young Men's Christian Association, and he was so
deeply involved in the Children's Aid Society and the Newsboys' Lodging House that during his deathwatch newsboys
and orphans gathered outside the Roosevelt home.[3] The fact
that Roosevelt Senior kept the family home in New York City
had an equally important influence. City life exposed the Roosevelt children to the leading developments of nineteenth-
century civilization. The technology needed to make a budding
metropolis function perhaps contributed to Theodore Junior's
later fascination with devices of all sorts, and the city's rise as a
media center may help to explain the importance that Roosevelt later placed on the press as a political instrument. Moreover, his father's attention to the other half of society, despite
the Roosevelt fortune, provided an example of how the rich
could make a connection to the poor, which could advance
charity but also serve as a practical political lesson about how
to reach beyond one's social class.

The upright character of Theodore Senior did contain one
major gap, at least as far as his eldest son was concerned. Thee
had failed to answer the call of his country during the Civil
War. In 1861 Roosevelt Senior was twenty-nine, yet he declined
to don a Union uniform out of consideration for his wife and
her southern brothers, who took up the Confederate cause.
A man of conscience, he could not let the two substitutes he
hired be the extent of his service. Rather, shamed, he enlisted
in a home guard cavalry unit to defend New York City, but, of
more consequence, he became an allotment commissioner and
traveled to encampments to convince soldiers to commit part
of their wages for the support of their families.[4] The younger
Theodore never commented on his father's choice. Although
he did not express his feelings, Roosevelt's actions as an adult
were revealing. The bellicose tones, the love of all things military, and his frantic efforts to secure a military position in 1898

all suggest that at some level he was compensating, if not over-compensating, for his father's refusal to fight. In a crisis, Thee, the model of manhood to his son, had used wealth and privilege to evade his masculine duty.

Although much of Theodore Senior lived on in the future president, his mother's southern heritage played a primary role in shaping Roosevelt's affinity for martial affairs. In his *Autobiography* Roosevelt describes his mother as the archetype for the southern belle. "My mother, Martha Bulloch, was a sweet, gracious, beautiful Southern woman, a delightful companion and beloved by everybody. She was entirely 'unreconstructed' to the day of her death."[5] She had grown up in Georgia until swept up by a traveling Theodore Senior, and her ties to the region remained strong during the Civil War. Her brothers, James and Irvine Bulloch, both served the Confederate States Navy, and tales of their exploits—rather than his father's—would thrill a young Theodore. Uncle "Jimmy" had helped to build the commerce raider *Alabama*, which destroyed millions of dollars of Union commerce on the high seas, while Irvine served aboard the vessel and took credit for firing the last shot in the *Alabama*'s final fight with the USS *Kearsarge*. The Bullochs thus provided a romanticized image of war. For a boy insulated from war's reality, the stories of uncles Jimmy and Irvine read like something from the hand of Sir Walter Scott, whose popular volumes romanticized the medieval knight. But no matter the period, for young Theodore Roosevelt war consisted of courageous men performing feats of derring-do amid great danger.

The Bulloch uncles added to their legendary status by remaining in England after 1865. Their involvement with the commerce raider *Alabama* had made them exiles. These Prince Valiants came alive for Theodore during a Roosevelt family tour of the continent in 1869. He met his famous relatives at Liverpool, and although James, the more prominent of the two, talked little of his wartime deeds, the meeting furthered his nephew's association of war with adventure. Standing before him were the objects of the stories of his earliest years. The connection would not end when the Roosevelts returned home, for his uncles would later assist T.R.'s writing on the naval war of 1812.[6]

More than just his uncles, the Civil War itself shaped young Theodore Roosevelt. Born in October 1858, Roosevelt naturally possessed only a child's recognition of the conflict. He would have been six years old when Robert E. Lee surrendered the Army of Northern Virginia in April 1865, so he was likely much older when the full weight of his father's failure to serve hit him. He did demonstrate awareness that a conflict was occurring despite his sheltered existence, and he also sensed the North-South split between his parents. At age three, as Aunt Annie Bulloch tried to fit him with a Zouave's outfit, Roosevelt reportedly beamed as he asked, "Are me a soldier laddie?"[7] Not too much should be read into such boyhood comments to explain Roosevelt's future fascination with war, but as he grew he demonstrated his awareness of the depth of feeling generated by the conflict. Looking back on these early years, he recalled, "Towards the close of the Civil War, although a very small boy, I grew to have partial but alert understanding of the fact that the family were not one in their views about that conflict, . . . and once, when I felt that I had been wronged by maternal discipline during the day, I attempted a partial vengeance by praying with loud fervor for the success of the Union arms, when we all came to say our prayers before my mother in the evening."[8] This episode might have been one of the first times, but certainly not the last, in which he invoked military affairs to make a point. Finally, the Union victory left an impression. In later years he would praise Lincoln's active and resolute leadership and call the sixteenth president "one of the two greatest of all Americans" (Washington being the other).[9] Roosevelt worshiped the idea that the Union sense of moral justice, along with material strength, had led to victory.

His admiration for strength and power grew from another conflict—Roosevelt's struggles with his own body. He may have had the good fortune to be born into one of Manhattan's richest families, but a variety of physical maladies plagued him. He suffered nausea, coughs, fevers, and diarrhea, but asthma afflicted him the worst of all. As a boy, Roosevelt tried to live the active life that his father wished, but crippling attacks often left him confined indoors and sometimes bedridden. His health grew only worse with age, and at twelve he reportedly became so thin and frail that he resembled a stork in appearance.[10] His eyesight weakened at the same time, and he endured the humiliation of relying on his younger brother Elliott for protection from other boys. Ashamed at his helplessness, he answered his father's call to "make" his body with relentless determination.

Roosevelt overcame his boyhood weakness through gymnasium workouts, boxing, hiking, and a host of other physical activities. His asthma never entirely disappeared, but it no longer controlled his life.[11] This physical accomplishment did not occur without affecting his character. He accentuated physical power and appreciated the effect of force on people. The once-scrawny Roosevelt never again yielded to bullying, especially after becoming a formidable lightweight boxer at Harvard. From this experience Roosevelt decided that strength could win respect and freedom from coercion. He would apply this principle on a national level as president when he pushed for military preparedness.

Roosevelt's struggle against physical frailty did encourage a negative quality. He exhibited contempt for people who chose not to develop or display their "muscular" or "primitive" sides. Such an attitude contributed to rhetorical excesses as he pounded the drum for war in the 1890s and later lambasted President Woodrow Wilson over the lack of American preparedness before entry into World War I. In 1896 he disparaged "unintelligent, cowardly chatter for 'peace at any price.'"[12] And in 1915 he assailed Wilson, Secretary of State William Jennings Bryan, and their supporters as "shivering apostles of the gospel of national abjectness" for refusing to embrace military readiness.[13] Such pronouncements still lay ahead for a young Roosevelt as he worked on his physique. By the time he left home and entered college in 1876, he could boast of a fine body.

Becoming His Own Man

On 12 February 1878 a sixteen-carriage funeral train carried the body of Theodore Roosevelt Sr. to the family plot at Greenwood Cemetery in New York City. His nineteen-year-old namesake grieved along with the many New York dignitaries who attended the services.[14] Although he felt the guidance of his father's example for the rest of his days, Theodore Roosevelt was coming into his own even at the time of Thee's death. In the late 1870s Roosevelt attended Harvard College and upon graduation would return to New York City in the early 1880s, where he began to establish a political career. During these years when he started to distinguish himself, he commenced, as well, to expound on national military policy, and he would experience his first taste of military service.

The stories about his seagoing uncles likely informed Roosevelt's choice of a topic for his senior thesis at Harvard. He researched naval actions between the United States and Great Britain during the War of 1812. The subject proved so compelling that he continued on it after graduation and published the manuscript in 1882, two years after he left Harvard. *The Naval War of 1812* represented a remarkable achievement.[15] Roosevelt's careful research and an appreciation for historical interpretation made for an authoritative account of the British and American naval contest. The publication of *The Naval War* led him to consider a career as a historical writer, and, although he never chose history as his vocation, this book launched him on a series of historical projects. Roosevelt had demonstrated not only his competence as a historian with *The Naval War* but also the rapid development of his thought about American military policy. He previewed many of the positions in naval affairs for which he later became well known.

Roosevelt published this first book just at the start of an American naval renaissance. Traditional thinking and tight budgets since the Civil War had dictated reliance on wooden hulls and sails even as the industrial revolution was beginning to transform sea warfare. Innovations in steam propulsion, armor, steel construction, and gun design bypassed the American navy, and European officers reportedly regarded the vessels of their American counterparts as little more than museum pieces.[16] Meanwhile, the iron monitors of the Civil War rusted from disuse and, in any event, were impractical on the open sea because of their low profile. During the presidency of Chester Arthur, Congress authorized four steel-hulled cruisers, which marked the beginning of the "new navy." Roosevelt crafted the preface of *The Naval War* to support naval modernization, and, in the fashion of so many of his coming public pronouncements, he pulled no punches. "At present," he wrote, "people are beginning to realize that it is folly for the great English-speaking Republic to rely for defence upon a navy composed partly of antiquated hulks, and partly of new vessels rather more worthless than the old." In condemning "new vessels," he was not blasting the steel cruiser program but, instead, likely targeting the wooden ships cobbled together for the Civil War or the decaying monitors. The text went on to point out the value of preparedness in securing American victories in single-ship encounters during the War of 1812 and stressed again the need to replace obsolete technology. In his summary Roosevelt also speculated about the impact that a few ships of the line would have had in the contest with Britain, given the generally capable performance of

American frigates and smaller vessels. His observations revealed an appreciation of the power of capital ships and anticipated his later advocacy of a large battleship fleet.[17]

The Naval War of 1812 also demonstrated an awareness of the relationship between world events, American national interests, and military power. Roosevelt showed that he and other Americans had started to contemplate the navy's part in a growing role for the United States in international affairs. Eight years hence these navalists would find their prophet in Capt. Alfred T. Mahan. In *The Influence of Sea Power upon History*, Mahan codified their thoughts into a full-blown geopolitical formula for achieving national greatness through sea power.[18]

Roosevelt's book exposed more than his navalism. It also revealed that he had developed a distinct philosophy of government during his Harvard years. If he had not stood in Alexander Hamilton's camp before he wrote *The Naval War*, then he resided there by the time he published the book. Roosevelt's study of the struggle with Britain convinced him of the importance of a strong central authority, especially to ensure proper military preparedness. In *The Naval War* he took particular aim at Thomas Jefferson's naval policy of small, dispersed gunboats rather than a force of large seagoing vessels. He labeled the gunboats "very worthless" and disparaged the whole scheme as "about on a par with some of that statesman's political and military theories."[19] Already, the historical lessons were clear for Roosevelt: decentralized force led to reverse and humiliation in battle and thus threatened national safety.

At the same time that he published his first book, Roosevelt gained a taste of military life. He joined the National Guard of New York in 1880 and remained a member until 1883. The move was a logical one. Roosevelt had completed his studies at Harvard and married Alice Lee, and he had recently returned to his hometown, determined to make a name for himself. What better way for a politically ambitious young man, with an interest in military matters, to establish a reputation for himself as civic-minded and a community leader than to join a local guard unit? The year after his enlistment, Roosevelt was elected to the New York state legislature.

In those post–Civil War years, the National Guard existed, chiefly, to keep public order. True, militia units lent a colorful splash to parades and other celebrations, but labor strife provided the impetus to organize the first recognizably modern guard units. In the last decades of the nineteenth century, guard units repeatedly suppressed strikes, and thus men of property looked favorably on the institution.[20] Roosevelt feared disorder but offered different reasons for enlisting. He joined the guard, he insisted, because he "did not intend to have to hire somebody else to do my shooting for me."[21] (This statement also might be the closest he ever came to criticizing openly his father's performance during the Civil War.) Roosevelt never fired a shot in anger as a guardsman, and his reasons for joining were likely more high-minded than he stated. He was demonstrating a sense of civic responsibility.

Relatively little is known about Roosevelt's experience in the guard. Befitting a man of his social standing, he became an officer and rose from second lieutenant to captain by the time he left the guard in 1883. He was responsible for Company B of the Eighth Regiment, which numbered no more than forty-seven men. The actual number may have been smaller, for an August 1883 letter, from what is apparently the quartermaster's office, asks Roosevelt to account for a discrepancy in the number of uniforms requisitioned for his unit. "I find you charged . . . 34 State Service Uniforms your company Roster Shows 47 noncommissioned officers & Privates."[22] Whether Roosevelt replied is unknown, for by that time he had already handed over command to another officer and departed the guard.[23] Also unknown was how well the men of Roosevelt's unit accepted him. During this period, as he began attracting attention as a legislator, Roosevelt was frequently ridiculed for his fancy clothes, squeaky voice, and dramatic manner.

If he had any problems with acceptance, then the character-istic energy with which he tackled his duties likely conquered them. One of Roosevelt's talents as a leader was his ability to reach individuals of more humble economic and social back-grounds despite his sheltered upbringing. He recalled nearly twenty years later, when he was governor of New York, how he had introduced the dispersed formations of a skirmish drill to his company when formal parade-ground drilling remained the standard of the day. He also assembled his men often and tried to make the training realistic: "I always used to drill my men as much as I possibly could to handle themselves as if the enemy were present. When they practiced firing drill in the compa-ny's room I would always prop up figures against the wall for them to aim at. I never wanted them to fire simply loose into the atmosphere."[24] The youthful Roosevelt doubtlessly enjoyed arms practice, and he also likely derived pleasure from wear-ing the guard uniform. The dress militia uniforms of that era were often eye-catching. Such garb would have appealed to Roosevelt, with his penchant for dressing like a dandy. The most notable occasion for which he wore the uniform actually occurred after he departed the guard. In July 1885 he dusted off the outfit, rejoined his unit, and marched in the New York City funeral parade for Ulysses S. Grant.[25]

Although he looked proudly back on his time in the guard, Roosevelt's stint in the New York forces was brief for a man who craved action and loved things military. Because the records of this particular episode in Roosevelt's life are scant, one is left to surmise several reasons for his departure from the guard. His personal and political life placed such demands on his time that even the famously energetic Roosevelt might have found guard drills to be an unwelcome distraction. By 1883 he had been elected to a second term in the New York legislature and had published *The Naval War.* He was planning a hunting trip to Dakota Territory, and he and Alice were expecting their first child. Other reasons, however, likely contributed to his decision to leave the guard. After three years he probably found the experience unrewarding, and it planted a distaste for state forces that would manifest itself in later years. He seemed to have concluded that the regular drilling was pointless. In life Roosevelt was always happiest when he could act, but he did not like action without purpose. The guard was not military enough for him, and it did not offer him the validation that he was performing deeds of much consequence in the community or work that might lead him to heroic feats one day. Reflecting on his experience in the New York guard, Roosevelt told an assembly of guardsmen in 1900: "The experience I had had, instead of being a blessing to me, would have been a curse [during the Spanish-American War]. . . . If I had thought it made me a finished soldier it would have been a curse to me; but inasmuch as I had no such idea it was of the greatest possible benefit. I was spared the two or three agonized weeks that some of the best men in my regiment [during the War with Spain] spent learning the drill orders." He concluded with the admonition to "remember how much is done by drill, but do not think the drill begins to be all."[26]

In essence, the guard did not provide him with the soldierly experience, the risk and trial, that he craved. There was something inherently unsatisfying in the repetitive marches of the parade ground, which was probably why Roosevelt had introduced the skirmish drill during his command of Company B. He desired the kind of service that would allow him, and others, to prove their manly virtue in a more trying and primitive environment. At best, in the settled East, he could hope to put down a labor dispute. Roosevelt sought harsher, less civilized ground on which to test his character and physical prowess and learn the soldier's art.

The School of the Frontier

Long before the 1880s "the West" had obtained mythical status. Mention of the West conjured scenes of vast plains, majestic mountains, and land teeming with game. This legendary West offered adventure and opportunity. For young Theodore Roosevelt the West also promised a test. This land was a place where a gentrified easterner could confront man, beast, and nature in their most savage forms. Men in Roosevelt's West had the chance to shed the garments of overcivilization to live the bold and often violent life of the frontier. For a man who dreamed of adventure, and yet had been derided as a fop, the West promised a chance to craft a new image. There he could prove his masculinity and live a life not far different from that of a soldier on a campaign. Finally, he could exorcize the demon of his sickly childhood and claim victory in his quest for health. In June 1884 Roosevelt wrote to his sister Anna that "I have been having a glorious time here, and am well hardened now (I have just come in from spending *thirteen* hours in the saddle)."[27]

Roosevelt plunged into the West for more than just a manly adventure. He wanted to make money. The bonanza era of ranching in the northern Badlands of Dakota Territory was at full height in the 1880s, and Roosevelt invested $80,000 to establish a herd. He also took up ranching to bury his grief after the tragic deaths of his young wife and his mother on the same day in February 1884. Roosevelt's Dakota venture turned out to be short-lived. Ferocious blizzards and relentless cold during the winter of 1886–87 decimated his cattle, and he decided to cut his losses and sell his holdings.[28] Although an economic failure, Dakota proved to be a boon to Roosevelt in other ways. The New York City politician succeeded in creating the image of himself as a cowboy, which helped to quiet ridicule that he was "our own Oscar Wilde" and added to his political appeal.[29] In a more practical political sense, his time in Dakota made him a better politician, for he had to win over rough-hewn westerners to his eastern ways. This period was, perhaps, just as crucial in the formulation of his military thinking. Here he determined many of the basic ideas that he would maintain for the remainder of his life.

Roosevelt left the West impressed with the military qualities that frontier living required of individuals. For him those qualities were straightforward. They exposed one to rugged living and taught practical skills necessary for survival. As Roosevelt put it, "You have got to know how to live in the open, to make your men as comfortable as circumstances will permit, to teach them to take cover and fight in open order, and above all you have got to teach them how to shoot, teach them how to hit; and you must have in them, and in yourself, the fighting edge." He claimed that hunting, in particular, proved valuable in learning such skills and would later recall from his experience in the Spanish-American War that "most of my men were accustomed to shooting game, which of course is a more valuable practice for warfare than shooting at a target because the conditions are more like those of warfare."[30]

Frontier life, in Roosevelt's opinion, supplied a military education that was as good, if not better, than the learning found in military academies. Thereafter, when he searched for leadership qualities in men, he often looked first for frontier experience. As early as 1886, after an incident on the Mexican border, he offered "to try to raise some companies of horse riflemen out here in the event of trouble with Mexico." He believed that the men with whom he lived and worked in Dakota Territory could jump instantly into the role of soldier, declaring, "I think there is some good fighting stuff among these harum-scarum roughriders out here." Later, as he was helping to organize the Rough Riders in San Antonio in May 1898, Roosevelt described the first major of the regiment, Alex Brodie, who was in the regulars, as "dandy" and a "grizzled old frontier soldier."[31] Brodie,

Roosevelt claimed, "had become a thorough Westerner without sinking the West Pointer—a soldier by taste as well as training."[32]

Ranching life imparted other basic lessons. The primitive surroundings of the Badlands taught Roosevelt the necessity of carrying adequate arms.[33] He had moved to territory that was only partially tamed, and on a variety of occasions he resorted to force. Once he knocked senseless a barroom bully with a swift flurry of punches. Another time he leveled a rifle to hold off five Native Americans whom he feared might rob and kill him. Roosevelt also served as a deputy sheriff and helped capture three cattle thieves.[34] Later in life he drew from such experiences to justify a more formidable national military. He projected the frontier environment on to international society and found both to be lawless places. Just as Roosevelt had carried weapons in Dakota, the nation required adequate armaments to ensure respect and security. He put it this way in 1908 during a fight for more battleship authorizations: "Don't hit at all if it can possibly be avoided; but if you do hit, hit as hard as you know how."[35]

The "perfect smashup" of the winter of 1886–87 may have led Roosevelt to jettison his ranch, but for him the future always lay to the east.[36] His western adventure had been important for shaping his image and thinking, but, if he were to achieve greater things, then he would need to seek his destiny in the settled confines of New York and Washington DC. Roosevelt understood this reality, and during the ranching years he returned to New York every winter to write and tend to political matters. He gained a reputation as a loyal Republican by supporting James G. Blaine for president in 1884, in spite of charges of corruption that tainted Blaine. He also became the party's sacrificial lamb in an 1886 campaign for mayor of New York that was hopeless from the start. In 1888 Roosevelt worked hard for Benjamin Harrison in a presidential campaign against incumbent Grover Cleveland. He promoted the Indiana senator as a "clean, able man," and such campaigning brought an appointment to the

U.S. Civil Service Commission after Harrison's victory.[37] Roosevelt served so well on the commission that Democrat Grover Cleveland, whom he had known when Cleveland was governor of New York, retained him after retaking the presidency in 1892. Roosevelt would spend a total of six years in Washington before he returned to New York City in 1895 to become a police commissioner. During these years he honed his political skills, gained administrative experience, and learned firsthand the pressures of the patronage system.[38] His location in New York City and Washington, two national centers of social and political life, did not hurt his prospects either. He would develop personal relationships that proved crucial to his career.

Gregarious, Roosevelt liked the company of many people, but he especially welcomed military officers into his circle. With those who had served in the West, he could swap stories, and they understood hardship and danger. Roosevelt was also drawn to men of intellectual accomplishment who were pushing the military services in more modern directions. In all, he liked to associate with army and navy officers because they personified, literally, the martial qualities that he most prized. They embodied "hardihood, manliness, and courage"; they tempered primitive violent tendencies with reason; and they symbolized loyalty to a higher cause: the protection and glory of the republic.[39] At least they possessed these qualities from the idealized perspective of a civilian outsider who looked admiringly at their lives. The values that these military men represented proved particularly compelling to Roosevelt during this time in his life. Whether he was in New York or at his civil service post in Washington, he witnessed corruption and influence peddling by the "glorified huckster or glorified pawn broker type" on an almost daily basis.[40] In contrast to the civilians with whom he dealt, military officers seemed incorruptible—indeed, the best of citizens. Thus, he often measured himself and others against a military standard.

During Roosevelt's service as a police commissioner in the mid-1890s, his closest ally on the New York City Police Board was a fellow commissioner who had military training. Avery Andrews was a Democrat, but he shared Roosevelt's commitment to rooting out dishonesty in the notoriously corrupt New York police force. Roosevelt praised Andrews for his "high-mindedness, disinterested courage and fidelity to duty," qualities that he might have credited, in part, to Andrews's time as a West Point cadet.[41] Andrews's honorable conduct impressed Roosevelt so much that after the Spanish-American War, in which both men participated, Andrews served as adjutant general of the New York National Guard during Roosevelt's governorship. The Andrews-Roosevelt relationship also led to the first meeting between two men whose lives would intersect again, with important consequences. Avery Andrews had roomed with John J. Pershing at West Point. Andrews had left the service but kept in contact with his friend. He introduced Lieutenant Pershing to Roosevelt one evening. The two men struck up an instant rapport as they traded stories of the frontier. Roosevelt impressed Pershing with his knowledge of frontier life and his admiration for the army's pacification of the West.[42]

Such social encounters delighted Roosevelt, but he also formed relationships with more practical considerations in mind. Francis Vinton Greene became a key contact. Greene first made a name for himself in the army with his account of the Russo-Turkish War of 1877–78. Later, in August 1898, he led the American assault on Manila. Between these wars Greene followed a path taken by many officers in the nineteenth-century peacetime army. He resigned his commission in 1886 and became a businessman in New York, where Roosevelt encountered him. Greene had something to offer Roosevelt, for he had maintained ties to military life, despite his civilian status. He was a general in the New York National Guard.[43] In the late 1890s, as tensions with Spain mounted, Roosevelt anticipated that

Greene would likely lead a New York contingent if war came, and he proposed a volunteer regiment under Greene's leadership. Nothing came of this particular plan—first proposed in September 1897—but the relationship with Greene endured. Greene acquitted himself well in the Philippines during the war with Spain and presided over the surrender of the Spanish army there. After becoming governor of New York, Roosevelt, ready to help a fellow New Yorker, advertised Greene's qualities. He awarded Greene his highest praise as "a born fighter; a born leader" when he recommended in July 1899 that Greene be put in charge of the entire Philippines. After the post of secretary of war opened, Roosevelt pushed Greene for that appointment, which ultimately went to Elihu Root, another New Yorker and Roosevelt family friend.[44]

Roosevelt's friendship with Leonard Wood was, without question, his most significant association with an army officer. From the 1890s through the end of World War I, the lives of Theodore Roosevelt and Leonard Wood were intertwined. This relationship was rewarding to both men and also something of a mutual admiration society. A complete discussion of this important political and military combination, however, is best left to the chapter on the Spanish-American War, for that conflict represented the "making moment" of each man's national career.

The Wood-Roosevelt relationship was special, but in general Roosevelt sought the comradery of naval officers just as much as he did that of army officers. He saw in navy officers the same qualities of fidelity to country, honor, and courage that he found attractive in army officers. Sailors could not make the claim of pacifying the western frontier, but they could point to challenges that were just as daunting. At sea they operated in an environment so hostile and alien that it could never be tamed, and the landscape of international politics in which they operated could be just as trying. Roosevelt's attraction to the brotherhood of naval officers was, perhaps, stronger than his affinity for army officers. He once gushed to his sister Anna, "I have a very strong feeling for the navy; I wish one of my boys could enter it."[45] He saw in the navy the fighting edge of an expansionist foreign policy. Moreover, as the author of *The Naval War of 1812*, he felt an intellectual kinship with navy officers that he did not feel to the same degree with army officers. Theories of sea power, after all, explained best for Roosevelt how the United States could create, and maintain, a destiny for itself as a great world power.

Roosevelt's enthusiasm for the navy, along with his historical work, led to a relationship with one of the navy's most prominent officers, Rear Adm. Stephen B. Luce. An advocate of professional education, Luce possessed an acute intellect. He pushed the creation of the Naval War College and became the school's first president in 1884. The admiral would remain an active influence in naval affairs into the early twentieth century, even though retired by that time.[46] Luce admired *The Naval War of 1812* and informed Roosevelt that War College students would use the book in their studies of that conflict.[47] At Luce's behest, Roosevelt made the first of many trips to the War College in August 1888 to lecture on "The True Conditions of the War of 1812." The association with Luce was long lasting. Roosevelt turned repeatedly to the sage admiral for advice and assistance throughout his years in official life, and Luce looked to Roosevelt for help on various administrative reforms.[48]

During the 1888 lecture trip, Roosevelt met Alfred Mahan. Captain Mahan, by then, was president of the Naval War College and soon to become America's foremost apostle of a big navy. When Mahan published *The Influence of Sea Power upon History* in 1890, the book excited the navalist in Roosevelt to the extreme. Here was a work that spelled out the key role of sea power for forging great nations. Roosevelt was so thrilled that he wrote Mahan in May 1890, "During the last two days I have spent half my time, busy as I am, in reading your book;

and that I found it interesting is shown by the fact that having taken it up I have gone straight through and finished it."[49] If Mahan had known Roosevelt better at the time, he might have expected a more effusive outpouring, but Roosevelt's admission about how he had devoured the work actually represented some of the highest praise he could deliver. His enthusiasm, in fact, led him to publish a review of the book that fall in the *Atlantic Monthly*. There, Roosevelt set the tone at the outset. "Captain Mahan," he argued, "has written distinctively the best and most important, also by far the most interesting, book on naval history . . . on either side of the water for many a long year." Mahan's writings, Roosevelt felt, furnished a vehicle to generate popular support for the kind of naval and foreign policy that he wanted. Thus, he delivered positive reviews of the captain's subsequent books in hopes of promoting a large battleship navy and overseas expansion. Roosevelt labeled *The Influence of Sea Power upon the French Revolution and Empire* "admirable," and *The Life of Nelson* as "the best book that he has yet written."[50] At this stage Roosevelt determined that if Mahan were the prophet of sea power, he would be a disciple spreading the word.

During the 1890s Roosevelt also became Mahan's advocate when he worried that the captain's pen might be stilled. In 1893 Mahan received orders to leave the Naval War College for a sea command. Part of the reason lay in the return to power of the Cleveland administration, which was less friendly to the expansionist tones of Mahan's writings. Mahan's main problem resided in the Navy Department's Bureau of Navigation. The chief of the bureau, Rear Adm. Francis Ramsay, placed little faith in the Naval War College and even less in Mahan's activities, because "naval officers do not write books."[51] Mahan enlisted Roosevelt's assistance in appealing the assignment to Secretary of the Navy Hilary Herbert. The Republican Roosevelt's voice had no effect on Democrat Herbert, and a frustrated Roosevelt wrote Mahan, questioning what "our prize idiots" were doing to the War College by removing the captain from his post.[52] Roosevelt helped again in 1894 when Mahan's squadron commander, Rear Adm. Henry C. Erben, questioned the captain's fitness.[53] From his civil service post in Washington, Roosevelt coordinated the case on Mahan's behalf, and the whole affair soon passed. Later as assistant secretary and then as president, he worked to implement Mahan's theories and continued to exchange ideas with the strategist.

Mahan's involvement with Roosevelt demonstrated that military officers welcomed Roosevelt's friendship for more than camaraderie and his similar outlook. He also represented a political asset. Throughout the nineteenth century, officers courted politicians to advance their careers or to promote favorite projects, and the practice remained alive at the century's end. Men such as Mahan were attracted to Roosevelt because he had obtained influence in the highest governmental circles by the late 1880s. Moreover, he held future promise as a rising figure in the Republican Party. When Luce invited Roosevelt to speak at the Naval War College, he had the well-being of the college in mind. He had heard of Roosevelt's influence with powerful members of the Republican Party and felt his support could help the struggling institution to survive.[54] Mahan also found a booster in the brash, young politician, as would others in the future.[55]

By the mid-1890s Roosevelt's involvement with the navy had moved beyond writing and advocacy. It had become a family affair. Anna, his older sister and confidante, startled Roosevelt when she announced her engagement to Lt. Cdr. William Sheffield Cowles in 1895. Roosevelt and the rest of his family had expected that his sister would not marry after having reached age forty that January, so he wrote that "we were dumbfounded" upon receiving the news. Then he went on to proclaim that he was "so glad it was'n't an Englishman! [She was in London at the time.] And I am glad it *was* a naval officer." After the marriage the brothers-in-law maintained an active correspondence. Roosevelt discussed a variety of topics that ranged from the Venezuelan crisis of 1895 to the armament of American battleships.[56] These exchanges deepened his knowledge of the navy by giving him an officer's perspective and also let him vent about his concern for preparedness in light of several foreign complications during the 1890s. After he became assistant secretary, Roosevelt worked on the behalf of Cowles, who eventually rose to the rank of rear admiral and served as one of Roosevelt's naval aides in the White House.[57]

A Time of Crisis

Roosevelt's dealings with military officers provided a welcome diversion from a crisis that T.R. believed had enveloped the United States by the 1890s. Popular culture would label the 1890s as the "Gay '90s," and there were things to celebrate. Chicago, for example, created a sensation with the great white city that was the World's Columbian Exposition. Acres of colonnaded, white stucco buildings made this world's fair *the* event of 1893. Outside the exposition, however, trouble brewed. Unhappiness with conditions on the farm triggered the political revolt known as populism, and discontent spread to industrial areas after the financial panic of 1893. The economic depression that followed in the panic's wake lasted for years and led to widespread unemployment, labor unrest, and the violent suppression of strikes. Many people, including Theodore Roosevelt, worried that the nation's political, economic, and social fabric was fraying. For Roosevelt, as well, other concerns compounded his sense of anxiety. During the first half of the 1890s, he confronted a family emergency and experienced grave doubts about his political and personal prospects. But by the end of the decade, thanks largely to the war with Spain, he saw a solution to his personal difficulties and to the problems confronting the United States.

The first years of the 1890s were the years of Theodore Roosevelt's discontent. To be sure, he had accomplished much in his life to that point. He had married childhood friend Edith Carow after his first wife's death, and the couple had a growing brood of children. Roosevelt had also added to his list of publications, so that by age thirty-three he had published a total of eight books. Yet he was frustrated. His income from the civil service and writing projects did not cover his family's yearly expenses.[58] In addition, he worried that his public career had hit a dead end. He could take pride that he had gone "into the actual battles of the political world," but his work as a New York state assemblyman, mayoral candidate, and civil service commissioner— all commendable—did not seem enough.[59] Roosevelt wanted to do bigger things; in fact, he felt he was destined to do great deeds. He doubted, however, whether he would have the chance to make a major impact. Roosevelt confessed to his friend Maria Longworth Storer his fear that his work on behalf of honest government may have alienated too many powerful people for him to go further in politics.[60] He conveyed a sense of helplessness when he wrote Storer in 1895: "After I have done my work here there will come a period in which I shall be whirled off into some eddy, and shall see the current sweep on, even if it sweeps in the right direction, without me."[61]

Even as Roosevelt wrote, luck had broken his way. In 1895 he won an appointment to the New York City Police Board. Newly elected mayor William Lafayette Strong wanted someone with a reformer's credentials to help clean up a police department notorious for corruption. The appointment seemed to be Roosevelt's ticket out of the obscurity of the Civil Service Commission. Although he was only one of four commissioners—Avery Andrews being another—Roosevelt possessed the strongest personality and soon became president of the board. Being addressed as "President Roosevelt" must have been very gratifying to him, and Roosevelt took full advantage of his new prominence. He knew how to attract attention, especially having returned to his hometown and one of the media centers of the country. Roosevelt would prowl the streets on "midnight rambles" to observe if officers were making their rounds. Thinly disguised, with his hat pulled low and his coat collar pushed high, Roosevelt would frequently undertake these forays with a member of the press in tow to ensure maximum publicity for the anticorruption crusade. These glory days were short-lived. His decision to enforce a Sunday closing law on saloons dented his popularity, especially in ethnic neighborhoods. Roosevelt determined to endure the controversy, but he could not counter the tactics of Andrew Parker, the other Democratic member of the police board along with Andrews. Parker may have acted for political reasons or because he resented Roosevelt's grandstanding, but whatever the purpose he took advantage of the police board's rule requiring unanimous votes in order to obstruct further reform work. Thus, soon again, Roosevelt found himself frustrated.

Roosevelt's worries over his younger brother Elliott could not have helped his mood. In their childhood Elliott had been the more physically robust of the two Roosevelt boys, and his older brother's defender. Elliott, however, also suffered from health problems. Seizures led to fainting and even delirium.[62] A much more serious problem plagued Elliott by the early 1890s. He had become an alcoholic. His behavior threatened to sully the family name when a servant girl charged him with fathering her child, and he consorted with still other women outside of his marriage.[63] Elliott also behaved erratically in public while intoxicated. In July 1894 Theodore relayed to sister Anna how their brother was recuperating from "a serious fall; while drunk he drove into a lamp post and went out on his head." Roosevelt had reached the point, after years of seeing his brother in sanitariums, where he felt nothing could be done. As he wrote Anna, "He [Elliott] can't be helped, and he must simply be let go his own gait."[64] The end lay near for Elliott. He died on 14 August 1894.[65]

So what, if anything, did Elliott's scandals have to do with Theodore Roosevelt's public life, beyond efforts to hide the younger Roosevelt's indiscretions? Theodore could easily project his brother's descent on to the United States. Like himself, Elliott was born of privilege but, unlike Theodore, had chosen to spend his life in pursuit of pleasure. Roosevelt worried that the United States, bursting with potential despite the depression, could fall into the same trap, especially with the frontier now gone. Put another way, Elliott's degradation symbolized a larger moral crisis facing the country. Having grown rich and increasingly powerful, Americans, in Roosevelt's mind, faced a choice. They could try to do good, hard work in the larger world and thereby accrue the moral benefits that such work would bring, or they could hunker down within the continental domain, become self-satisfied, and indulge in the pursuit of luxury. If Americans chose the first path—the path of imperial duty—he felt optimistically that "our nation is that one among all the nations of the earth which holds in its hands the fate of the coming years." However, if Americans chose the latter path, they risked, on a societal scale, the degradation that consumed Elliott. The contrast between the two Roosevelt brothers comes to mind when Theodore wrote of the United States in 1894: "We enjoy exceptional advantages, and are menaced by exceptional dangers; and all signs indicate that we shall either fail greatly or succeed greatly."[66]

Roosevelt reflected the intellectual currents of his day in this thinking. He had imbibed social Darwinism, and although he did not agree with all adaptations of Charles Darwin's thinking, he did believe that some peoples were more "fit" than others in international society. Roosevelt also believed that without vigilance a people could slip into moral, physical, and mental decay. For America he warned darkly, "if we lead soft and easy lives, concerning ourselves with little things only, we shall occupy but an ignoble place in the great world drama of the centuries that are opening."[67] He also assigned blamed to the people who "would bring this country down to the Chinese level." They were the "moneyed and semi-cultivated classes, especially of the Northeast." It was telling that he singled out people in one of the most settled regions of the country. Overcivilization, in his opinion, produced flaccid minds and bodies. At the same time, he was targeting people who came from the same economic and intellectual elite as himself, yet who opposed his muscular rhetoric and his belief that a little bloodshed, from time to time, was good for a nation. He railed frequently at the "mere money-getting American," "the idiot peace-at-any-price individuals," and "the futile sentimentalists."[68] Roosevelt, for example, hurled brickbats at Harvard president Charles Eliot and at Carl Schurz, the Civil War general and politician, for their advocacy of arbitration, rather than war, as a means to resolve international disputes. Their position, Roosevelt charged, "bears its legitimate fruit in producing a flabby, timid type of character, which eats away the great fighting features of our race." And without such qualities in its population, Roosevelt warned, the United States would fall to the level of China or the Ottoman Empire, among the "sick men" of the world.[69] Greatness, he proclaimed, came only through continuous struggle, admonishing that "it is only through strife—righteous strife—righteously conducted, but still strife, that we can expect to win to the higher levels where the victors in the struggle are crowned."[70]

Roosevelt's words almost dripped with blood, and his overheated rhetoric masked the complexity of his thinking. He may have harbored romantic notions about men rushing to battle, but he also acknowledged the reality of modern industrial and urban society. In a review of Brooks Adams's *The Law of Civilization and Decay*, he called the book a "marvel of compressed statement" but went on to take exception to Adams's argument that decay began in a civilization when economic priorities trumped martial considerations, or, in short, "economic man" prevailed over "martial man." Given Roosevelt's rhetoric about "fighting qualities," one might have expected him to side with Adams on this point. Roosevelt's dedication to historical accuracy prevented him from adopting such a stance, and he also felt compelled to acknowledge that a civilization's vitality rested on economic power. To do otherwise would have been to deny the impact of the economic changes that he had witnessed within his own lifetime. Therefore, Roosevelt did not subscribe to the notion that Western civilization would soon end up in the ash can of history because of the rise of industry and commerce. He found evidence that such "military" values as honor, courage, duty, and patriotism still existed in Western civilization. For him, the dilemma lay in how to preserve those virtues in a "great modern State."[71]

The solution, Roosevelt found, came with the recognition that economic man and military man were not mutually exclusive. "There are," he wrote, "great branches of industry which call forth in those that follow them more hardihood, manliness, and courage than any industry in ancient times." He pointed to the railroad industry as an example, and he turned to history for validation. Recently, the Germans had married economic and military success in the creation of the Second Reich. Over a longer period, the English had produced some of their best warriors in the Duke of Marlborough, Adm. Horatio Nelson, and the Duke of Wellington at a time when economic attributes had supposedly overshadowed martial tendencies. The modern state, he therefore observed, could achieve and maintain greatness if it possessed "thronging millions" who earned wages, but, in time of war, could "put into the field armies, composed exclusively of its own citizens."[72] For Roosevelt imperial ventures combined the best of both the economic and martial worlds. Overseas expansion would present economic challenge and opportunity, court the twin risks of danger and death, and breed a sense of larger responsibility and duty that could only strengthen civic virtues and military qualities. For proof, Roosevelt wrote to his friend, the British diplomat Cecil Arthur Spring Rice, "India has done an incalculable amount for the English character."[73]

When Theodore Roosevelt wrote to Spring Rice, it was 1899, and American imperialism had become an accomplished fact. His problem before that time was how to remove the obstacles that barred the way to his own destiny and that of his country. For Roosevelt the frustrations and anxieties of the early and mid-1890s suddenly cleared as the decade neared its close. The path lay open, and Roosevelt sensed that the chance for a greater destiny for himself and his nation had arrived.

2

In the Arena

In the late winter of 1897, Theodore Roosevelt busied himself with a debate. The matter at hand was not serious, for the fate of the letter *u* hung in the balance. Novelist Marion Crawford demanded a continuing pride of place for the *u* in words such as *honour*. The sanctity of the English language versus efficiency and modernization were at issue. Roosevelt argued for discarding the *u* in such words and sought linguistic precedents to use as ammunition. The debate was lighthearted—Roosevelt called it a "futile controversy"—and a welcome diversion from what was really nagging at him: his future.[1] That winter he determined that he could do no more good as a New York police commissioner. He confessed to his sister Anna, "I can not now do so very much more in my present position."[2] He hungered for word from the newly elected McKinley administration. Would he be selected to become the assistant secretary of the navy? Friends who had influence with William McKinley were working hard on his behalf. Maria Storer had helped McKinley out of financial difficulties earlier in the 1890s and pressed Roosevelt's case, as did Henry Cabot Lodge, senator from Massachusetts since 1893.[3] On 6 April the word arrived. Theodore Roosevelt was McKinley's choice for assistant secretary of the navy.[4]

The veil of pessimism lifted only slowly from Roosevelt. After years of wondering about his prospects and family finances, he confessed doubts that he would go further than his new position in the Navy Department. He confided to Anna that the assistant secretary's post "would mean four years work" at least, and to William Mantius, the American consul in Turin, Italy, he wrote, "I am glad to be in a position where I can do work of which I am genuinely fond, but I guess this will be the last position of importance I will ever hold under the government."[5]

Roosevelt could not know at the time that a meteoric rise had started. He had begun not just four years of work but twelve, during which he would be busy indeed, and in increasingly higher office. Those years, from the beginning of his time as assistant secretary to the end of his presidency, marked the years when he would have the most impact on the American military establishment. And much of what he would do during that time lay rooted in his year as assistant secretary of the navy and then the months that followed in 1898, when he served in the Rough Riders and became governor of New York.

During this crucial period, he packed in a variety of valuable experiences. Roosevelt gained familiarity with managing a government bureaucracy, one that tied the military to industry because of the new steel navy. He helped to formulate national military policy, and he gained greater familiarity with both high-ranking and junior officers in his duties at the Navy Department. Roosevelt also worked on war plans and the problems of preparing a force for imminent conflict. His time in the Rough Riders not only furnished the test of battle that he craved but also exposed him to the workings of the army— and its failures—from the perspective of an officer in the field. Finally, Roosevelt's tenure as governor of New York brought him back into close contact with the National Guard, and he would confront, he believed, fundamental flaws with state forces. Altogether, during these last years of the nineteenth century, Roosevelt proved he was a quick study in military affairs, and the experience proved to be excellent preparation for being commander in chief.

The Assistant Secretary

The newly appointed assistant secretary could hardly wait to start his duties in April 1897. President McKinley had nominated him for the job on 6 April, and by 19 April he was in Washington and at his desk in the Navy Department. The doubts and anxieties of recent years finally fell away, once Roosevelt took over his new responsibilities. A temporary separation from his wife and children was hard, but Roosevelt was happy. He had "always taken a great interest in the Navy," and, more important, he could act.[6] Roosevelt was happiest when he could wield power. Moreover, he performed work of national significance in the Navy Department. True, as assistant secretary, he was the second man in the department, but in the American government of that day, when the secretary of the navy was a member of the cabinet, Roosevelt's position contained some prominence in its own right. Moreover, there seemed to be opportunity for him to maneuver within the department, for Secretary of the Navy John D. Long of Massachusetts provided a serene contrast to his eager assistant. Roosevelt, in fact, called Long a "perfect dear," a label he seemed to reserve for older men whom he felt were beyond their physical and mental prime.[7]

For Roosevelt, Long had the gratifying habit of taking frequent trips to his home in Boston, which left the assistant secretary in charge. Within three days after Roosevelt took office, Long departed on such an excursion and made Roosevelt the acting secretary of the navy. The assistant secretary's enthusiasm, and his desire to impress, leaped off the page in a 26 April 1897 letter to President McKinley that detailed ship deployments. Roosevelt noted in detail the capabilities of different vessels for a possible deployment to the eastern Mediterranean. Unrest in the Ottoman Empire might warrant action to protect American interests, but Roosevelt advised against sending a battleship "unless we intend to make a demonstration in force, in which case we should send certainly three or four armored vessels, and not one." In a nod to his subordinate position, Roosevelt also reported his activities to Long that same day.[8]

When not filling the secretary's shoes, Roosevelt assisted Long in the day-to-day business of the navy. The force they oversaw consisted of more than six battleships and sixteen cruisers. Numerous smaller craft, navy yards, coaling stations, the U.S. Marine Corps, and the bureaucracy of the Navy Department all fell under their supervision. Roosevelt found that, among other things, he needed to become quickly familiar with personnel policies, ship design, weaponry, gun targeting, and war planning. Although he had helped manage a major city's police force, the Navy Department represented his first experience with the administration of an organization on a far-flung scale. The experience would acquaint him with some of the problems confronting government at the turn of the twentieth century. The United States was attempting to run an increasingly complex naval force with methods more appropriate to the age of wood and sail. No matter the problem or intensity of the job, Roosevelt reveled in the work. He wrote to Cecil Arthur Spring Rice—"Springie"—on 29 May 1897 and reported, "I have been a month in office now, and I heartily enjoy the work."[9]

The work may have been rewarding, but the Navy Department offered its own set of frustrations. Roosevelt soon discovered that the department was a clumsy instrument for ensuring preparedness. The Navy Department consisted of eight bureaus that performed specific tasks in areas such as personnel, ship deployments, construction, repair, supplies, accounts, steam engineering, and medicine. Over the years bureaus had been tacked on as various needs arose, but little attention had been given to how the whole apparatus would function together. In short, individual bureaus tended to perform their separate functions well; the problem stemmed from coordination. The only officials who could provide oversight were the secretary and assistant secretary, and, as political appointees, they were often not expert enough, nor did they serve long enough, to supply effective supervision. As a result, the chiefs of the various bureaus grew used to operating with a good deal of independence. They were jealous of their authority and frequently refused to discuss their actions with other bureau chiefs, which led to confusion and inefficiency.

Roosevelt confronted just such a situation in September 1897 when two bureaus failed to communicate. As acting secretary, he had ordered the gunboat *Newport* from the navy yard at Portsmouth, New Hampshire, to the Boston navy yard based on the recommendation of the Bureau of Navigation. Boston had a work crew that could complete the refitting of the vessel faster. Roosevelt discovered, however, "that the Bureau of Navigation had not consulted the Bureau of Construction."[10] (The Bureau of Navigation, among a variety of duties, handled ship deployments, and the Bureau of Construction and Repair held responsibility for ship design.) The matter might have gone unnoticed, except that jobs, constituents' jobs, were at stake. The Portsmouth facility sat on the Maine–New Hampshire border and, soon enough, the Speaker of the House of Representatives, Thomas Reed of Maine, contacted the assistant secretary about the *Newport*'s transfer. With this added complication, Roosevelt began referring to the *Newport* as "that infernal gunboat."[11] To help prevent confusion in the future, he instructed the head of the Bureau of Navigation, Capt. Arent Crowninshield, "that always hereafter the Bureau of Construction should be consulted."[12] In this episode, despite the messy political fallout, Roosevelt did ultimately work out the difference between the bureaus, but it was likely just a temporary solution. For as would indeed be the case with Roosevelt, the tenure of assistant secretaries tended to be shorter than those of the officers who headed the bureaus. Once an official like Roosevelt had departed the scene, old habits in the Navy Department reasserted themselves.

The assistant secretary thought any problems with the Navy Department lay in the departmental staff and not so much with the organization of the department itself. Roosevelt had grown up in an era—and household—in which personal morality counted the most, and he had seen that people of good character who acted with the best of intentions could bring concrete results. Although his father had been part of the business world, he had not, and thus he had no meaningful exposure to the organizational revolution that had begun as businesses burgeoned in the late nineteenth century. Roosevelt did not think much about bureaucratic abstractions such as "systems" or "rationalization." For him, efficiency stemmed not so much from proper organizational structures but from people of sound intellect, good morals, and manly bearing. In September 1897, for example, he reflected on proposals to reorganize the Navy Department bureaus: "I believe that the organization of the Yards and Docks Bureau for business purposes is at present bad, but I think the main trouble comes in not having at its head someone like Captain Folger or even Captain Brownson."[13] Captains William Folger and Willard Brownson apparently possessed the qualities that he valued, and such individuals would remain his preference during his time as assistant secretary and in the years following. As a result, Roosevelt relied on certain naval line officers for advice rather than the expertise of the bureaus.

Roosevelt maintained most frequent contact with Alfred T. Mahan and, of course, William Cowles, with whom he exploited family ties. He made Captain Mahan a confidant on his more grandiose ideas regarding sea power and imperial expansion. In one letter, which Roosevelt charged "must, of course, be considered as entirely confidential," he laid out an ambitious imperial agenda stretching from Hawaii to the Caribbean. Regarding Hawaii, he confided, "If I had my way we would annex those islands tomorrow. If that is impossible I would establish a protectorate over them." As part of a robust naval policy in general, he professed, "I believe we should build the Nicaraguan canal at once, and in the meantime that we should build a dozen new battleships, half of them on the Pacific Coast." He went on to recommend that the United States "turn Spain out" of the West Indies and "acquire the Danish Islands [the Virgin Islands]."[14]

As much as Roosevelt enjoyed sharing his strategic vision with the prophet of sea power, he welcomed the views of younger officers on more technical matters. He took particular notice of one officer: Lt. William S. Sims, perhaps the most gifted officer in the U.S. Navy at the time. Elting Morison, his biographer, observed of Sims's vision and energy: "Admiral Sims could imagine reality. It was this that gave him his distinction and driving power. He remembered Pearl Harbor before it happened."[15] At Sims's death in 1936, Franklin Roosevelt praised his career as "brilliant and colorful" and said that Sims himself was "dynamic and forceful . . . admired and respected by friend and foe alike."[16] In 1897 Lieutenant Sims was a naval attaché in Paris. He reported to Assistant Secretary Roosevelt on European improvements in ship design and gunnery. An impressed Roosevelt urged an investigation into the comparative deficiencies in American designs and performance, but hostilities with Spain delayed the probe. Sims's name, however, would surface again after Roosevelt entered the White House, when they formed a partnership with significant implications for the navy and for Sims's career.[17]

Roosevelt valued autonomous voices such as Sims's. They supplied a check on the navy's bureaus, which line officers like Sims charged sometimes followed an agenda that placed their own well-being before the service's as a whole. Roosevelt would continue this practice during his presidency, despite the creation of the General Board of the U.S. Navy in the aftermath of the Spanish-American War. This board of naval officers offered independent advice but could not, in its very nature as a collective body, be the kind of hard-charging force that Roosevelt favored.

The assistant secretary wanted to make sure that the right people got into command positions. Bureaucrats and their agencies were one thing, but Roosevelt wanted to ensure that the best men went to sea. And it would not hurt if they reflected Roosevelt's image of himself as a man of action and also functioned as allies inside the navy. They were to be fighters, the officers who would take the navy into battle and decide America's destiny on the seas. He wanted to make sure that when the U.S. Navy went to war "the men who have dared greatly" were at the helm.[18] Roosevelt held up Civil War admiral David Farragut as the ideal naval officer. Farragut, he claimed, "offered an example, not only of patriotism, but of supreme skill and daring in his profession. He belongs to that class of commanders who possess in the highest degree the qualities of courage and daring, of readiness to assume responsibility, and of willingness to run great risk. . . . He possessed also the unwearied capacity for taking thought in advance, which enabled him to prepare for victory before the day of battle came."[19]

To move such officers into commands, the assistant secretary embraced personnel reform. This cause was not a new one for Roosevelt. He had fought for years on the New York City Police Board and as a U.S. civil service commissioner for promotion by merit. For inspiration, Roosevelt could even look back to the time when his father had stood against the New York political machine of Roscoe Conkling.[20]

In the Navy Department Roosevelt headed a body, soon known as the "Roosevelt Board," charged with personnel reform. This entity faced two major tasks: examine promotion policy and try to resolve a bitter rivalry between engineering officers and naval line officers, the men who commanded a vessel in the line of battle. The latter problem proved to be the most controversial, and the board's proposed solution led some navy officers to denounce the assistant secretary. Bickering between line and engineering officers was relatively recent, but the dispute tapped into ancient naval traditions. In the age of sail, the line officers not only fought the vessel but also were the ones who made it go. They were masters not just of war, but of seamanship. They knew the winds and their vessel's capabilities. The coming of steam power challenged that world. Engineers played an increasingly important role in moving ships. They wanted recognition of their importance and complained that line officers belittled them.[21] Line officers, indeed, felt that grimy "mechanics" did not merit equal status. This squabbling hurt morale, so the Roosevelt Board attempted to reconcile line-engineering differences. The board recommended the amalgamation of the line and engineering corps, a solution that aroused much line indignation.[22] The Roosevelt Board was proposing what line officers most dreaded: engineers would become one of them. One officer complained that the proposal injected too much leveling and grumbled that "someone should kick . . . Rosevelt! [sic]"[23] Rear Adm. Thomas Selfridge declared that the engineers just wanted line officers' titles and deemed amalgamation a disservice, as neither line nor engineering officers could perform the duties of each other.[24] In actuality, the board's recommendation represented the only reasonable way to remedy the line-engineering dispute over the long term. Retention of a separate engineering cadre of officers, even if their status had somehow been elevated, would have remained an invitation to continuing division and derision. As hard as this problem had been to solve, another major personnel issue proved to be more intractable.

The Roosevelt Board threatened another hallowed military tradition in its reform of personnel policies. During peacetime, promotion strictly on the basis of seniority guided officer advancement in both the navy and army for much of the nineteenth century. For officers the system offered benefits. They would move to the higher ranks if they survived long enough, and because seniority was an objective standard, promotions in the regular ranks could remain relatively free from the potential disruption of outside political interference. The system, however, contained some "evils." Officers might advance to the top ranks, but at a snail's pace.[25] As a result, many who reached the highest ranks were elderly and unable to serve for a long period. Roosevelt pointed out the precise problem as he reflected on the navy's experience during the Civil War: "indifference prevented any reorganization of the *personnel* of the Navy during the middle of the [nineteenth] century, so that we entered upon the Civil War with captains seventy years old."[26] The demands of war shook out the old mariners but did not help the rate of promotions in the long term. Naval ranks swelled during the war, with a large portion retained after 1865. For Naval Academy graduates in the years that followed, promotions moved at glacial speed, as Civil War veterans clogged the ranks above them. Sometimes decades passed before an officer moved to the next rank. Fifteen years as an ensign, or twenty as a lieutenant, were not unusual. And the ranks stayed plugged because the Civil War veterans could remain in the service for forty years or until they reached age sixty-two.[27] Well before Roosevelt's time in the Navy Department, efforts were undertaken to alleviate the problem, but to little effect. In the 1880s Congress reduced the number of academy graduates who received commissions and extended the time that a midshipman spent in school from four to six years.[28]

As its solution, the Roosevelt Board recommended "selection-out." The board proposed only a limited change, but one that, in principle, would speed promotions and get younger, and presumably more capable, officers into the higher ranks. Selection-out would involve the forcible retirement of officers from each rank, but only "in case there shall not be a certain proportion of vacancies occurring from natural causes."[29] If such a condition developed, then a board of admirals would convene, and it would evaluate officers on the basis of merit. The proposal, therefore, defined carefully when selection-out would be implemented. Although Roosevelt would likely have preferred that such a system operate at all times, and not just under certain circumstances, a more sweeping scheme would have aroused greater opposition. Many officers feared the potential for abuse of a promotion system based mainly on merit. Absent the strict seniority standard, some of their comrades, they feared, might use social and political connections to make their case for advancement, a practice that could provoke jealousies just as destructive to morale as the line-engineering dispute.[30] The Roosevelt Board itself split over this proposal. Three members objected to merit being the basis of selection; instead, the *Washington Post* reported, they wanted selection to be "based on chance."[31] Apparently, these members felt that any criterion other than random chance for moving officers out, or up, would poison feelings within the ranks.

Naval officers need not have worried much, for Congress accepted only part of the Roosevelt Board's recommendation. The Personnel Act of 1899, which legislators based on the board's proposals, established the principle of selection-out, but only for the rank of captain. It was a limited reform, but a start. The law also sanctioned line-engineering amalgamation, although bickering erupted again in the naval ranks during Roosevelt's presidency.[32] Nevertheless, the law represented progress and moved the navy toward personnel practices that would be adopted wholesale during the twentieth century.

Roosevelt's interest in personnel reform demonstrated how he brought together the thinking of the nineteenth century, which emphasized the personal and the moral, with the trends of the twentieth century to come, in which abstraction, the impersonal, and systems would be more operative. Roosevelt did not have much patience for tinkering with bureaucracies, but he did recognize that if sound practices were to be perpetuated beyond the tenure of a good person, then institutions or processes had to be established that would maintain that vision. For personnel he wanted a system that moved up people of proven merit—and for him that included his idea of manly virtues—and removed those who had become deadwood. In short, he adopted the thinking of a managerial and organizational ethos to promote the traditional values that he venerated.

With the interruption of the war with Spain, the Personnel Act did not pass until after Roosevelt had departed the Navy Department. In the absence of some type of merit system, Roosevelt leaped into the void. He used his own influence to push forward men whom he judged to possess Farragut-like qualities. Roosevelt championed Cmdre. George Dewey, in particular, for an important command. The assistant secretary wanted Dewey in charge of the Asiatic Squadron in case war erupted with Spain. "I urged it," he explained in 1899, "upon the specific ground that whoever was sent there might have to go into Manila and that Dewey would certainly do it."[33] Roosevelt had determined that Dewey was a man of action. He based this judgment not on his direct personal knowledge of the man, although the two had met. Rather, Dewey's actions during the Chilean crisis of 1891–92 impressed him. War fever had erupted in both the United States and Chile after rioting in Valparaiso had targeted sailors from the uss *Baltimore.* Further confrontation and American demands for an apology aggravated the situation. Dewey had refueled his ship during the crisis before he received departmental orders, and Roosevelt felt that an officer who had shown such initiative was the man to take Manila if there was war.[34]

The name of Cmdre. John Adams Howell, however, had also been forwarded for command of the Asiatic Squadron, and Howell had an important backer in Sen. William Chandler of New Hampshire. Chandler possessed the added distinction of being a former secretary of the navy. Roosevelt tried to deflect Chandler from supporting Howell. He informed the senator that Howell's recent performance on the navy's armor board convinced him that the commodore was unfit for a responsible position. Roosevelt did not mince words: "I hardly know of a man of high rank in the Navy whom I should be more reluctant to see entrusted with a squadron or fleet under peculiar circumstances, such as actual or possible hostilities with Spain. He is irresolute; and he is extremely afraid of responsibility."[35]

In distinct contrast to Howell, Roosevelt believed that Dewey had great fighting instincts—a new Farragut. To improve Dewey's chances, he encouraged the commodore to recruit his home state senator, Redfield Proctor of Vermont, to his cause.[36] Ironically, the assistant secretary was playing a political game of preference at about the same time that members of the Roosevelt Board were warning against the politicization of personnel matters. His hypocrisy seemed even more pronounced, given that soon after he had assumed his post he had written, "Lobbying is a disgrace, and I am rendered really uneasy by the effort to get influence or 'pull' for certain naval officers."[37] Although Secretary Long would claim that the decision on command of the Asiatic Squadron occurred before either Proctor or Chandler had exerted pressure, Roosevelt demonstrated that he would readily sacrifice standards for promotion by merit when he felt that military efficiency appeared threatened. In the end, Dewey received the Asiatic Command and went on to become the "Hero of Manila Bay," while Howell assumed command of the European Squadron.[38]

The imperative of military readiness, Roosevelt doubtlessly believed, overrode concerns about political influence. War with Spain over Cuba loomed as a distinct possibility, and to the assistant secretary America's success in such a conflict weighed in the balance. Although getting fighters such as Dewey into critical commands was a priority, Roosevelt believed that he could render an even greater service as assistant secretary. He would act as a conduit for transmitting war plans to Secretary Long and for pushing the secretary to ready the navy along the lines proposed in those plans. Roosevelt appeared at Long's door so often that the secretary complained, "He bores me with plans of naval and military movement, and the necessity of having some scheme of attack arranged for instant execution in case of an emergency."[39]

Roosevelt did bombard Long with war plans during 1897. The assistant secretary worried that tensions with Spain over Cuba would boil over, sooner rather than later, and he wanted the navy prepared for every eventuality. In an attempt to prod Long, who worked to restrain his rambunctious assistant, Roosevelt reminded the secretary of an important political reality: "If . . . war should suddenly arise, the Navy Department would have to bear the full brunt of the displeasure of Congress and the country if it were not ready."[40] With such statements the assistant secretary demonstrated not only his anxiousness to push preparations forward but also that he, like Long, a former governor of Massachusetts, had his share of political seasoning. Roosevelt was not pushing his own ideas but instead promoting materials generated by the Office of Naval Intelligence, the Naval War College, and various special boards. Together these bodies constituted the principal parts of the Navy Department's pre-1898 mechanism for war planning.[41] As Roosevelt put it, he "used all the power there was in my office to aid these men in getting the material ready."[42] He took it upon himself to risk provoking Long.[43] As Roosevelt explained, just before he departed his post to go to war, "My chief usefulness has arisen from the fact that . . . I have continually meddled with what was not my business, because I was willing to jeopardize my position in a way that a naval officer could not."[44]

What plans for war with Spain did Roosevelt propose? The plans followed Captain Mahan's recipe for sea power. Roosevelt laid out how Long could concentrate the fleet by assembling vessels from far-off stations. In fact, the schemes Roosevelt proposed contained such details about ship locations and capabilities that Secretary Long must have surmised that the true source was not his assistant but officers in various Navy Department agencies. The plans differed in their specifics, but basically war planners wanted the fleet deployed off Cuba soon after hostilities commenced and pushed for a "flying squadron" of vessels to harass the coast of Spain. This force of swift vessels would occupy the Spaniards at home and free Americans to conduct operations against Spanish colonies without interference. Plans also included an attack on Manila in the Philippines, a naval blockade of Cuba, and an army expedition to Cuba, which Roosevelt felt would speed Spanish surrender. Later, after the battleship *Maine* exploded, planners dropped the idea of a flying squadron. The navy could not spare the vessels for such a raiding force. As Roosevelt explained to Alfred Mahan, "when we had seven armored ships against the Spanish fleet, I thought a flying squadron might be of use; at present we have six against eight, and I don't think so."[45]

Some of Long's impatience might have come from the assistant secretary's insistence on presenting war plans for countries other than Spain. Planning for various contingencies was not bad in itself, but Roosevelt anticipated some sort of trouble with Japan, perhaps even Japanese collusion with Spain. He looked west across the Pacific at the prompting of Mahan. Because of their past collaboration, the captain looked forward to having a like-minded soul at the top layers of the Navy Department. Mahan, with Roosevelt's encouragement, supplied ideas to the assistant secretary to help him fulfill America's destiny as a sea power. He fixed on the Hawaiian Islands and the need to acquire them as an advanced outpost before Japan seized them. Mahan sounded the alarm in May 1897, soon after Roosevelt occupied his new office in Washington. "Japan is a small and a poor state, as compared to ourselves; but the question is are we going to allow her to dominate the future of those most important islands because of our lethargy." He also recommended that "your best Admiral needs to be in the Pacific," which perhaps led Roosevelt to take up Dewey's cause.[46]

When Mahan wrote, the sun was indeed rising on the Japanese empire. In the mid-1890s Japan had defeated China in a short war and ended Chinese claims over Korea. The Japanese had also acquired Formosa and other island possessions. Roosevelt admired the Japanese for their military abilities. During the suppression of the Boxer Rebellion in 1900, he would exclaim, "What extraordinary soldiers those little Japs are!" and, more respectfully, "What natural fighters they are!"[47] Japan's ascent had raised Roosevelt's and Mahan's fears about Hawaii. The islands had, indeed, become a potential flashpoint. Possession of Hawaii represented a chance for both countries to improve their political and military positions in the Pacific, but the stakes were even higher than the acquisition of a geographically advantageous territory. Both peoples had deeper interests in the islands. A growing Japanese population lived there, but since 1893 American planters had ruled Hawaii as a republic. They had overthrown the native monarchy of Queen Liliuokalani and looked forward to annexation by the United States but had waited in vain during the antiexpansionist presidency of Grover Cleveland.

Although Roosevelt worried much more about the tensions over Cuba than Japan, he wanted to hedge against the possibility of the Japanese "chipping in" if the United States went to war with Spain.[48] In May 1897 he contacted Capt. Casper Goodrich, the president of the Naval War College, and requested the students there tackle a "Special Confidential Problem," war with Japan over Hawaii. Roosevelt wanted to know, especially, "What force will be necessary to uphold the intervention, and how shall it be employed?" He also instructed Goodrich to keep "in mind possible complications with another Power on the Atlantic Coast (Cuba)." The War College responded with alacrity and provided the assistant secretary with a plan by mid-June. Roosevelt was not entirely happy with the result, which emphasized an army expedition to the islands. Instead, in true Mahanian fashion, he wrote Goodrich that "it seems to me that the determining factor in any war with Japan would be control of the sea. . . . In other words I think our objective should be the Japanese fleet."[49] Commander Goodrich defended the plan, which accounted for the anticipated weakness of American naval forces in the Pacific.[50]

Whether Japan or Spain was the object, Roosevelt's fixation on war planning represented one way that he recognized modern war's emerging nature. He understood that with increasing mechanization and the resources of industrialized states to back war machines, warfare was becoming more complex. As a result, more planning and preparation was required. In June 1897 he declared,

> Ships, guns, and men were much more easily provided in time of emergency at the beginning of this century than at the end. It takes months to build guns and ships now, where it then took days, or at the most, weeks; and it takes far longer now to train men to the management of the vast and complicated engines with which war is waged. Therefore preparation is much more difficult, and requires a much longer time; and yet wars are so much quicker, they last so comparatively short a period, and can be begun so instantaneously that there is much less time than formerly in which to make preparations.[51]

At this point, prior to the war with Spain, Roosevelt was not yet contemplating a centralized war-planning agency. The navy's existing system seemed to work as long as energetic, dedicated individuals were on the scene to direct planning. From his statement, though, the urgency that he attached to planning for war, particularly with Spain, becomes more understandable.

Similar to many of his generation, he assumed that the execution of war between nation-states in the industrial age would be much swifter than in the past. Since the end of the American Civil War, all evidence seemed to confirm this impression. The wars of the earliest years of the twentieth century would do so as well. Roosevelt, just as so many others, did not foresee the long stalemate of World War I.

If Roosevelt considered war planning to be one of his top duties, then he worked equally hard to prepare warships for action as the prospect of hostilities with Spain increased over the course of 1897. Here the "hot-weather Secretary," as he described himself to President McKinley, a reference to Secretary Long's absences in the summer, delved directly into naval policy as he pushed for fleet expansion. In doing so, Roosevelt risked John Davis Long's displeasure, for, as he confided to Mahan, "Secretary Long is only lukewarm about building up our Navy, at any rate as regards battleships."[52] Long was more open to battleship building than Roosevelt surmised, but the navy secretary was not ready for the construction program that his enthusiastic assistant wanted. On 30 September 1897 Roosevelt presented a case for rapid fleet expansion to Long. He cited the rise of the Japanese and German navies and expanding American interests in the Pacific, along with the need to uphold the Monroe Doctrine. Roosevelt then went on to press, "I believe that Congress should at once give us six (6) new battleships, two (2) to be built on the Pacific and four (4) on the Atlantic; six (6) large cruisers . . . and seventy-five (75) torpedo boats."[53] The assistant secretary did not anticipate, however, how to supply crews for so many ships, which would be a perennial problem during his presidency, nor did he consider the reality of funding. In a typical pattern Roosevelt acted as if the ships, crews, and money would simply show up if he willed them to do so. He focused on the vision of sea power and its most tangible expression—the ships. Such a higher-level approach would be

more appropriate when he was president, but, as assistant secretary, he was expected to deal more with the details of naval
operations than was his inclination.

Much of Roosevelt's fixation on naval preparedness, and
general enthusiasm for his job, stemmed from the feeling that
he was doing important work. Part, as well, came from the fact
that he was having fun. When he was not writing missives to the
secretary of the navy, he was conducting inspections, exploring
ships, and observing maneuvers. Contemporaries commented
on the boyish side of Roosevelt, and he was able to indulge boyhood fantasies as assistant secretary. Roosevelt craved action,
and as assistant secretary he could literally go places. He also
must have been delighted at the deference and ceremony that
accompanied his office. In May 1897 he visited the Brooklyn
navy yard and caused quite a stir when he arrived a half hour
early. A resulting comical series of incidents doubtlessly amused
Roosevelt and pleased him as well, for they underscored that
he was the center of attention—where he liked to be. A surprised gatekeeper, not recognizing him, demanded, "Who d'ya
want see?" while the guard of 150 marines and the navy yard
band scrambled to get in position to present arms and regale
the assistant secretary with "Hail to the Chief." The aide to the
yard commandant threw himself into his uniform to escort Roosevelt.[54] The assistant secretary was even more excited when he
could get aboard ship. In September 1897, after returning from
open-sea maneuvers of the North Atlantic Squadron, Roosevelt
declared, "I have never enjoyed three days more than my three
days with the fleet." He got to watch gun turrets in action and
witnessed night firing exercises. As an added bonus, the weather
was calm, for he worried about sea sickness.[55]

Roosevelt naturally thrilled to the spectacle of battleships at
sea. These vessels expressed both grace and power in action.[56]
During the maneuvers seven battleships and two armored
cruisers—the bulk of American naval hitting power at the time—

would drill.[57] Roosevelt deemed it his task that as many people as possible gained the same impression that he had of American naval might. He understood the politics behind a big-navy policy. Popular enthusiasm could spur congressional generosity toward the navy budget.

Fleet reviews and maneuvers were natural objects for the press, and Roosevelt excelled at generating media attention. He already had practice with the reporters who had congregated at the New York City police headquarters when he had been on the police board. Therefore, when it came to the navy, the assistant secretary helped reporters get their stories. He made special room for them in his arrangements for squadron maneuvers in September 1897. Most captains did not welcome reporters aboard ship, but Roosevelt demanded adequate press representation. Moreover, he wanted to ensure favorable press coverage, so he recruited reporters who he knew would be friendly toward the navy. Roosevelt approached Paul Dana, editor of the New York *Sun*, a paper that was reliably Republican under Dana, and requested the services of Richard Oulahan, the *Sun*'s reporter at the Navy Department. Oulahan, according to Roosevelt, was "a gentleman and a thoroughly trustworthy fellow." Roosevelt also sought to enlist his old comrade from his police board days, Jacob Riis, telling the reform-minded correspondent, "You will have a rather primitive bunk, but I think you will be comfortable enough, and it would be the best kind of spree."[58] At that time journalists often reported events without a critical eye, and Roosevelt was making certain that the squadron exercise had the best possible coverage from the navalist point of view.

The press coverage of the maneuvers must have pleased the assistant secretary. Carrier pigeons brought advance word of the activities, but a full account had to wait until Roosevelt and his party of reporters returned to shore. Then the wire services broadcast a glowing story of the maneuvers. Readers learned of the "excellent" gunnery practice and movements conducted with "splendid precision" by "crack" cruisers and battleships carving the waves with "resistless power." Not surprisingly, as well, the assistant secretary of the navy earned a prominent place in the portrayal of the action. Roosevelt, after all, had handpicked the correspondents, who already knew he made good copy. He took advantage of the opportunity to push naval growth, proclaiming upon his return, "At last we are beginning to have a navy fit to uphold the interests of our people, a navy which, though too small in size, need not fear comparison with no other as regards the quality of its ships and men."[59]

Pictures accompanied the words, which intensified the impression that American naval power had come of age. Frederic Remington accompanied the squadron, and Roosevelt looked forward to the artist applying the same dramatic style he used to capture scenes of the American West to renderings of the North Atlantic Squadron: "I am very glad . . . to have had you along with the squadron; and I can't help looking upon you as an ally from henceforth on in trying to make the American people see the beauty and majesty of our ships, and the heroic quality which lurks somewhere in all those who man and handle them."[60]

Roosevelt seemed most thrilled with the technology he had seen. He did not possess much mechanical aptitude, but like many Americans of his era he liked gadgets. He also believed it his duty to stay abreast on technological matters to advise Secretary Long or function as acting secretary himself. He never felt entirely comfortable in dealing with technological details but did develop enough expertise to make informed choices on new designs and equipment. He told Henry Cabot Lodge that during his visit to the North Atlantic Squadron, "I saw for myself the working of the different gear for turning turrets— electrical, hydraulic, steam, and pneumatic." As a result, he became an advocate for the electrical system.[61] Roosevelt also investigated other technological issues such as the armament of new battleships, gunnery targets, torpedo boat design, torpedo tube placement, and the torpedo itself.[62] Making informed choices was critical because the navy was a technologically oriented service. A torrent of technological change brought yearly developments in gunnery, armor, machinery, and design, which made vessels rapidly obsolete.

Roosevelt's interest in technology stemmed from more than his official duties or a personal fascination with gadgets. Technology, especially to Americans in the late nineteenth century, reflected progress, material evidence of the superiority of their society and of Western civilization as a whole. Good reason existed for highlighting the implements of the industrial revolution at the Columbian Exposition and, before it, at the Philadelphia Centennial Exhibition of 1876. The technological development of the present promised a better future and accelerating advances.

Roosevelt possessed an imaginative enough mind to grasp this sense of potentiality, and during his tenure at the Navy Department he worked on behalf of technological invention and innovation. By his time human beings could move across the land and the surface of the sea at increasing rates of speed, but they remained, for the most part, bound to the face of the earth. Ever inquisitive, Roosevelt became interested in the possibilities of flight. Professor Samuel Langley's aviation experiments attracted his notice. In 1896 Langley had built two steam-powered "aerodromes" that flew but were unmanned.[63] Roosevelt brought Langley's flying machine to the attention of Secretary Long in March 1898 and urged action. "It seems to me worth while," he told Long, "for this government to try whether it will not work on a large enough scale to be of use in the event of war." Roosevelt recommended that Long appoint two officers of "scientific attainments" to investigate Langley's work. Nothing came of this initiative. The War Department had anticipated the navy's interest and had already appointed an investigatory team.[64] More significantly, Roosevelt, Long, and the rest of the American military would soon have much more to worry about than attempts at flight. It was the spring of 1898, and the final crisis with Spain had arrived. Langley would continue his work, but ultimately the Wright brothers would produce a successful aircraft.

Roosevelt would revisit aeronautics as president, as he would many other matters packed into his one year as assistant secretary. He learned much during that time about the navy that would serve him well as commander in chief. He had undergone an intensive technical, administrative, and political education that honed his skills at dealing with bureaucracies and balancing competing interests, whether they involved civilian or military matters. He may have learned, as well, that power brought responsibility. In June 1897 Roosevelt had delivered a speech to officers at the Naval War College in Newport, Rhode Island, that was rife with bellicose statements such as "no national life is worth having if the nation is not willing, when the need shall arise, to stake everything on the supreme arbitrament of war, and to pour out its blood, its treasure, and its tears like water, rather than submit to the loss of honor and renown."[65] Secretary Long objected to Roosevelt's rhetoric and restrained his assistant from other such pronouncements. At the time Roosevelt bridled, but complied, because, as he told Long when he departed the department, "I have grown not merely to respect you as my superior officer, but to value your friendship very highly."[66] Finally, Roosevelt's service in the Navy Department had allowed him to develop personal relationships in Washington that would serve him well in the future.

The Rough Rider

On 19 November 1897 residents of Washington DC witnessed the assistant secretary of the navy peddling his bicycle furiously through the streets. He was on an urgent mission. Theodore Roosevelt needed a doctor and nurse, and he needed them quickly, for his sixth and final child, Quentin, was arriving, and coming fast. Roosevelt succeeded, and reported to his sister Anna two hours after the baby's birth that both Edith and the child were doing well.[67] Roosevelt's frantic search for medical help was symbolic of the next few years of his life. The pace of events would quicken, and Roosevelt would find many of his long-delayed dreams of a greater destiny suddenly fulfilled. During this same period he would also cement his basic conceptions about the American military establishment. These ideas would have everything to do with his service in the Spanish-American War and the fact that he later preferred to be addressed as "Colonel Roosevelt" when he was not being called "Mr. President."

As assistant secretary, Roosevelt was familiar with the diplomatic maneuvers that accompanied the heightened tensions with Spain over Cuba. Since the Cuban revolt against Spanish rule had broken out in 1895, Americans had recoiled at the reports—often sensationalized—of Spanish brutality. In late 1897 a new worry emerged, when Spanish loyalists on the island rioted and posed an apparent threat to American lives and property.[68] Roosevelt determined that if war broke out he would be on the front lines. "I don't want to be in office during war," he wrote insistently. "I want to be at the front."[69]

Roosevelt used both his New York and Washington connections to secure a place for himself in the army that might be mobilized. The assistant secretary courted, especially, the adjutant general of the New York National Guard, C. Whitney Tillinghast. He knew that if war came he would most likely need to associate himself with a state to be part of the volunteer forces that would be the bulk of any wartime army. Traditionally, states had raised the units that fleshed out federal forces in an emergency. But Roosevelt had a problem. He would be in Washington, and not on the scene in New York if tension boiled over with Spain. Thus, he worked to ingratiate himself with Tilling-hast by offering a quid pro quo. He would be Tillinghast's man on the inside in Washington, if the New York adjutant general would look on him favorably should volunteer regiments need officers. In Christmas greetings to Tillinghast in 1897, Roosevelt informed the general in plain terms, "I shall not forget to warn you if I think there is any danger of trouble. . . . And I shall ask you and every other friend I have to help me arrange matters so that I can go." He also reminded Tillinghast on more than one occasion that he had prior military experience to qual-ify him. Roosevelt's three years in the National Guard had not given him much satisfaction, but now he was going to play up the experience for all it was worth. As he told the adjutant gen-eral, "I have had a good deal of experience in handling men." Roosevelt also threw in for good measure that he had "acted as sheriff in the cow country!"[70]

These appeals to Tillinghast were revealing. At first glance Roosevelt's fawning behavior belied his proclamations that "lob-bying is a disgrace."[71] When he condemned individuals who tried to use "pull," however, he made a distinction from his own circumstances. In the case of military officers, police offi-cers, or members of the civil service, the use of political influ-ence—or worse, bribery—to gain advantage represented one of the great "evils" in public life. Roosevelt had fought for the principle of merit in public service for much of his career. By contrast, he viewed his determined efforts to line up a military commission for himself as the ultimate civic expression and in keeping with the best of American traditions. He would be the service-minded citizen, ready to drop all to perform gallant duty for his country. Therefore, in an interesting twist, he saw his flagrant use of influence as high-minded and nothing resem-bling the base sort of influence peddling that he condemned. His messages to Tillinghast also reinforced the notion that Roo-sevelt believed that military ability came from more than just formal military training. He stressed his National Guard training, but, for him, his experience with frontier law enforcement counted for just as much.

As 1897 turned to 1898, Roosevelt worried that his chance to go to war would not come. The old sense of frustration began to return, especially after the USS *Maine* blew up in Havana harbor on the evening of 15 February 1898. The *Maine* had been dispatched to signal the determination of the United States to protect American lives and property in Cuba after the recent rioting. Before the *Maine*'s destruction, Roosevelt had praised President McKinley's measured policy toward Spain and the Cuban insurgents. He wrote Philemon Sherman, son of Gen. William T. Sherman and a New York lawyer, that McKinley had treated the "Spanish business . . . admirably." Roosevelt explained "that the President has handled this Spanish question so as to avoid the necessity of war, and yet to uphold the honor of our country."[72]

After the *Maine* sank Roosevelt grew impatient. Intemperate outbursts were rare, such as the famous blast that McKinley had the backbone of a "chocolate eclair"; rather, Roosevelt grew increasingly nervous that the president's strong desire for a peaceful resolution with Spain might prevail. On 6 March 1898 he told Douglas Robinson, the husband of his sister Corinne, "We are certainly drifting towards, and not away from, war; but the President will not make war, and will keep out of it if he possibly can."[73] By the end of March 1898, Roosevelt was close to throwing McKinley into the camp of the "sentimentalists" and arbitration advocates, whose masculinity was questionable, in his opinion. He wrote Robinson again, this time stating, "The President is resolute to have peace at any price."[74]

What Roosevelt was unwilling to acknowledge was McKinley's own war record. The president had witnessed the carnage at Antietam Creek in 1862 and did not wish to plunge the nation into war. Roosevelt, though, implied that McKinley's manly will to fight must have dissipated with age. The assistant secretary held out hope that McKinley would have to accede to the tide of prowar sentiment building in Congress.[75] By this point, he could scarcely contain himself, telling William Cowles, "Personally, I cannot understand how the bulk of our people can tolerate the hideous infamy that has attended the last two years of Spanish rule in Cuba; and still more how they can tolerate the treacherous destruction of the *Maine* and the murder of our men!"[76]

Roosevelt also fretted that family concerns might deny him his war. Here the chords of memory sounded a familiar tone. Roosevelt was eager to make up for his father's failure to serve. Edith was, however, deathly ill. Complications after Quentin's birth left her increasingly weak, until by March 1898 Roosevelt, fraught with anxiety over his wife, wrote, "Edith is not strong enough even for me to read to her much."[77] With his wife in a perilous state, Roosevelt knew he could not leave if war came. Doctors soon located the cause of the trouble. An abscess had formed in the muscle outside the pelvic cavity, and after an operation Edith was soon on the mend.[78] His eldest male child and third to bear the name "Theodore" was also recovering from a malady. A nervous disorder had taken hold of Ted. Apparently, T.R. had been pushing his ten-year-old son too hard and caused some sort of breakdown. He pledged, thereafter, "I shall never press Ted either in body or mind."[79]

As Roosevelt cared for his family and waited on the president's diplomacy, he pursued his duties at the Navy Department with even more zeal. He was determined that the navy would be ready for battle. The day after the *Maine* blew up, Roosevelt, who still referred to the incident as an "accident," advised Secretary Long to recommission several Civil War–style monitors and the ram *Katahdin* to help make up for the loss. A few days later Roosevelt recommended that the navy equip itself with "at least one hundred torpedo boats" and that Long ask Congress to authorize four new battleships immediately. He also urged the rapid completion of the battleships *Kearsarge* and

Kentucky.[80] Roosevelt bombarded Long with so much advice on war preparations that he feared the secretary regarded him as persona non grata.[81]

Most famously, Roosevelt took advantage of Long's absence from the Navy Department on the afternoon of Saturday, 25 February, to issue a host of orders to raise the navy's state of readiness. Orders flowed to procure ammunition, enlist sailors, and distribute ships. Upon his return, Secretary Long reversed several of the orders as ill-advised, but he let stand one in particular that Roosevelt had sent to Cmdre. George Dewey, now the commander of the Asiatic Squadron: "Order the squadron, except the Monocacy, to Hong Kong. Keep full of coal. In the event of declaration of war [on] Spain, your duty will be to see the Spanish squadron does not leave the Asiatic coast, and then offensive operations in the Philippines. Keep Olympia until further orders."[82] Roosevelt could not know at the time that with this order he would provide fodder to historians who would see the assistant secretary taking advantage of temporary authority to set in motion an imperial adventure in the Philippines. Roosevelt's own prior discussion of war plans, however, counters such notions. A move to neutralize the Spanish position in the Philippines had been long contemplated in the Navy Department, and Roosevelt's action was militarily prudent. Secretary Long, a much more deliberate man, affirmed his assistant's judgment on this point when he supported this order, even as he withdrew others.[83]

Timing represented the key question in the issuing of the orders to Dewey, as historian David Trask has argued. Trask supported the idea that Roosevelt was simply executing long-contemplated orders and not acting on behalf of some imperialist conspiracy. The assistant secretary had just decided when they should be issued.[84] Of course, the effect of the orders on American-Spanish relations should not be overlooked. The case may be persuasive that the orders to Dewey reflected prior military planning, but they also contributed to the breakdown between the United States and Spain. Dewey's movements made American intentions clear. On 2 March 1898 newspapers published a dispatch from Shanghai, China, about the concentration of the Asiatic Squadron at Hong Kong. The following day there was excitement in Madrid: "The public is much exercised over the report of the presence of a squadron of United States warships at Hongkong, as it is presumed the vessels intend to threaten Manila . . . in the event of war between the United States and Spain."[85] Roosevelt's intentions may have been to ensure naval preparedness in case of war, but the orders to Dewey apparently still played a role, albeit a small role, in bringing about that conflict.

During this time of preparation, Roosevelt continued to pump for more. He described to Brooks Adams how he had preached to McKinley and the cabinet that "the blood of Cubans, the blood of women and children who have perished by the hundred thousand in hideous misery, lies at our door; and the blood of the murdered men of the *Maine* calls not for indemnity but for the full measure of atonement which can only come by driving the Spaniard from the New World."[86] Roosevelt's rhetoric had reached the highest level of self-righteousness because he had convinced himself that a war with Spain would be fought for the best of reasons. It would be a moral crusade. This campaign would not be just for the salvation of the Cubans or revenge for the *Maine* but for moral improvement for the American people. War would give "them something to think of which isn't material gain." Strategically, as well, one more European outpost would be removed from the Americas. And, if he needed further justification, Roosevelt pointed to the practical effect of a war on the army and navy. War would test the army and navy in actual combat. Roosevelt wanted to land, for example, an army expeditionary force in Cuba, "if only for the sake of learning from our own blunders."[87] If he could have foreseen the experiences of the actual Cuba expedition, he might not have hoped for such a lesson. He did not need to wait long to find out how American forces would perform, for President McKinley soon bowed to political pressure and requested authority to intervene in Cuba. On 25 April 1898 McKinley signed a joint congressional resolution authorizing military action. Theodore Roosevelt had his war.[88]

If events had not seemed to move fast enough for Roosevelt during the run-up to war, now he was caught in a whirlwind of activity. From April through November 1898, the pace became furious: he would help prepare the navy for battle, resign his post in the Navy Department, gain an officer's commission in the volunteer cavalry, organize and train a regiment, embark to Cuba and fight in two battles, return to the United States, resign from the army, run for the governorship of New York, and win the race for governor. During these few months Roosevelt transformed himself into a national hero and set himself on the path that would lead to the highest office in the land. During 1898 he would also complete his basic military education. His year at the Navy Department had furnished him with the practical knowledge of administering a large bureaucracy. The weeks that he would spend in the army familiarized him with that service but would also confirm his notions about military life as a supremely masculine and romantic experience. In addition, his time in the army volunteers demonstrated to him the need for reform if the United States were to have a military worthy of the imperial mantle it claimed in the war with Spain.

For Theodore Roosevelt, when war came, the choice was simple. He had to be in the fighting. Friends and associates urged him to reconsider. After all, he had a family to think of, and that family was not entirely well at the time. Roosevelt devoted pages in his correspondence to justifying his decision to seek a volunteer officer's commission. He felt driven to live up to the expansionist doctrines that he had preached. His moral code could permit no other course, for he confessed to a "horror of the people who bark but don't bite."[89] To do less, in his opinion, would appear to be craven and unmanly. He also countered arguments that he could do more good by remaining in the Navy Department. Roosevelt claimed disingenuously that "my office is essentially a peace office. The Assistant Secretary has properly nothing to do with military operations." Instead, he contended that the officers of the navy would "assume their proper importance" and "be the real directors of military operations."[90] In other words, Roosevelt was arguing that his role of promoting ideas on behalf of naval officers ended once the guns sounded. He was obviously rationalizing and overstating his uselessness. By remaining as assistant secretary, he could have helped mobilize the navy's bureaus to support operations. Such work was critical to the fleet's success, even if it did not involve direct control of forces in battle. Roosevelt had been a prominent voice for preparedness before the war, and, ever irrepressible, he doubtlessly would have attempted to influence operations during wartime. After all, before he resigned as assistant secretary, he chaired the Naval War Board, a special body established to guide strategy.[91]

Roosevelt's ambitions for future office also played a part in his decision to enter the war. He had to live up to the interventionist policy he had advocated if he wanted to advance his political fortunes. If he failed to act, political opponents could dismiss him as an "armchair and parlor" jingo, damaging his public standing.[92] In any event, by April 1898 it would have been hard for him to reverse course. He had made his mind up long ago and had been working behind the scenes to line up a military appointment.

Roosevelt had been lobbying for something at the state level, but his position in Washington would secure for him the officer's commission that he coveted. His prewar efforts with the New York National Guard bore no fruit, and he worried that he might miss his chance when initial plans signaled that only existing National Guard units would be used to supplement the regular army. If that were the case, he announced, "I shall try to get on the staff of one of the Generals."[93] Opportunity soon beckoned that April when Congress authorized three regiments of cavalry to be drawn from a national pool of volunteers. Roosevelt took immediate advantage of his proximity to power. He knew Secretary of War Russell Alger and claimed that Alger was fond of him and sympathetic to him because the secretary had felt the same way when he had fought in the Civil War. If that were not enough to persuade Alger, then Roosevelt had someone else on his side, the secretary of war's family doctor, Capt. Leonard Wood.[94]

Theodore Roosevelt had numerous political and social contacts, but in 1898 Leonard Wood was one of the best connected men in Washington DC. He was married to Louisa Condit Smith, who had been the ward of Supreme Court justice Stephen Field. Moreover, not only was he Secretary Alger's physician, but Wood also attended to William and Ida McKinley. Wood had earned a military reputation, when, as an army doctor in 1886, he had commanded troops in the campaign against Geronimo.[95] Roosevelt met Wood in June 1897, and the two became fast friends. He idolized Wood's reputation as a Native American fighter and admired the doctor's capacity for remarkable feats of physical exertion. They soon became regular playmates and scrambled around Washington's Rock Creek Park to keep in shape and test their bodies. The two men could also be seen enjoying the "solemn kicking of [a] football round an empty lot."[96] This association proved to be fortuitous for both men, for it helped carry them to the tops of their respective pursuits. With Wood added to the picture, Secretary Alger acceded to Roosevelt's request for a commission. The secretary of war, according to Roosevelt, wanted to make him the colonel of one of the volunteer cavalry regiments, with Wood as lieutenant colonel. In an act of self-denial that demonstrated he was not the supreme egotist that his contemporaries often portrayed, Roosevelt insisted on the reverse, for he wanted the more experienced Wood in command. As Roosevelt put it, "I did not wish to rise on any man's shoulders."[97]

Roosevelt's commission confirmed his ideas about the nature of military command. These conceptions would remain ingrained even though increased professionalization was fast making them obsolete. Roosevelt recognized the importance of training and experience in leading troops into battle but felt an industrious individual could learn such skills quickly. He did not believe that field command necessarily demanded long years of education and promotion through the ranks. In his view an officer needed to know only basic organizational principles: drill, marching formations, and the charge. These elements remained secondary to the characteristics that made for sound military leadership. Among other things an officer should be aggressive, courageous, honorable, just, and inspiring. Roosevelt believed that he was blessed with an abundance of these qualities. His idea of effective officership would always continue to emphasize character over training and education, even though he was familiar with professional developments in the military. In 1898 he could not foresee that the day was almost past when inspired amateurs could rise to field commands.

If Roosevelt needed any validation of his beliefs, then he needed to look no further than Leonard Wood, who did not possess a formal military education. He held a degree from Harvard Medical School and had joined the army as a contract surgeon. Wood's lack of a West Point background made no difference to Roosevelt. Rather, he felt that Wood demonstrated that factors other than years of study at a military academy made the soldier. Looking back on the Spanish-American War, Roosevelt would write, "He [Wood] had every physical, moral, and mental quality which fitted him for a soldier's life and for the exercise of command."[98] By that he meant that Wood was a "man of high ideals" who was "by nature a soldier of the highest type" and who "scorned everything mean and base."[99] Altogether, Wood was an officer who "combined . . . the qualities of entire manliness with entire uprightness and cleanliness of character."[100] This solid core was complemented by Wood's experience battling the Apaches in the West, and Roosevelt considered western life a prime school of warfare.

Roosevelt's time as a soldier also confirmed his notions about the proper configuration of the American military establishment. In 1898 he and Wood, along with thousands of others, were participating in an honored tradition, the rush to the colors. The Americans who had fought the Revolutionary War had been distrustful of a large standing military force, given their experience with the British army and government. They had another model of defense to draw on that fit better with their republican ideals. The idea of a citizen obligation to defend the state had a long lineage in English and colonial history. In colonial America, militia forces had represented the first defense, and often the only defense, against Native American raids, slave revolts, and other threats to public order. During the War for Independence, patriot militias provided a crucial, if often unreliable, supplement to the Continental Army. The new nation maintained a national army after the war, but kept it small, owing to worries about the dangers to liberty that large standing forces represented and because of costs. In case of war, forces needed to expand rapidly, and the organization of volunteer units proved expedient. That practice applied much more to the army than the navy, because of the technical requirements required for sea service. By the end of the nineteenth century, the technological complexity of modern steel warships made it even more the case. Captains could no longer readily convert vessels from peacetime to wartime use, as had been possible in the past.

For Roosevelt the act of volunteering represented more than a practical measure to expand the army. Volunteering was a noble gesture and spoke volumes about an individual's mettle. Volunteers were demonstrating civic-mindedness, courage, and honor—in short, all the qualities that Roosevelt defined as manliness. He did not feel that war was necessary to develop such traits, but, if conflict occurred, a quantity of men would gain from the character-building aspects of military life and thus serve as a civic inspiration to the next generation. The values that had built the country were thereby to be perpetuated. As Roosevelt put it in 1897, "The fight well fought, the life honorably lived, the death bravely met—these count for more in building a high and fine type of temper in a nation."[101]

What Roosevelt could not see at the time, and resisted acknowledging in the future, was that the patriotic rush to the colors did not lend itself to an era that increasingly placed a premium on systems and efficiency. The mobilization of mass armies, similar to the industries that sustained large-scale forces, would increasingly resemble the organization of the factory system. To be sure, Roosevelt recognized the necessity of military preparedness. He stressed George Washington's adage "that in time of peace it is necessary to prepare for war."[102] Roosevelt would also witness many of the shortcomings of the mobilization for the war with Spain, yet the reforms he would support later as president were designed to fix the immediate problems of administration and preserve the time-honored system of mobilization. Such an approach was hardly unique. Many of the reforms of the Progressive Era—whether they were directed at breaking up business trusts, ending corruption in government, improving the moral and economic condition of the poor, or solving some other issue—aimed often to maintain, or restore, the values of a preindustrial nineteenth-century society.

If anything, Roosevelt resisted the notion that the industrial age called for machinelike military methods. Quite to the contrary, he sought to preserve the established volunteer system to counter the very force of standardization. Soon after the Spanish-American War, he would describe the superiority of the American method of mobilization: "The battalion chief of a newly raised American regiment . . . has positively unlimited opportunity for the display of 'individual initiative,' and is in no danger whatever either of suffering from unhealthy suppression of personal will, or of finding his faculties of self-help numbed by becoming a cog in a gigantic and smooth-running machine."[103]

Of course, why would Roosevelt want to change a system from which he derived so many benefits? His political and personal pull had won him his desired officer's commission. Moreover, after he had received his lieutenant colonel's rank in the First U.S. Volunteer Cavalry, he stayed on in Washington for a time, not only to complete his duties as assistant secretary but also to expedite the organization and equipping of his unit. As a result, the Rough Riders would get things that other units never received. Roosevelt related how he secured modern carbines that fired new smokeless powder. These were the same weapons used by the regular cavalry, and they were superior to the outdated black powder weapons that National Guard units used. He compared the guard weaponry to "crossbows and mangonels." Roosevelt also possessed the advantage of a direct appeal to Secretary of War Alger when a War Department bureau chief proved obstinate. Alger, he said, "helped me in every way" when the War Department tried to issue winter clothing for campaigning in the tropics and, again, when the department slowed the regiment's requisitions for horses, wagons, and other supplies. Without such help the Rough Riders might not have gone to Cuba, and Roosevelt would have missed his long-desired appointment with glory.[104] He did not admit that his unique access to the corridors of power worked to his special advantage. Rather, for him, his ability to equip the Rough Riders came down to personal traits, his energy and intelligence, both of which he did have in abundance.

After Roosevelt resigned as assistant secretary on 6 May 1898, he began his military education in earnest. He also commenced it in style, with a lieutenant colonel's uniform from Brooks Brothers.[105] He loved the process of organizing and drilling the regiment at San Antonio, Texas, telling Senator Lodge that if it were not for homesickness, "I should really be enjoying myself thoroughly."[106] After all, the First U.S. Volunteer Cavalry brought together both his worlds. It combined easterners known for their Knickerbocker Club affiliations with rough-hewn westerners. Roosevelt's military education also included firsthand exposure to the consequences of the army's failure to prepare sufficiently for war. T.R. understood that difficulties would occur even before the declaration of war. He wrote to Capt. Robley Evans on 20 April, "If only the Army were one-tenth as ready as the Navy we would fix that whole business in six weeks."[107] In his war diary he was more candid: "I have the Navy in good shape. But the army is awful. The War Dept. is in utter confusion. Alger has no force whatever, & no knowledge of his department."[108]

Roosevelt's boasting about naval preparations and his criticism of the army might have been attributed to an enlarged ego, if not for the fact that the War Department was not as prepared for war as the navy. Roosevelt would soon learn the depth of the problem when the Rough Riders deployed to Florida and then, as part of the Fifth Corps, embarked to Cuba. As a result, he would develop a list of shortcomings to be addressed after the war. To be fair, Roosevelt would acknowledge that much of the fault lay in thirty-three years without a major conflict and "the condition of red-tape bureaucracy which existed in the War Department," but he also felt many problems could have been avoided, or quickly remedied, with "men of push and intelligence" in charge—that was, men of his own stripe. He condemned "various bureau chiefs . . . who doubtless had been good officers thirty years before, but who were as unfit for modern war as if they were so many smoothbores."[109]

Roosevelt grew especially alarmed at the confusion that plagued the deployment of forces to Cuba. The railway journey from San Antonio to Tampa, Florida, the expedition's embarkation point, took four days rather than two because of problems with organizing the train. Roosevelt was up every night to direct the watering and feeding of the regiment's horses, and the trip was hot and dusty, although he did find some time to read Edmond Demolins's *Supériorité des Anglo-Saxons.*[110] The conditions that he found in Tampa appalled him, and he spoke of the "wildest confusion."[111] On 10 June he began a correspondence with Senator Lodge that would last throughout the campaign and represented the best record of his private horror at the problems that he witnessed. Lodge, he hoped, would be his surrogate before administration officials, although he wanted his name kept out of any discussion.[112]

Upon arrival at Tampa, the Rough Riders received no food for twenty-four hours, and nobody showed them where to establish camp. Port Tampa was ten miles away, and a single rail line connected it to the camp, even though, as Roosevelt complained, "troops have been gathering here in a country where lines of temporary railroad could be laid down for miles in 24 hours." When the regiment deployed to the port, the troops spent an entire night waiting for a train, and then the trip took twelve hours to complete. Mule trains moved faster alongside the track. The regiment arrived at a wharf jammed with troops, trains, and boats—the picture of bedlam. No officers met the unit to assign a transport, and Wood and Roosevelt located the depot quartermaster, Lt. Col. Charles F. Humphrey, only after some difficulty. Humphrey advised that they seize their transport because another regiment, the Seventy-First New York, had received orders for the same vessel. Roosevelt took four hundred men and raced the Seventy-First for the transport, securing it with the "most vigorous and rather lawless work." Once on board the men found themselves in cramped, sweltering quarters. Roosevelt likened the lower holds to being "unpleasantly suggestive of the Black Hole of Calcutta," a situation made more unbearable by a failure to sail for several days. He appealed to Lodge to use his influence to get the expedition moving. If they were to leave Tampa and get into action promptly, he would forgive the early bungling.[113]

Problems continued to plague the expedition in Cuba. In July Roosevelt wrote that the troops still suffered as a result of administrative shortcomings. He complained to Lodge that "our condition is horrible in every way," and to his brother-in-law Douglas Robinson he raged, "I cannot get even rice and oatmeal for the sick. . . . My men are in tatters and their shoes like those of tramps. . . . The few delicacies—if beans and tomatoes can be called such—which they have had I have had to purchase myself."[114]

Roosevelt blamed this situation on a lack of transportation. The army had assembled too few small craft, wagons, and mule trains to land material from the transports and then carry it to forward units. Hospital care, Roosevelt charged, was even worse. He reported that "the mismanagement of the hospital service in the rear has been such that my men will not leave the regiment if they can possibly help it."[115] Some of the Rough Riders spent forty-eight hours at the hospital before they received food, and they depended on the walking wounded to bring water. Roosevelt's criticisms were not limited to administration, as he also registered complaints about the artillery and the engineers; nevertheless, he directed most of his anger at the army's organizational failures.[116] The difference in prewar preparation between the navy and the War Department stood fully revealed to him. As Roosevelt lamented, "Oh the difference in the Departments and the men in the higher ranks."[117]

His anger was understandable but not entirely fair to the army's top officials and officers. Roosevelt viewed their performance from the vantage point of a regimental officer, and, rightfully, he placed the welfare of his troops above all else. From his perspective the Cuba expedition's difficulties grew out of incompetent leadership. Roosevelt's natural tendency was to blame individuals first rather than the inadequacies of the institution or past national disinterest in military affairs. Now in the midst of battle and the tropical heat of Cuba, his longer view about the gap in time between the Civil War and the current conflict disappeared. Also, at the moment he had nothing else with which he might compare his experience. He was, after all, part of the first expedition of the conflict and thus was witness to some of the worst features of the entire wartime mobilization. Far fewer problems occurred during the later expeditions to the Philippines and Puerto Rico.[118] Roosevelt only knew at the time that his men were suffering.

He could rail against distant War Department administrators, but the top officers of the expeditionary force presented much more visible targets. They seemed to embody all that Roosevelt found wrong with the army's leadership. As a group, he found them to be old, physically and mentally debilitated, and not the men of "push and intelligence" that he valued. The commanding officer of the Fifth Corps was the worst offender. Sixty-two years old and weighing more than three hundred pounds, Maj. Gen. William Shafter presented an ungainly figure who inspired ridicule rather than respect.[119] He was not the assertive and energetic commander that Roosevelt expected. Rather, Shafter suffered in the tropical summer, and soon Roosevelt was charging that Shafter had brought the expedition to the verge of disaster. He labeled Shafter as "utterly inefficient" and "panic struck," and in one especially ferocious blast he wrote that "not since the campaign of Crassus against the Parthians has there been so criminally incompetent a General as Shafter."[120] Specifically, Roosevelt found Shafter to be useless in battle because he was "too unwieldy to get to the front," and therefore, Roosevelt claimed, the engagement at the San Juan Heights had basically "fought itself under . . . brigade and regimental commanders" such as Wood and himself. The top commanders, he believed, had little to do with the success. Roosevelt also faulted Shafter for not pressing for adequate supplies and for considering less than the unconditional surrender of Spanish forces.[121] Shafter seemed to symbolize the worst features of promotions made strictly by seniority. He had received his rank and command because he was the next in line.[122]

Other senior leaders also failed to inspire confidence. Maj. Gen. Joseph Wheeler had been a Confederate warhorse but was well past his prime as leader of the expedition's dismounted cavalry. President McKinley had appointed him to promote North-South reconciliation, but the best that Roosevelt could say was that "Wheeler is an old dear; but he is very little more fit than Shafter to command."[123] Wheeler was sixty-one years old at the time, and his health deteriorated quickly during the campaign.

The condition of the expedition's senior officers would encourage Roosevelt to focus on overhauling the system of army promotions after he became president. He may have determined to fight against future "Shafters," but in 1898, during the heat of the moment, he was unfair to the general. Shafter had his problems, but the colonel of the Rough Riders (Roosevelt received a promotion during the Cuba campaign) showed little concern for the broad nature of the difficulties that confronted the commander. Shafter may not have been suited to the demands of his job, but the army as a whole lacked experience at organizing a large expedition, and Shafter did not have much chance to establish order before the departure for Cuba. He was not the complete military incompetent that Roosevelt suggested. Before 1898 he had won a reputation for aggressiveness and toughness from his work on the frontier.

His weight and lack of energy in the tropical heat were problems, but his irresolution in Cuba stemmed largely from poor intelligence about the state of enemy forces, which happened to be in even worse condition than his own, thanks to the work of Cuban insurgents.[124]

If Cuba taught Roosevelt about the army officer corps, then it also provided him with a lesson about the nature of modern warfare. Before the war he had expected to whip the Spaniards easily, and early indications suggested that the Americans would have little problem doing so. On 24 June they pushed back Spanish forces at Las Guásimas on the way to Santiago de Cuba. Unknown to the Americans, the Spanish commander had previously decided on a retreat before the engagement at Las Guásimas.[125] The 1 July attack on the San Juan Heights told a different story. Roosevelt earned his crown of glory in the twin assaults on Kettle and San Juan Hills, and although he exalted at what he had done, the triumph had come at considerable cost. The Rough Riders suffered nearly 20 percent losses during the attack, and, in the days immediately following, Roosevelt became almost frantic. He had seen the face of modern battle, and it did not match his prewar romanticization of warfare. Two days after the attack on the San Juan Heights, Roosevelt wrote to Lodge in urgent tones: "Tell the President for Heaven's sake to send us every regiment and above all every battery possible. We have won so far at a heavy cost; but the Spaniards fight very hard and charging these intrenchments against modern rifles is terrible. We are within measurable distance of a terrible military disaster; we *must* have help—thousands of men, batteries, and *food* and ammunition."[126]

The force of modern firepower had impressed Roosevelt, and at the time he wrote Santiago de Cuba, which sheltered a Spanish naval force and was protected by an army garrison, still held out. He had to wonder what price would be paid for taking the city. Roosevelt and his troops were spared the answer, for the same day that he wrote Lodge, the Spanish squadron attempted to break through the American naval blockade and was decimated. By mid-July the Spaniards surrendered Santiago.[127]

For Roosevelt the rapid conclusion to the campaign meant that the hard reality of war did not make a deep impression. He attributed most of the hardship to human folly and mismanagement, and he chose to celebrate his "regiment on the crowning day of its life" rather than dwell on the bloody nature of the fighting. Before July 1898 was over, his prewar bravado had returned. Now the battle of 1 July had become the "bully fight at Santiago," and the "charge itself was great fun." The belief that he had killed a Spaniard "with my own hand" signaled to him that he had entered an exclusive brotherhood, the brotherhood of the warrior. By the time of World War I, his old assumptions of war's glory continued to burn brightly, and he would wish his sons their "crowded hours" as well.[128]

Roosevelt's experience with war helps to explain such thinking. The Spanish-American War was a brief struggle, with only 114 days of fighting.[129] For Roosevelt personally, the war came down to one day of skirmishing at Las Guásimas and one day of hard fighting on the San Juan Heights. He risked much, but his time on campaign paled, by comparison, to what many veterans of the Civil War had endured over the course of four years.

The fact that the Rough Riders prevailed in spite of command, transport, supply, and medical problems confirmed for him that valor and human spirit would triumph in the end. During the desperate days after the San Juan fight, when the normally buoyant Roosevelt was worried, his confidence in his men never flagged. He said of his regiment, "I am as proud of it as I can be." And his book about the war, *The Rough Riders*, belied satirist Finley Peter Dunne's witticism that a better title would have been *Alone in Cubia*. Roosevelt, in fact, filled the text with praise for the officers and troops who served with him. He relayed, for example, how Capt. Albert Mills "had been shot through the head" during the assault on the San Juan Heights, but that "he would not go back or let any man assist him." Troopers John Waller and Fred Bugbee, both westerners, demonstrated their resolve when each man received a flesh wound in the head, yet "neither of them paid any heed to the wounds." Such performances, especially from the troopers of the West, validated for Roosevelt the notion that hard experience and personal fortitude, rather than a formal military education, provided the best school of the soldier. He wrote of his command: "They were natural fighters, men of great intelligence, great courage, great hardihood, and physical prowess. . . . It must be remembered that they were already good individual fighters, skilled in the use of the horse and the rifle, so that there was no need of putting them through the kind of training in which the ordinary raw recruit must spend his first year or two."[130]

Roosevelt gave plenty of credit to his men, but he remained the center of attention, and news of their exploits added luster to his political fortunes. Throughout the war he was a darling of the press. Roosevelt knew how to make himself part of the story. He always seemed ready with a colorful quip or about to perform a dramatic feat. Reporters who wanted to be part of the action felt they needed to be near the most famous Rough Rider. Richard Harding Davis of the *New York Herald*, whose embellished accounts of the Cuban insurgency and Spanish brutality before 1898 had helped create the conflict, now trooped alongside Roosevelt and recorded his exploits.[131] Roosevelt was also gratified that General Wheeler intended to nominate him for the Medal of Honor because of his actions on the San Juan Heights. The medal would have represented a tremendous political asset, but Roosevelt apparently craved the award as a tangible symbol of his courage and service: "I think I earned my Colonelcy and medal of honor, and hope I get them; but it doesn't make much difference, for nothing can take away the fact that for the ten great days of its life I commanded the regiment, and led it victoriously in a hard fought battle."[132] The nomination for the Medal of Honor reaffirmed Roosevelt's sense of his gallantry, but the award never came during his lifetime. His own penchant for controversy worked against him.

Although newly promoted to colonel, Roosevelt assumed a prominent place in the withdrawal of the expedition after the fighting. At the end of July 1898, he worried that disease would soon decimate the troops, more than Spanish bullets had ever done. The yellow fever season was soon on the Americans, and the disease threatened to kill men "like rotten sheep." Malarial fever had so weakened the command that when "yellow jack" hit, Roosevelt claimed, over half the army would die.[133] He had good reason for concern, as disease had devastated Caribbean invaders in the past. Other officers shared this worry, and General Shafter informed Washington of the danger, asking for permission to relocate to the United States.[134] Roosevelt wrote a strong letter to Henry Cabot Lodge in favor of withdrawing the expedition and railed against Secretary Alger for exposing the troops to yellow fever. He condemned Alger's inaction as "this particular form of murder."[135] Roosevelt's signature was also on the famous "Round Robin Letter," which the expedition's division and brigade officers submitted in support of Shafter's plea.[136] Both letters reached the press and made national headlines on 4 August, the same day that the administration announced the return of the expedition. These simultaneous events created the impression that McKinley and Alger had neglected the welfare of the victorious troops until anxious commanders had bypassed normal channels to get action. In fact, the president had already decided on the removal based on Shafter's communication and first learned of the Round Robin and Roosevelt's letter in the morning newspapers. The affair embarrassed the administration, which had not yet revealed the poor conditions in Cuba and was engaged in negotiations with Spain. Secretary Alger blamed Roosevelt in particular, and thereafter the colonel's chances for a Medal of Honor dropped precipitously.[137]

Governor of New York

On 7 August 1898 Colonel Roosevelt, on horseback, led the Rough Riders to the waterfront of Santiago de Cuba. Worn out, the regiment was going home. The troops boarded their transport, the *Miami,* and eight days later arrived at Montauk, Long Island, where they were to recuperate. An enthusiastic crowd waited and surged toward the dock with "tumultuous cheering" and "loud shouts of 'Welcome Home.'" Roosevelt was the star attraction, and he did not fail to perform. He thrived on the attention and seemed also to have drawn strength from the war, as the press noted that "his manner had lost none of its old-time vigor. His complexion was ruddy and healthy, and it did not seem as if he had lost a pound of flesh." The colonel, dressed in a new khaki uniform, gave the crowd just the kind of remarks it craved. When asked how he was feeling, Roosevelt replied, "Well, I am disgracefully healthy. Really, I am ashamed of myself, feeling so well and strong, with all these poor fellows suffering and so weak they can hardly stand. But I tell you we had a bully fight. This is a fine regiment, all a lot of crack-a-jacks." In comments delivered later that afternoon, Roosevelt again lauded the Rough Riders and reinforced the notion that hardy living, rather than the classroom, forged true soldiers. He praised individual members of the regiment and asserted that the Rough Riders succeeded because "ninety-five percent of my men had at one time or another herded cattle on horseback, or hunted big game with the rifle."[138]

Roosevelt was riding a massive wave of popularity. The "Roosevelt boom" had started even before his crowded hour on the San Juan Heights. Some New York Republicans mentioned him as their best hope to retain the governor's chair following the scandal-plagued administration of Frank Black. After the San Juan Heights, the talk included the presidency. In August 1898 one crowd shouted, "We'll make you President yet."[139] The signing of a peace protocol with Spain on 12 August had assured that Roosevelt would be free to run for the New York prize, which, if claimed, might indeed make him a contender to follow McKinley in 1904.[140]

Roosevelt won the New York governor's race by 17,194 votes, a respectable but not wide margin. The political tide had shifted against the Republicans, but Roosevelt had helped save the governorship for the Grand Old Party.[141] He would serve as governor for two years, until William McKinley picked him for vice president. For an analysis of Roosevelt and the military, the gubernatorial years are significant. His campaign for the office, made possible by his military service, would also be complicated by Roosevelt's actions in Cuba. And as New York governor, he had military responsibilities as "Commander in Chief of State Military and Naval Forces."[142] He would have close dealings with the state National Guard, and the relationship was tense. The experience would reinforce his impressions about the weaknesses of that military arm.

If Theodore Roosevelt emerged from the Spanish-American War convinced of his own virtue and of the rectitude of volunteers such as the Rough Riders, he was equally convinced that the National Guard lacked leaders of the same moral and military caliber. Both in the training of troops and in the fighting, Roosevelt witnessed National Guard troops in action and found defects in their preparation, equipment, and leadership. Soon after the war he recounted how former guardsmen in the Rough Riders had sometimes been more of a burden than a benefit. Although most took well to the training of the regiment along with their fellow volunteers, some former guardsmen entered the federal service with the attitude that they had already mastered soldiering. As Roosevelt put it, "the man was a curse to me who had been a National Guardsman and came in with the impression that there were very few who could give him points—he knew it all."[143] "If he realized," Roosevelt later observed in his *Autobiography*, "that he had learned only five per-cent of his profession, that there remained ninety-five per cent to accomplish before he would be a good soldier, why, he had profited immensely." Roosevelt faulted the guard's emphasis on parade-ground drill for not training men to handle the stress of war. "If the man had merely served in a National Guard reg-iment, or in the Regular Army at some post in a civilized coun-try where he learned nothing except what could be picked up on the parade ground," then that man might be harmed, just as much as helped, by such limited experience.[144]

Such preparation apparently made units composed mostly of guardsmen almost worthless in battle, at least according to Roosevelt. He arrived at this sweeping conclusion based only on his limited exposure to combat. Shortly after the action on the San Juan Heights, he wrote to Secretary of War Alger to lobby for redeployment of the Rough Riders. He wanted them assigned to the expedition that would invade the Spanish col-ony of Puerto Rico. Bursting with pride for his unit and its accomplishments, Roosevelt bragged about its quality, but at the expense of state troops: "We earnestly hope that you will send us—most of the regulars and, at any rate, the cavalry division, including the Rough Riders, who are as good as any regulars, and three times as good as any State troops—to Porto Rico." Still exuberant from winning glory on the San Juan Heights, Roosevelt continued to thump the guard: "We could land at Porto Rico in this cavalry division close to 4,000 men, who would be worth easily any 10,000 National Guard, armed with black powder, Springfield, or other archaic weapons." Alger rebuked him for making "invidious comparisons," and Roos-evelt explained that he had acted primarily in a "spirit of cal-culated imprudence" to call Alger's attention to the obsolete black powder weapons that the War Department had provided to state forces.[145] This excuse masked nothing. His original letter to the secretary had betrayed deep disdain for state troops rather than concern about the quality of their weaponry. Additionally, Roosevelt's desire to put the Rough Riders in action again in Puerto Rico displayed more exuberance than sound military judgment, given the deplorable state of their health.

T.R. would soon regret belittling the National Guard. After the publication of the Round Robin letter, Alger, in a fit of anger, released Roosevelt's criticism of state troops. According to one observer, Alger "threw a boomerang" politically by attacking the popular Rough Rider and for violating the confidentiality of Roosevelt's communication with him. Alger, though, might have taken pleasure at how his action affected the New York governor's race that fall. In a tight contest, the alienation of the New York guard might prove decisive, and the candidate knew it. With over nine hundred officers and more than thirteen thousand troops, New York maintained the largest state force in the country. Moreover, with an annual budget of one million dollars the New York guard was a potent force for political patronage. Roosevelt's outward buoyancy betrayed an inner pessimism when he confessed to Senator Lodge, a few days before the election: "I have no idea how this fight is going. It is evident that the National Guard will give a majority against me, partly on account of my letter to Alger, but more on account of the fact that they were really not very good soldiers and are sore and angry and mortified about the hardships they have encountered."[146] The guardsmen's hostility simply strengthened Roosevelt's opinion that they lacked the same kind of soldierly virtue that he and the Rough Riders had exhibited in Cuba. For a man who constantly measured others against a lofty personal code and preached his views in self-righteous tones, he was close to a wholesale declaration of the guard as morally defective.

Roosevelt's first weeks in office would do nothing to reverse that attitude. As governor, he was commander of the New York National Guard, and in that capacity he inherited a case against officers of the Seventy-First Regiment. This New York guard unit had entered federal service during the war with Spain and, like the Rough Riders, had seen action in Cuba. During the charge at the San Juan Heights, senior field officers of the Seventy-First failed to lead their troops in the rush on the Spanish lines. Two privates later testified before a court of inquiry that they found one of their officers "one mile back behind a tree" and another two miles behind the lines.[147] As a result, the unit "did very badly."[148] Proceedings against the officers were occurring when Roosevelt took office, and his experience with the court-martial further convinced him of the unmilitary nature of the guard.

Lt. Col. Clinton Smith, Maj. John H. Whittle, and Maj. Elmore F. Austin faced charges for cowardice and incompetence.[149] By almost any measure, but certainly by Roosevelt's, these officers failed the test of soldierly virtue. As Roosevelt put it to William Conant Church, editor of the *Army and Navy Journal*, "Do you think that at Pittsburgh Landing [in the Civil War] there were many Colonels, Lieutenant Colonels and Senior Majors who ran when their regiments stood, or stood when their regiments went forward . . . ?"[150] Not only had these men failed to conform to the standard of leadership that Roosevelt himself had met on the San Juan Heights, but he also considered the proceedings against them to lack a proper military quality. More precisely, he felt that the men would not face the justice they deserved because the court was following more "the methods of the town meeting than those of military service."[151] This criticism went straight to the heart of Roosevelt's attitude toward the guard. It served too many state and local political priorities to make it an effective military instrument. The New York guard, with its large budget, was organized to provide maximum benefit to state officeholders who wanted to dispense favors.

Moreover, units elected officers, which sometimes meant that soldiers felt that they could replace, or refuse to obey, an officer with whom they disagreed. Two days after taking office in January 1899, Roosevelt imposed a military tone on the proceedings by expanding the authority of the military court. Two of the charged officers then resigned their commissions, but the third, Lieutenant Colonel Smith, persisted. A new military board then convened just to try him, and when Smith appealed to the New York Supreme Court to prevent the trial, Roosevelt intervened and denied the civil court's right to hear the case. He was determined that Smith face military justice.[152] The court of inquiry would find Smith guilty, and he was removed from command of the Seventy-First.[153]

Roosevelt's actions toward the officers of the Seventy-First New York triggered a vehement response, which doubtlessly convinced him further of the hopelessly unmilitary nature of the guard and its partisans. In 1900 Col. Alexander Bacon published a brochure that defended the Seventy-First New York and leveled charges that Roosevelt had been a "quitter" at the San Juan Heights. According to Roosevelt, Bacon was a former guardsman who had been a counsel to the officers of the Seventy-First during the court-martial proceedings. Bacon employed material from the report of the inspector general of the U.S. Volunteers to make his accusations. Supposedly, Roosevelt had commented on the debilitated state of his command after the battle and had said, "No man can decry me or my regiment but we must accede to the next proposition from the enemy." Roosevelt questioned the authenticity of the statement and, in turn, accused Bacon of resorting to "blackguardism" after the ruling against the officers of the Seventy-First. Although he considered Bacon "too unimportant of vermin for me to take notice," Roosevelt contemplated releasing the letters that recommended him for a Medal of Honor if the attempt to darken his reputation went any further.[154] The governor hesitated to counter Bacon directly if he could avoid such action, for such a move would call attention to the charges and deepen the controversy: "I have not thought it worth while to take any notice of Bacon who is simply a prime blackguard engaged to do dirty work for some men who flinched at Santiago."[155] Instead, he relied on the testimonials of others about his actions in Cuba. His nomination for the vice presidency in 1900 also likely deflected attention and helped to deflate the controversy.

Roosevelt perhaps reacted so strongly because there was some truth to Bacon's charge. He had seemed near panic at the increasingly desperate supply and medical situation in the days following the victory on the San Juan Heights.[156] Bacon's charge also threatened his heroic public image, which, if not refuted, could foreclose on his chances of even higher office. In addition, Roosevelt would have to admit to himself that he had harbored feelings that seemed to defy the masculine standard he had set for himself.

The controversy over the officers of the Seventy-First did not mean that Roosevelt gave up on the New York National Guard entirely. He could not, even if he had wanted, because politically the guard was there to stay. Roosevelt even conceded that the National Guard possessed a degree of usefulness. As he would later observe in 1917, he felt militia forces should be left "to do the necessary and important state duty which the National Guard is peculiarly fitted to perform."[157] In other words, Roosevelt viewed the guard as a valuable supplement to local police forces, but not much else, certainly not as the first reserve for the army. He would employ the guard, like so many other governors—before and since—to help maintain, or restore, public order. During the spring of 1900, for example, workers at the Croton Aqueduct struck to protest low wages and poor working conditions. Roosevelt dispatched the state militia to keep order as tensions rose, for he had been "very much concerned over the situation" and did not want "any riot."[158] Feelings had indeed reached the boiling point, and the situation led to the death of one guardsman, who was killed by an unknown assailant. The strike soon collapsed, as contractors refused to meet the protesters' demands, and Roosevelt contributed fifty dollars to a fund to help the family of the slain guardsman.[159]

A dedicated reformer, Roosevelt launched a campaign to improve the guard. If he was forced into a marriage with the guard as governor, then he determined to make the guard into a better partner. He chose his old ally from the New York City Police Board, Avery Andrews, to become adjutant general of the New York forces. Now that Roosevelt had Andrews by his side, he proclaimed, "confidence in his [Andrews's] ability to build up the National Guard to its former standard."[160]

If reform were to occur, then a plan was needed, and the governor wanted more than just the New York guard improved. Roosevelt pushed an initiative to reform the guard at the national level. The reform of one guard organization, even if it was the largest in the country, would be meaningless if other guard organizations failed to follow suit. Roosevelt used his contacts in high places and urged Secretary of War Elihu Root, the old Roosevelt family friend, to promote the idea of a report on reserve systems. The report would examine militia forces in other countries, especially in Britain; discuss their principles of organization; and investigate their practical workings. By demonstrating the practices of other nations, such an investigation could provide legitimacy for reserve reform proposals within the United States and draw public and congressional attention to the need for change.

President McKinley agreed to the proposition and asked Col. William Cary Sanger to carry out the task. Sanger was the inspector general of the New York guard, and his appointment recognized the project as a New York initiative. Roosevelt also ordered Sanger to provide the state government with a copy of his findings. In his charge to Sanger, the governor left open the possibility that the reserve force need not be the guard: "It is true that the Army of the United States should have an effective reserve and that the relation of the State forces to the army should be definitely settled."[161] In this one line the governor suggested another avenue of reform: stronger federal control of the guard. The Sanger Report appeared in late 1900, but by then Roosevelt was contemplating his elevation to the vice presidency. When Roosevelt moved suddenly into the White House, the Sanger Report helped lay the basis for militia reform during his presidency.[162]

Roosevelt's stay at the governor's mansion was too short for him to have much of an impact on militia reform. He soon had a more important mission. Roosevelt needed to help William McKinley win a second presidential term, and the war-hero governor could best perform that service as McKinley's running mate. The "Easy Boss" of New York's Republican machine, Sen. Thomas Collier Platt, had also decided that the vice presidency provided the perfect place to ease the reform-minded Roosevelt out of New York politics and prevent further damage to the party machinery. Roosevelt understood that the vice presidency was an empty position and protested, "I would a great deal rather be anything, say professor of history, than Vice-President."[163] Roosevelt craved action, and he understood that the vice presidency would relegate him to obscurity for four years. Ideally, he would have preferred to run again for governor and then perhaps make a bid for the White House in 1904—anything but the boredom and political frustration that the vice presidency offered. But Roosevelt remained a good soldier for the Republican Party. He knew that without faithful service to the party's power brokers, he would also be condemned to political oblivion.

Senator Platt gleefully went to Washington in March 1901 with the new governor of New York, Benjamin Odell, to see "Teddy take the veil." He could not know that in a little more than six months, Theodore Roosevelt, at age forty-two, would become president of the United States. Though youthful, Roosevelt, with his early start in politics and long and varied public service, was well prepared for the nation's highest office. He seemed especially ready to be commander in chief of the army and navy, thanks to his work in the Navy Department and service in the Spanish-American War. During his nearly eight years in the White House, he would refer constantly to those experiences as he pursued his vision of a proper military establishment for a newly emerged great power.

3

The New Hand on the Helm

Almost one year after William McKinley died, the victim of an assassin, Americans worried that they might lose another leader. President Theodore Roosevelt was on a speaking tour to Massachusetts in early September 1902. On 3 September a streetcar smashed into his carriage in Pittsfield. The impact tossed Roosevelt, the governor of Massachusetts, and others from the carriage. Fortunately for the president and his companions, they landed on a pile of soft earth. Roosevelt came away with a cut lip, a bruised face, and a battered leg. His bodyguard, Secret Service agent William Craig, was not so lucky. Craig, known as the "giant of the Secret Service force," fell under the wheels of the streetcar and died instantly. After being thrown from the carriage, the president "was on his feet in a flash. He assisted the others to arise, and his first words were a question as to the condition of the other members of the party." Reportedly, he also confronted the streetcar operator, yelling, "This is the most damnable outrage I ever knew," while shaking his fist. Despite the tragedy, his injuries, and pleas to cancel the rest of his schedule, Roosevelt resumed the trip after a half hour. He said that large crowds had gathered and that he should greet them, although he refused to deliver any more speeches and "wished no demonstrations on account of the terrible accident."[1]

By September 1902 Americans knew that they had a different sort of president. Theodore Roosevelt painted the political canvas with bold strokes, and he lived life as fully in the White

House as he had before becoming its occupant. Roosevelt realized life was short. He was forty-three years old at the time of the collision, and death had stolen his father at age forty-six. Roosevelt was now in the place where he could most advance his country's destiny. His view of the presidency was as expansive as his outlook on America's new role in the world as a great power with overseas interests and possessions. He would employ the powers of the office in a way not seen since Abraham Lincoln and would leave a modern, activist cast to the executive branch. Roosevelt believed that the army and navy had a key role to play in assuring American greatness, and he would use his authority and influence as commander in chief to modernize and enlarge the armed forces.

As telling as his emergence from the streetcar crash was for the style of Roosevelt's presidency, his itinerary for the day prior to the accident illuminated his conduct of military affairs. When it came to things military, Roosevelt was going to be a hands-on president, sometimes literally, at least when it came to matters for which he cared most deeply. The president visited Springfield, Massachusetts, on 2 September 1902. Seventy-five thousand people greeted the chief executive, who made the U.S. Armory at Springfield his first stop. After a twenty-one gun salute, Roosevelt headed to the armory's offices, where he was "keenly interested" in a new model of rifle. The arsenal's latest product was supposed to be an improvement over the army's current rifle, the Krag-Jørgensen. The president "carefully examined every detail of the mechanism, and finally asked, 'What of its accuracy?'" When told that the new rifle was much more accurate than an older Springfield model and "somewhat better" than the Krag, Roosevelt responded "that this was an important consideration."[2]

Later that day he spoke to a crowd of twenty-five thousand in Springfield's Court Square. There he championed an expansionist foreign policy and defended the conduct of American soldiers in the Philippines. Charges of American atrocities against Filipinos had riled opponents of American expansion, and Roosevelt wanted to play down the charges. He admitted wrongdoing on the part of a few but pledged that "wherever it has been possible to find them out the offender has been punished." He also reminded the audience that while the troops were fighting a "treacherous foe in the heartbreaking work of jungle warfare," any crimes had been occasional and committed under stress. "On the whole," Roosevelt proclaimed to applause, "the men who for three years in those islands have followed the flag of the United States have added a new page to the honor roll of the Nation." He drew even louder applause when he taunted critics, implicitly casting doubt on their manliness: "I think that the men who sat at home could have afforded to be more lenient in bearing judgment."[3]

On that day in Springfield, Roosevelt donned the two hats that he wore most commonly as commander in chief. One was the campaign hat that he wore in Cuba, the hat of the colonel of the Rough Riders. In his visit to the Springfield armory, the president was interested in the intricacies of weaponry. This Roosevelt was the one who dealt in minutiae, simply because military matters of all kinds fascinated him. He was also the man with leftover business. Roosevelt had been exposed to a number of things during his short stint in the army and during his year at the Navy Department, and there were many unfinished tasks. He stood now in the best possible position to complete that work or address problems that he had seen. The other hat that he wore was the top hat of the policy maker and the leader who would keep the eyes of the American people focused on grand goals for themselves and for their country.

No matter the headgear, Roosevelt would bring to the task his formidable powers of persuasion and strength of purpose. He had honed his skills at public relations over the years. This ability represented, perhaps, the most important weapon in his political arsenal. Without effective persuasion, he would be unable to realize old goals or accomplish new ones. His emphasis on media, image making, and public outreach added another feature to the portfolio of the president: advocate in chief. Roosevelt's role as advertiser, then, merits examination first, for from it all other things flowed.

The Bully Pulpit

Theodore Roosevelt's first day working at the White House began a new era for the presidency. Roosevelt would be something Americans had never before witnessed in the presidential chair: not only was this president going to be the object of news; he was also going to create and manage stories about himself. According to the *New York Times*, on the morning of 22 September 1901 Roosevelt walked to his office from his sister Anna's home. Throughout the morning he met members of the House and Senate, and he paid special attention to the southerners. To Sen. Hernando D. Money of Mississippi, the president, in an attempt to establish the national appeal of his new administration, declared, "I am half Southern . . . and I have lived in the West, so that I feel I can represent the whole country." At 1:30 p.m. he departed the White House, accompanied by Gen. Leonard Wood, now governor general of Cuba, for a brisk walk back to his sister's residence for lunch. Later that afternoon he and Wood mounted horses at the White House for a ride to the northwest section of Washington. Press reports detailed the president's attire—a black cutaway coat, soft felt hat, tan riding gloves, trousers buckled at the instep, and small hunting spurs—and noted how he "presented a handsome figure on his spirited animal." "He . . . handled his mount like a skilled and veteran horseman." The story of the president's first day at the White House also noted that not since President Chester A. Arthur had a chief executive rode horseback regularly.[4]

From his first day at the White House, Roosevelt demonstrated that he was going to manage his own public relations—and that he was a master at generating publicity. He almost always had ready the quotable line, as in his quip to Senator Money about his countrywide appeal. Roosevelt knew even better how to make himself the story, especially with his flair for action. His public horseback ride with Leonard Wood illustrated that Roosevelt, simply through the act of living his life, was going to establish a politically advantageous image of himself. This president would live life in the White House to the fullest, and he would call attention to himself and the goals for which he worked.

Roosevelt possessed great personal appeal. He was naturally gregarious with his infectious smile, good humor, and boundless energy, and he loved to be at the center of everything. As his daughter Alice would observe, "My father always wanted to be the corpse at every funeral, the bride at every wedding, and the baby at every christening."[5] Roosevelt's well-heeled upbringing also instilled in him a confidence that put him at ease in dealing with people, and reporters delighted in his informal style. Certainly, none of this was new for him. By the time he reached the presidency, he was an old hand at dealing with reporters. They had followed his exploits in Cuba, and, as assistant navy secretary and a member of the New York City Police Board, he had courted reporters to advance the causes of navalism and police reform.

As president, Roosevelt continued to curry the favor of reporters. He encouraged coverage by establishing the first White House press room and by conducting frequent news conferences and interviews. Reporters loved the access and being privy to inside information, and Roosevelt exploited that sentiment. During weekdays he would invite favorite correspondents to attend his 1:00 p.m. shave, during which he would banter with the reporters. Roosevelt was also aware of the reporters' deadlines and credited himself with discovering that Monday was

a slow news day and thus a day when he could steal the headlines much more readily. Roosevelt's attentiveness worked, for
reporters—flattered at the attention and charmed by the man—
befriended not only Roosevelt but also his policies. If the president was not available, then his secretary, William Loeb Jr.,
fulfilled the same function of a present-day press secretary and
supplied White House news to the press.[6]

Accessibility to the president helped to shape stories, but
Roosevelt and his staff worked even more assiduously to craft
an appealing image. For example, the White House encouraged coverage of the president's hikes and hunts, his so-called
scrambles, because such activities reinforced an image of rug-
gedness and vigor. Depictions of the chief executive in ten-
nis attire, however, were forbidden, as they seemed less than
manly, even though Roosevelt was an avid player. The president
would also punish journalists who ran unfavorable coverage by
denying them the information that they coveted. He harbored
a special animus toward the *Boston Herald*, for as he wrote in
December 1904 to its editor, Edwin Haskell, "it has been difficult for me to avoid the conviction that in the editorial columns of the *Herald*, and in the letters written for it . . . there is
deliberate falsification."[7] On this particular occasion Roosevelt
objected to a 24 November article that accused his children of
tormenting a turkey on the White House lawn while he supposedly looked on and laughed. Roosevelt called the story "delib-
erately invented" and said he would not have paid attention
to it "had it not attacked my children, accusing them and me
of outrageous cruelty."[8]

He condemned reporters who committed such perfidy to
the Ananias Club, which he named for a liar in the Bible who
died for his transgressions. Correspondents relegated to the
club had, in Roosevelt's opinion, spread falsehoods or revealed
a confidence and were banned from the White House. Despite
his claims that he overlooked most slights, Roosevelt never took

criticism well, and the Ananias Club symbolized well the self-righteous anger that contrary news could provoke in him. In the case of the *Herald*, Roosevelt banished all of its representatives from the White House until the paper apologized. He relented only after the *Herald* issued a retraction.[9]

Roosevelt knew what the press was writing, for he closely monitored its coverage. He filled his letters with reactions to various news stories. In October 1904, for example, he wrote his son Kermit about the contrary positions of the New York *Evening Post* and *Collier's Weekly* on his position about race and imperialism: "The *Evening Post* . . . profess[es] loud sympathy for my attitude toward the colored man of the South, but in spite of this oppose[es] me because of my attitude toward the Filipinos. On the other hand, *Collier's Weekly* and a much larger body of men profess great sympathy with my attitude toward the Filipino, but attack me because of my attitude toward the colored man of the South."[10] Roosevelt understood something that many of his peers had not yet grasped. National magazines and mass-circulation newspapers had come into their own, and they were the vehicles through which he could reach a wide audience. Roosevelt had latched on to one of the most potent sources of presidential power in the twentieth century: the appeal to the public.[11] Or, as he put it, the presidency provided him a "bully pulpit" for preaching his messages. He often turned to the citizenry to pry legislation out of Congress, and this tactic was essential to the advancement of his military policies. Moreover, his use of the media signaled a larger trend. The link between the media and the presidency would grow increasingly strong over the course of the twentieth century. Advances in electronic communication have only enhanced the chief executive's ability to make public appeals to the point that the presidential image, words, and voice can instantaneously appear before citizens on a variety of devices. The perceived intimacy between people and president has not been entirely positive, for concurrent with the power of the press to influence is its power to destroy. Americans could view their presidents celebrating political victories or twisting in the winds of controversy. Roosevelt attracted his share of bad press, but when he departed office the public decided that it had enjoyed the ride. His ability to grab headlines and cultivate popularity set a standard that his successors did not match until Franklin Roosevelt.

Off the Front Porch and into the Fray

In 1896 William McKinley had run a typical front-porch campaign for president. He had preserved the dignity of his candidacy by letting surrogates such as Theodore Roosevelt carry on the actual campaigning. Such was the accepted practice for presidential candidates. McKinley's Democratic rival that year, William Jennings Bryan, broke precedent by personally headlining his national campaign with hundreds of speeches on a rail tour. Roosevelt despised Bryan's politics, which he denounced as a "terrible menace to the country," but he embraced the man's style.[12] He would not be a front-porch president. Although convention would bind him when he ran for the presidency in his own right in 1904, Roosevelt sought to bring his message directly to the people as much as possible. He had much to say, whether the topic was conservation of natural resources, regulation of business trusts, spelling reform, or an expansionist foreign policy. In his public appearances he devoted much time to military affairs because they were close to his heart, but also because he shrewdly recognized the political benefits to be derived from his close association with a strong defense, both for the services and for himself. His personal popularity would add luster to the image of the armed forces, while national pride in a powerful military would enhance his reputation and extend his popularity.

Roosevelt delighted in appearing at military celebrations because such events gave him a forum for spreading his message about a vigorous military policy. Such ceremonies allowed him to invoke the nation's martial past to arouse support for modern-day forces. For example, he journeyed to Sharpsburg, Maryland, in September 1903 to dedicate a monument to New Jersey soldiers who fought at the Battle of Antietam in 1862. Roosevelt took full advantage of the occasion because the 1904 presidential election was almost one year away. On the rail trip Roosevelt greeted crowds at Chambersburg, Pennsylvania, and Hagerstown, Maryland, before he joined nearly one thousand New Jersey Civil War veterans at the battlefield. As he dedicated the monument, a forty-foot granite column topped by the figure of a Union officer, the president recalled the sacrifices made during the Civil War and the War for Independence and told the assembled veterans, "it was because you . . . triumphed in those dark years that every American now holds his head high." With such rhetoric Roosevelt stressed the notion of the grand things that could be won on the field of battle. He went on to equate deeds of good citizenship with feats of past military valor, taking advantage of the moment to remind his listeners about present-day American troops "who uphold the honor of the flag in far tropic lands." A savvy politician, Roosevelt wanted to wrap the expansionist venture in the Philippines in the cloak of the two great military struggles of American history. The crowd devoured his words and also his performance. A drenching rain hit during Roosevelt's remarks and saturated the president and his listeners. He waved off an umbrella and then declared, "If they can stand it I can." Near the end of his remarks, he expressed concern about his listeners and promised to conclude soon, but one member of the assemblage shouted back, "Oh go on. Keep it up until to-morrow."[13]

The sky was again overcast a month later at the unveiling of a statue of Gen. William T. Sherman in Washington DC. No rain, however, marred the event. Flags, along with red, white, and blue banners, decorated Pennsylvania Avenue, and a parade

of soldiers, sailors, marines, and District of Columbia guardsmen entertained a crowd of thousands. Adm. George Dewey
appeared in full dress uniform, and the president's cabinet
attended as well. Amid the pageantry, Roosevelt made an even
more direct connection between the military glories of earlier
generations and the duties of present-day citizens when he proclaimed, "No man is warranted in feeling pride in the deeds of
the army and navy of the past if he does not back up the army
and navy of the present." Roosevelt then proceeded to call for
"no let-up" in the expansion of the navy and for making "our
small regular army" an effective nucleus of much larger wartime forces. His message received extensive coverage in the
Washington Post, which splashed the ceremony across the front
page and recorded the president's comments in full.[14]

The press practices of the time and the general spirit of the
age eased Roosevelt's job in promoting his views. Crowds were
receptive because he was the president, and although scandals
had erupted around earlier administrations, the office itself
remained an object of veneration and not yet subject to the
skepticism and cynicism that would follow in the wake of the
Vietnam War, the Watergate affair, and other such episodes.
Americans of Roosevelt's era were nationalists, even if a strong
antimilitary strain ran through the culture, and many opposed
an imperialistic foreign policy. Strong military forces represented
national power and cultural superiority. In short, the president
was preaching to a receptive audience. Finally, despite hostile
editorials and the falsehoods that so disturbed Roosevelt, press
reports tended to be much less critical compared to the coverage of the later twentieth century and beyond. Visual media
remained limited, so description was at a premium in press
reports. Detailed accounts of an event allowed the public to
visualize the atmosphere surrounding something that had trans-
pired, and newspapers would print verbatim the president's
remarks so that the broader public could know what was said.

The bigger the event meant the greater the public attention, and Roosevelt had the advantage as commander in chief of staging grand spectacles and thrusting himself in the middle of them. The most thrilling of all would be the departure and return of the "Great White Fleet" on the world cruise near the end of his presidency, which is discussed in a subsequent chapter, but there were other less spectacular, yet still significant, events that served a similar purpose.

Roosevelt loved naval reviews because he could dramatize the value of big ships and show off his handiwork in pushing naval expansion. He also simply enjoyed watching the navy at work, and politically such appearances paid dividends, for they tied him closely to the powerful vessels that were being displayed. A review in Long Island Sound in September 1906 was representative. Twelve battleships, eight cruisers, and a host of lesser vessels—forty-five ships in all, one for every state in the Union at that time—gathered in three long columns. One hundred thousand spectators crowded the shore for what the *New York Times* trumpeted as "the greatest naval display America ever had." The president sailed in the middle of it all aboard the yacht *Mayflower*. Members of the House and Senate Committees on Naval Affairs accompanied him, as did representatives of the media. After the review Roosevelt descended from the bridge of the *Mayflower*, "his face wreathed in smiles," and he threw his arms around the shoulders of several senators and representatives who were gathered in a group. He proclaimed that the mighty fleet was their handiwork and that "it has all been done within the past ten years." He also applauded their "wisdom in the appropriations for the target practice, for there is where the American Navy excels." By giving Congress credit in such an emotional atmosphere, the president wanted to sustain support for the navy at a time when enthusiasm for naval expansion was starting to wane. An evening light show capped off the review.[15] Roo-

sevelt could not have hoped for a better exhibition of American naval power and later exulted, "I defy anyone with a spark
of national pride . . . not to feel moved at such a sight."[16]

T.R. also worked to shape press coverage, just as he had when
he had been a junior public official. During the naval review
Roosevelt invited two prominent writers to be among his special guests on the *Mayflower.* James Brendan Connolly penned
stories of the sea, but Finley Peter Dunne was even more of a
favorite. Dunne was the most influential satirist in turn-of-the-
century America. He had become famous for the observations
made by his character Mr. Dooley, who was an Irish bartender.
The day after the review, Roosevelt informed Elihu Root that "I
wanted both Dunne and Connolly to grow to have a personal
feeling for the navy—to get under the naval spell—because I
want them both to be our allies in keeping the people awake
to what it means to have such a navy."[17] In short, the president
was stroking both men with an eye to future benefits. Members
of the press also had their turn with the president at the review.
The signs that announced the press boat teased Roosevelt for
his attempt to revise American spelling along phonetic lines.
Instead of "Press Boat," the billboards read "Pres Bot." Roosevelt laughed loudly when he spotted the signs.[18]

The president employed personal appearances to advance
other military policies too. He escorted his wife and daughter
Alice to Sea Girt, New Jersey, in July 1902. The usual enthusiastic crowds gathered, and Roosevelt delighted in the reception, gushing at one point, "Oh, I'm so glad I'm an American."
There to inspect a National Guard encampment, Roosevelt
rode a black horse as he reviewed a regiment of soldiers and
an artillery battery. But his remarks targeted a larger audience.
Public appearances, especially at military gatherings, gave Roosevelt great pleasure, but they pleased him more when they
produced results, legislative results. Militia-reform legislation
had passed the House of Representatives, and to help secure

Senate passage the president wanted to highlight the need for the bill. The measure would allow the national government to provide more equipment and assistance to the guard. Roosevelt also seized the occasion to promote his ideas about the link between the good citizen and the good soldier. He praised the guardsmen for their volunteer service and reminded them that "the same qualities that make a man a success, that make him do his duty decently and honestly in a National Guard regiment, are fundamentally the qualities he needs to make him a good citizen in private life." The Rough Rider in him, however, could not entirely shake the contempt for the guard that he had exhibited during the war with Spain. He lectured that "any one who joins the National Guard only to have a good time, pretty surely has a poor time and certainly makes a poor hand at being a Guardsman."[19]

Whether reviewing troops, witnessing naval maneuvers, or dedicating a monument, Roosevelt stole the spotlight. He was a single figure on whom the press and public could fasten. Roosevelt did, however, often share the military stage with others, for he welcomed allies in his efforts to promote the military services. Like-minded navalists, for example, formed the Navy League in 1902 "to advance the interests of the Navy in every practicable way, and to keep the public informed regarding its needs and its accomplishments."[20] League members published a journal, but the organization's influence remained limited during Roosevelt's administration despite support from the president and the Navy Department. The navy even bought five hundred copies of the Navy League's journal every month to help boost the organization.[21] Within the government Elihu Root, when he was secretary of war during Roosevelt's first years in office, joined Secretary of the Navy William Moody in promoting their respective services. The navy benefited, in particular, from having such notables as Admiral Dewey and Alfred T. Mahan in its ranks.

Roosevelt and the other advocates of the armed forces did not occupy the field of public debate alone. Many members of Congress rejected the president's policies as militaristic, expensive, and undemocratic. An active peace movement campaigned against military expansion, arguing that international arbitration represented a more enlightened way to settle disputes. Some of the most well-known Americans promoted the peace approach, including Carl Schurz, Andrew Carnegie, Washington Gladden, David Starr Jordan, Jane Addams, Ida Tarbell, Lincoln Steffens, and Booker T. Washington. At an international peace conference in 1907, Carnegie, as president of the Peace Society of New York City, spoke about a future without war, in which, "the frown of the world would sober any Government tempted to plunge into the mad excess of bloody contest."[22] Administration officials were not necessarily set against the peace movement. Admiral Dewey endorsed arbitration; Elihu Root later headed the Carnegie Endowment for International Peace; and Roosevelt accepted the honorary presidency of the Practical Peace League in 1908. They found international arbitration an acceptable goal, but only if the nation had adequate armaments to protect against aggression.[23] As Roosevelt told Carl Schurz in 1905, "Hitherto peace has often come only because some strong and on the whole just power has by armed force, or the threat of armed force, put a stop to disorder."[24]

In private the president was not so polite toward the peace movement. Roosevelt described peace advocates as the "Carnegie crowd" to his British friend Cecil Arthur Spring Rice. He observed of their efforts: "Everybody ought to believe in peace and everybody ought to believe in temperance; but the professional advocates of both tend toward a peculiarly annoying form of egotistic lunacy."[25]

The emergence of a scandal in late 1901 over American actions in the Philippines would test the new chief executive's ability to shape events. Soon after Roosevelt became president, fresh concerns flared about the war to enforce American control over the Philippines. The conflict had already lasted nearly three years, stoked the anti-imperialist movement, and distressed peace advocates. Continuing resistance to American rule and reports about atrocities against Filipinos led to calls for a congressional investigation.[26] Dispatches relayed how American forces were prepared to reconcentrate the population of Batangas Province to combat the insurrection there. The parallel to Spain's earlier campaign in Cuba was clear, and the *Baltimore Sun* reminded readers how many Cubans had died as a result and how "orators in Congress . . . demanded that the United States intervene and save the Cubans from extermination."[27] Even more disturbing were reports of Americans torturing and summarily executing prisoners. Press accounts described use of the "water cure" to force confessions about insurgent activities. Soldiers would usually drain three or more jugs of water into an insurgent's stomach, and then if the man failed to cooperate they would stand him up and hit him in the jaw or his distended belly. On one occasion a ten-year-old boy was subjected to the treatment when he would not inform on his father, a paymaster in the Philippine army.[28]

Public attention fastened on the pacification of the Philippine island of Samar and on two figures in particular: Gen. Jacob Smith and Maj. Littleton Waller. Resistance to American occupation remained strong on Samar, a fact made clear when Filipinos ambushed the American garrison at Balangiga on 28 September 1901, killing forty-eight. Newly appointed to command on Samar, General Smith made the suppression of resistance his top priority, and, after Balangiga, harsh measures fit the mood of many. Smith allegedly voiced orders to make Samar a "howling wilderness," and many of his officers acted in accord with that sentiment. Major Waller, commander of a marine battalion, ordered the execution of twelve Filipinos without investigation or trial. The killings occurred after an ill-advised and poorly prepared march into the interior. Eleven of Waller's men died from the conditions, and blame was directed at the Filipino porters. They allegedly had hoarded food and committed other acts of treachery. In truth, however, Waller's incompetence caused the disaster.[29] At home headlines broadcast, "Smith's Cruel Order" and "Waller Asked Vengeance," and terms such as "barbarous," "savagery," and "brutality" characterized American actions.[30]

Roosevelt clearly faced a problem. Charges of American atrocities threatened to discredit the imperial project that he deemed vital to national well-being. The president would need to marshal administration resources and rely on allies in Congress and the press to restore confidence in military actions. On Capitol Hill Henry Cabot Lodge provided vital assistance as chair of the Senate Committee on the Philippines. He worked to limit the political damage, but even he could not contain a flood of reports about American abuses. In an effort to stem cries of outrage, the administration announced that men responsible for excesses would be tried in military court. Roosevelt and others also attempted to play down any criminal activity as the work of individuals who had become carried away in difficult conditions. Trials were held, but punishments were mild. General Smith was tried, found "guilty of conduct to the prejudice of good order and military discipline," and retired. Proceedings against Major Waller led to an acquittal, an action that historian Brian Linn characterized as a miscarriage of justice.[31] Denunciations of American policy remained, and Secretary of War Elihu Root received stinging criticism over statements in which he had asserted that the American army had conducted itself with "scrupulous regard for the rules of civilized warfare."[32]

The administration and its allies fought back with a public relations effort that shaped its own version of events. Even as he stated an American commitment to civilized conduct, Secretary Root was crafting a response to the concerns about atrocities. He argued that most American troops maintained discipline, but he did acknowledge that some soldiers had acted beyond the bounds. Those cases were "few and far between," Root claimed, and he added that such incidents should no more define the army "than the deeds of lawless violence which constantly occur in every large city characterize the people of the city."[33] Senator Lodge took the same line in stating that the guerrillas' cruelty may have forced a few otherwise civilized men to cross moral boundaries, but that the nation should still honor the army as an institution.[34] Former members of the Philippine revolutionary government also appeared in Washington. Gen. Felipe Buencamino, who had been Filipino secretary of state, came to the capital in May 1902 to praise the "really wonderful work for good" of the American civil administration and army and to discredit stories of cruelty as "either wholly untrue or greatly exaggerated."[35] The president made the same case in a Memorial Day speech at Arlington National Cemetery. There amid the graves of the fallen, he lauded troops fighting for "the triumph of civilization over forces which stand for the black chaos of savagery and barbarism." He went on to lament how some men had forgotten themselves but declared that for every one heinous act by Americans the insurgents had committed hundreds. Roosevelt pledged to punish the guilty and "to take, if possible, even stronger measures than have already been taken to minimize or prevent the occurrence of all such instances in the future." This pledge, along with a promise to grant the Philippines independence one day, earned the president praise for the wisdom of his approach.[36]

The combination of these efforts did much to allay public concerns about the conduct of the war in the Philippines. Roosevelt, Lodge, and Root had adroitly managed a scandal that threatened to tarnish them and the American imperial experiment. They downplayed appalling actions, further demonized the Filipino insurgents, and presented themselves as agents of justice. Strong nationalist sentiment and a general popular faith in the new president helped, along with the relative isolation of the Philippines because of distance and slow communications.

The Philippines controversy would hardly be Roosevelt's last, and, as in many episodes, he attempted to turn a matter that could be a liability into a strength. All in all, his ability to frame a message served his military policies well. He could not succeed in all that he set out to do, but he did much, thanks in large part to his powers of persuasion. Expansion of the navy accelerated, and reforms reshaping the army from a frontier force moved apace during his tenure. Sometimes the individuals who benefited the most from Roosevelt's intense interest in martial matters—military officers in particular—bristled at what they saw as the president's interference. Still, they could not have asked for a better friend in the White House for painting positive images of the services before the public and the world.

New President, Old Priorities

Just as Theodore Roosevelt brought his skill at public relations to the presidency, he also brought a to-do list that he had developed as assistant navy secretary and as a cavalry commander, experiences only three years in his past and still fresh in his mind. Some of this prior business—in particular, personnel reform—stretched back further, to when he was a New York City Police Board member and a civil service commissioner, but that topic is so extensive as to warrant treatment in another chapter. His top priorities early in his presidency would be matters that he considered essential to maintaining a vigorous foreign policy, so he focused on his favorite service, the navy. Less lofty affairs also absorbed his attention. Roosevelt was something of the ultimate dilettante, with a bent for technical detail when it came to things military, and he could not resist dabbling in all sorts of matters, large and small. Whether the proposal involved a major policy or a minor issue, Roosevelt would employ his powers of persuasion to advance as many military projects as possible during his first term. A special sense of urgency compelled him to do so. As an "accidental" president and one with strong reformist tendencies that frightened the Republican Party old guard, he worried about his chances for securing the nomination in 1904 and obtaining four more years to achieve his goals.

Roosevelt was hardly installed in the White House when he began to follow up on something that had nagged at him since the Cuba campaign. In early October 1901 he complained to the assistant secretary of war about army uniforms. The president, incidentally, knew the assistant secretary well because he was William Cary Sanger, the same man who had studied European militia systems when Roosevelt was the governor of New York. Roosevelt pointed out the inadequacies in the army's service uniform as a result of "my own experience at Santiago and the experience of practically every officer I have ever met who regarded a campaign as a business." He felt that the first requirement in the service uniform was "absolute ease and freedom. Anything that binds the body, particularly the knees, hips and arms, and anything that confines the neck, is all wrong." The president particularly objected to stand-up collars, for which he felt there was "no possible justification." Rather, he declared, "the service blouse should have a turndown, open collar, and instead of the white shirt collar there should be a handkerchief knotted around the neck." Roosevelt also objected to the color of the flannel shirt that soldiers wore. "Dark blue," he wrote, "is one of the worst possible colors for actual campaign use." Better colors, he claimed, would be gray or brown because they were more neutral.[37] Here the president reacted to the changes in the nature of battle that he had witnessed. Before the age of smokeless powder, commanders needed bold-colored uniforms to help differentiate their troops from the enemy's, but in an age of smokeless power such garb made soldiers more obvious targets. The carnage wrought by Spanish Mauser bullets had left an impression.

A year later Roosevelt had a similar recommendation to make, but this time he directed it to the secretary of war. Even more than Sanger, the president was familiar with the head of the War Department. Elihu Root was more than a carryover from the McKinley administration. Before coming to the cabinet, he had been a corporate lawyer in New York and helpful to the Roosevelt family. Root had been a friend of Theodore Senior and had backed T.R. when he first ran for the New York Assembly. Root had also saved Roosevelt's candidacy for the New York governorship when questions rose about his residency. The two men enjoyed a warm relationship that went beyond mutual admiration of their abilities, for they frequently exchanged jokes with each other. (Root continued as secretary of war for much of Roosevelt's first term and served as secretary of state during his second.) In October 1902 Roosevelt wanted the secretary of war to look into something that again reflected the president's days in the cavalry. He asked whether cavalry troops could be fitted for a "smaller spur, by preference one fitting into the heel." Roosevelt desired a spur that would "interfere as little as possible with their walking."[38] Records do not indicate if the War Department acted on a new spur, but typically these presidential requests led officials to study the proposal to see if action was warranted.

These episodes were revealing of Theodore Roosevelt as commander in chief. His tendency to dabble surfaced here, as well as a belief that a few months in the army had imparted a certain expertise. However, although he was dealing with minor matters for a man of his responsibility, his interest in uniforms and spurs actually touched on profound developments in combat and his thinking about warfare. Roosevelt may not have cared to admit it, perhaps not even to himself, but the Cuba campaign had stripped much of the romance out of war for him. He saw just how deadly the modern battlefield had become. Thus, his recommendations to Sanger and Root, especially on the color of the military shirt, were completely practical. Indeed, when the United States entered World War I in 1917, American soldiers and marines wore earth-colored hues into battle. Roosevelt would also get the looser fitting service blouse that he wanted, but only after he overruled a War Department decision against the looser collar.[39]

A Fleet in Fact, as Well as Name

Army officers in the tropics would appreciate changes to the field uniform, but they could not serve in distant locations without the service that was Roosevelt's prime interest, the U.S. Navy. He had departed the post of assistant secretary of the navy in May 1898. Three and a half years later, he would pick up where he had left off in the Navy Department. Except this time, he would be the secretary of the navy in all but name. Counting his old boss, John D. Long, whom he inherited from McKinley, Roosevelt would go through six secretaries of the navy during his seven and a half years in office. Although some were able men, others were nonentities, or they used the office as a way station to a more desirable appointment. William H. Moody, who succeeded Long, served ably from 1902 to 1904 before becoming attorney general. Paul Morton, described by one naval officer as a "bag of cold mush," was a former president of the Atchison, Topeka and Santa Fe Railroad and viewed his job as a stepping-stone to the Treasury. When a scandal forced Morton out after a one-year tenure, Charles Bonaparte took over but looked forward to becoming attorney general upon Moody's appointment to the Supreme Court. Former California congressman Victor Howard Metcalf served from December 1906 to November 1908 but wanted simply to be left alone.[40] Roosevelt's final navy secretary, Truman H. Newberry, filled the office for the last four months of Roosevelt's presidency. None of this rapid turnover mattered because Roosevelt intended to run the navy himself.

Above all, whether he was an assistant secretary or president, Roosevelt wanted one thing for the navy, battleships—and plenty of them. Battleships were the queen of naval battle. For sea power advocates these floating fortresses would decide control of the sea and, therefore, which nations dominated commercially, diplomatically, politically, and culturally. In short, battleships, above all other naval instruments, would determine the fate of nations. Alfred T. Mahan had popularized such thinking, but Roosevelt could rightly believe that he had helped contribute to this recipe for national greatness, beginning with *The Naval War of 1812*. His conclusion to that work hypothesized how much better the U.S. Navy might have performed against the Royal Navy, "had Congressional forethought been sufficiently great to have allowed for a few line-of-battle ships to have been in readiness some time previous to the war."[41] Now, as president, Roosevelt was in the best possible position to help American sea power reach its highest expression. The United States possessed the international outposts that Mahan had called for with the annexation of Hawaii, the takeover of the Philippines, and the protectorate over Cuba. Roosevelt also wanted to realize the age-old dream of an interoceanic canal in Central America.

The United States, in his view, needed yet a first-rate battleship force to protect these interests and the safety of the nation as a whole. As he put it, "to be rich, aggressive, and yet helpless in war, is to invite destruction."[42] To be sure, Roosevelt wanted more than battleships. In November 1901 he declared, "I want cruisers, gunboats, and torpedo boats in addition [to battleships]; and above all I want men."[43] But battleships were the first priority because, "No fight was ever won yet except by hitting; and the one unforgivable offense . . . is to hit soft. Don't hit at all if it can possibly be avoided; but if you do hit, hit as hard as you know how."[44]

Roosevelt was fond of this adage. It helped him to argue the necessity of a strong navy, but it also took him back to his Dakota days when he had to flatten a bully in a bar. As he recollected the story in his *Autobiography*, Roosevelt had sought shelter in a "primitive little hotel" one cold night. When Roosevelt entered the hotel's bar, a "shabby individual," who had been shooting up the saloon's clock, immediately fastened on the bespectacled newcomer. The bully demanded that "four eyes" treat, but when he came too close, Roosevelt put an end to the affair with a "right just to one side of his jaw, hitting with my left as I straightened out, and then again with my right."[45] At sea the great guns of battleships equaled for him the knockout punches he had thrown in the Dakota barroom. For Roosevelt, if he deemed the cause to be just, then force, depending on the circumstances, might be employed to uphold justice. Indeed, his arguments for more warships frequently invoked the lessons of western life. The untamed West, for Roosevelt, was analogous to the unsettled environment of international life, and his experiences on the frontier seemed entirely appropriate to understanding the potential dangers that confronted the United States abroad.

Soon after he took office, Roosevelt mounted a lobbying campaign to push more battleship construction. After the war with Spain, Congress had authorized a total of eight battleships to add to the existing nine vessels. Roosevelt did not think this number sufficient, and, moreover, he worried that a decision in 1901 not to authorize additional battleships sent the wrong signal to other nations. He fretted, for example, about German ambitions in the Western Hemisphere: "I find that the Germans regard our failure to go forward in building up the navy this year as a sign that our spasm of preparation, as they think it, has come to an end; that we shall sink back, so that in a few years they will be in a position to take some step in the West Indies or South America which will make us either put up or shut up on the Monroe Doctrine."[46] In November 1901 he talked about requesting three more battleships for the coming fiscal year, although he felt four ships would be ideal.[47] He delivered his first annual message to Congress a month later, and as part of a lengthy list of priorities he urged a larger navy. Roosevelt did not ask for specific numbers of ships in this message; rather, he sought to establish a general case for continued naval expansion. He invoked a number of themes. The United States required an even larger navy to protect against European ventures to colonize in the Americas. The Monroe Doctrine, he declared, "should be the cardinal feature of the foreign policy of all the nations of the two Americas." He also turned to new American responsibilities in the Pacific and the Caribbean, along with his desire for a canal linking the Atlantic and Pacific. But the appeal to national pride represented his most potent argument. "The American people," he proclaimed, "must either build and maintain an adequate navy or else make up their minds definitely to accept a secondary position in international affairs."[48]

Such rhetoric helped, for Roosevelt got the ships he wanted. During his first term, Congress agreed to add eight more ships to the seventeen vessels that were built or under construction. That meant that the United States had more naval tonnage under construction than any other power, except for Great Britain.[49] The six ships of the *Connecticut* class each displaced sixteen thousand tons and boasted main batteries of four twelve-inch guns, while the two ships of the *Mississippi* class were smaller at thirteen thousand tons but carried the same number of twelve-inch guns as the *Connecticuts*.[50] With no small amount of hyperbole, journalists predicted that the *Connecticut*, near the time of its launch in 1904, was "destined to prove one of the most formidable fighting machines ever constructed."[51] This kind of report was just what Roosevelt needed to foster continued enthusiasm for naval expansion.

Foreign events, or, more precisely, the Venezuelan crisis of 1902–3, assisted him as well. Venezuela suffered from a problem all too common to Latin American republics in that era. It had taken out too many foreign loans, was drowning in debt, and could not repay its obligations. Germany and Great Britain headed a consortium of creditors that demanded payment. Both German and British leaders professed that their countries would respect the Monroe Doctrine. They wanted only money, and not territory. Roosevelt remained unsure of the Germans. Hungry for "a place in the sun" for the Second Reich, Kaiser Wilhelm II might, the president worried, demand compensation in land from a destitute Venezuela. In a note to the British, the Germans had, after all, noted the possibility of a "temporary" occupation of Venezuelan ports. A similar arrangement in China had resulted in Berlin obtaining a ninety-nine-year lease at Kiaochow.[52]

Roosevelt maintained an affinity for Germany, based in part upon his childhood visits there. "After all the Germans," he stated, "in their fundamental, not their superficial qualities, are essentially the same as ourselves . . . and a war would be a great misfortune."[53] The Kaiser was a different story. Roosevelt viewed him as "altogether too jumpy and too erratic" and found his policies to be the same way, full of "wholly irrational zigzags." Wilhelm respected the United States, in Roosevelt's opinion, only because he believed Americans would fight if threatened and because "we have a pretty good navy with which to fight."[54] Caribbean naval maneuvers already planned for late 1902 worked, coincidentally, to strengthen Roosevelt's hand during the Venezuelan crisis, especially after the Germans destroyed three Venezuelan gunboats. Those maneuvers, to be described shortly, were also important for instituting a new fleet formation. The Venezuela matter ended in an agreement to arbitrate the debt problem, but the affair also lent urgency to the president's requests for more battleships.[55]

More ships were better, in Roosevelt's opinion, but large numbers of battleships alone did not a sea power make. If the U.S. Navy was going to take on a front-rank naval power like Germany—as opposed to a decrepit one like Spain—then it required a combined force at the outset of hostilities. Roosevelt understood the benefits of concentrated naval power. Captain Mahan had argued that only a consolidated fleet could seize control of the sea and thereby maintain access to markets in wartime. For his part, Roosevelt, as assistant secretary, had helped assemble naval units for the war with Spain. He had watched anxiously as the battleship *Oregon* raced from the Pacific, around the horn of South America, to bolster the forces in the Atlantic and help recoup the loss of the *Maine*. When he became president, Roosevelt wanted to apply lessons learned from the war with Spain, and from the writings of Mahan, to fundamentally alter American naval policy.

In 1901 the American navy was a fleet in name only. Mahan may have popularized sea power theory over a decade before, but when Roosevelt replaced McKinley the distribution of the U.S. Navy did not conform to navalist ideas of a concentrated fleet. Rather, dispersed squadrons remained the standard deployment, and they covered broad swaths of water around the globe. The term *squadron*, in fact, often had little basis in reality. It conveyed an image of ships cruising together, but in actuality a squadron was frequently more of an administrative designation. Ships belonging to one of five squadrons sailed independently of one another to patrol as much ocean as possible.[56] The scattering of vessels had been the rule throughout the nineteenth century, as the navy dispatched ships to various parts of the globe to explore, demonstrate a national presence, and protect American access to overseas markets. This practice meant that in wartime the navy needed to assemble far-flung vessels hastily. The officers and crews of these ships had little practice acting together in units as large as squadrons, much less as a fleet. Roosevelt, along with naval professionals, believed that such a force could not hope to perform effectively against an opponent that had trained together for many years. Fully alert to this fact, he made a concentrated fleet one of his top goals.

The process of consolidation began during Roosevelt's first year in office. In 1902 the navy established the North Atlantic Fleet and the Asiatic Fleet, which were to be the focus of American naval power in the Atlantic and the Pacific. These two fleets would divide between them the navy's prime hitting force—the growing battleship armada—a decision that demonstrated the importance of the new stations. Navy planners hoped ultimately to move all battleships to the Atlantic. Mahan had preached, after all, that the greater the concentration of force the better. Indeed, the biggest potential danger lay in the Atlantic. Large European fleets plied the waves there, but one navy above all others aroused American suspicion, the German High Seas Fleet. Britain may have ruled at sea, but the Kaiser's bid to build a world-class naval force and his quest for overseas possessions seemed to pose the most likely threat to American dominance in the Western Hemisphere, especially after the Venezuelan affair. In 1902, however, Adm. Henry Taylor, chief of the Bureau of Navigation, was reluctant to remove all battleships from the Pacific, given the commitment to the Philippines, other American interests in the region, and brewing trouble between Russia and Japan in northeast Asia. Secretary of the Navy Moody concurred, and letters from Rear Adm. Stephen Luce and Rear Admiral Mahan confirmed the decision to retain battleships in those waters, despite Mahan's own stated principle of concentration.[57]

A war was required to complete American fleet consolidation. That war, however, was one the United States watched from the sidelines. In 1904 Russo-Japanese tensions boiled over into conflict, and Japan's besting of Russia in 1905 changed the strategic equation in the Pacific. With Russian naval power eliminated from the region, and Japan and Britain in an alliance, the United States looked like the only potential great power rival of the Japanese empire. Racial discrimination against Japanese in California quickly soured relations the year after Japan's victory over Russia. Prudence dictated the transfer of the Pacific battleships to the Atlantic, lest a divided force fall victim to a unified Japanese fleet. Armored cruisers would replace battleships at the Asiatic station. The faster cruisers stood a better chance of escaping a Japanese naval descent, while the battleships could be preserved for a unified thrust from the Atlantic to the Pacific. Thus, only well into Roosevelt's second term would the process of fleet formation be completed. In 1907 all operational battleships were attached to the Atlantic Fleet, a designation established the previous year. Meanwhile, in the west, further consolidation occurred when the Asiatic Fleet and Pacific Squadron were joined to form the Pacific Fleet.[58]

For a man of strong convictions such as Theodore Roosevelt, fleet concentration was a prime article of faith. Without a true fleet formation, the building of battleships would have been essentially pointless. With other nations closely following Mahan's prescriptions, would the prophet of sea power's words go unheeded in his own country? Since the 1890s, despite anti-imperialist sentiment and the denunciation of economizers, navalists like Roosevelt had won the day. He wanted to make sure the United States took this next crucial step toward true naval power. Thus Roosevelt seized every opportunity to remind the country of the importance of a concentrated fleet. His annual messages trumpeted how "our officers and enlisted men are learning to handle the battleships, cruisers, and torpedo boats with high efficiency in fleet and squadron formations."[59] And when he left office in 1909, the one piece of specific advice that he gave to president-elect William Howard Taft was "under no circumstances divide the battleship fleet between the Atlantic and Pacific Oceans prior to the finishing of the Panama Canal."[60]

In fact, Roosevelt's devotion to a concentrated battle fleet was so strong that at one point in his presidency he erupted at none other than Alfred Mahan when the author dared question his commitment to the principle. On 10 January 1907 Mahan read in the morning newspaper "that four of our best battleships are to be sent to the Pacific" and, he confessed, that this report about the division of the battle fleet "has filled me with dismay." He then proceeded to lecture Roosevelt about the necessity of a unified battleship force: "In the case of war with Japan what can four battleships do against their navy? In case of war with a European power, what would not the four battleships add to our fleet here?"[61] Although Mahan apologized for perhaps reading too much into a newspaper report, an irritated Roosevelt had no patience for a tutorial from the admiral and shot back, "Don't you know me well enough to believe that I am quite incapable of such an act of utter folly as dividing our fighting fleet?" He entertained "no more thought of sending four battleships to the Pacific while there is the least possible friction with Japan than I have of going thither in a rowboat myself." In fact, he declared, he would pull every warship from the Pacific if war looked possible, so that "our whole navy could be gathered and sent there in a body."[62]

Not only did this exchange demonstrate the president's dedication to a concentrated battle fleet, but it also exposed the nature of the Roosevelt-Mahan relationship. As Richard Turk has written, the two men had an ambiguous association.[63] In the early to mid-1890s, when Roosevelt was outside naval circles looking in, and Mahan had scored a hit with *The Influence of Sea Power*, he did all that he could to promote Mahan's ideas to advance a navalist policy. After mid-September 1901 Roosevelt was in a better place to promote sea power than the admiral. He no longer needed Mahan as much and kept him more at arm's length, although the navy's most famous writer could still help build a public consensus for fleet expansion. The president was now driving naval matters and definitely felt no need in 1907 for a reminder from Mahan about the importance of a concentrated fleet. He had drawn many of the same lessons in *The Naval War of 1812*, but just had not wrapped them into a comprehensive recipe for national greatness like Mahan had.

Navy Maneuvers

A fleet might be created, but it would only be a fleet in name unless the vessels, officers, and crew that composed it worked together. The complexities of handling ships in formation, signaling, gunnery, and various other operations all needed to be practiced if the new American fleet were to be a truly formidable force. Over the previous twenty years, a few naval officers had pushed for large-scale exercises, but their appeal had gone unanswered until Roosevelt took command. He recognized the need for training as close to actual warfare as possible and ordered naval maneuvers for 1902. Although headlines associated Rear Admiral Taylor with the exercises, Roosevelt claimed primary credit in making them happen. "The plan was not Admiral Taylor's" he asserted, "it was mine."[64] Roosevelt directed the General Board of the U.S. Navy to prepare for the operation during the summer of 1902, and the exercises were to commence in December of that year, which happened to coincide with the Anglo-German pressure on Venezuela. The North Atlantic Fleet and the European and South Atlantic Squadrons would assemble at Culebra, off Puerto Rico, and practice battle formations and search problems, remaining there into early 1903. Seven battleships would form the core of the gathered force.[65] The president gave the maneuvers the highest priority, and Secretary of the Navy Moody made sure that the rest of the Navy Department knew of Roosevelt's feelings.[66]

Once Roosevelt ordered the fleet exercise, he worked mainly to remove political obstructions that threatened to derail the operation. For example, Sen. Thomas Platt, the Republican Party boss of New York, objected that the exercises might interfere with his plans for a favorite officer. Platt wanted to expend some patronage on Rear Adm. Arent Crowninshield, whom he hoped would take command of the European Squadron. The president assured Platt that Crowninshield would, indeed, head the squadron and that it would return to its Mediterranean station following the exercises. Roosevelt knew Crowninshield and played on the admiral's professionalism in responding to Platt. He guessed that Crowninshield, as a good sailor, would "jump at the chance of seeing the American fleet gathered together to maneuver at Culebra."[67] Later that year Sen. Matthew Quay of Pennsylvania, another Republican powerbroker, raised a much more serious concern. In June 1902 miners of anthracite coal had struck for shorter hours, better pay, and recognition of their union, and in response mine operators had shut down their mines. After summer had turned to fall and the impasse between owners and miners continued, Senator Quay suggested that the maneuvers be cancelled because of the coal shortage and the impending winter. Roosevelt replied that he had considered that step but was reluctant to halt the maneuvers unless the circumstances were dire. The president conveyed to Quay the same sense of priority that he had impressed on the navy: "For six months great trouble and some expense have been incurred in making ready all the plans for these maneuvers, and they are essential for the proper development of the navy. I do not believe that the amount of coal saved would be proportionate to the great damage done, and I am confident that it would mean serious demoralization in the navy to stop the maneuvers."[68] In the end, Roosevelt's successful mediation between owners and miners alleviated the situation.

The Rooseveltian political touch was most evident in the man chosen to command the fleet exercises. At the time no other man represented the American navy more than the hero of Manila Bay, George Dewey. In 1902 Dewey was nearly sixty-five, but as admiral of the fleet he remained active as head of the navy's general board. Even though Dewey often nodded off at inopportune times, Roosevelt knew that putting him in command of the maneuvers would underscore their importance and attract greater attention to them. Such popular notice could work only to the navy's benefit at appropriations time. The flying of the admiral's four-star pennant above the fleet also served the president's diplomatic purposes when tensions mounted over Venezuela. Dewey's distrust of Germany was well known ever since 1898, when Vice Adm. Otto von Diederichs had assembled a powerful squadron in Manila Bay and seemed too eager to snap up the Philippines from the Americans.[69] In making the appointment, Roosevelt explained to Dewey that his direction of the fleet "will be a good thing from the professional standpoint; and what is more, your standing, not merely in this nation but abroad, is such that the effect of your presence will be very beneficial outside of the service also."[70] The admiral could hardly decline, especially considering the debt of gratitude he owed Roosevelt for securing him command of the Asiatic Squadron in 1897.

Dewey played his part well, just as Roosevelt had hoped. The admiral's presence drew favorable attention, and after the maneuvers he helped to publicize their success. The admiral claimed that the navy had achieved a higher state of development now that it had practiced for a fleet engagement. Officers and sailors had performed efficiently so that the exercises concluded without "a hitch of any kind, not an accident of any description, and [with] the most enthusiastic morale in the entire fleet." Such work, Dewey stated, had increased the reputation of the navy and the nation. The United States had demonstrated that it could mobilize a fleet 1,500 miles from its shores and produce an effect on other powers, as it had during the Venezuela crisis.[71]

Making Shots That Count

Roosevelt wanted more ships, he wanted them concentrated, and he wanted them to sail together. But for battle formations to be of much use, they also had to be able to hit the enemy. During his first years in the White House, Roosevelt returned to another piece of work that he had been unable to complete as assistant secretary of the navy: naval gunnery. Navy gunners had an abysmal record of hitting targets when Roosevelt took office. Upon learning the degree of the problem, he made gunnery practice a priority throughout his presidency. In fact, naval gunnery became one of his pet military interests, and Roosevelt's involvement with gunnery demonstrated the extent to which he was willing to use his authority on matters he saw as crucial to America's defenses.

Lt. William S. Sims had first called Roosevelt's attention to European gunnery practices in 1897. The Spanish-American War had cut short Roosevelt's career at the Navy Department, but before the war he had made some effort to follow up on reports and messages from Sims. Posted in Paris, the lieutenant was highly critical of American gunnery and hoped for action from Roosevelt. He knew his man, for the assistant secretary already understood the importance of effective gunnery. Roosevelt had credited superior gunnery as a key factor in the few victories that the puny American navy had scored against Great Britain in the War of 1812.[72]

Roosevelt's quest to learn more had inspired him to attend the squadron maneuvers off Hampton Roads in September 1897. For three days the assistant secretary viewed battleships and armored cruisers maneuvering and firing.[73] He broadened his experience the following month aboard the dispatch ship *Dolphin* by stepping behind the sights himself and blazing away with a rapid-fire six-pound gun. He related his technique: "I could do best by shooting when the ship's side was rising, getting the gun in position, and then, just as the front sight touched the target on the way up, pulling the trigger." In his typical fashion, he found the whole exercise to be "great sport." He discovered, in the process, the principle that "the number of *hits* is what counts," not the rapidity of fire.[74] Seeking more objective data in November 1897, he wanted Rear Adm. Montgomery Sicard to report on gunnery during the September maneuvers and desired to know results for both large and rapid-fire guns, as well as the efficiency of turrets. Foreign data was also of interest, and Roosevelt studied reports on the practices of other navies.[75]

The reformer in him, that part of Roosevelt that held there was usually something better to be obtained, decided that naval gunnery needed to improve. The assistant secretary planned a special gun practice with Admiral Sicard's squadron, in which the best trained gun crews would test four-, five-, six-, and eight-inch guns. Presumably such an exercise would establish a high standard from which to measure the performance of other vessels. Roosevelt also proposed a board of inspectors that would visit both the navy's gunnery ship and Sicard's squadron to observe gun practice. Composed of experts, the board could combine knowledge of foreign methods with the results of American practices and suggest improvements in marksmanship. Finally, Roosevelt recommended that competition between ships might produce results. "It would seem to be well if we could give prizes for the men who have done best with their guns." Such awards would recognize accomplishment and hopefully spur others to achieve the same level of excellence.[76] Roosevelt proposed these ideas in late 1897 and early 1898, but war with Spain soon intervened. The sweeping American victories that followed at Manila Bay and off Santiago suggested to him that Sims had taken a "most pessimistic view of our marksmanship" and was an "alarmist."[77]

The fact that "the Spaniards proved so much worse than we were" masked the poor record of American gunnery in the war and contributed to complacency after the fighting ended.[78] Hitting a moving target at sea, during combat, was no easy feat. At Manila Bay, just 2.42 percent of the American shells fired hit home. That is, Dewey's men counted a total of 5,859 shells expended but only 142 hits. The numbers were similar for the sea battle at Santiago. There, 123 shots hit the four armored Spanish vessels in the battle.[79] That the Americans had bested the Spaniards counted the most, but the high ratio of shells fired for those that actually hit disturbed thoughtful officers like William Sims, who worried what would happen if the next opponent was better prepared than Spain.

In 1901 Sims was still a lieutenant, but he was now on duty at the China Station. He decided, after some hesitation, to contact Roosevelt directly in November 1901 about continuing problems with American naval gunnery. Sims did so at considerable risk. For a lieutenant to address an assistant secretary of the navy was one thing, but for a junior officer to write directly to the commander in chief was quite another. Sims had stepped far outside the chain of command and risked charges of insubordination if his uniformed superiors found out about his letter to the president. The gamble paid off, in large part because Roosevelt already knew Sims. The lieutenant also fit Roosevelt's own mold. Sims was bold, energetic, forceful, and intelligent, and in writing Roosevelt he seemed only to want to serve the navy and the country. The president also valued opinions that came from outside bureaucratic channels. He had witnessed the workings of both the Navy and War Department bureaucracies in the run-up to the war with Spain and had been appalled at the inefficiency of certain officers. Sims was just the sort of man who could serve as a personal conduit for information that bureaucrats had dismissed or might not want to be heard.[80]

Sims appealed to Theodore Roosevelt because he wrote in a hard-hitting style. The president liked people who were direct, as long as their cause seemed just and they were not hurling criticism at him. Given his strong self-righteous streak, Roosevelt rarely took criticism well. Sims did not cause offense because he acted apparently with only the good of the navy in mind, even though he was criticizing a service to which Roosevelt had great personal attachment. His letter to the president rammed home American inferiority in naval gunnery, along with problems with weaponry and ship design. The lieutenant reminded the president of the attempt to improve marksmanship while Roosevelt was assistant secretary and then went on to describe a looming American naval disaster. In alarmist tones, Sims warned what would happen if the U.S. Navy confronted a major naval power: "I have . . . been forced to the very serious conclusion that the protection and armament of even our most recent battleships are so glaringly inferior . . . to those of our possible enemies, including the Japanese, and that our marksmanship is so crushingly inferior to theirs, that one or more of our ships would, in their present condition, inevitably suffer humiliating defeat at the hands of an equal number of an enemy's vessels."[81] Sims recognized the seriousness of his charges but supported them by pointing to his long study of the subject, numerous reports to the Navy Department, and the results of a special target practice. The North Atlantic Squadron had recently demonstrated poorer marksmanship than Sims "could have imagined possible." Five ships had each fired for five minutes at a target 2,800 yards distant. They made only two hits altogether.[82]

Sims's letter rang with urgency. His words conveyed a sense of danger reminiscent of Roosevelt's own rhetoric in the 1890s, when he felt his country faced a political, moral, and economic crisis. Now under the burden of high responsibility, Roosevelt responded with a restraint that contrasted his younger self. In an earlier time he might have raged against the thickheadedness or timidity of the officials who had allowed such a situation to develop. While president, Roosevelt understood the need to preserve the aura of dignity that surrounded the office and worked to control his impulse—at least in public—to lambaste those he deemed effete, inefficient, and unintelligent. Recognizing in Sims an impulsiveness that exceeded his own, Roosevelt first worked to rein in the lieutenant. In his reply he told Sims outright, "I think you unduly pessimistic," for Roosevelt still looked to the victory over Spain as an affirmation of the basic quality of American gunnery. He recalled the lieutenant's anxieties at the start of the war, "when, as you may remember, you took a gloomy view of our vessels even as compared with those of Spain." But Roosevelt avoided discouraging Sims too much and asked him to write again, "in criticism, or suggestion."[83] He did not want to silence this independent source of information. Voices like Sims's would help him to run the navy himself, without being a complete captive of the Navy Department bureaucracy. Moreover, Sims represented just the sort of leader Roosevelt wanted at the top of the armed services, if Sims's energies could be properly channeled. It also did not hurt that Sims was relatively young. He had been born only about two weeks before Theodore Roosevelt in 1858, so the two men were nearly the same age.[84]

Roosevelt had responded in characteristic fashion. He sought more information. Contrary to caricatures of him as a cowboy or Rough Rider using six shooters to enforce his political will, he was a thoughtful, cautious executive. He preferred to have all facts and to weigh various points of view before he acted. Roosevelt sought help in running the navy, for while he understood the ideas behind sea power, he knew that he was beyond his depth in many technical matters, especially when it came to ballistics, targeting, and ship design. In this case he turned to advice from his brother-in-law, William Cowles, who was now a captain and the president's naval aide, and from Rear Adm. Henry Taylor, soon to be the chief of the Bureau of Navigation. The president considered Sims "a good man, but a preposterous alarmist," especially in his worries about American ship design; however, Roosevelt was "inclined to think we are deficient in target practice." He requested, specifically from Taylor, "some plan of improving our gun pointing."[85]

The president was right to probe more deeply; Sims had overstated his case. Sims's criticism of American gunnery rested, in part, on a new British system of gun pointing known as continuous aim firing. Yet the British Admiralty, whether out of conservatism or some other factor, had not fully embraced this method that had so impressed Sims. Until the British changed their way or some other navy adopted a superior gun-targeting system, the American navy was not in as "crushingly inferior" shape as Sims portrayed.[86] Moreover, other voices in the American navy provided strong arguments that contradicted Sims, and Roosevelt could not ignore them. In April 1902 Rear Adm. Charles O'Neil, the chief of the navy's Bureau of Ordnance, took specific exception to Sims's criticism of inadequate gun mounts, telescopic sights, and other materials required for accuracy. O'Neil contended that the human element was the one variable that could still be substantially improved. Technology could only do so much, and accurate hitting ultimately depended on the skill of the gun crew.[87]

For his part Admiral Taylor responded to the president's query with a proposal that anticipated Admiral O'Neil's emphasis on the human factor. He relayed to Roosevelt a plan on naval gunnery that the West Indies Squadron would test. The scheme involved progressive instruction. Lieutenants would work on the performance of their gun divisions every week, captains would try to improve the results for their ships every month, and admirals would strive for improvement in their squadrons every quarter. The Navy Department would inspect the West Indies Squadron on 1 May 1902 to measure the results.[88] Crews were to be better trained, but the changes to gunnery techniques and technology that Sims wanted were not mentioned.

A passionate and driven man, Sims was not one to make his

point and then drop it. He wrote to the president again on 11 March 1902 and stressed, at length, the defects in naval gunnery and the navy's complacency regarding target practice. For example, Sims compared British and American target practices and found that American vessels performed abysmally. The British battleship *Majestic* fired twice as fast as the *New York* and outclassed the American ship in rapidity of hitting by much larger margins.[89] Such statistics helped to convince Roosevelt of the true gravity of the problem, and he told Admiral Taylor, "I am really very much impressed with Sims' letters."[90] Then the president took on a role he relished, the youthful crusader battling vested interests. Sims had persuaded him that backward thinking in the navy had blocked a solution to a clearly evident problem with marksmanship. Roosevelt moved "to overcome the inertia of bureau chiefs, especially of the elderly men . . . reluctant to adopt new ideas."[91] He instructed Taylor, who was sympathetic to change, to prepare a memorandum that embodied all of Sims's arguments. He also wished to go over the details of the subject in person with the admiral. Roosevelt was ready for decisive action, informing Taylor that "we must take all possible measure for correction."[92] Naval gunnery would now be a top priority.

Taylor more than took Roosevelt's words to heart. He decided to put the faultfinder himself in charge of gunnery improvements. He recalled Sims from China Station a year early and made him the inspector of target practice. Senior officers, including the president's brother-in-law, disapproved, but younger officers applauded the choice. From late 1902 to early 1909, Sims served in this post. He would be helped in his quest to improve gunnery because of his special channel to the president. Roosevelt had made gunnery a priority, so whenever Sims felt that he faced obstacles, he could turn to his patron in the White House. The relationship grew even closer when Roosevelt made Sims a presidential naval aide in November 1907. Until March

1909 Sims would have direct and regular access to the president. Roosevelt, determined to achieve results, decided that the best way to obtain improvements was to put the right man in the right place. With Sims he could bypass the procedures and conservatism of the Navy Department, as he perceived it, and force the navy's bureaucracy to respond to the reformer. This arrangement was ad-hoc and would effectively expire in 1909, when Roosevelt left office, but he kept Sims as inspector until his administration had almost expired in the hope that the changes in gunnery training would take deep root.[93]

Sims's demand for new gun sights showed how the relationship operated. Improvement could go only so far without better equipment, but the navy bureau responsible proved slow to supply them. The Bureau of Ordnance remained headed by Rear Admiral O'Neil, the man who had expressed skepticism in April 1902 about Sims's claims for a better system of gun aiming. O'Neil would retire in 1904, but his attitude toward Sims remained alive in the bureau. (Roosevelt had wanted O'Neil assigned to sea duty in 1903 but let him remain until his retirement the following year.[94]) The swift adoption of continuous aim firing had also caught bureau officials off guard, and, while Sims could work out a new training system rather quickly, the bureau required more time to develop suitable equipment. In short, the bureau failed to provide equipment that was either fast enough or good enough to satisfy the impatient Sims. He reported the problem to the president, who in turn sought information from both sides. Roosevelt ruled in favor of Sims after the Navy Department estimated that it would require seven years to install the new sights. Such a timetable apparently struck Roosevelt as bureaucratic foot-dragging, so he presented the Navy Department officials with a choice: "either they must find the money to resight the Navy with the best possible design of instruments or I shall take the matter up with Congress and tell them that the Navy's sighting devices are obsolete and inefficient."[95] In short, he threatened bureau officers with public embarrassment. His intervention worked, for navy officials found the required resources and the entire fleet received new sights within two years.[96]

Results in gunnery practices would ultimately be needed to prove Sims right. By 1907 the navy had nearly doubled the percentage of hits made by all guns. In 1903 gunners had hit their targets 40 percent of the time. Four years later they could boast of 77.6 percent.[97] For this work, Sims climbed the ranks, until in 1909 Roosevelt rewarded him with the coveted command of a battleship, the *Minnesota*.

Sims took the leading role, but numerous others played a part in improving American gunnery. Gun crews made Sims's ideas a reality, and even navy bureaucrats, whom Sims condemned as obstacles, assisted. Without the Bureau of Ordnance the new range finders and sights that he wanted would have been harder to obtain. Henry C. Taylor, the top uniformed bureaucrat as chief of the Bureau of Navigation, deserved particular recognition. He had brought Sims back to Washington as inspector of target practice and supported his work.

This action was just one of several that Taylor undertook to make the navy a more modern and effective fighting force. He began, for example, the implementation of a true fleet organization, and he fought for a naval general staff to improve war planning and command. Taylor was an older officer. In 1902 he was fifty-seven years old, but in other ways he fit Roosevelt's mold for the model military leader. He was intellectually gifted and was a past president of the Naval War College. Taylor was also a warrior. During the Spanish-American War he had ably commanded the battleship *Indiana* at the sea battle off Santiago. Taylor, however, would be fated only to see change begin. In July 1904, while visiting his son in Canada, he was stricken and died suddenly.[98] Roosevelt would miss him. The admiral, as head of the most important navy bureau, had thought along the same lines as the president, which had made it easier for Roosevelt to oversee the navy.

Where naval gunnery was concerned, Roosevelt demonstrated just how much of a hands-on commander in chief he could be. His deep interest was natural. Battleships were central to his conception of a robust foreign policy, which in turn was crucial to maintaining American national greatness. If those ships could not hit a foe, then a serious defect existed in the entire military, diplomatic, and cultural edifice that he had constructed. As a consequence, Roosevelt watched carefully for improvement in naval gunnery. He eagerly awaited the results of target practices and thoroughly consumed the reports when they arrived. He was thrilled to learn that Sims's work was producing change. In March 1903 he told Assistant Secretary of the Navy Charles Darling, after the first practice using continuous aim firing, "I am greatly pleased with these papers on target practice. I not only value the improved showing of this practice aboard our ships, but I value the zeal and intelligence with which the high officers . . . are handling the subject."[99] He hungered for as many details as the Navy Department and Sims could provide and pressed constantly for even more information. For example, Roosevelt asked Admiral Taylor for a comparison with German naval gunnery in September 1903, and in April 1904 he questioned whether the Navy Department had taken steps to improve marksmanship on cruisers as well as battleships. "It is the cruisers," he remarked, "that would have to do most against torpedo boats, and I am particularly anxious to know how they are doing with guns of six-inch calibre or less."[100] He kept up the pressure even after American hitting ability equaled, or surpassed, the performance of other navies. In October 1907 he queried Sims about the possible difference in hits between eight-inch guns mounted in turrets superimposed on the main battery and eight-inch guns positioned elsewhere on ships.[101]

Roosevelt was not content merely to read reports. During the war with Spain, he had criticized officers who had not been in the thick of the fighting. As president, he planned to continue to lead from the front. Roosevelt wanted to see for himself, just as he had when he was assistant secretary, and he attended practices as often as possible.[102] For example, in August 1902, while at home in Oyster Bay, New York, he boarded the *Mayflower* to observe gunners at work. The *Mayflower* often served as a presidential yacht, but it also carried ten six-pound guns and two one-pound guns. Roosevelt watched from the bridge as each of the gun crews fired for two minutes on an oblong canvas target one thousand to two thousand feet distant. According to press accounts, the expressive chief executive "was generous in his applause when the projectiles struck the white canvas of the targets," and when shots missed "there was a look of sorrow on his face." After the first gun crew missed the target entirely, Roosevelt shouted advice: "Your elevation was excellent, but you shot to the left and did not count. It's the shots that hit that count."[103] He awarded a prize to the best gun crew and then commented about the need for improvement, teamwork, and expert gun pointers. His message was not aimed just at the *Mayflower* crew but at the entire navy and indicated the standard that he wanted all ships to achieve.[104]

Roosevelt not only lent his public presence to draw attention to naval gunnery but also supported a system of rewards for naval gunners if they improved their performance. Two days before he witnessed the *Mayflower*'s demonstration, Roosevelt was thumbing through the navy's target regulations and observed to Secretary of the Navy William Moody that "it seems to me that a prize and certificate for marksmanship should be given to those responsible for the best shooting with the big guns."[105] On the *Mayflower* he did just that. Roosevelt congratulated each member of the best gun crew and, as he did so, pressed five dollars into each man's hand. The best gunner of the day, W. J. O'Donnell, received twenty-five dollars in gold from the president.[106] Nine months later, in May 1903, Roosevelt suggested that superior gun pointers receive more pay. Pay advances were eventually implemented for gun pointers, but the main incentive remained ship-to-ship competition, the winners of which received trophies.[107] Finally, the day after viewing the *Mayflower* demonstration in 1902, Roosevelt proposed that the ship be employed as an experimental vessel for marksmanship. It would serve as a vehicle for ascertaining the best system of gunnery and would supply examples of marksmanship for other ships to emulate.[108] William Sims's arrival as inspector of target practice that October, with his sweeping revision of gunnery procedure, apparently supplanted this idea.

Without Roosevelt's dedication to the gunnery program, it might not have survived its greatest crisis in April 1904. An accident occurred that led some observers in the press and the Navy Department to condemn the new system of gunnery. During target practice, an explosion ripped through one of the turrets on the USS *Missouri* and claimed thirty-three lives. An accident of this scale had never happened before in the new steel navy. The *Missouri* was the newest of the American battleships and was commanded by a man with very close ties to the president, William Cowles. Apparently, as the crew engaged in the rapid firing of one of the main batteries, a charge of powder ignited, perhaps because of hot gasses from a previous shot or the cloth cover of the charge had caught fire. If not for Cowles's quick action in flooding the ammunition magazine, the entire ship might have been lost.[109] One "naval expert," unnamed in the *New York Times*, summed up the sentiments of those skeptical of the new gunnery program: "I fear," he commented, "that enthusiasm at making world records has led us past the danger line. In our anxiety to surpass the world in the rapidity of big gun fire I fear we have permitted our enthusiasm to get the better of our judgment."[110] Suddenly all of Sims's work seemed to be in danger, for his emphasis on rapid firing did entail some risk. Sims countered by placing the blame on defects in the design of turrets, but he required help from higher places to weather the storm.[111]

Roosevelt weighed in decisively on the side of Sims and the new system of gunnery. Word reached Sims soon after the accident "that the President . . . while insisting upon every safeguard, will not sanction nor order any measure that will tend to check our advance in efficiency."[112] Roosevelt himself pronounced his unqualified commitment to rapid firing in a letter to Secretary Moody on 10 May. The president declared, "There must of course be no decrease in the practice for rapidity of fire. We cannot do well in battle unless we practice in peace. The test is not the number of ill-aimed shots, nor the percentage of hits among shots fired slowly, but the number of shots that hit in a given time." Roosevelt went on to praise the conduct of the *Missouri*'s officers and crew in the aftermath of the accident and to state his appreciation for the speedy resumption of target practice. Such strong statements ended the threat to Sims's system of gunnery and also absolved Captain Cowles of responsibility.[113] A few years later Sims would join other reformers in using the *Missouri* accident to support charges of battleship design defects.

Roosevelt's strong stand demonstrated again just how dedicated he was to the new gunnery program. Once he had decided something was right, and essential, his crusader's instinct would kick in and he would defend against all opposition with bulldog tenacity. Furthermore, although Roosevelt practiced politics as the art of the possible, he would reject compromise if he felt opposition stemmed from uninformed opinion or reactionary motives. In the case of the *Missouri* accident, he would regret the loss of men, but he could also point to results to justify continuation of the gunnery program. In 1907 he would boast of how marksmanship had become five times better since the start of reform in 1902.[114] Perhaps the greatest validation came after Roosevelt left office. Sims's gunnery program remained in place—recognition of the fact that it had brought improvement.

Roosevelt was most effective as commander in chief when dealing with a matter such as naval gunnery. Few budgetary or political fetters bound his efforts to improve this basic part of naval preparedness, and he could measure progress easily through the results of target practices. He embraced the project with a zeal seen in few secretaries of the navy, much less presidents. Roosevelt endorsed a new operational policy, learned its technical outlines, and kept a close watch over its implementation, to the point of reading target-practice regulations, studying the results of firing exercises, and personally reviewing gunnery practices.[115] For him this task was easier to complete than convincing Congress to add more ships to the fleet, and he also had the satisfaction of watching the big guns in action.

Roosevelt's enthusiasm for improving gunnery ran so deeply that it inspired him to think about more than just shots fired at sea. He wondered how well army gunners could hit their targets. In August 1907 he turned his attention to the army's artillery. He decided that the accuracy of the army's gunners could likely stand improvement if the navy's performance had risen so markedly since 1902. After reading a comparison of army and navy accuracy, he told Secretary of War William Howard Taft that he wanted improvements in army artillery and ordered Taft to send the report to the army's general staff for study, the results of which he wanted to see. War Department officials subsequently called attention to artillery improvements since 1900 but, just like their naval counterparts had done earlier, declared the need for better fire-control equipment.[116]

Whether gunnery was the matter at hand, or fleet concentration and maneuvers, Theodore Roosevelt's involvement in naval operations represented a level of immersion in technical military matters that most chief executives, before or since, would be hard-pressed to match. Only another former assistant secretary, Franklin Roosevelt, could claim superior experience with naval affairs, because of his eight years in the Wilson administration. Additionally, while the majority of presidents during the twentieth century could point to some military service, few demonstrated Roosevelt's unsurpassed enthusiasm for military affairs and only two, Dwight Eisenhower and Jimmy Carter, came with professional military training. Roosevelt's intervention in operational matters signaled a change for the presidency in the twentieth century. Whether chief executives wanted to or not, over the course of that century they would increasingly play an active role in national-security affairs. Two world wars, the Cold War, and the rise of the United States as a global power gave them little choice. Advances in technology would narrow their options even further. By the second half of the century, a president who lacked basic familiarity with space and missile technology, for example, would do so at the peril of his political future and the security of the country.

When Theodore Roosevelt became president, he had resumed important military business left over from the 1890s, and naval affairs were a major part of that effort. He felt that the navy needed continued improvement and expansion, but he also believed that, on the whole, American naval forces were capable. The U.S. land forces remained a different story.

4

Arms and the Men

"Those who have not seen the President in some time remark . . . that he has grown heavier," a press clipping noted in August 1902, nearly a year after Theodore Roosevelt had assumed the presidency. The story went on to comment that Roosevelt's collar size had increased from 16¾ to 17¼, a delicate way of noting that the presidential waistline had grown proportionately.[1] Theodore Roosevelt preached the strenuous life, but he also enjoyed eating. His military aide, Capt. Archie Butt, observed firsthand Roosevelt's "wholesome appetite." In a letter to his mother, Butt confided, "You think me a large eater; well, I am small in comparison to him."[2]

Roosevelt knew he was getting portly and complained about the weight. He also grumbled about a "good deal of rheumatism" and his advancing age. He fought the extra pounds in the only way he knew how: hard-paced exercise. The president chopped wood, took long walks, and enjoyed roughhousing with his children. The White House became his gymnasium, as he practiced Japanese wrestling and boxing. Wrestling led to the spectacle of the president being thrown "over an opponent's head and batted down on a mattress," while boxing caused an injury that contributed to Roosevelt's eventual blindness in one eye.[3] When Leonard Wood was present, the two men enjoyed playing singlestick together. This "play" consisted of covering themselves in padding and then beating "one another like carpets." "Now and then by an accident," Roosevelt commented, "one or the other of us gets hit where there is no protecting armament." After one especially hard rap on the arm, the president ended up with a possible bone fracture.[4]

Roosevelt also enjoyed his "scrambles." These lengthy hikes more often resembled obstacle courses, and the president relished making them competitive. He delighted in challenging government officials and foreign dignitaries to accompany him. Rock Creek Park in northwestern Washington was a favorite site, but Roosevelt also liked walks that took him to the Potomac River, so that he could swim to the Virginia side and then back. Captain Butt recollected one journey that involved climbing, and he worried for the president's safety, as they passed "along the outer faces of rocks with hardly enough room in the crevices for fingers or feet." His fears were nearly realized when Roosevelt tumbled off one cliff and into a creek. Fortunately, the president landed in shoulder-deep water and laughed off the fall.[5]

On more than one occasion, the president took senior officers of the army with him, and what he saw concerned him. Many could not keep up. Two generals and a colonel, according to Butt, "showed such evident fatigue and distress as to make them unfit, he [Roosevelt] feared, for active service in the field."[6] Memories of Cuba and the obese William Shafter doubtlessly flooded back. General Shafter's poor physical condition represented a greater problem than Roosevelt had originally suspected. The officer corps seemed rife with older and physically unfit leaders.

One of Roosevelt's many crusades was to remake the army officer corps. The twenty-sixth president embraced numerous causes during his tenure, but the campaign to remake the army officer corps sprang from a special source: Roosevelt's self-image. Just as he believed that he was his own best pick for secretary of the navy, he styled the ideal army officer after himself: intelligent, resourceful, physically active, youthful, and devoted to duty. Roosevelt cited his playmate Leonard Wood as the ideal, but looking at Wood was really like looking into a mirror. Each man had frontier experience, which, as far as Roosevelt was concerned, accounted for a unique American spirit. They also possessed Harvard degrees and a devotion to vigorous exercise. Moreover, both represented a new generation of political and military leadership. Wood was born in 1860, only two years after Roosevelt, so each man embodied a post–Civil War outlook. From the late 1860s until 1901, every president had served, or been of military age, during the Civil War. With Roosevelt and Wood, power shifted to individuals shaped more by the final settlement of the West and industrialization than by the sectional conflict. Thus, in seeking to reform the army officer corps, Roosevelt faced a daunting task. He was attempting to displace one of the most honored generations of officers. The result would be civil-military tension and a good measure of presidential frustration.

Roosevelt embarked on this effort for reasons beyond the practical need for commanders who could withstand the physical rigors of a military campaign. Such causes were satisfying to him, because even if he lost he could claim the moral high ground of having made the good fight. Moreover, although he would need legislation for some of what he wanted to accomplish— namely, a new system of promotion—he could also have considerable effect wielding his powers as commander in chief. But something more profound motivated Roosevelt. The physical decay of older officers seemed symptomatic of a condition that the president believed threatened the American republic as a whole. That is, Roosevelt's old fears from the 1890s of a cultural, social, and political crisis continued to play on him. Although a young nation by historical standards, the United States had reached a new stage of development with rapid industrialization and urbanization, and Roosevelt fretted that the imperial spasm of the Spanish-American War had not been enough to prevent Americans from being absorbed with luxuries and becoming physically soft. He worried especially when he saw unfit and older army officers. If any Americans could provide an example of rigorous living, then, according to Roosevelt's image of officership, it should be men who were charged with the ultimate physical experience of battle. Army officers were the ones who should be drilling their men and leading by example. In short, Roosevelt wanted officers in command who would be exemplars of the strenuous life.

For Theodore Roosevelt the physical equaled the virtuous. To him outward vigor was a manifestation of a strong inner character. Hence Roosevelt's rhetoric and public persona were steeped in muscular themes and imagery, as he preached "the great virile virtues of strength, courage, energy, and undaunted and unwavering resolution."[7] The best citizens were those individuals who acted, whether the activity was physical, which would fortify the soul, or in the public arena, which would benefit the common good. Military officers were already pledged to serve the nation and that, in Roosevelt's opinion, made them among the best of citizens. But they were not yet the paragons of physical virtue that he hoped would inspire others. For Roosevelt there were still too many Shafters and not enough Woods in the service. A guiding hand, his own, was needed to enforce on army officers the physical rigor that would make them truly objects worthy of veneration and imitation. This line of thought would also lead Roosevelt to support more realistic training exercises and reform of the militia. The state forces, from his vantage, needed the benefit of federal guidance if they were to serve effectively, and better training, in coordination with federal authorities, would only help to achieve that goal.

Roosevelt's thinking on army leadership echoed an earlier generation of Americans. His worries about the dissipating effects of wealth and soft living recalled the hopes of Revolutionary-era leaders that the newly founded United States would become a

"Christian Sparta." This vision, much like Roosevelt's, was of a land of austere, public-spirited, and heroic people.[8] Roosevelt also demonstrated his particular regard for Alexander Hamilton. The fact that Hamilton's economic practices contributed to latter-day commercial excess did not trouble Roosevelt. He liked the power and respect that a thriving economy brought the United States at the turn of the twentieth century. Roosevelt realized that economic growth cut as a double-edged sword and made it a public mission to warn people about crass commercialism. Rather, what Roosevelt embraced about Hamilton was the first secretary of the treasury's goal of a strong federal government orchestrating the political, diplomatic, and economic affairs of a free nation. Roosevelt would certainly use the prerogatives of the presidency in an expansive fashion, and he could hardly say enough against the states' rights view of Thomas Jefferson. Roosevelt's vehemence knew few bounds when it came to the third president, "Heaven knows how cordially I despise Jefferson," whom he regarded as "the most incompetent chief executive we ever had."[9] By contrast, Roosevelt would push to the limits his powers of commander in chief. In the case of the army officer corps, he fought to advance men that he deemed of the right stripe, and he supported greater federal oversight of National Guard units.

New Leaders for the Army of Empire

When Theodore Roosevelt assumed the presidency, he knew that he was an accidental president. He did what leaders before and since have done following a fallen chief executive. The new president sought to reassure the country and pledged to pursue his predecessor's policies. Yet Roosevelt being Roosevelt, he would soon come to own the office, well before he ran for the presidency in his own right in 1904. On one of Roosevelt's first days in the White House, he indicated as much to Henry Cabot Lodge: "It is dreadful to come into the Presidency this way; but it would be a far worse thing to be morbid about it. Here is the task, and I have got to do it to the best of my ability."[10]

Within two months after taking office, Roosevelt revealed what he had in mind for army officers. He nominated Capt. William Crozier to become the new chief of the Bureau of Ordnance in the War Department. If confirmed, Crozier would rocket to the rank of brigadier general. The nominee embodied the innovative, intelligent, and younger type of officers that Roosevelt wanted at the head of the army. At forty-seven Crozier was relatively youthful, and he was physically vigorous. He would accompany Roosevelt on his hiking expeditions. On 4 June 1904 Roosevelt reported to Leonard Wood how "just yesterday, Crozier and I had a three hours' scramble."[11] Besides being able to endure the president's excursions, Crozier possessed numerous professional attainments that commended him. He was an ordnance specialist who had been co-inventor of the disappearing gun carriage. Crozier had also distinguished himself as the American military representative at the Hague International Peace Conference of 1899. He played a crucial role in bringing about an agreement setting more humane standards for the conduct of war. Finally, Crozier appealed to T.R. because they were like-minded about personnel reforms. In 1899 Crozier had approached Roosevelt, then governor of New York, with a proposal for merit promotions. He wanted Roosevelt's support, but nothing came of the initiative.[12]

Crozier's rise from captain to brigadier general naturally sparked opposition. No one questioned his qualifications, but merit was not all that counted. Other ordnance officers would be denied the chance of a general's stars if Crozier remained on the job until he retired. Because he was relatively young, Crozier could hold his appointment, considered permanent, until 1919. Other members of the ordnance branch could look forward only to lesser positions because Crozier would block them from the top spot for nearly two decades. Morale would suffer, and resentment might build. Similar concerns would surface throughout Roosevelt's presidency when he made more such appointments. Nonetheless, T.R. would persist because he wanted younger, more capable officers in the top ranks. Crozier's nomination, early on, set the terms of the debate.

In promoting Crozier, Roosevelt could claim that he was simply tapping into the legacy of William McKinley. After the war with Spain, McKinley moved a number of men out of their turn to brigadier general. He and Secretary of War Elihu Root recognized the same problem that Roosevelt had witnessed in Cuba. Officers came to top commands too old and stayed for too short of a time. As Root noted, timeservers departed and talent moved forward only after war erupted, but "at the expense always of treasure and of life, and sometimes of temporary failure and humiliation."[13] The culprit was the seniority system of promotion. Officers advanced only if the billet above them opened, and openings were rare. The situation had been worse at one time. Before 1890 captains and lieutenants had to wait for a vacancy in their regiment before they could move forward, while majors and above depended on openings in their combat arm. Promotions were allocated according to combat arms for all ranks after 1890. In staff positions, however, faster advancement was possible with an appointment to a bureaucratic post.

Officers who lived long enough could look forward to advancement eventually, but the pace was glacial because of another factor. The Civil War had swelled the regular ranks, so all those men who joined after 1865 faced a wartime "hump" of officers that blocked promotions. As a result, the average first lieutenant was forty-five years old in 1891, and the average artillery captain was slightly over fifty years of age.[14] The adoption of a mandatory retirement age of sixty-four in 1882 was the only measure taken before 1900 to help break the logjam. Still, the Spanish-American War demonstrated that the system had problems. McKinley and Root decided to use executive powers to attempt a patch.

They called first for a promotion system based on merit. Officers who did not advance from one rank to another in a certain amount of time would be "selected out" and retired. But the proposed reform required legislation, and Congress refused to move. Many members had cozy relationships with War Department staff officers, who, in exchange for protection of the bureau officers' domains, supported military projects in home districts. Also they were aware that many of the first officers to be selected out would be Civil War veterans. Many senators and representatives were themselves veterans of the war, and because of emotional ties were unwilling to displace former comrades who still wore the uniform. Even if they were tempted, the Grand Army of the Republic, *the* veterans' association of the day, was a politically potent watchdog of veterans' interests.

Existing law did allow McKinley some room to maneuver. Moreover, expansion of the army after 1898 to police the new American empire also added some flexibility. Under the current military code, strict seniority governed the ranks from lieutenant to colonel. A president, however, could nominate anyone for a brigadier general's slot, although no one had done so since 1873. Moreover, the Army Reorganization Act of 1901 opened more possibilities.[15] The number of major generals in the line of the army increased from three to six, and brigadier generalships climbed from six to fifteen.[16] In 1900 McKinley broke precedent when he moved three men, out of the regular order, into brigadier generalships. He bumped up Arthur MacArthur, William Ludlow, and Joseph Wheeler. All three were Civil War veterans, and all three were also generals in the volunteers. Then in 1901 McKinley broke decisively with tradition when he pushed ahead James Franklin Bell, Frederick Funston, Frederick Dent Grant, and Leonard Wood. None could claim Civil War service, and two, Wood and Funston, lacked a Military Academy education. In fact, Funston had no background in the regular service at all. Moreover, before their promotions, both Wood and Bell held the permanent rank of captain. Bell made the most spectacular leap, jumping over 981 senior officers. To recommend the promotions, all four men were brigadier generals in the volunteers, and three wore the Medal of Honor. Taken together these appointments sent the message that McKinley was prepared to award meritorious service.[17] The path, indeed, seemed blazed for Theodore Roosevelt's own promotion program.

Roosevelt, who often encouraged controversy to advance a proposition, should have taken pause from the fact that the genial McKinley's promotions sparked criticism. True, the president and Root tried to smooth the way by giving some old soldiers a star. That effort was not enough to prevent protests. One of the loudest voices belonged to the commanding general of the army, Lt. Gen. Nelson Miles, who could boast of proud Civil War service and had gone on to important commands during the pacification of the western frontier. He also possessed one of the great egos of his day. Roosevelt called him a "brave peacock," and during the Spanish-American War satirist Finley Peter Dunne described the transportation needed to carry Miles's gold-encrusted uniforms as "specyal steel protected bullyon trains fr'm th' mint, where they've been kept f'r a year."[18] Miles was adamant against McKinley's promotions. He wanted generalships to reward past service and remained wedded to strict seniority promotions.[19]

Although Miles rarely shied from publicity and harbored political ambitions (at one point he had courted Roosevelt as part of an ill-conceived plan to unseat McKinley in the 1900 election, and in 1904 he would seek the Democratic nomination), he did seem to speak for many other officers in this case.[20] They resented the fact that less "seasoned" men than themselves had skipped so quickly to the top while they had waited years for advancement. The promotions of Frederick Grant and James

Franklin Bell aroused less antagonism because they were graduates of West Point, and Bell was a respected student of military affairs.[21] Officers, however, denounced Frederick Funston's elevation. Because Funston could point to no regular service, his promotion appeared to be due solely to his capture in March 1901 of Emilio Aguinaldo, the principal leader of the Philippine nationalist forces. Aguinaldo's capture helped to break the back of Filipino resistance to American rule and save McKinley from a tight political spot. Leonard Wood's promotion over 530 other officers smelled of favoritism. Reportedly, fellow officers felt that his military experience was too limited to justify the appointment. In their minds he remained Dr. Wood, who owed his rank to two very important patients, William and Ida McKinley. Wood's obvious executive ability, first as administrator in Santiago de Cuba and then as military governor of Cuba, helped to counter his critics.[22]

When his turn came, Roosevelt did not blink at the protests against McKinley's promotions. In the end, had not McKinley gotten his way on every nomination? Roosevelt's natural combativeness and crusading instinct also compelled him to enlarge on McKinley's precedent. The new president, after all, was a man who believed that when life ended "it would be pleasant," among other things, "to know that on the whole one's duties have not been shirked, that there has been no flinching from foes."[23] When he moved, beginning with Crozier's nomination, Roosevelt characteristically acted with more drama than the comparatively placid McKinley, who had nominated men who were already generals in the volunteers and confirmed them in that rank in the regulars. Roosevelt would put forth officers who were not volunteer generals. Sometimes these men held a temporary rank higher than their permanent grade, but none had the experience at command of McKinley's nominees. Indeed, in some cases Roosevelt awarded a junior officer with a brigadier generalship. As a consequence, his promotion policies would prove more controversial and, in particular, upset other army officers and provoke the Senate Military Affairs Committee, which had to approve all nominations. Roosevelt also found it harder to make such promotions seem vital with the problems of the Spanish-American War fading from memory.

T.R. hoped that by making nominations such as Crozier's he would plant like-minded allies in the War Department, and he would help build the case for promotion-by-merit legislation. Such an action made sense for a man with Roosevelt's political style. He believed in leading by example, and there seemed no better way to demonstrate the benefits of younger leaders than by putting them in top commands. In addition, he was acting with bold strokes by putting in men who had never before worn a general's stars. Such a move would only help attract attention, even by way of criticism, for the larger reform goal: a complete overhaul of the promotion system. As much as he liked rewarding men who fit his image of a general, Roosevelt understood that meaningful change would occur only if the overall system changed. Otherwise, he might succeed in peppering the higher command ranks with a few younger officers, but the passage of time and the continuation of strict seniority promotions would undo the good he and McKinley had done. Thus at almost the same time that he nominated Crozier, he pushed for legislation to overhaul the promotion system.

Less than two weeks after he had nominated Crozier to be the new chief of ordnance, Roosevelt called for promotion reform in his first annual message to Congress. The entire message was one of the longest a president had ever sent to Capitol Hill. The chief executive did not deliver it himself; rather, the clerks of the House and Senate read it to their respective chambers. In the Senate the reading required two-and-a-half hours to complete. For members who endured the entire reading, at about three-quarters of the way through the president discussed reform of the army promotion system. He bluntly identified the basic problem with army promotions: "It is very undesirable," Roosevelt stated, "to have the senior grades of the army composed of men who have come to fill the positions by the mere fact of seniority. A system should be adopted by which there shall be an elimination grade by grade of those who seem unfit to render the best service in the next grade."[24] This was not just the president of the United States writing these lines, but also an assistant secretary of the navy and cavalry leader who had seen firsthand the problems that occurred when officers were too old and stayed for too long in their commands.

The former civil service commissioner and police board member were also evident in the message. Roosevelt wanted a promotion system free of political influence. He reminded Congress of the evils of political maneuvering in personnel matters: "Pressure for the promotion of civil officials for political reasons is bad enough, but it is tenfold worse where applied on behalf of officers of the army or navy." He spelled out more how the new system would reward only merit and not political pull—an effort to counter arguments that seniority was the only possible objective measure and free of political gamesmanship. The president acknowledged an even larger consideration when he addressed the need to provide "justice to the veterans of the Civil War who are still in the army." He recommended that a law be passed giving them the same privileges as their naval colleagues. When navy officers retired, they advanced by one grade. Such a measure would honor them with greater status and a larger pension. And then, like any American politician, he tried to make merit promotion in general an irresistible proposition with some lofty rhetoric. "The merit system of making appointments," he wrote, "is in its essence as democratic and American as the common school system itself."[25]

In spite of the length of Roosevelt's first message, members of Congress received it well. They should have. Roosevelt had shared advance drafts with Republican leaders, and they had edited portions of the manuscript.[26] They were not, however, any more willing to change the army promotion system for Roosevelt than they had been for McKinley. If anything, they may have been less inclined. The patronage link to War Department bureau officers remained as strong as ever, and the problem of discharging Civil War veterans became more sensitive when Roosevelt proposed it than when McKinley had done so. McKinley, as a Union veteran, could claim standing as a comrade-in-arms. Roosevelt represented a new generation, and to the graying veterans—both in and out of uniform—he would have been seen as a military upstart. He had endured one day of hard fighting along with several other days of being in a combat zone. Many Civil War veterans had survived months and years of hazard.

More than political interests and concern for an honored generation seemed to be at issue. The good order of the army officer corps appeared to be at stake. Merit promotions, by nature, would operate on a much more subjective standard than promotion strictly by seniority. Officers and interested partisans could much more easily manipulate what amounted to merit on behalf of a favorite than they could the objective record of one's time in service. Roosevelt had argued forcefully in his annual message that the system he had in mind would guard against favoritism because he knew that partiality represented one of the strongest arguments against changing the existing system.

In the end, Congress was willing to consider change only on the margins of the current promotion system. Overall reform remained out of the question during Roosevelt's presidency— not that Roosevelt ever abandoned his call to discard the old promotion system. He repeated the request until the end of his presidency. His annual message of 1908 was perhaps the most succinct: "Our men come too old, and stay for too short a time, in the high-command positions."[27] If he were to accomplish anything on this front, then Roosevelt would have to approach Congress on a case-by-case basis, for legislators, if McKinley's precedent was any indication, appeared willing to entertain individual nominations, if for no other reason than courtesy to the chief executive. As a new president following a fallen leader, Roosevelt had some goodwill that he could count on from Congress and the country.

"Jumping Up" His Own Men

In 1902 the president decided to give William Crozier some company. He nominated two men to become brigadier generals out of their regular turn. The appointment of Tasker Bliss echoed McKinley's promotions. He was already a brigadier general in the volunteers, although he retained the permanent rank of major in the regulars. As a result, his promotion would raise him over the heads of 271 seniors. Just like Leonard Wood, Bliss had earned praise for administration in postwar Cuba. He had brought order to the collection of Cuban customs and thereby helped give the new nation sound finances. Bliss also possessed a keen intellect. He had taught at the Naval War College as a young army officer and later helped develop the army's general staff. He was a master of four foreign tongues—Spanish, French, German, and Russian—and was called "the army's most finished product."[28] At less than fifty years old, he also fit Roosevelt's age requirement. The president's other choice for an extraordinary promotion in 1902, William Carter, had a similar profile. He had not yet reached fifty and had impressed Secretary Root with his ideas for army reform. He would go on to become one of the primary architects of the general staff. Carter's talents had already won him promotion to colonel as an assistant adjutant general, and as result he passed only 89 others on his way to brigadier general.[29]

Carter's and Bliss's promotions were two of the easiest for Roosevelt to secure. Although Bliss jumped over a considerable number of senior officers, senators realized that he had pulled off a significant accomplishment in reorganizing Cuban finances and that his knowledge of Cuba's economic affairs would be crucial for shaping relations with that republic. Carter was leaping over far fewer officers, and he also was regarded as the protégé of Adjt. Gen. Henry Corbin, who was among the most respected figures in the War Department. As adjutant general, he managed personnel matters and therefore would have commanded considerable attention from patronage-minded members of Congress. One journalist referred to Corbin as "the chief of the military politicians."[30]

The fact that Roosevelt kept the promise in his first annual message to take care of Civil War veterans also helped smooth the way for Bliss and Carter. He followed the practice outlined in his message to Congress. Civil War veterans who retired would receive a promotion. The president commenced this practice on his own authority but hoped legislation would be forthcoming to regularize the arrangement. Twenty-five officers took advantage of the offer in 1902, and, of them, twelve were senior colonels. Members of the Senate liked the program and encouraged its expansion. Roosevelt fostered goodwill with an additional nod to older officers. Along with Bliss and Carter, he awarded stars to five of the seven most senior colonels in the army.[31]

In 1903 Roosevelt determined on his most dramatic elevation yet. He wanted to bump up a man who, Leonard Wood aside, was his ideal of American officership. The prospective nominee was in his forties and possessed a Military Academy education. He also had experience on the western frontier and had proven himself a man of action in Cuba and then against Filipino insurgents. Moreover, the president already knew him. Roosevelt had met John J. Pershing in the 1890s and then seen him in action at the San Juan Heights. In 1903 Pershing was a captain and had just completed a successful pacification campaign on the Philippine island of Mindanao. Pershing had attacked strongholds of the rebellious Moros as head of a force of infantry, cavalry, and artillery, but he had won their allegiance to the United States with few American casualties. One news headline summed up Pershing's accomplishment best: "Seven Moro Forts Taken: Twenty-Five of the Enemy Killed, While American Loss Is Nil." Or as another article put it, "Capt. John J. Pershing, of the Fifteenth Cavalry, is a man who 'does things,' and that is a sure passport to the admiration of President Roosevelt."[32]

Roosevelt was indeed paying attention and wanted to reward Pershing's performance and put him on the track to higher command. In July 1903 he praised Pershing's "striking bit of service in the Philippines."[33] Roosevelt, though, decided to back away from the appointment before the end of the month. Some thought the reward of a brigadier generalship was excessive, and Secretary Root recommended that the president jump another officer before he push up Pershing. Root wanted Thomas Barry moved up and also doubted whether Roosevelt should elevate Pershing "over the head of another man—A. L. Mills, Superintendent of West Point."[34]

In the end, Roosevelt decided that Pershing could wait and instead honored his deeds in the Philippines by mentioning the captain by name in his annual message for 1903. On 7 December, as part of Roosevelt's yearly appeal for a merit system of promotion, members of the House and Senate heard how John Pershing represented the perfect example of earning promotion because of worthy deeds. "When a man renders such service as Captain Pershing rendered last spring in the Moro campaign," the president wrote, "it ought to be possible to reward him without at once jumping him to the grade of brigadier-general."[35] A degree of combativeness crept into the statement. Rather than just asking for promotion reform, he appealed to Congress to give him merit promotions not just to reward an officer like Pershing but to stop him from the practice of jumping good officers far above the heads of their seniors. He implied that he would continue until Congress acted. As time passed, however, Congress would become less and less tolerant of Roosevelt's dramatic moves.

The man who received the promotion originally slated for Pershing, Thomas Barry, was an assistant adjutant general and forty-seven years old in 1903. His case for promotion was advanced simply because it involved less controversy at a time when resistance to leaping men above others was building. Barry had amassed a good military and administrative record since graduating from West Point, and his file, unlike Pershing's, contained endorsements from general officers. Moreover, Barry would pass only thirty-six other officers. Secretary Root also claimed that Roosevelt did not have to wait long to reward Pershing. He could promote the hero in 1904, when four vacancies would occur.[36]

With Barry's promotion the president relayed openly his criteria for picking generals. Roosevelt weighed experience and looked at an officer's age, but his perception of an officer's character represented the decisive factor. Roosevelt told Barry as much when he wrote him in July 1903: "From my association with you I believe you have the energy, the intelligence, the courage, and the power of immediate decision in any crisis, no less than the willingness to take responsibility, which are vital to welldoing."[37] Thus, T.R. told Barry, he believed him to be a man of action and that the new general needed to continue to meet the president's expectations. In the phrase "from my association with you," Roosevelt also admitted that he was picking men with whom he was personally acquainted. Absent a merit system of promotion, the only standards in which he had confidence were his own. He wanted to make sure that the men he selected, and staked his political reputation on, would succeed. Hence the qualities that he admired in Barry again reflected the president's own core virtues for good civic behavior.

As an assistant adjutant general, Barry did represent an exception to one of Roosevelt's rules of promotion. He was not a cavalryman. Roosevelt most often chose men from the part of the army that he knew the best—his former branch of the service, the cavalry. The imbalance was so striking that the War Department's general staff noted in April 1906 that the cavalry was receiving a disproportionate share of the appointments to brigadier general.[38] Roosevelt not only knew officers in the cavalry but also felt that the cavalry supplied the best warriors. For him cavalry combined the qualities of the past with the ability to meet the martial demands of the future. Cavalry recalled the West, Roosevelt's great forge of soldierly and individual character, and mounted troops also offered flexibility in the conduct of war. As Roosevelt observed in 1901, looking at conditions in the Boer War in South Africa, "modern warfare demands not cavalry as found in the English army . . . but cavalry of exactly the type we have in our army; that is, cavalry who are trained to a very high standard of horsemanship, who are taught to maneuver as cavalry, and in case of necessity to charge as cavalry, but who are expected normally to fight on foot with the rifle or carbine."[39]

Because of Roosevelt's partiality toward the cavalry and the men in it, the charge of favoritism began to be leveled against his promotion program. Indeed, although the president would say he was picking the best men—and he did promote officers who served well—he was also selecting individuals whom he knew, and thus his promotions did smack of personal preference. Ironically, the favoritism that Congress feared would accompany merit promotions instead appeared in the informal process that the president established because of the absence of congressional action.

The charge of favoritism first began to stick because of the enmity of one man. Lt. Gen. Nelson Miles had disliked McKinley's promotions because they lifted men out of their turn. He objected to Roosevelt's promotions for the same reason, but he also resisted them because of Roosevelt himself. Miles increasingly resented the new president, and Roosevelt returned the feeling. In 1900 he had rejected the general's political overtures, and he now held the office that Miles coveted. Moreover, Roosevelt remained the military upstart to the veteran of the Civil War and Native American campaigns, and the general also did not like the president's imperialist policies. T.R.'s avid support of army reform further antagonized Miles, as the proposed creation of a general staff threatened to wipe away his very position. The fact that the two men had oversize egos did not help relations either. In 1901, after Miles inserted himself into a dispute between two admirals over credit for the naval battle off Santiago in 1898, Roosevelt publicly upbraided the commanding general. A censure was forthcoming from Secretary Root, in which he told Miles, "You had no business in the controversy, and no right, holding the office which you did, to express any opinion."[40]

Relations between Roosevelt and Miles deteriorated from there. In March 1902 Miles testified before the Senate Military Affairs Committee against a general-staff bill, calling it "an effort to adopt and foster . . . a system peculiarly adapted to monarchies having immense standing armies. . . . It would seem to Germanize and Russianize the small Army of the United States."[41] Later, in June, Roosevelt's coldness toward Miles was apparent at ceremonies celebrating the centennial of the Military Academy. The president made a point to make as little contact with the general as possible. At a review of the Corps of Cadets, Roosevelt ignored Miles, except when he "turned suddenly, extended his hand, and then turned away again."[42]

Because of this animosity, Miles's condemnation of Roosevelt's promotions probably came as no surprise to the president. In a move calculated to appeal to fears of Roosevelt's robust executive style and the possible problems with a merit-promotion system, the commanding general claimed that the president and secretary of war were trying to make the army into a personal organization. With the general also working to discredit the administration's policies in the Philippines, Roosevelt seethed that Miles was "the most dangerous foe and slanderer of the army."[43] He could not, however, dismiss the politically prominent and well-connected officer.

Roosevelt would deal with the Miles problem in another way. He could not make the general take back his damaging words, but he could make it harder for the general to be heard. Miles wished to go on an inspection tour of the Philippines. Roosevelt granted the request. Although Miles could still stir up trouble—he had made much of the charges of American atrocities in the Philippines—he would, at least, be far from Washington and less likely to derail army-reform efforts.

The Battle Intensified

Even with Miles absent from Washington, the charges of favoritism grew only stronger because of another promotion. The promotion, in this case, was not for an officer who was jumping over others. Rather, the problem lay in the man Roosevelt wanted to promote. T.R. planned to move Leonard Wood from brigadier general to major general. He claimed that Wood was moving up in his turn and that the general had performed well in every position of authority that he had held. He had served ably as military governor of Cuba and, following Cuban independence, as commander of the Department of Mindanao and governor of the rebellious Moro Province in the Philippines.[44] Wood's ability was not in question. Rather, Wood came in for criticism because he had already benefited greatly from personal preferment. The "Captain Doctor" had served one president as a physician and was the playmate of another. If promoted to major general, a scant few years after becoming a brigadier, he would stand only six places away from lieutenant general, the top position in the army. His close association with Roosevelt also made him the perfect target for rivals who wanted to embarrass the president.

Two senators led the charge to deny Wood the promotion. Sen. Henry Teller, Democrat of Colorado, made the most vocal protests. Teller had been an expansionist in 1898, but even then he had pushed the amendment that pledged the United States to Cuban independence at the start of the war with Spain. Colorado produced sugar beets, and competition from Cuban sugarcane was unwelcome. Wood's belief that Cuba might one day become American territory would not have endeared him to the senator. Furthermore, Teller, who had once been a Silver Republican, disliked Roosevelt's support of the gold standard, and he recoiled at the president's assistance to Panamanian revolutionaries to expedite the building of an interoceanic canal.[45] Much more ominously for the president, Sen. Marcus Hanna of Ohio went into opposition on the Republican side. Hanna was the kingmaker of the Republican Party. He had managed William McKinley's political fortunes and was mentioned as Roosevelt's most likely rival for the Republican presidential nomination in 1904. Hanna was unlikely to unseat Roosevelt, but he could cause trouble as the guiding hand of the Republican old guard in the Senate, a group that distrusted the president's reformist impulses.[46]

The assault on Wood was fierce in the Senate Military Affairs Committee. Teller denounced a promotion in which favoritism played such an obvious role. He accepted Wood's promotion to brigadier general as recognition of his civil services in Cuba but felt that further advance was unwarranted. Teller warned that the promotion set a dangerous precedent because it put a man without formal military education and little field experience into the highest echelons of command. If applied overall, the practice would damage army morale and could bring wartime disaster. Officers would lose spirit as they watched men bypass them for no better reason than political "pull." In Wood's case promotion had come "by the partiality of the Executive . . . and not from merit."[47] All in all, Teller echoed officers' concerns that promotions such as Wood's threatened the professional integrity of the officer corps. For his part, Hanna attacked the work that had made Wood renowned, his service as military governor of Cuba. Hanna wanted Wood condemned for unlawful interference in the conviction of Estes G. Rathbone for fraud. A friend and constituent of the senator, Rathbone had run the Post Office Department in Cuba until Wood had him arrested and imprisoned for embezzlement. The committee heard Rathbone's testimony but eventually vindicated Wood.[48]

The Senate hearings presented Roosevelt with a dilemma. If he failed to get Wood's promotion confirmed, then he would suffer a personal and political reverse going into a presidential election year. If Roosevelt, however, waged an assertive campaign on behalf of his friend, then he would be validating charges of executive bias. The nomination fight was also an unwelcome distraction, for at the same time that the Senate hearings occurred in November and December 1903, Roosevelt was fighting for ratification of the treaty with Panama that would allow work to begin on a canal. This project would fulfill his navalist dreams and secure his place in history. Opponents such as Henry Teller delighted in the opportunity to attack Roosevelt on two matters about which he cared so much, his compatriot Leonard Wood and his Panama policy.

Roosevelt decided to make a fight for Wood. He would fight so hard that he would lend further ammunition to opponents of his promotion practices. The president's friendship with Wood played a role in his decision to fight, although he never admitted as much. He did, however, blast the attacks on Wood as "base and cruelly unjust."[49] Roosevelt would play down his relationship with Wood in any event, for, as in so many of his crusades, he had convinced himself of the rightness of his cause. As far as he was concerned, Wood's accomplishments spoke for themselves and justified the promotion. Moreover, Roosevelt was not about to suffer a political setback going into the 1904 presidential contest, especially at the hands of Mark Hanna.

Therefore, well before the Senate hearings, sensing that "the fight will be on from the very beginning," the president directed Secretary Root to collect documents relevant to Wood's services in Cuba and his participation in the expedition against Geronimo in 1886.[50] Roosevelt also ordered Wood to "give me all the information . . . that you can think of and . . . anything else which you think any scoundrel may say against you or any well-meaning fool believe." In orchestrating this effort, T.R. further recommended that Wood do exactly what he had said should not occur under a merit system of promotion. He wanted Wood to mobilize his political contacts in Washington. "Is there any way," Roosevelt wrote, "that you could get any influence with Senator Proctor? If so, exert it." Redfield Proctor was a former secretary of war and a Republican member of the committee. In addition, Roosevelt told Wood to court Sen. Francis Cockrell of Missouri, a Democratic friend on the Military Affairs Committee.[51]

Such tactics might win Wood's promotion, the short-term objective, but would work against the larger goal of merit-promotion legislation by playing straight into the hands of the critics of such a system. True to his usual practice, Roosevelt carefully monitored press coverage of Wood's nomination and rated the *Sun* and the *Evening Post* as the "most bitter" among the New York newspapers. He also informed Wood that "the Southern democratic press so far as it is against you is simply desirous of doing anything it can to annoy the administration." To counter such sentiment, he sent an elaborate seven-page defense of Wood and the administration's promotions policy to Oswald Garrison Villard, editor of the *Evening Post*. Later Roosevelt claimed that only lobbying by Root and himself had brought the *New York Tribune*, the *Philadelphia Press*, the *Outlook*, and the *Review of Reviews* over to the administration's side.[52] If any doubt remained how strongly Roosevelt wanted the promotion, it ended when word came from the White House that the vote on Wood would be seen as a test of party loyalty. Secretary Root reportedly informed the Military Affairs Committee that a negative report on Wood would be interpreted as a break with the administration.[53] Roosevelt explained to Wood, "I think most of the Republicans will not want to split off with the President who seems likely to be the candidate for President next year."[54] Despite mention of a challenge from Hanna, he knew most Republican senators would not want to weaken their best hope to keep the White House in 1904.

The administration's exertions paid off. The Senate Military Affairs Committee voted eight to three to endorse the promotion on 4 January 1904, and the entire Senate acted on 18 March to confirm Wood by a margin of twenty-nine votes. Mark Hanna's sudden death on 15 February 1904 removed a possible obstacle to Wood's second star and the president's own political fortunes. According to former secretary of war Russell Alger, now a senator from Michigan, Roosevelt was "very, very happy" with the vote for Wood.[55] The victory came at a cost. The president himself realized that Wood's "confirmation was due only to the straining of every nerve by the Administration."[56] After the fight the promotion policy slowed down, and Roosevelt won fewer victories. In fact, he would dare to leap very few officers in a dramatic fashion after the battle over Wood.

For the remainder of his first term, Roosevelt moved up only one more officer out of turn, and in the wake of the bruising Wood fight, the effort nearly failed. He decided to promote an officer who had been with him on the San Juan Heights. Albert L. Mills was a captain of cavalry who had impressed Roosevelt "as absolutely cool, absolutely unmoved or flurried in any way." During the battle a bullet had struck Mills in the head, destroyed one of his eyes, and blinded him temporarily in the other. Nevertheless, Roosevelt recorded in *The Rough Riders* that Mills "would not go back or let any man assist him, sitting down where he was and waiting until one of the men brought him word that the hill was stormed."[57] After the war, with his wound healed, Mills became superintendent of the Military Academy. In fact, on the day that Roosevelt celebrated the academy's centennial in 1902, he spent much of his time conversing with Mills, even as he snubbed General Miles.[58] As superintendent, Mills held the temporary rank of colonel, yet his permanent rank remained that of captain. If Roosevelt were to make him a brigadier general, Mills would leap over about 350 other officers.[59]

Congress gave the Mills nomination a chilly reception. Senators decided that the time had come to restrain the White House. They appeared incredulous that Roosevelt would make such a nomination so soon after the tempest over Leonard Wood.[60] After the stand that Roosevelt had taken on Wood, the time had arrived to send an unmistakable message down Pennsylvania Avenue. In March 1904 the Senate Military Affairs Committee seemed prepared to vote against Mills's confirmation. The *Army and Navy Journal* reported that senators were ready to make a statement against the promotion of any more junior officers to field ranks. Committee members had decided that these promotions were too harmful to army morale. They met with Roosevelt to request that he withdraw the nomination or that he retire Mills immediately after promotion. The president refused to do either but offered the senators a pledge in return. After Mills, he reportedly promised, the administration had no intention of elevating lower ranking officers to generalships.[61] Roosevelt's exact words were not recorded, but he apparently felt he left himself room to maneuver, because within two years he would again be pushing the case of John J. Pershing. T.R. may have made a pledge in 1904 that he had no immediate plans for another extraordinary promotion, but in 1906 he would decide that enough time had passed for him to violate the spirit of the agreement.

Roosevelt's pledge had the intended effect and assured the majority of the committee, which then endorsed Mills's nomination. However, Sen. Nathan B. Scott, Republican of West Virginia, was not satisfied. A committee member, he had been absent during the committee's deliberations but returned in time to block the vote in the Senate until the Fifty-Eighth Congress adjourned.[62] Roosevelt gave Mills a recess appointment in the interim, which lasted until December 1904, when the Senate at last granted approval.[63]

Roosevelt, for a time, honored the senators' feelings about extraordinary promotions. He understood that he had tested the limits of congressional tolerance and that seniority must receive more consideration. The primary cause of discontent, he believed, remained Wood's promotion. Getting Wood confirmed, Roosevelt wrote, "left a very bitter feeling in the Senate, for which Mills paid the penalty." Whatever the cause of unhappiness, the president recognized that he needed to acknowledge political realities for a while. His next brigadier general would be a colonel or an officer whose seniority approximated a colonel's. Roosevelt, never happy about a retreat, grumbled to Wood "that the public naturally cannot know who the best officer is, and all the mutton heads in the army . . . naturally object to anything resembling promotion by merit." If Mills's nomination had come before Wood's, Roosevelt felt no such trouble would have occurred.[64] Here, then, was a president, certain in the ultimate correctness of his goals, who was prepared to confront Congress again, once he sensed that he could prevail. His belief was a testament to his faith in his political ability.

The promotion policy seemed almost to have run its course by the time Roosevelt stood for election in November 1904. He had achieved limited success. He had leavened the upper ranks with younger officers who could serve years instead of months in command. The number of "honorary" generals had declined. Altogether, Roosevelt elevated thirty-nine officers who would serve at least a few years as general, if not more in some cases, before retirement. He had also managed to suggest a standard for promotion based on fitness for command, a criterion that stood in distinct contrast to seniority as the sole basis of advancement.[65] As the end of his first term neared, Roosevelt had failed to obtain his primary goal: promotion by selection for all ranks on the basis of merit. Congress grudgingly accepted his nominees for general but refused to break with the seniority system of promotions. Ties were too strong to army officers who had an understandable interest in protecting the old system. That arrangement provided security and increased their chances for promotion, even if it came slowly. Roosevelt might dismiss army opponents as mutton heads, but he also noted while reflecting on the opposition to Wood's appointment, "Root and I were astounded to find how overwhelming this sentiment . . . was, both among the people at large . . . and among the army."[66]

Although stymied on promotions by 1904, Roosevelt and Root did achieve a significant success that helped to improve army personnel. They may have faced a difficult time promoting younger officers to higher commands, yet there was another route to securing a more youthful officer corps: retirements. At the same time that Mills's confirmation stalled, Congress sanctioned the administration's practice of retiring Civil War veterans. Senators and representatives did so only after some pressure. When Congress first refused to lower the minimum age at which veterans could receive pensions to sixty-two, Roosevelt implemented the rule through executive order. An amendment to the Army Appropriations Act of 1904 gave the measure legislative sanction. The new law permitted the president to promote Civil War veterans one rank upon mandatory retirement at age sixty-four, upon voluntary retirement at age sixty-two, or upon voluntary retirement after forty years of service.[67] Officers already retired were included under the act, as were former volunteer generals of the Civil War or the Spanish-American War. Older officers left in droves as a result, with 134 retiring from the active list by 1906. The law affected 115 active and retired colonels and therefore lessened pressure to reward long-serving men with general's stars. Unlike the promotion policy, the retirement policy proved popular. It honored men for past service and, with the promise of a higher rank upon retirement, gave them an incentive to leave the service on the best of terms. No one lost with this balanced proposition, unlike the promotion policy, which seemed unfair to many.[68]

Building a Better Militia

As biographer Kathleen Dalton put it, by 1904 Roosevelt had shown himself to be a strong man in a weak state.[69] He had taken on large business trusts, secured a canal treaty, and resolved the anthracite coal strike of 1902. Roosevelt had put the presidency at the forefront in a way not seen since Abraham Lincoln. In breaking up J. P. Morgan's Northern Securities Company, he asserted the supremacy of federal power over the barons of American finance and industry. In Panama and with the coal strike, he used executive power with equal force. To prevent Colombia from suppressing a revolt in Panama in November 1903, and hence interfering with his plans for an interoceanic canal, Roosevelt dispatched the USS *Nashville*. He helped settle the coal strike by threatening recalcitrant mine owners with the use of the army to seize and operate the mines. Roosevelt had taken the reins of power firmly and had also captured the public's imagination. The bold, colorful, and often controversial chief executive, with his young family, charmed even those individuals who did not agree with his tactics or policies. He had shown how he was willing to use the strong arm of the executive to bring change, and this was equally true with his efforts to build a more modern military establishment. T.R. had certainly demonstrated how active he could be in his attempt to improve the army officer corps. His involvement with the National Guard would show another side of his work as commander in chief.

In keeping with his other reforms, Roosevelt held that the militia would benefit from the guidance of the federal government. As a professed Hamiltonian, he would build the reform of state forces around an extension of central authority. Although he did not fully endorse Alexander Hamilton's economic ideas, he embraced the first treasury secretary's beliefs about robust national governance. Roosevelt did so because he liked to wield power but also because the vigorous use of the federal government seemed to be the best way to produce a stronger, more respected country and to induce economic and political reform. In general, then, the militia legislation of the Roosevelt administration followed the twenty-sixth president's typical pattern of reform and use of power. Expanded federal oversight would help build a more reliable reserve for the greater good of the American people.

Militia reform, at the same time, also fell outside Roosevelt's usual pattern for military matters. Examination of this effort is useful because it illustrates what Roosevelt was *not* as commander in chief. In most areas of military affairs, he took a detailed interest and put his personal stamp on policy. By contrast, Roosevelt was not especially concerned with the fortunes of state forces. He assumed this attitude in part because he thought such matters could be delegated to others. His relative lack of involvement, though, also had deeper origins. A nationalist by inclination, and with the office of the president enforcing a national outlook, Roosevelt would much rather deal with the navy and the regular army, which were under his direct authority, than share with state authorities the direction of more than forty militia organizations, which maintained various degrees of preparedness. He seemed to view guard forces as a necessary evil, a relic of the decentralized Jeffersonian impulse that he despised. T.R. would tolerate the guard because the army needed a reserve, but state forces were not his preference, so he never made militia reform a top priority. In short, he would not "strain every nerve" to involve himself with the militia and to win reform legislation.

Theodore Roosevelt, of course, had first gained a taste of military life in the New York National Guard in the 1880s, but after his experience with guardsmen during the Spanish-American War and as governor of New York, he had soured on the institution. He had, as noted in an earlier chapter, promoted a militia-reform effort during his brief tenure as governor of New York. The Sanger Report that resulted analyzed English and Swiss militia models and would help support militia reform during Roosevelt's presidency.[70]

Two men were most responsible for militia reform during Roosevelt's administration. One was the man Roosevelt leaned on the most in his cabinet, Elihu Root, who possessed an agile mind and sarcastic wit and had already proven to be one of the most able secretaries of war. When McKinley had appointed Root in 1899, Roosevelt had derided the decision. He confessed to Henry Cabot Lodge, "Personally, the desire to have a lawyer in the War Department seems to me simply foolish," although Roosevelt did regard Root as an "absolutely upright and able man." His attitude may have stemmed from the belief that McKinley might offer him the job, as he had fantasized about how he would handle the insurrection against American rule in the Philippines.[71] Roosevelt soon altered his assessment after Root presided over a range of reforms in response to the army's problems during the war with Spain. By the time Roosevelt took office, Root had accomplished changes to the officer education system, increased the size of the army, and revised bureau appointments, along with laying the groundwork for a general staff corps. He had also contemplated an improved system of reserves for expanding the army in wartime.[72] Charles Dick was the other chief agent of militia reform.

Dick served in the House of Representatives from Ohio. He was well positioned to help guide militia legislation through Congress. Dick chaired the House Committee on the Militia, and he was a major general in the Ohio National Guard and president of the National Guard Association.[73]

The Militia Act of 1903, which was more commonly known as the Dick Act, put the National Guard on the track to federalization. Federal arms, training with regulars, and inspection would all follow a governor's request for aid. Moreover, although the law designated guard units as the first to be called into federal service, it made no guarantee that state guard units would be preserved once mustered into the army. Root had also wanted, as part of the Dick Act, the creation of a national reserve of a hundred thousand, which would have no connection to the National Guard. Jealous of being the first reserve, the National Guard opposed Root's provision, and senators such as Edmund Pettus of Alabama contended that the reserve force "was a direct infringement of the authority given to the States by the Constitution." Faced with failure of the entire bill, Root withdrew the section on the federal reserve.[74] After passage of the bill, the *New York Times* lauded the Dick Act for putting "the National Defense upon a much sounder basis." The *Times* recognized the greater federal presence in guard affairs and hoped "that the efficiency of the National Guard in the States in which it is greatest will be improved under this measure, and that, in the more backward States, the standard will be gradually but steadily raised under the pressure of the law."[75]

Roosevelt confined his role on the militia act to providing limited publicity. He kept himself out of the congressional debate and left Root to manage the legislation. Roosevelt displayed nowhere near the interest that he had when leavening the army officer corps with younger generals. To be sure, he had enough to worry about during the summer and fall of 1902, as the militia bill moved through Congress. Injuries from the

Massachusetts streetcar accident slowed him, and the anthracite coal strike was his top priority. His July 1902 visit to the National Guard encampment at Sea Girt, New Jersey, did call attention to the proposed reform. While enjoying the enthusiastic crowd of citizens and soldiers and reminding the guardsmen that each man was there to "work with his whole heart to do his duty," the president informed the assembly, "I am happy to say that a bill has passed through the lower House which will enable the National Government materially to aid the National Guard of the States." Roosevelt then roused the assembly further when he proclaimed his belief that the Senate would pass the bill during its next session and that he would "guarantee the signature of the President."[76] His annual message for 1902 echoed those comments when he, in a short paragraph, asked for "prompt attention and action" so that a "practical and efficient system should be adopted."[77]

Beyond Sea Girt and his annual message, Roosevelt was almost invisible on the topic of militia reform. A president need not, and in fact cannot, devote equal energy to all the affairs of state. The pressures of the office, even in Roosevelt's day, were simply too great. With Elihu Root and Charles Dick at work on militia reform, Roosevelt could afford to direct his attention elsewhere. Yet for a man fascinated with so many aspects of military matters—no subject seemed too trivial when Roosevelt was interested—he displayed a notable lack of passion when it came to the militia. In his Sea Girt speech, for example, he was careful not to laud the troops for their soldierly ability. Instead, he encouraged them "to try to come up to a high standard" and reminded them that they were not "play soldiers."[78] These sentiments reflected more Roosevelt's opinion of the guard during the Spanish-American War and his own experience as a guardsman than someone who truly believed that militia-reform legislation would transform the guard into a reliable and efficient reserve force.

So why did Roosevelt back the militia law at all? He was a practical politician, and this reform represented the best he could get at the time. A federalized reserve force lay outside his grasp. The political influence of the National Guard, at the state level and in the form of the National Guard Association, was simply too strong. His preference remained a truly national reserve. This body would be something on the order of the volunteer forces that had rallied to the flag during wartime crises throughout the nineteenth century, except that this federal reserve would remain organized and available during peacetime. Such units would reflect the national spirit that Roosevelt himself embraced. Although he would acknowledge the guardsmen's good citizenship, Roosevelt could not shake his own bias, which lay rooted in his New York years. To him guardsmen were playing at soldiering, and state guard organizations, such as the one in New York, had become little more than instruments for dispensing patronage.

Roosevelt was careful not to voice such sentiments as president. He was always more circumspect when he felt the responsibility of power. Later, long out of office, he voiced feelings that seemed to have run as a constant subtext whenever he had mentioned the guard from the 1880s to the 1910s. During World War I Roosevelt would unload his feelings about the National Guard on Secretary of War Newton Baker. In April 1917, as he sought permission to raise volunteers on a scale much grander than in 1898, Roosevelt criticized the Wilson administration's calling up of the National Guard, and he did so in a tone that suggested he would be a better wartime manager than Baker or Woodrow Wilson. "Nothing more completely divorced from sound military policy," he wrote, "can be imagined than this attempt to utilize the national guard." Roosevelt pointed to a recent mobilization of the guard as a response to troubles on the Mexican border: "the actual experience on the border has shown that the attempt to do what was done in Mexico, (and what it is now proposed to do in Europe) with the National Guard inevitably produces waste, extravagance, military inefficiency and cruel injustice. Last summer you tried to mobilize the guard. You were not able to mobilize much more than half of it; and of this half three-fifths had practically no training, and only one-fifth could shoot."[79]

Granted, Roosevelt made these remarks well into his retirement and during a period when he seemed particularly intemperate. Still, his contempt for the guard had appeared before, most notably in the late 1890s, and this attitude had likely lain under the surface during his presidency, a time when he worked harder to restrain his public outbursts to preserve the dignity of his position. No matter his feelings on the guard, Roosevelt knew that he would have to work with it as president, so he determined to make the National Guard and the army the most efficient instruments that circumstances would permit. The circumstances that he had in mind included more than just reform legislation. They would involve a new program of training.

Training for War

On 27 September 1902 two armies clashed on American soil. The army of the Browns battled the army of the Blues at Fort Riley, Kansas. Neither force was large. The Browns numbered about 2,500 soldiers, while the Blues had approximately 4,500. No one died that day, for the battle was a mock one. The troops were participating in an American attempt to conduct European-style maneuvers. When the umpires called a halt to the day's activities, the troops, whether they knew it or not, had opened a new era of realistic training. Secretary of War Root praised the maneuvers as a grand success, especially because they helped break down "jealousy, superciliousness . . . and bad feeling between regular and volunteer officers."[80]

The push for large-scale army maneuvers was not new, but the army had not been in a position to conduct them before Roosevelt's time. Many obstacles blocked regular exercises before the war with Spain. In the late nineteenth century, army units were widely dispersed among various coastal forts and scattered frontier outposts. Numbering fewer than 30,000 men until 1898, the army rarely assembled the companies of a regiment, much less conduct regular maneuvers with larger units. Regimental exercises took place on occasion beginning in the 1880s, and Brig. Gen. Wesley Merritt had organized brigade-sized maneuvers in 1889, but efforts to organize such undertakings more often than not went begging in the years before 1898.[81] No apparent foreign foe threatened, and the army had suppressed Native American resistance against being relocated to reservations. Given those circumstances, little interest existed in enlarging the army, concentrating its units, or pouring resources into sham battles.

The army's problems in 1898 paved the way for many reforms, but they did not generate immediate improvements in peacetime training. The authorized strength of the army did increase to over 88,000 in 1901, which would create the larger mass necessary for maneuvers.[82] In 1899, as part of his reform program, Elihu Root called for "the exercise and training of the officers and men of the Army in the movements of large bodies of troops by brigade, division, and corps under conditions approaching as nearly as possible those to be anticipated in . . . war."[83] Large-scale maneuvers, though, had still not taken place by the time Roosevelt proclaimed in his first annual message: "It is our duty to see that . . . training is of a kind to insure the highest possible expression of power to . . . units when acting in combination."[84]

T.R. was the right person, at the right time, to make maneuvers a reality. After his experience in Cuba, he was convinced that American officers needed the practice. The higher the rank, he felt, the more unprepared the officers had been for their duties in Cuba. In fact, Roosevelt had written in 1901, it was "a blessing that fighting in open order . . . resulted in the company officers getting out of touch with their battalion and regimental commanders!"[85] His interest in maneuvers, however, stemmed from more than his time in Cuba. Although he was not a natural athlete, Roosevelt's physically active lifestyle led him to frame things in terms of sports. He approached military preparations in the same way that an athlete would train for a contest: the more training the better and the more strenuous the training the better yet. Using language that evoked physicality and alluding to his own time as a collegiate boxer, Roosevelt spoke of "decisive blows," coming as the result of "long years of practice" and "special training applied to men of exceptional physique and morale."[86] Finally, Roosevelt was well aware of what European armies had been doing for years. With time spent traveling and studying abroad, he was something of a world citizen, even as he remained a uniquely American politician. Reports of German military maneuvers particularly impressed him and encouraged his belief that the American army required more rigorous training.[87]

Roosevelt believed that Europeans had much to teach Americans about the conduct of maneuvers. In July 1902 he confessed as much to a German friend, who was one of his "playmates." Hermann Speck von Sternberg—"Speck" for short—shared with the president a "fondness for sport, for riding, shooting and walking." He also had influence in the kaiser's court and would later become the German ambassador to the United States. Roosevelt informed Sternberg that "thanks to the kindness of the Emperor [Wilhelm II], I shall send three of my army officers, including General Wood, to see the German maneuvers this year. I am very anxious to start maneuvers on a small scale here, and I would like some of our men to see your army at work." Later that year Roosevelt could point to the Fort Riley exercises as the start of American maneuvers, but he could not take credit for being the first to send a military delegation to view foreign armies in action. The precedent already existed for ordering officers to foreign shores. The Delafield Commission had observed the Crimean War in the 1850s, and Lt. Gen. Philip Sheridan had witnessed the Franco-Prussian War of 1870–71. More recently, Lt. Gen. Nelson Miles had viewed fighting in the Greco-Turkish War of 1897 and then reviewed troops across Europe, from Russia to Britain.[88]

Roosevelt's interest in European maneuvers did not end with the dispatch of the army mission in 1902. American observers returned to Germany repeatedly to witness military exercises. Also, at least once, in 1905, a delegation of officers visited French maneuvers. These missions were not minor affairs and often consisted of the highest-ranking American officers. The observers who went to France in 1905 included Adna R. Chaffee, the chief of the general staff; J. Franklin Bell, commandant of the General Service and Staff College at Fort Leavenworth; and William Crozier, chief of ordnance. In 1906 and 1907 the president of the Army War College, Thomas Barry, headed the American delegation to German maneuvers.[89]

Roosevelt wanted to make sure the public knew that American maneuvers had begun and used his bully pulpit to call attention to them. Memories of the problems of 1898 remained fresh enough that mention of maneuvers would send the message that the administration was working to assure a better-prepared force for any future conflict. During a western trip in 1902 (which would be cut short because of a knee infection caused by injuries from the streetcar accident), Roosevelt told a crowd in Indianapolis, "It is our purpose, beginning with the present year, to institute a series of manoeuvres which shall offer some opportunity for training our officers to handle their men in masses." This type of training appealed to Roosevelt because it was practical, it took men into the field, and it stressed both physical and mental challenge. Maneuvers represented, as Roosevelt put it, "the kind of training that counts, the kind of training that makes a man fit for work when he is called out to do the work, so that a man who has an [*sic*] uniform and a rifle will know how to march, will know how to take care of himself in the open, and know how to handle that rifle."[90]

The 1902 Fort Riley maneuvers were just a start. Roosevelt wanted the exercises expanded and continued on an annual basis. In every annual message from 1901 to 1907, he emphasized maneuvers as an essential part of army preparedness, in part to ensure that congressional funding would be forthcoming. For example, he told Congress in 1902, following the Fort Riley maneuvers, that "without such manoeuvres it is folly to expect that in the event of hostilities with any serious foe even a small army corps could be handled to advantage. Both our officers and enlisted men are such that we can take hearty pride in them. . . . But they must be thoroughly trained, both as individuals and in the mass."[91] Such messages helped, for during the following year the War Department organized a larger set of maneuvers. About nine thousand troops gathered at Fort Riley, and an additional ten thousand assembled at West Point, Kentucky. The chief umpire of these maneuvers, Col. Arthur L. Wagner of the general staff, recommended afterward that the War Department hold annual maneuvers for the regulars and militia in each of the army's geographic divisions and that regular troops be allowed to spend a longer period of time in encampment.[92] The War Department followed up in 1904 with maneuvers at Camp Atascadero, California; American Lake, Washington; and Manassas, Virginia. At Manassas more than twenty-six thousand troops took part in the operations. Roosevelt's concern about funding was not trivial because a lack of appropriations prevented maneuvers in 1905, but the exercises resumed in 1906 with seven major joint exercises involving a total of nearly fifty thousand men—about twenty thousand of them were regulars and the rest were militia. Two years later the army conducted eight major maneuvers.[93]

Roosevelt believed that maneuvers would be especially beneficial to the National Guard. If the guard were to be the first reserve, then maneuvers could expose the troops to battlefield operations, and they would benefit from the hardening effects of hunger, fatigue, and outdoor living. The Militia Act furnished guard troops with better weapons. (Looking once more to 1898, Roosevelt proclaimed in 1902 that "I feel thoroughly ashamed every time I see a National Guardsman with a black powder musket.") Now guard troops had to practice using the newer armaments.[94] The presence of guardsmen at maneuvers would also supply regular army officers with larger numbers to command at each exercise. Army size remained small during Roosevelt's presidency. The authorized force numbered forty-five thousand in 1909, and a sizable portion of that remained stationed overseas in places like the Philippines. Guard participation in maneuvers had longer term implications as well. Mutual disdain sometimes resulted from such contact, but just as often army-guard maneuvers bred associations between state forces and their regular counterparts that lasted for years, helped break down prejudices, and encouraged army officers to provide training at summer guard encampments.[95]

Participation in maneuvers did not do much to improve the standing of the National Guard in Roosevelt's eyes. His preference remained for a federal reserve. No amount of militia reform could change the fact that the guard would always be, first, a creature of the states. Roosevelt continued to look to the great pool of citizens outside the guard as the nation's main reserve. Federal institutions, he believed, could shape these inspired souls into an effective fighting force.

Army maneuvers in general encouraged Roosevelt's tendency to manage the details of military affairs. With them he played commander in chief, commanding general, and party leader all at once. In 1904, for example, he requested either that Texas be a site for maneuvers that year or that Texas troops at least have the opportunity to practice elsewhere. He felt strongly that "the South should have one set of maneuvers." Such exercises would satisfy more than military necessity. They would sit well politically in the South. General Chaffee, chief of the general staff, could not stage maneuvers in Texas, but he did recommend that militia from that state be ordered to attend operations planned for the Pacific division.[96]

Past experiences also influenced Roosevelt's interest in maneuvers. Memories of Cuba flooded back when the president received a plan for a joint army-navy exercise that would take place in September 1902. Mock assaults in Narragansett Bay, at the eastern end of Long Island Sound, and at New Bedford would teach the navy about attacking forts and batteries, while the army would learn about the defense of coastal sites, communications, supply, the use of armaments, fire control, outlooks for spotting enemies, and other practical matters.[97] Confusion accompanied the actual event, when the navy reported that its ships had successfully run a gauntlet of forts in Narragansett Bay, and the army claimed, "We sank them all."[98] Undaunted by the interservice dispute, the president conceived even more ambitious plans for combined maneuvers in the future. He wanted to practice the embarkation, transport, and landing of a substantial expeditionary force along the coast of the United States. The problems of 1898 replayed in Roosevelt's mind, for he realized that the United States would likely need to mount a large expedition again, owing to its geographic position and the far-flung nature of its interests. Specifically, the president told General Chaffee in July 1905 that he wanted the general staff to plan for deploying a division, or at least a brigade, and suggested that the expedition depart at Galveston and land somewhere in Florida. Again stressing active work over mere planning, he declared that only exercises "conducted under actual war conditions . . . could test what is designed to be used in war."[99]

The mock expedition never left port, but Roosevelt's conception did prove to be sound. A lack of available transports compelled General Chaffee to abandon the operation, but not before the army general staff had gained valuable experience planning a large-scale operation. The general staff aimed to concentrate a force of about three thousand at Newport News, Virginia; transport them to the Maine coast; land them near Portland; and march them about 250 miles to Fort Ethan Allen in Vermont. The experience of planning the mobilization and transportation of a large force did not go to waste because the army faced the problem of dispatching a major expedition only a year later when Roosevelt ordered a second intervention in Cuba.[100]

Finally, Roosevelt's interest in army training went beyond large-scale maneuvers to include smaller tactical exercises. The former colonel wanted more realistic tactical training for the cavalry and infantry. In August 1903 he suggested to Gen. Samuel B. M. Young, then the army chief of staff, that the cavalry should adopt more realistic training methods for charges. Roosevelt wanted to know if it would "be practicable to arrange a row of dummies so that at the culminating moment of the charge the cavalry could actually ride home and hit the dummies?" He felt that having horse and rider shy away at the last instant "was a positive disadvantage from the standpoint of actual fighting" and wanted Young to "see if this dummy idea cannot be worked up."[101] Nearly a year later he encouraged General Chaffee to conduct infantry marches and encampments under war conditions to determine the amount of equipment that troops could carry. At the same time Roosevelt argued the superiority of the rifle over the bayonet on the modern battlefield, provided that troops were properly trained to handle rifles in close quarters. He contended that a "bayonet man will only win against . . . a man with a loaded firearm who gets rattled."[102] His faith in the rifle again reflected his regard for the American frontiersman who had won the West with rifles, and it stood in contrast to the "cult of cold steel" being preached in other countries.

By the time his first term expired, Roosevelt had worked to ensure that the army, like the navy, was better practiced at actual operations. He had seen how thirty years between major contests could lead to atrophy and believed that the nation could not afford the blunders and confusion that had characterized the early stages of so many American mobilizations during the nineteenth century. Like many, Roosevelt subscribed to the notion that the industrial age had transformed warfare. To be sure, there was always room for individual heroics in his mind, but the time for them had grown compressed. "Modern war of a serious kind," Roosevelt stated in 1902, "is determined quite as much by what the antagonists have done in advance of the outbreak as by what they do afterward."[103] His own experience with war confirmed such ideas. After all, the conflict that brought T.R. glory had lasted only a few short months. One of the watchwords of the day was "efficiency," and Roosevelt believed that field practice would make for a more efficient army. He had also done much to install men of his own stripe in higher commands. This effort went right along with his support for maneuvers. To this point in American wars—most notably the Civil War—incompetent officers needed to be weeded out until the right commanders emerged. The shortened time span of the Spanish-American War had not allowed this process to take hold, so Roosevelt determined that it must occur now in peacetime with a selection-out system. He wanted no more "Shafters" in top commands when war erupted.

This work to improve the army was incomplete when Roosevelt's first term approached its end. He had not won a promotion system based on merit, and his improvised system had generated increasing controversy and resistance. Moreover, the maneuvers that were instituted remained small in scale, especially compared to European military exercises. The early American maneuvers also concentrated on battlefield tactics at the expense of logistics, but they represented a beginning and were better than nothing. Taken together, Roosevelt's efforts, along with the Root reforms, helped put the army on a more modern footing. One other change begun during Roosevelt's first administration would mark a major departure for the army: the creation of a general staff. The discussion of that initiative, along with a similar push for the navy, belongs to the next chapter.

5

The Institutions of Command

In the summer of 1906, troubles in Cuba again thrust the island to the forefront of Theodore Roosevelt's thoughts. Headlines such as "Cuba in Throes of Rebellion" and "Whole Island in Ferment" alarmed Roosevelt.[1] Factionalism, nationalism, and a strained economy led to a revolt against the government of Tomás Estrada Palma in August 1906.[2] This time Roosevelt did not want to send American troops. There was no glory to be won in 1906. This Cuban war was a civil war, and the American public, after the long fighting in the Philippines, had become less tolerant of imperial ventures. Somewhere in the back of Roosevelt's mind likely lay memories of the travails of the 1898 expedition. T.R. emphasized his reluctance to intervene. He wrote British historian George Trevelyan during early September 1906, "In confidence I tell you that I have just been notified by the Cuban Government that they intend to ask us forcibly to intervene in the course of this week, and I have sent them a most emphatic protest against their doing so."[3] Despite Roosevelt's objection, he knew the Platt Amendment to the Cuban constitution might oblige him to do exactly what he did not want to do.

Negotiations led to a peaceful settlement in the end. American troops would enter Cuba, but as an army of occupation and not one of forcible intervention. U.S. administration of the island would last until 1909, when Cuban rule was again restored. The peaceful resolution of affairs in Cuba lifted a burden from Roosevelt. The performance of the army in this second expedition to Cuba was another bright spot. Within a few weeks the army had readied an initial force of 5,632 and assembled men "from nine widely different sections of the country."[4] Although the mobilization was not without difficulties, the 1906 expedition seemed the model of efficiency compared to the effort of 1898. The creation of an army general staff between the two interventions represented one of the reasons that the second Cuba expedition performed better than the first. With a general staff the army had a body to provide the planning and oversight that had been lacking in 1898. It also possessed an institution that provided a layer of modern management, which would help the army prepare for a new century of warfare.

Theodore Roosevelt lived in an era that was giving rise to what has been termed the "organizational society" and the "administrative state."[5] Rapid industrialization and urbanization had spawned a rising set of demands on businesses, government, and private institutions. Complex and sprawling businesses required new methods of management, as did governmental agencies and other organizations. The turn of the twentieth century was a time when supporters of organizational change spoke of "rationalizing" institutions, "efficiency," and adopting new methods of management. Bureaucratization increased, and another feature of modern life began to appear with greater frequency—the impersonal society. No wonder that Roosevelt fought so hard to protect "frontier virtues." He sensed that the individuality that he so treasured was slipping away. Paradoxically, he would fight to protect individualism with his stress on manly and virtuous behavior, but at the same time he would promote the rise of an organizational society. In this way Roosevelt was a true turn-of-the-century man, a man who resided in two worlds. He embraced nineteenth-century Victorian values with his emphasis on inner character, while at the same time he sought to give governmental administration a more modern cast. His involvement with the general staff of the army and the quest—ultimately futile—to install a similar agency in the navy helps to illustrate the two sides of Theodore Roosevelt and may also explain why his involvement with new institutions of command would be accompanied by both accomplishments and shortcomings.

This chapter explores Roosevelt's role in developing the administrative state through his efforts to create new institutions of command, as well as his use of such agencies. Roosevelt's effort would involve, in particular, the establishment of the army general staff, a failed campaign to create a naval general staff, and the employment of an existing naval advisory body, the General Board of the U.S. Navy. The president would depend heavily on military advisory bodies at times, but at others he would show a decided lack of interest in their development. Perhaps, in the end, like many leaders, Roosevelt preferred to measure success in tangible ways. The number of battleships built, officers promoted, maneuvers conducted, and the like counted for more with him—and the public—than the realignment of administrative architecture.

The Brain of the Army

The drive to establish an army general staff was long and often difficult. Although the general staff began operations during Roosevelt's watch, T.R. does not deserve primary credit for its creation. Rather, the man whom he called a "corker," "admirable," and "splendid," Secretary of War Elihu Root, was most responsible for winning the fight for a general staff.[6] Root laid the basis for general-staff legislation well before Roosevelt assumed office, and he orchestrated the campaign to win congressional approval. As with militia reform, Roosevelt delegated responsibility to an individual whom he trusted thoroughly and regarded as the most able member of his cabinet. The president, therefore, stood on the sidelines during the campaign for a general-staff bill, except when Root needed the force of his personality and the weight of the presidency to assist him.

Only after the general-staff law took effect in 1903 would Roosevelt take a more direct role with the new agency.

So what was the concept behind the general staff that Root proposed and Roosevelt endorsed? The general staff would stand near the pinnacle of the military hierarchy, one step below the secretary of war. The chief of staff would be the leading military adviser to the secretary and the president on army matters. This official was to preside over other officers who drew up war plans and ensure that the army was ready to implement them. The idea of a staff was not new. Prussia's Great General Staff had gained fame during the wars of German unification, and other European countries imitated the Germans' example during the late nineteenth century. In the United States Col. Emory Upton, a brilliant yet troubled officer, had called for a general staff along Prussian lines about twenty years before the Spanish-American War.[7] Upton's words went unheeded, and, struggling with mental illness, he silenced his own voice through suicide. Nevertheless, adherents such as William Harding Carter and Adjt. Gen. Henry C. Corbin kept Upton's ideas alive and introduced them to Elihu Root when he became secretary in 1899.

In his first annual report as secretary of war, issued in 1899, Root alluded for the first time to a general staff. He did so as part of a wide-ranging set of proposals designed to modernize the army and prevent the problems of 1898 from reoccurring. Root proposed improvements in training and officer education, an effective system of reserves, and personnel reform. He included in this list the need for the "systematic study by responsible officers of plans for action."[8] Root went no further at this time. He did not mention a general staff by name because he knew that the very idea of such an entity might provoke resistance among some members of Congress, the public, and even the army itself.

The idea of a general staff both raised philosophical concerns and threatened patronage interests. Together, those two factors formed a powerful combination. Philosophically, a general staff ran contrary to the American heritage of divided power. Just as the constitutional system worked to keep authority from accumulating in one branch of government, the states and national government had shared military power at the start of the federal era. Moreover, the regular army would be kept small to guard against tyranny. This arrangement made sense to a revolutionary generation that had fought the British army and saw large standing militaries as a threat to liberty. A general staff ran counter to this tradition. Such a body represented centralization and was intended to counter the excessive dispersion of power. One hope of twentieth-century reformers was that the general staff would coordinate the various bureaus that composed the War Department. Although the bureaus shared a common home in the War Department, they often functioned as separate fiefdoms under their respective chiefs as secretaries of war came and went. To reformers a general staff would bring greater efficiency, but to foes it was just one of the dangerous consequences of imperial expansion. In short, opponents saw it as a sign of creeping militarism. William Jennings Bryan warned of "empires . . . bowed beneath the weight of their own armaments."[9]

Patronage interests compounded the situation. Long-serving bureau chiefs maintained close ties to members of Congress, especially senators and representatives who sat on military-affairs committees. Each group cultivated the other for their mutual benefit. Bureau chiefs could facilitate projects in home districts in exchange for congressional protection of their positions. A general staff with the goal of military efficiency might upset this relationship.

The War Department's glaring deficiencies during the first weeks of the war with Spain provided a window of opportunity for change. Continued revelations of problems with the mobilization furnished additional ammunition. President William McKinley had appointed a commission under former Civil War general and railway president Grenville Dodge to investigate the conduct of War Department officials during the conflict. In early 1899 the commission heard sensational charges about "embalmed beef" being supplied to the troops, and one news report claimed that some of the suspect canned beef killed a cat that had eaten a "good-sized portion." The Dodge Commission dismissed the worst of these charges about chemically treated beef, but Roosevelt, then governor of New York, wrote how the canned beef had been "thoroughly bad."[10] Such scandals captured the headlines, but, beyond the beef controversy, the Dodge Commission recommended a number of changes to make War Department operations more efficient. Proponents of a general staff believed that a new command structure would accomplish just that goal, but they also knew that time was limited before public and congressional attention drifted to other matters, and resistance again built to the proposed reform.

It is unlikely that an American army general staff would have been established after the war with Spain if Theodore Roosevelt had not become president. Roosevelt may have deferred to Root in the campaign for a general staff, but his coming to the presidency added crucial support to the fight. President McKinley had installed Elihu Root in the War Department and supported his postwar reform program. McKinley, however, believed that a general staff would be too controversial. Theodore Roosevelt backed the project without reservation.

More than the difficulties of the Cuba expedition inspired Roosevelt to lend his support. He appreciated prewar planning. Before the war with Spain, he had shaped the navy's plans and, as a volunteer army colonel, witnessed the consequences when planning proved inadequate. Roosevelt's brief service on the Naval War Board from March to May 1898 also exposed him to war planning. This temporary body provided the secretary of the navy with advice on strategy. Even before he left the Navy Department, Roosevelt, who was ever eager to boast, proclaimed the superiority of the navy's ad hoc planning process compared to the army's relative lack of preparation. "We have our plans for the Navy," T.R. wrote in April 1898, "and beyond that there is absolutely nothing."[11]

Unlike his predecessor, President Roosevelt gave open assistance to a general staff. His 1901 annual message was brief but unambiguous: "A general staff should be created." In 1902 he went a bit further, but not by much. "I urgently call your attention," Roosevelt declared, "to the need of passing a bill providing for a general staff."[12] His brevity might be explained by the fact that the general staff remained a controversial proposition and he did not wish to complicate Root's task. Nevertheless, by making such clear statements in his annual message, he let Congress know where the executive stood. He did not, however, take to the bully pulpit to rally public support. The general-staff campaign remained Root's to win or lose.[13]

Roosevelt may have seemed uncharacteristically reserved on the general-staff bill, but he did provide crucial help. He usually acted at Secretary Root's request. Root enlisted the president's aid, for example, after Rep. John Hull of Iowa, head of the House Committee on Military Affairs, warned the secretary of a possible danger. Other members intended to attach amendments to support personal interests, and these additions could make the bill unacceptable to the House, although no party opposition existed to the core proposition of a general staff. Root wanted Roosevelt to approach Democrat James Richardson of Tennessee, a member of the House Committee on Rules, for his support in preventing personal amendments. Such intervention paid off, as did Roosevelt's assistance in dealing with the commanding general of the army, Nelson Miles.[14]

Miles presented a problem in the fight for the general staff. The general-staff bill proposed the elimination of Miles's position in favor of a chief of staff, and the prickly general naturally opposed that proposition. Casting Miles aside would doubt-lessly have given Roosevelt and Secretary Root great personal pleasure. Miles had whipped up controversies in recent years designed to embarrass the executive branch and elevate his own standing. The elimination of his post, however, also made organizational sense. The commanding general occupied an anomalous position. Secretary of War John C. Calhoun had established the office in the 1820s as a way to focus the service on peacetime preparations, but the commanding general pos-sessed no authority to coordinate War Department bureaus. Frustration became a principal part of the job.[15]

Miles had used the commanding general's post to insert himself into political matters and nettle the Roosevelt admin-istration. The president's every impulse told him to discharge the general, for, in Roosevelt's opinion, Miles had ceased to serve the public interest and was pursuing only his self-interest. Miles's opposition to the general-staff bill confirmed Roosevelt's belief. In March 1902, as the first attempt at general-staff legisla-tion moved through Congress, Roosevelt complained to Secre-tary Root. "General Miles," the president fumed, "has made it abundantly evident by his actions that he has not the slightest desire to improve or benefit the army, and . . . his actions can bear only the construction that his desire is purely to gratify his selfish ambition, his vanity, or his spite." Later that month the president seemed ready to dismiss the general, declaring, "General Miles' usefulness is at an end and he must go."[16] Polit-ical realities dictated otherwise, and Roosevelt, after venting his fury, chose discretion in dealing with Miles. The general could count on many senators and representatives for help. Accord-ing to the *New York Times*, "the men who rule the Senate—are friendly to Miles." George Frisbie Hoar, John Spooner, and Nel-son Aldrich were all Republicans, but Miles's support was bipar-tisan. "Most of the leading Democrats," the *Times* went on to report, "are also friendly to Miles."[17] A direct attack on the commanding general would obviously risk a political storm that could sink the general-staff bill or any other proposed army reform.

Under such circumstances Roosevelt proceeded with care. He did not summarily dismiss the general. Roosevelt wanted to, especially after Miles testified against the first general-staff bill before the Senate Military Affairs Committee in March 1902, and the bill subsequently failed. Instead, he decided to "consult two or three of the leading members of the Senate and House, as to whether it will not be well to avoid complicating the passage of the Army bill . . . by refraining from acting in the Miles business until that is out of the way." Senator Spooner advised Roosevelt to wait until army legislation had passed.[18] The president heeded his advice.

After the defeat of the general-staff bill in 1902, the administration adjusted its approach. Secretary Root trimmed the legislation to make it more acceptable to senators. He cut, in particular, sections that proposed the abolition of the inspector general's department and the creation of a single Department of Supply that would have combined the Quartermaster's Department, the Subsistence Department, and the Pay Department. The new bill also stipulated that the general staff would not be established, nor would the commanding general's position be eliminated, until General Miles retired in August 1903. Roosevelt provided a boost by agreeing to send Miles far from Washington. The general had wanted to go to the Philippines. He got his wish and more. An extended inspection tour that took him to the Philippines, Guam, Japan, and other places in East Asia would make it hard for Miles to sabotage the second attempt at a general staff. With all these elements in place, the general-staff bill became law in February 1903.[19]

The President and the General Staff

After the general staff began functioning, it soon became more Theodore Roosevelt's creature than Elihu Root's. In fact, Root guaranteed that others would oversee the development of the general staff. The president's indispensable man decided that the general staff would be the last major reform that he would push. Root tendered his resignation in August 1903 and departed the War Department in 1904, after nearly five years of service. Roosevelt would replace him with another confidant, William Howard Taft, the man who in 1908 would become T.R.'s chosen successor. (Roosevelt's relationship with Taft represents something of a puzzle. Although affable and possessed of a sharp intellect, physically the portly Taft failed to fit Roosevelt's ideal of a man of action.) The new secretary of war was capable enough, but he lacked Root's energy and interest in departmental reform. He had been governor of the Philippines and saw his new position as a way to continue his work on the colonial experiment there. Roosevelt would not be his own secretary of war—certainly not in the same way that he acted as his own secretary of the navy—but he would play a significant role in the early years of the general staff.

An examination of Roosevelt's involvement with the new general staff may provide insight into his understanding of the modern forms of administration emerging at the turn of the twentieth century. Beyond even military affairs, Roosevelt grasped that more complex organizations required increasingly sophisticated management. He sponsored the Committee on Department Methods, better known as the Keep Commission, after the head of the committee, Assistant Secretary of the Treasury Charles Keep. In 1905 the commission studied ways to improve business methods in executive-branch departments.[20] At a time when general staffs in other countries were still trying to define their proper function—including the Great German General Staff, the model for other nations' staffs—Roosevelt demonstrated a basic comprehension of the usefulness of such an institution. Still, he could have done more to develop and support the general staff as its members worked to establish a place within the existing War Department bureaucracy. In particular, Roosevelt would depart from his overall mission to improve the quality of top-level commanders when he selected chiefs of staff to preside over the new agency.

The general staff was a small and simple organization at the start. A chief of staff directed the forty-five officers composing the staff corps, most of whom held assignments outside Washington in the headquarters of the army's geographic departments, where they assisted with the administration of military duties.[21] In theory, the chief of staff occupied the third most important spot in the army hierarchy. The reality was something quite different in the earliest years of the general staff. The General Staff Act and army regulations charged the chief of staff with implementing the president's military policies, dispensing advice, supervising field forces, and directing the departmental bureaus.[22] But a legislative grant of powers did not mean that the chief of staff could actually wield them. The early general staff faced the problem of fitting into a well-established War Department bureaucracy. For example, the supervision of the bureaus never materialized in the way that Elihu Root had envisioned. Politically well-connected bureau chiefs resisted subordination, and neither the early chiefs of staff nor Secretary Taft were particularly interested in asserting the authority of the new institution.

Perhaps the greatest way that President Roosevelt could influence the early fortunes of the general staff was through the people he chose to head the new organization. All in all, Roosevelt's first choices for chief of staff failed to speed the development of the general staff. Roosevelt, in fact, seemed to revert to the strict seniority system in making his picks, despite the fact that he was dedicated to inserting younger officers in the tiers below the chief of staff. His first three chiefs of staff were all lieutenant generals, then the highest rank in the army, which was held by only one individual at a time. At first, such selections appeared wise. The lieutenant general held the most authority in the army, other than the secretary of war. Making the lieutenant general the chief of staff, however, did not necessarily help the general staff develop as an institution. The lieutenant general possessed authority, but that fact alone did not invest the office that he administered with the same stature. In other words, the power of the chief of staff did not necessarily increase from the lieutenant general being in the position. The choice of lieutenant generals, in fact, created a problem. These officers were near the end of their careers, and they lacked the time or interest to enforce the authority of the general staff within the War Department. Younger individuals would have been more likely to view the development of the general staff as an investment in their careers and would have had more years to devote a full four-year term to the task.[23]

Roosevelt's first choice for chief of staff illustrated how he wanted to reward men near the end of distinguished service. Not surprisingly, Samuel B. M. Young also had a reputation as a fighter and had been a comrade-in-arms with Roosevelt. The president had known Young in Cuba because the general had commanded the brigade to which the Rough Riders belonged. Young had led at Las Guásimas when Theodore Roosevelt first experienced battle. In the *Rough Riders*, Roosevelt wrote that "General Young was—and is—as fine a type of the American fighting soldier as a man can hope to see" and went on to portray him as a courageous combat leader.[24] Young's military career, like so many others, had begun during the Civil War, in which he distinguished himself in the cavalry and emerged as a boy colonel. After the Cuba campaign, he had fought in the Philippines before he chaired the army's War College Board, which served as something of a proto–general staff. Given Roosevelt's fondness for Young and given the general's seniority and his experience at the War College Board, his selection as the first chief of staff was not unexpected. However, Young's age made for a short tenure. He served only about half a year before retiring in January 1904.[25]

Adna R. Chaffee and John C. Bates were next. Both fit the same mold as Young. Chaffee and Bates had started out in the Civil War. Both became brigadier generals after the outbreak of war with Spain, served in Cuba, and went on to assume temporary command of divisions. Roosevelt was acquainted with each man. He had joined them in signing the round-robin letter to extract the expedition from Cuba. Chaffee gained special distinction after the war when he led the American component of the Chinese relief expedition during the Boxer Rebellion and then commanded in the Philippines, where he waged a tough campaign against remaining Filipino resistance. He was a fighter, a "soldier through and through," as Taft described him to Roosevelt.[26] As chief of staff, Chaffee filled his time mostly with personnel matters and other routine duties. Neither he nor Bates occupied the chief of staff's chair for a four-year term: Chaffee stayed for nearly two years, while Bates lingered for only two months.[27]

In Bates's case Roosevelt treated the appointment as an honorary one. He planned initially to have Bates and Maj. Gen. Henry C. Corbin, the former adjutant general, retire with the rank of lieutenant general. Because Young and Chaffee had simultaneously served as lieutenant general and chief of staff, it seemed only natural to award Bates and Corbin with both titles. Chaffee would retire in early 1906, and Roosevelt wanted Bates and Corbin to succeed Chaffee, in turn, before they also retired later that same year. The president then planned to pick another officer who could give the office the benefit of longer service. Corbin, however, backed out in the best interests of the army. A tall, powerful man, he received one of the great compliments of the day. Gen. James Parker described him as a "man of force and great intelligence." Corbin also was known for the long hours that he worked.[28] Except for his age, he represented a good choice to be chief of staff. He indicated his willingness to become lieutenant general but asserted that the architects of the General Staff Act had never intended that the lieutenant general automatically become chief of staff. "On the contrary," Corbin claimed, "it was considered exceptional that he would be."[29] He felt that the position should go to a less senior officer who could devote at least four years to the job. Thus Corbin bowed out, and, after Bates took his short turn as chief of staff, Brig. Gen. J. Franklin Bell assumed the job in 1906 and held it until 1910.[30]

Roosevelt contradicted himself in pushing Bates and Corbin for chief of staff. His actions regarding the two officers ran contrary to his distaste for strict seniority promotions. He had pushed for promotion by merit but was unwilling to make a conspicuous example of one of the highest posts in the army. To be sure, Bates and Corbin had meritorious careers and would not serve long before Bell assumed the duty, but Roosevelt showed little concern for precedent and was operating mainly on the principle of seniority, the practice that he was working against in the advancement of other officers. Politics also played a role. Members of Congress wanted to see favorites honored, and Roosevelt made his choices carefully so that he would not alienate Capitol Hill.

Corbin's self-sacrificing gesture provided an alternative that met Roosevelt's desire to reward good service and yet strengthened the post of chief of staff. Lieutenant general alone was a high honor; Roosevelt did not need to couple it with the office of chief of staff. As Corbin advised, the president needed to install a chief who could devote many years to the job. For the first three years of the staff, T.R. did not seem to accept that the office of chief of staff required vigorous and consistent leadership if it were, as the *New York Times* claimed, "to amount to anything."[31]

J. Franklin Bell was Roosevelt's kind of soldier. He was a man of action, who had performed daring feats in battle, and he

also possessed a sound intellect. Frank Bell, as his army comrades called him, had rocketed to prominence, much like his
commander in chief. Bell was a long-serving first lieutenant in
the cavalry when war broke out with Spain. The conflict in the
Philippines transformed his career. He left on the second expedition to the Philippines in June 1898, and before he returned
Bell would receive one of President McKinley's extraordinary
promotions to brigadier general. During the Philippine War
he made his reputation by conducting reconnaissance missions
that often led to the capture of the town that he was just supposed to scout. His motto was "All you need to go anywhere
in the islands . . . is a handful of men who will keep a-shout-
ing and revolvers that will keep a-shooting." At Bamban in the
autumn of 1899, Bell led eighteen shouting and shooting men
against an entrenched enemy and took the town. He went on
to govern Batangas Province, where, to much criticism back
home, he instituted a policy of population reconcentration.
His methods, however controversial and reminiscent of Spanish practice in Cuba, proved effective. Such actions probably
helped his cause with Roosevelt, for again Bell had proven he
was a fighter and could take stern measures when necessary.
His next assignment helped him to live down charges of cruelty. When he returned home, Bell directed the army's school
for rising officers, the old Infantry and Cavalry School, at Fort
Leavenworth, Kansas, which became the General Service and
Staff College. There he displayed his intellectual talents when
he designed the curriculum of that institution.[32]

Despite Bell's record, his name was not the only one mentioned for chief of staff. Bell himself had expected that Gen.
Arthur MacArthur would get the nod after Corbin removed
himself from consideration. MacArthur was in line to become
lieutenant general, so Bell's assumption was logical. Bell was
wrong, for MacArthur may have been an excellent soldier, but he
lacked sound political instincts. He had alienated the adminis-

tration by opposing the creation of the general staff, and he had clashed with Secretary of War Taft in the Philippines, when Taft was governor and he was military commander. Later MacArthur earned a presidential rebuke "for speaking ill of the Germans." MacArthur had predicted impending war with Germany in a published conversation.[33] In all, MacArthur's liabilities were too great, and so were Leonard Wood's, but for different reasons. Wood was also mentioned for chief of staff, but after the bruising fight over his recent promotion to major general, the president could not consider his friend for the job. Neither would T.R. look at Brig. Gen. Frederick Dent Grant, despite speculation about his possible appointment. Grant had opposed Roosevelt when both served on the New York City Police Board, and if that were not enough, the president regarded Grant as an "absolute zany," a "very stupid man," and "one of blunted moral susceptibilities."[34] As a consequence, Bell came to the position of chief of staff, not necessarily as Roosevelt's obvious choice but because others were unacceptable. Later, after Bell's appointment, Roosevelt reportedly found him to be personally irritating, which did not help interactions between the chief of staff and the president. Still, with Bell's appointment, the precedent had been set for making a younger man, who was not necessarily the top-ranking officer in the army, the chief of staff.[35]

Bell's work was cut out for him. His predecessors had not stressed the function of preparing for war, nor had they asserted the general staff's authority within the War Department. To be fair, they had been charting unknown waters, and time was required for any institution to develop a sense of its proper function and insert itself within a well-established bureaucracy. The reality, nevertheless, remained that for three years the general staff had focused more on matters of petty administration than pursuing its intended function. General-staff officers devoted considerable time to the distribution of annual reports, the design of cook wagons, and the proper use of belts on military evening wear. These activities were familiar to officers who were unsure how a general staff should proceed. Some mastery of administrative detail would also help to establish the general staff's position vis-à-vis the bureaus and acquaint it with the details of equipping and supplying the army. But routine administration could also prove to be a trap. Officers could work hard and point to accomplishments but not advance the more important functions of a general staff.[36]

The situation amounted somewhat to a return to the days of the commanding general, when the bureaus and the secretary decided departmental business and the commanding general was largely an irrelevancy. The architects of the general staff wanted to interpose that body between the secretary and the bureaus, requiring that bureau officers consult the chief of staff before a matter reached the secretary for a decision. Such an arrangement would keep the chief of staff well informed about departmental affairs and allow him to give sound military advice to the secretary. The new system would work if the secretary refused independent contacts from the bureaus, and if the chief of staff asserted his authority to hear bureau business. Taft showed little interest in such administrative issues, and Chaffee was content to leave the bureaus alone. In sum, the General Staff Corps drifted into high-level isolation.[37]

Theodore Roosevelt did little to lift the general staff out of that state in the first years of its existence. The task rightly belonged to the secretary of war and the chief of staff, but Roosevelt might have been expected to intervene, given his avid interest in military affairs. He did direct a large amount of business to the War Department and even sent some items straight to the general staff, bypassing the secretary. But too often Roosevelt dispatched work that reinforced the tendency of the General Staff Corps to focus on administrative trivia or on military tactics rather than its place in the army bureaucracy or on the higher levels of war planning. The latter omission seemed particularly striking. Roosevelt had been struck by the War Department's lack of prewar preparations in 1898. He did, on occasion, remind the general staff of its proper function, but his messages proved contradictory. His actions reflected a low appreciation of bureaucratic problems, which was not unusual when presidential duties permitted little time to master them. Even so, for a man who was closely acquainted with the operations of Washington and the military bureaucracy, and who dabbled in all kinds of military business, the lack of involvement was notable.

In the general staff's early years, Roosevelt often recommended projects that betrayed both a fascination for military minutiae and a sense of expertise based on his brief military service.[38] His special interest in the cavalry surfaced in Roosevelt's initial contacts with the general staff. T.R.'s first recommendation was the August 1903 suggestion in which he wanted cavalry training to be more realistic through the use of dummies.[39] Two years later his attention centered on weaponry. He suggested a sword for officers to "cut or thrust with" but did not see much use for the bayonet in the cavalry, "even though the modern cavalry man is nine times out of ten on foot."[40] The president's inquiries demonstrated his concern for preparedness but kept the energies of the general staff focused on relatively minor matters.

The Russo-Japanese War of 1904–5 had stimulated Roosevelt's interest in small arms. Accounts of trench warfare and hand-to-hand combat inspired his discussion of the sword and bayonet. Besides rejecting the bayonet as a cavalry weapon, he felt that the ramrod bayonet was "about as poor an invention as [he] ever saw" and favored instead a short triangular design. He wished also that all officers would carry rifles and wanted thorough tests conducted of the twenty-four-inch and thirty-inch versions of the new Springfield rifle.[41] This recommendation doubtlessly stemmed from his own familiarity with firearms. The general staff formed a special committee in response to the president's letter. On the question of the sword alone, the committee deliberated throughout 1905 and produced extensive reports before finally settling on definitive models. It also delivered studies on the rifle and bayonet.[42] Although such matters were important to battlefield performance, they need not have consumed so much of the time of the general staff's limited personnel. The Bureau of Ordnance could have conducted the investigation, and the general staff could then have considered the findings and accepted or rejected them. Officers of the general staff, however, doubtlessly felt that they could not properly ignore a commander in chief's wishes, even if they had been inclined to refer the matter elsewhere.

Roosevelt did use the general staff for more than indulging his inner soldier. Unfortunately for the staff, much of that work involved service as a political clearinghouse. Members of the administration sent numerous inquiries, which often had little relevance to military affairs and more to do with placating constituents and members of Congress. Such assignments again diverted the attention of the general staff to areas outside the main mission of preparedness. Upon the president's request, for example, the First Division of the general staff considered the proper disposal of a Confederate flag in October 1903. The flag had belonged to a post of the Grand Army of the Republic, and the general staff determined that it should go to the museum at West Point upon certification of authenticity.[43] In a matter that was a bit weightier, Roosevelt asked the general staff in 1904 to consider the case of Maj. Joseph Wham, a retired officer for whom the Grand Army wanted relief. After a review of Wham's circumstances, Lt. Col. James F. Kerr, the acting chief of the First Division, recommended against helping the major.[44] Such matters may not have required much effort from the general staff on an individual basis, but cumulatively they were time consuming and distracted from other duties.

On the whole Roosevelt's early involvement did not seem to

assist the development of the general staff very much. He distracted the staff from duties that focused directly on war planning and thereby, it might be said, detracted from the new institution's development. The reality was more complex. Roosevelt's dual nature emerged in dealing with the general staff. To be sure, his recommendations on swords and bayonets looked back to an earlier day when the management of organizations, similar to the command of soldiers, was conducted on a more personal basis. Yet, on occasion, the president's forward-looking persona emerged, and he made attempts to put the general staff on the right course. For example, he warned General Chaffee about blindly imitating the Japanese after their success over Russia, just as the fashion had once been to copy all German practices after the Franco-Prussian War. He cautioned, "Not all of the things they have done have been wise, and some of the wise things *they* have done are not wise for *us*."[45] In other words, the general staff should apply only those lessons from the Russo-Japanese War that fit with American military tradition.

He could not, however, simply leave Chaffee with that lofty principle to guide war planning. His proclivity to indulge in his personal enthusiasms pulled too hard. Roosevelt resumed his discussion of the bayonet in his instructions to Chaffee and, in fact, devoted a good share of his message to it. The president was certain that rifle training suited American soldiers better than training with the bayonet. He was "firmly convinced that it is out of the question ever to teach our soldiers as a body to do effective work with the bayonet, while it is comparatively easy to teach them to use the firearm well as a firearm." He went on to discount the so-called cult of cold steel that had gained currency in other countries. Soldiers were supposed to quail and lose spirit when confronted with a foe determined to spear them. Roosevelt recognized "the moral effect of the bayonet" but believed "it would be far easier to teach our men to disregard this moral effect than it would be to make them efficient with the bayonet or sword." From a practical standpoint, he felt that the rifle usually trumped the bayonet because "a really good man with a loaded rifle who has no bayonet will at close quarters normally beat a really good man who relies on the bayonet." This discourse on the bayonet, all in all, certainly contained interesting insights into Roosevelt's perceptions on the military culture and practice of his day. But on the matter of the general staff and its development, he had weakened the force of his advice to Chaffee with a subject of less significance.[46]

So to what degree should Roosevelt be faulted for not putting the general staff on its intended track? No one, it seemed, knew exactly what a general staff should do. Roosevelt, however, was not without insight into the proper role of such an agency, and he could have done more than he did. He possessed a degree of familiarity with the leading American military planning institutions of the day, a knowledge that few others could claim. The Naval War College, the Naval War Board of 1898, and the General Board of the U.S. Navy all preceded the army's general staff in existence. Roosevelt knew well the operations of the Naval War College, and he had served briefly on the Naval War Board, which was the predecessor to the general board. Based on his one year of service in the run-up to the war with Spain, Roosevelt understood the value of such a body. He would convey as much when he supported a proposal to give the general board congressional sanction and make it a full-blown naval general staff, a topic that is discussed later in this chapter.

Forces beyond Roosevelt's control played an even bigger role. Few things bring focus more than a crisis. Nations, institutions, and people are tested, and they either measure up or are found wanting. The general staff's drift into routine administrative matters might have stemmed, in part, because no major crisis erupted in the first few years that would galvanize and challenge it. From 1903 to 1906 the United States enjoyed a respite from the foreign problems that had drawn its interest abroad in the late 1890s. Cuba had gained independence, and most U.S. troops had evacuated the island. The army had broken Filipino resistance to American rule, and the pacification of the Moros on Mindanao was the only fighting of any consequence that still occurred. A direct European challenge to the Monroe Doctrine receded in early 1903 with the agreement of Germany, along with Britain and Italy, to arbitrate financial claims against Venezuela. The Russo-Japanese War flared during this period, but the conflict was distant, and Roosevelt mediated a peace that provided for a regional balance of power, thereby preventing one belligerent from gaining dominance and threatening the Open Door Policy in China. American worries about Santo Domingo's foreign debt did prompt a fiscal protectorate over the island but not a major mobilization of troops. The geographic isolation of the United States doubtlessly contributed to the sense of complacency during this period of relative tranquility. After all, no major land powers bordered the United States, and nobody seriously conceived of a World War I–style mobilization at that time. Moreover, no one believed that the army would replace the navy as the mainstay for defending American interests beyond the continental mainland.

All the above may have been true, yet Roosevelt and the War Department hierarchy were not so easily excused. He and those beneath him in the chain of command possessed the soldier's pessimistic view of human nature: that conflict was unavoidable. Back when he was thumping the drum for war in 1897, Roosevelt had proclaimed to officers at the Naval War College that "Peace is a goddess only when she comes with sword girt on thigh."[47] War, in his view, was part of the human condition, so soldiers and sailors needed to prepare for it in peacetime. Although Roosevelt professed the desirability of peace, he felt that war would inevitably come. The period after 1903 was calm, but no one believed that a great power clash was outside the realm of possibility and that the army would play only a minor role in such a conflict. Civilian officials and military officers alike were mindful that the slightest tensions might lead to a blowup, even with supposedly friendly powers, in the competitive international climate of the day. A number of flashpoints existed. Negotiations over the Alaskan-Canadian border disturbed Anglo-American relations for a time; there were continued fears of European, especially German, violations of the Monroe Doctrine; Japanese-American ties became strained after 1905 as a result of exclusionary immigration policies; and the United States had its stated interest in China. Prudence suggested that army expeditionary forces would be required in the future and that they might well be needed to protect American interests against another great power.

The army did undertake planning but composed only a few scenarios. Most noticeably, planning for possible future complications with other great powers remained undeveloped. Students at the Army War College, which fell under the Third Division of the general staff, practiced war planning as part of their program of study. They considered a war with Mexico, a deployment to Cuba, the system of recruitment for regular and volunteer forces, and general American preparedness for war. Thus, the army did have some plans for contingencies that might erupt close to home and were based on historical experience. To not have developed such plans would have made the general staff and the War College almost entirely remiss in a key duty in preparing for possible conflict. The United States, after all, had granted itself the right to intervene in Cuba under the Platt Amendment, and, as historian Allan R. Millett has noted, there was also the compulsion to get the expedition of 1898 right this time, at least on paper. None of these early plans, though, reflected the entry of the United States into the arena of the great powers. They reflected interests that the country had asserted even before the war with Spain, including the concern for Cuba's fate, and did not involve complications arising from competition with another major nation. The war-plans file remained thin because the general staff was still in its formative years, but also because the priorities that it set, and the assignments that it received, took it in the direction of administrative and political work.[48]

Roosevelt's appointment of J. Franklin Bell as chief of staff did much to alter the culture of the early general staff, but the simultaneous return of foreign crises perhaps did even more to help orient the general staff toward the mission envisioned by its creators. Upon taking up his new duties, Bell found an organization too absorbed in routine administration. He determined that strategic planning and intelligence gathering needed more attention, and, unlike his predecessors, the fifty-year-old general was not near retirement and would have a full four-year term to put his stamp on the general staff. Disturbances in China, renewed trouble with Venezuela, and, in particular, the insurrection in Cuba would assist him in refocusing the work of the general staff. In China a boycott of American goods had led to riots and attacks against American merchants and missionaries. In Venezuela the government of Cipriano Castro refused to settle debts with Americans, in the same way that it had resisted European claims in 1902–3.

Crises provided clarity, and Roosevelt knew how to use the general staff in such situations. The disturbances in China led to a presidential request for possible operations against Canton (Guangzhou). Roosevelt wanted to be able to mount an expedition of up to twenty thousand troops to back up demands for redress. He believed that the Chinese army was more formidable than it had been during the Boxer Rebellion, and thus he wanted to "be absolutely certain that we provide amply in the way of an expeditionary force." He cautioned Secretary of War Taft, "We ought not to take any chances. We cannot afford a disaster." Before pushing for coercion, Roosevelt wanted to ascertain whether the War Department could deliver the forces. Military action proved unnecessary in the end because the boycott ended and the Chinese met claims for damages.[49] The Venezuelan episode also never led to armed intervention, and Roosevelt's inquiry to the general staff amounted to no more than a planning exercise. The renewal of trouble in Cuba would put the general staff, and the rest of the army, to a sterner test.

In August 1906, when a long smoldering feud between the government of Tomás Estrada Palma and its Liberal opponents burst into open insurrection, a second American intervention in Cuba threatened.[50] From the onset of the crisis, Roosevelt relied heavily on the general staff. The situation happened, fortuitously for the general staff, to fit precisely two of the studies it had prepared. The Army War College had already examined the possibility of an intervention in Cuba, and, moreover, the general staff had studied exercises for the deployment of a large-scale expedition in 1905. As a result, when messages asking for advice arrived from the president's summer quarters at Oyster Bay, General Bell could confidently advise him about a possible intervention. Bell also drew on his experience of fighting in the Philippines. In their conversations he counseled Roosevelt about the difficulty of confronting insurgent forces. Bell's testimony and the advice of Brig. Gen. Frederick Funston, another old hand at battling insurgents, apparently convinced the president to request more mobile forces—cavalry—in proposals for an expeditionary force. By mid-September 1906 the general staff had completed plans for an intervention. Roosevelt approved, having been satisfied on the amount of cavalry being deployed.[51]

The crisis of 1906, difficult as it was for the Cuban people and their aspirations for self-government, proved a boon to the general staff. As one of the contingencies for which the general staff was prepared, it provided an opportunity to demonstrate the true potential of the staff corps. A sudden flare-up with a great power would have been much more taxing and might have led to far different results for the reputation of the general staff.

As August 1906 passed into September, Theodore Roosevelt lamented the dilemma that Cuba presented. He abhorred the disorder occurring on the island. But Roosevelt remained reluctant to intervene and face the possibility of fighting insurgent forces and a long occupation. Such a course could involve a major commitment of troops, fierce antiguerrilla operations, and a political storm at home. He unburdened himself to George Trevelyan on 9 September: "In Cuba, what I have dreaded has come to pass in the shape of a revolt or revolution. We of course kept everything straight and decent in the island while we were running the government. . . . Now a revolution has broken out, and not only do I dread the loss of life and property, but I dread the creation of a revolutionary habit, and the creation of a class of people who take to disturbance and destruction as an exciting and pleasant business." Roosevelt thanked Trevelyan for being patient while he vented his frustration and sought to achieve some kind of solution: "All this is of course for your private eye and represents merely the fact that I have to blow off steam by making a wail to somebody. I guess I can work it out all right somehow, but I do not yet quite see how."[52]

The solution arrived in the form of an American peace mission to Havana. Roosevelt wanted to broker an arrangement between all parties, so that if an intervention were required American troops could enter the island peacefully. As the negotiations proceeded, general staff officers continued planning for the use of force, in case the talks failed. They drafted orders for the bureaus and told the quartermaster general and the chief of the Ordnance department to begin assembling supplies for an expedition. In the end, the peace mission averted a war. An American provisional administration would assume control of Cuba until elections were held. The staff officers' work did not prove useless, however, for an army expeditionary force would support the authority of the provisional administration. They and the president were doubtlessly glad that the reception for the expedition promised to be a peaceful one.[53]

The work of the general staff did not end there. Members of the staff were ubiquitous in the occupation of Cuba. A general staff representative directed the assembly and embarkation of the troops, and General Bell served for a time as commanding general in Cuba. After Bell returned home, another general staff officer, Brig. Gen. Thomas Barry, succeeded him. Barry was a former head of the Army War College and had served as acting chief of staff during Bell's absence. He would remain as commander of army forces in Cuba until American forces withdrew in the spring of 1909. Throughout the occupation a general staff officer acted as Bell's and Barry's chief of staff, while other members of the general staff served in the provisional government. Troop commanders confirmed the importance of the general staff to the success of the enterprise. They did not resent its activities but instead felt that the general staff could have exerted more influence, especially in the launching and landing of the expedition.[54]

Theodore Roosevelt was also delighted with the general staff's performance. In early September 1906, in the midst of the Cuban difficulties, he complimented General Bell for his sound advice, proclaiming that "the propositions that you make represent the kind of proposition which makes it worth while to have a Chief of Staff."[55] He later used the platform of his annual message for 1906 to laud the general staff, describing the intervention as a "fine demonstration of the value and efficiency of the General Staff."[56] Roosevelt must have been particularly gratified that the general staff was demonstrating its usefulness in another intervention in Cuba. The conduct of the second expedition contrasted markedly with that of the first and made the general staff's achievement seem that much greater. He probably, as well, derived pleasure from the fact that the performance of the army had improved markedly during his watch compared to its performance under his predecessor—under far different circumstances, of course.

Despite Roosevelt's praise and the overall success of the Cuba operation, the general staff's performance was not flawless. Some of the old problems of 1898 remained. Staff officers had not controlled closely enough the embarkation of the expedition and its debarkation in Havana. Orders were issued too late and lacked detail. The result was confusion; however, the disorder did not compare to the chaos of 1898. On the whole general staff officers demonstrated that they could manage an operation such as the Cuba intervention, but they did not yet seem ready for war with a more powerful enemy. The fixation on administration remained, and they tended to deal more with operations than with military strategy. General Bell himself believed many deficiencies remained. The general staff did not execute the Cuba operation as well as he would have liked.[57] A conflict with a great power would demand more than operational expertise. It would also place a premium on strategic forethought. Operational and tactical ability could be wasted— with tragic results—if the overall strategy was flawed.

The general staff's battles within the War Department were not ended either. In fact, they had only begun. The intervention doubtlessly heightened the institutional esprit de corps of the general staff, for its members had performed work that represented their reason for being a distinct corps. They did not, however, notably increase their status in the War Department. Bureau officers remained as powerful as ever and just as determined to defend the position of their individual agencies. For example, four years later, after Roosevelt had vacated the White House and Bell's term as chief of staff expired, the new chief of staff, Leonard Wood, attempted to reduce the authority of the most powerful bureau chief. Wood wanted to consolidate the muster rolls that Adjt. Gen. Frederick Ainsworth controlled. A clash resulted that would ultimately leave the general staff weakened on the eve of American intervention in World War I. Ainsworth struck back with the help of congressional allies. Legislation cut the size of the War Department's general staff to thirty-six in 1912, and the National Defense Act of 1916 slashed it even more. The Defense Act did raise the overall size of the general staff to fifty-four officers, but it attached strict limits to the number assigned to Washington. In April 1917, just nineteen general staff officers worked in the War Department.[58]

President Roosevelt also did not help the general staff to maintain an emphasis on war planning after the Cuba emergency had passed. Rather, he reverted to his old behavior during the remainder of his second term. He would ask on occasion for war plans but just as often request that officers work on a pet project. For example, he did consult with the general staff about the defense of American possessions in the Pacific after immigration policies sparked tensions with Japan in 1906. General Bell was doubtful about the army's ability to protect insular outposts without the presence of the battleship fleet in the Pacific.[59] At the same time, Roosevelt returned to one of his favorite topics, the bayonet. He pressed the general staff for more information about the use of the bayonet, even though it had explored the topic in-depth several years previously. He also revisited the subject of horsemanship, a topic he had first broached after the installation of the general staff in August 1903.[60] In the end, unless the matter involved a crisis or a technology or technique that attracted his notice, Roosevelt's interest soon flagged. That was certainly the case in institutional matters for which there was little emotional appeal and scant political credit to be collected.

Roosevelt and a Naval General Staff

When the army's general staff had come into being in August 1903, Theodore Roosevelt was enjoying his summer at Sagamore Hill near Oyster Bay, Long Island. Forty-four years old, but ever boyish and irrepressible, he enjoyed playing with his children. His antics included "bouncing over hay-ricks" in an old barn as part of a romp demanded by his nine-year-old daughter, Ethel, for her birthday. Even as he roughhoused, rode horses, and otherwise relaxed, business remained on Roosevelt's mind. During his summer retreat he reviewed the fleet and contemplated other projects.[61] He had to prepare for the following year when he would run for the presidency in his own right. Before then, he wanted to get a Central American canal underway, in part so that the rapidly expanding navy could make the transit much more swiftly from the Atlantic to the Pacific. Roosevelt also had something else in mind for his beloved navy. He wanted it to have a general staff like the army and planned to make a pitch for such an agency in his December annual message. The outcome of this campaign, however, would be different than the one that established the army's general staff. The navy would not get a general staff on the same standing during Roosevelt's presidency. That might have been because the president's approach toward securing such an agency was strikingly similar to the effort for an army staff corps. There were bursts of enthusiasm, but he deferred chiefly to others to get the work done. As a result, the service that he deemed essential to his foreign policy, as well as his cultural vision for the country, would, in the end, possess a command structure less coherent than that of the army.

The proposal for a naval general staff originated from two men whom Roosevelt regarded highly, Rear Adm. Stephen B. Luce and Luce's protégé, Capt. (later Rear Adm.) Henry C. Taylor. Luce was one of the fathers of the modern American navy. He helped found the Naval War College at Newport, Rhode Island, in 1884, because he wanted naval officers who were specialists in the conduct of war. Luce inspired other officers, such as Henry Taylor, to fight for improvement of the navy, and he remained the intellectual godfather of naval reform throughout

Roosevelt's presidency, even though he was retired from active service. Taylor was one of the turn-of-the-century navy's most capable leaders. He was also one of its most personable and politically astute officers.[62] A thoughtful man, Taylor had lectured at the Naval War College after its inception and became its president in the 1890s. During the war with Spain, he had commanded the battleship *Indiana*. A fellow officer declared that Taylor was "eminently fitted for command" because his "active brain [was] ever at work," and he displayed "the happy results that lie in the clever grasp of the iron hand in the velvet glove."[63]

The conflict with Spain had impressed Taylor with the need for a body dedicated to planning and preparation for war. Although the navy's mobilization proceeded more efficiently than the army's, problems still hampered naval preparations in 1898. There was too little smokeless powder, the quality of coal was inferior, the fleet lacked auxiliary vessels, and a shortage of personnel existed. The navy possessed four plans for war against Spain, but these plans were the product of different offices and lacked consistency in assumptions and strategy.[64] As a result, Secretary of the Navy John D. Long commissioned a study on a naval general staff and gave Taylor the assignment.[65]

Taylor proposed two boards that together would form a naval general staff. A planning body would draft war plans and present them to a nine-member general board, which would meet at least one month each year to rule on the planners' work. The chief of the Bureau of Navigation, the preeminent bureau chief, would present the board's work to the rest of the Navy Department and thus would act as the secretary's chief military adviser. In effect, he would be the naval chief of staff.[66]

Secretary Long worried that Taylor's scheme went too far in eroding civilian authority. Long did not administer the Navy Department with the flare that was so characteristic of his former assistant secretary, nor did he share Theodore Roosevelt's navalist passions. The more mature and politically seasoned secretary did provide steady, competent leadership in both peace and war. He, after all, had reined in Roosevelt when the assistant secretary had become overly bellicose. Long was not about to weaken civilian control of the navy, especially when there was no compelling reason to do so. Had not the navy covered itself with glory in the recent war with Spain? The secretary desired professional advice but was not prepared to see the chief of the Bureau of Navigation gain so much power, nor was he willing to establish a permanent naval board. He wanted to avoid a body of officers that might someday usurp the civilian secretary's influence in the department. Instead, he decided to institute a board strictly on a trial basis. The General Board of the U.S. Navy came into being on 13 March 1900, but it existed at the secretary's pleasure and could be abolished at the stroke of a pen.[67] The general board would offer advice only and possessed no powers to enforce its decisions on the rest of the navy. The new board, therefore, fell short of the general staff that Taylor advocated.

Although he did not get all that he wanted, Taylor viewed Secretary Long's decision as a positive development. He believed that a naval general staff would be achieved only through an evolutionary process. The general board, he stressed, needed to show first its value as a war-planning agency. If it produced "solid, well studied, authoritative plans of war," he told George Dewey, "'all things' as the Bible says 'will be added unto us.'" Taylor wanted the current board sanctioned by law, for "a change of administration may easily wipe us off the slate."[68] Then he hoped to move gradually toward authorization of a naval staff with power to enforce its will on departmental bureaus.[69]

Theodore Roosevelt's unexpected ascent to the presidency changed that equation. Roosevelt's dedication to the navy and his forceful political personality generated hopes that he would both speed expansion of the navy and spearhead the overhaul of the Navy Department. Then the American navy would not only be among the world's largest but also have efficient direction and supply. Such change seemed even more likely when John Long resigned as navy secretary in 1902. Long had waited a respectful time after McKinley's death before departing because neither he, nor Roosevelt, were temperamentally suited to work together now that the one-time assistant secretary had become the senior official, and especially when the president intended to run the navy himself.

Roosevelt did not replace Long with a nonentity. William Henry Moody was a man suited to Roosevelt's tastes. The president had known Moody since both were undergraduates at Harvard, and, unlike Long, the new secretary shared Roosevelt's navalist vision regarding American sea power. He also possessed an agile mind and had a reputation "as a great worker and a man of excellent executive and judicial ability." (The unsuccessful prosecution of Lizzie Borden for murder was Moody's most famous legal case.)[70] Moody, the strongest of T.R.'s picks for navy secretary, was, however, merely biding his time until the post that he really desired became available—attorney general. All in all, he fit well Roosevelt's expectations for a navy secretary. He possessed political ability, having served as a member of the U.S. House before his selection; he endorsed naval expansion; and he represented his causes with conviction. Yet Moody was not so familiar with naval affairs when he took office, nor so supremely interested in making a lasting mark as navy secretary, that he would resent his boss's involvement in the day-to-day management of the fleet.

The campaign for a naval general staff unfolded in a way reminiscent of the fight for the army's general staff. Much as he had deferred to Elihu Root at the War Department, Roosevelt turned to his able subordinates at the Navy Department, Secretary Moody and Henry Taylor, who had become chief of the Bureau of Navigation in 1902, to lead the drive. Roosevelt did intend to launch the effort before turning it over to Moody

FIG. 1. Assistant Secretary of the Navy Theodore Roosevelt at the Naval War College in 1897. Naval History and Heritage Command, Washington DC.

FIG. 2. (*opposite top*) Maj. Gen. William Shafter, commander of the expedition to Cuba. Library of Congress, LC-USZ62-114705.

FIG. 3. (*opposite bottom*) After his "crowded hour": Roosevelt and the Rough Riders atop San Juan Hill. Library of Congress, LC-USZ62-7626.

FIG. 4. (*above*) Cdr. William S. Sims—one of Roosevelt's "men of push and intelligence." Bain Collection, Library of Congress, LC-DIG-ggbain-00696.

FIG. 5. Capt. John J. Pershing, prior to his promotion to brigadier general. Library of Congress, LC-USZ62-131533.

FIG. 6. The active president, shaking hands while doing one of his favorite daily activities, horseback riding. Library of Congress, LC-DIG-ppmsca-35831.

FIG. 7. (*opposite top*) The submarine *Plunger* underway at Oyster Bay,
New York, with crew members atop the vessel. Bain Collection, Library of
Congress, LC-USZ62-89964.

FIG. 8. (*opposite bottom*) Orville Wright demonstrating the Wright Flyer at
Fort Myer, Virginia, in 1908. Library of Congress, LC-DIG-ppmsca-19075.

FIG. 9. (*above*) USS *Louisiana*, the new battleship that took Roosevelt
to Panama in 1906. NH 59575, Naval History and Heritage Command,
Washington DC.

FIG. 10. USS *North Dakota*, the object of alleged design defects that triggered a drive to reform naval administration late in Roosevelt's presidency. NH 44729, Naval History and Heritage Command, Washington DC.

FIG. 11. (*opposite top*) The world cruise departs Hampton Roads, Virginia, 16 December 1907. Roosevelt saw the fleet off from the presidential yacht, *Mayflower*, the single-stacked vessel in the right foreground. Detroit Publishing Company Photograph Collection, Library of Congress, LC-DIG-det-4a15932.

FIG. 12. (*opposite bottom*) The world cruise returns. The president welcomes home the crew of the USS *Connecticut*, 22 February 1909. NH 1836, Naval History and Heritage Command, Washington DC.

FIG. 13. Theodore Roosevelt and Leonard Wood at the Plattsburg training camp, 1915. Library of Congress, LC-USZ62-28470.

and Taylor. In September 1903, after being prompted by Alfred T. Mahan, he asked Taylor, "Will you write me a paragraph for my [annual] message on the General Staff bill?" Taylor must have been excited when he read Roosevelt's next line: "I shall push for it all I know how."[71] With the president's energy behind a naval general-staff bill, the chances of congressional acceptance appeared considerably brighter.

On 7 December 1903 Congress received the statement sandwiched between presidential requests for a naval base at Subic Bay in the Philippines and approval of a canal treaty with the new republic of Panama. Members of Congress heard "that there should be provided a naval general staff on lines similar to those of the General Staff lately created for the Army" and that "we need the establishment by law of a body of trained officers, who shall exercise a systematic control of the military affairs of the navy, and be authorized advisers of the secretary concerning it."[72]

The president had made his wishes clear, and by adopting Taylor's language, he seemed ready to support the admiral and Secretary Moody in all ways. Taylor might, however, have been given pause by the thrust of the letter in which Roosevelt asked the admiral to draft those lines for his annual message. The request came as a brief afterthought to Roosevelt's reaction to results from the new system of target practice. He was delighted at Taylor's report of improvements in firing and remarked how he was "especially struck at the radical difference between ships like the *Chicago* and *Panther*, which have not tried the new system, and the others which have tried it."[73]

Roosevelt revealed here where his real interests lay: in the measurable results that came from building up a fleet and having it practice. Such priorities were understandable. Bureaucratic change did not provide the symbols of national power with which Roosevelt could identify. It did not appeal to the sense of the dramatic that he treasured, and it would not go

into battle, although institutions could certainly affect the outcome of wars. A nation first had to have ships and properly
trained crews if it were to protect itself at sea. Moreover, Roosevelt could reap more political benefit by pointing to a great
force of white and buff-colored battleships than he could by
highlighting bureaucratic reform. The historian and publicist
in Roosevelt understood that legacies were built not by tinkering with administrative structures but by performing big deeds.
And he would not be able to continue to carry out such feats
unless he secured the presidency in his own right in 1904. If
there were a goal that he would work for "all I know how," then
it was his election. Thus, although Roosevelt sympathized with
the proposed change in naval administration, he basically left
the reform effort to its own fate after December 1903.

In so doing, the president was acting the part of a practical
politician. He may have tested the political winds and decided
they were blowing too stiffly against obtaining a second general staff in less than a year. Sensitivities remained high in some
quarters about creeping militarism, overseas expansion, and
executive aggressiveness. Also the fact that the navy had performed well in the recent war did not provide the same compelling incentive that had produced change in the army.

The strongest center of opposition lay in the Senate Naval
Affairs Committee. Sen. Eugene Hale, a Republican from Maine,
chaired the committee. If Hale wanted to halt Roosevelt's plans
for the navy, he was in a powerful position to do so. He had
become a reluctant supporter of rapid fleet expansion, but he
was openly hostile to reform of the Navy Department. The senator harbored a blend of competing ideas regarding the navy,
American foreign policy, and congressional influence that made
dealing with him a delicate matter. He had promoted the new
steel navy in the 1880s and 1890s but disliked the overseas expansion that had followed. Hale subscribed to the philosophy that
imperialism corroded the democratic virtue of the nation and

lowered America to the debased condition of European monarchies. Although he thought overseas acquisition misguided,
he did accept that the United States needed a large navy to protect itself in case an imperial squabble turned into something
larger. Thus Hale, even as he helped expand the fleet, maintained deep differences with the big-navy, expansionist Roosevelt. In February 1904 the president would complain about
how Secretary Moody was "being harried by Hale in naval matters until he feels like crying."[74]

Hale's reservations about Roosevelt went beyond naval policy.
The senator also had problems with the president's aggressive
executive style. He saw himself as a guardian of congressional
power and regarded the young, active president with suspi-
cion. Hale regarded naval affairs as his special province. Presidents came and went, but long-serving members like Hale
gained expertise, and they came to regard navy matters as
more their domain than the chief executive's. Roosevelt represented a challenge with his background in naval administration, along with his determination to run the navy directly.
He, in short, threatened Hale's influence. Hale's reach, however, stretched beyond the Naval Affairs Committee. The senator also served on the Appropriations Committee and sat on
the Steering Committee. When combined with his oversight of
navy yards, these assignments meant, as George Kibbe Turner
of *McClure's Magazine* put it, that Hale had "his hands on two-
thirds of the financial patronage that goes out of Congress."[75]
To cross him would be perilous.

Hale and other members of the Senate Naval Affairs Committee cared especially about navy yards. Of the ten members
of the committee, eight had navy yards in their states. These
facilities represented important sources of political patronage,
and committee members protected them fiercely. (A similar
conflict of interest did not occur in the House of Representatives because Speaker of the House Joseph Cannon refused to

appoint members with navy yards in their districts to the House Naval Affairs Committee.) A naval general staff loomed as a threat, at least in the minds of senators who had navy yards in their states. The rhetoric used to advance a general staff promoted the idea of greater military efficiency. Senators worried that a general staff would rule against keeping open navy yards that no longer served a vital military purpose. (After all, the United States maintained eleven navy yards to six for Britain and three for Germany.) For example, the navy yard at Kittery, Maine, in Senator Hale's home state, was one often mentioned that could not meet the needs of the largest battleships. Combined with ideological concerns about creeping militarism, rising costs, and the executive's manner, senators like Eugene Hale were not about to sacrifice a political benefit to military efficiency.[76]

Roosevelt and other members of his administration understood the situation and worked hard at winning Senator Hale's favor. They stroked the senator by showing him special attention. In February 1902, when Roosevelt entertained Prince Henry of Prussia at the White House, he invited Hale to attend the state dinner in the prince's honor. Roosevelt went to Maine later that year to deliver a series of speeches. As host, Hale was one of the president's traveling companions. At one event Roosevelt praised Hale for helping to provide the ships that fought in the war with Spain and declared that the senator was one of "the men who rendered that victory possible."[77] Hale had already joined Secretary Moody in early August 1902 to witness the cruise of the North Atlantic Squadron, and he was also with Moody at the Naval Academy at Annapolis in January 1903 to inspect new buildings. Unfortunately, a seventeen-gun salute frightened the team of horses pulling the two men's carriage and sent it careening through the academy grounds. The incident left Hale unhurt, but Moody was knocked unconscious for a time after he leaped from the speeding vehicle.[78]

The efforts to curry Hale's favor were intended primarily to secure expansion of the fleet, which was always Roosevelt's first priority in naval affairs, not reform of the Navy Department. Roosevelt would have been happy to gain approval of a naval general staff during his presidency, but he was thrilled whenever Congress authorized more ships. He was doubtlessly gratified at the news in February 1903 that the campaign to cultivate Senator Hale had paid off when the Senate Naval Affairs Committee approved four new battleships and two armored cruisers.[79]

The big push for a naval general staff began soon after Roosevelt's annual message of 1903. Admiral Taylor and Secretary Moody decided that a full-fledged general staff stood no chance of passing at that time. The opposition, lodged most deeply in the Senate, remained simply too strong. Taylor's evolutionary approach seemed to be the best way to make headway. Secretary Moody forwarded a bill that asked chiefly for legal sanction of the general board. The board would remain an advisory body, but the bill would mean that the board existed beyond the tolerance of the residing secretary. Moody's bill would also give the board a head who resembled a chief of staff in all but name. With this official in place, the general board would be a little closer to being a general staff.[80]

Moody and Taylor hit a stone wall in Congress. They could not even get past hearings in the House of Representatives. Members recoiled at anything even loosely resembling a general staff. Philosophical concerns combined with practical politics to kill the measure. During committee hearings, members spoke mainly in high-minded terms, leaving unstated their worries about state patronage. John Rixey, Democrat of Virginia, voiced the common complaint that the bill would give military men too much influence in the conduct of naval affairs. He feared that a general board sanctioned by law might act independently and compete with the secretary's authority. Adolph Meyer, Democrat of Louisiana, seconded Rixey's concern about undue military influence, wondering whether an ignorant or lazy secretary would rely excessively on the board.[81]

Secretary Moody, Admiral Taylor, Admiral Dewey, and others appeared before the House in April 1904, but their testimony could not surmount the opposition. The coup de grâce came when other members of the Navy Department testified against the measure and told many committee members what they wanted to hear. Assistant Secretary of the Navy Charles Darling reinforced the beliefs of committee members who fretted about a military grab for more power. He lambasted the legislation, claiming that it would reduce the secretary to a figurehead and that it smelled of European militarism. Several bureau chiefs echoed this sentiment and emphasized their worries about a reconstituted general board.[82] They left unspoken their concerns about their status in a reorganized Navy Department.

Navy opponents testified with Secretary Moody's permission because he wanted a free airing of all opinions. At least one did so at personal cost. In the White House the president doubtlessly fumed over the testimony of general-staff opponents. To him their attitudes likely reflected the same conservatism and wooden behavior that he had witnessed in the War Department during the early days of the Spanish-American War. He could not easily displace the bureau chiefs due to their close congressional relationships, but he could take action against Assistant Secretary Darling, whose opposition to the naval general staff probably irritated him the most. Darling occupied T.R.'s old post at the navy, and he had helped stop a measure that the president deemed good for the service. When Moody resigned to become attorney general in 1904, Roosevelt refused to elevate Darling to the top post at the Navy Department, in spite of pressure from Senator Hale and Darling's home state senator, Redfield Proctor of Vermont. The president acknowledged that Darling was "upright, honest, and capable." The assistant secretary had been a judge in Bennington, Vermont, before his appointment in 1901. Roosevelt questioned his vision to be the civilian leader of the navy. The assistant secretary, he said, "instead of regarding the industrial efficiency of the navy as of value in so far as it provides for the military efficiency of the fleet, . . . regards it as an end in itself, and would like to sacrifice the military efficiency of the fleet by stopping its mobility by preventing the incessant exercise at sea of ships, men and guns, because under such circumstances hulls, engines, and ordnance cost much more money than if they are not used."[83] In short, Darling was unable to ensure the navy's military readiness. His testimony before the Senate Naval Affairs Committee had proved that he was not the man to continue the campaign for a naval general staff. Roosevelt stressed after the defeat of Moody's bill the continued need for "legislation to establish such an advisory board on military questions." Darling, the president implied, belonged to those "men who believe in the old system of quiet and rest."[84]

The assistant secretary had exhibited a grave failing in T.R.'s eyes. He had not demonstrated the qualities of push and intelligence that Roosevelt treasured, and thus he remained as assistant secretary only until 1905. Darling would go on to be collector of customs at Burlington, Vermont, an appointment that would have helped placate Senator Proctor.[85]

The president did not believe in 1904 that the campaign for a naval general staff had ended. Moody and Taylor had confronted a serious setback, but the first attempt at an army general staff had also failed, and then victory came with the next try. Roosevelt likely hoped for a similar scenario for the naval general staff in 1905, when the presidential election campaign was over, and he, presumably, occupied the White House in his own right. It was not to be. Unlike the drive for the army general staff, when Secretary Root remained to lead the lobbying effort, the chief architects of the naval general-staff campaign departed the scene after the rejection of their proposal in 1904. Moody left for the attorney generalship, but Taylor's death in 1904—one account blamed peritonitis—was unexpected.[86] Taylor's death was the more serious blow to naval reformers' hopes for a general staff. The admiral had provided a prestigious, thoughtful voice and had conceived not only of plans for the staff itself but also of the campaign most likely to win congressional approval.

Roosevelt did charge Moody's successor at the Navy Department, Paul Morton, with renewing the battle. The president instructed Morton, shortly before the new secretary took office, that "there should be legislation to establish . . . an advisory board on military questions, evolving this board from the General Board. . . . Only in this way is it possible to give full force to the military efforts of the navy." Morton proved to be a disappointment. Similar to Moody, he hoped to graduate to another cabinet post, the Treasury, but, unlike his predecessor, Morton did not demonstrate strong leadership while at the Navy Department. If he had such aspirations, they may have been cut short by Roosevelt, who made it clear to Morton that he intended to run the navy himself. Roosevelt wrote the incoming secretary a few days before he would take his position, "As you know, there is no other Department with which I have kept in as close touch or with which I am so familiar as the Navy Department, because I hold that this Department should be treated . . . as of literally vital concern to the Government."[87] Then a financial scandal cut short Morton's tenure at the Navy Department, and his successors—Charles Bonaparte, Victor Metcalf, and Truman Newberry—lacked either the time or interest to push administrative reform.[88] Thus, after 1904 the naval general-staff campaign seem hopelessly stalled. The effort would be revived later in Roosevelt's presidency but not from the top levels of the Navy Department;

rather, maverick officers would lead the campaign to shake up naval affairs. This part of the story, however, belongs to a later chapter.

Many circumstances combined to halt naval administrative reform. Congressional opposition was strong, and the reform effort lost its key leaders, Moody and Taylor, after the first attempt to strengthen the general board. Responsibility also lay at the president's doorstep. Roosevelt promised to push all he knew how for a naval general staff, but he did not lend his formidable powers of persuasion to the cause after endorsing it in his annual message. He also did not pick men for secretary of the navy whose first interest was the development of the service. Moody was capable and a strong leader, but he was not completely dedicated, and Morton proved to be an embarrassment. Roosevelt was the de facto secretary; however, the navy was one part of a thick presidential portfolio. If Roosevelt had to set priorities, then he was going to concentrate on building more ships and reviewing them and their crews. Ships were impressive, while training exercises were visible and exciting.

Big ships and big guns appealed to Roosevelt's romantic streak. He liked action and pageantry. They were also more satisfying because he stood to reap much more political credit from building them than from securing a naval general staff. The public could see, as Winston Churchill poetically labeled battleships, "gigantic castles of steel," but naval administrative reform remained an abstraction.[89] Images and legacies were not built on such accomplishments. Presidents, from time to time, have attempted to reorganize the executive departments with the hope of gaining more control and squeezing more efficiency out of the administrative apparatus. Such efforts have often seemed more like exercises in futility because of resistance from members of Congress interested in protecting patronage and from officials determined to defend their own domains. To his credit, Roosevelt recognized the importance of more modern forms of management, but, being a politician, he also discerned that little lasting political gain would come from bureaucratic reform. For Roosevelt, being a man standing astride the nineteenth and twentieth centuries, if there were a problem, a few energetic people of good character could address it more swiftly and easily than altering the administrative architecture. Why get bogged down in obscure matters when he was getting ready to enjoy a second term in his own right?

6

In the Fullness of It All

The fourth of March 1905 was Theodore Roosevelt's day. Sunshine warmed a slight breeze as thousands crowded Washington DC to witness the inauguration of a once-accidental president. The previous November Roosevelt had swamped his Democratic opponent, Alton B. Parker, collecting 336 electoral votes to Parker's 140. Parker had proved to be an uninspiring candidate, but Roosevelt fretted until the returns arrived. Then he gushed to his son Kermit, "I am stunned by the overwhelming victory we have won. I have the greatest popular majority and the greatest electoral majority ever given to a candidate for President."[1] On Inauguration Day Roosevelt's joy knew no bounds, and he could barely contain himself during the festivities. When a band from Pennsylvania played "There'll Be a Hot Time in the Old Town, To-Night"—the song that had sent the Rough Riders off to war—the president swayed in time to the music, and when he saw West Point cadets and Annapolis midshipmen march by, he declared, "Those are the boys. . . . They are superb." He also joked with other dignitaries on the reviewing stand, referring to criticism during the recent campaign that he had dictatorial tendencies: "I really shuddered slightly to-day as I swore to obey the Constitution!"[2] That evening he attended the inaugural ball at the Pension Building, which was crammed with twelve thousand celebrants.[3] There he had an equally splendid time. The only damper on his joy came from within him. As he told his uncle Robert two days after the inauguration, "How I wish Father could have lived to see it too! You stood to me for him and for all that generation, and so you may imagine how proud I was to have you here."[4]

Presidents who win second terms often find that their return to office comes at a price. Their influence wanes as people begin to think about the next occupant in the White House, and political alliances start to realign in anticipation of the change. Second-term presidents are also known quantities to members of Congress, the press, and the public. Actions that might have inspired admiration or praise early on become habits that are expected, perhaps even predictable. Moreover, economic, political, and diplomatic troubles that erupt during a second term cannot be passed off easily as problems inherited from a predecessor. Theodore Roosevelt would have his share of the difficulties that so often seem to accompany second-term presidencies. An economic panic would occur, relations with Congress soured, and foreign crises occupied the president's time. Roosevelt, with his ample endowment of self-righteousness and ego, was rarely reluctant to retreat from a fight and thus would sometimes prove to be his own worst enemy in whipping up controversy. Yet no matter what troubles he might face during his last four years in the White House, he could always bask in the approval given him by the American people in November 1904 and know that he remained popular with them.

When the pressures of the presidency became too much, Theodore Roosevelt sought various forms of release. The perpetual motion machine that was Roosevelt turned to intense physical activity, especially during times of stress. For example, he engaged in his singlestick jousts with Leonard Wood after the anthracite coal strike was resolved and while he nursed the leg injury sustained in the September 1902 streetcar accident. He also vented anger through frequent outbursts, but in private so as not to sully the public dignity of his office. Opponents became the objects of insults. He, for instance, blasted

Sen. George C. Perkins of California, for having "no more back-bone than a sea anemone," and also disparaged him for his "usual feeble timidity," referring to Perkins as a "wretched crea-ture." Roosevelt's contempt stemmed from the senator's oppo-sition to naval expansion, even after a crisis erupted with Japan over the exclusion of Japanese schoolchildren from California schools. Sen. Benjamin Tillman of South Carolina earned the Rooseveltian epithet of being "one of the foulest and rotten-est demagogs in the whole country."[5]

In gentler moods Roosevelt would seek solace with his fam-ily, especially Edith, for she was, he wrote, "so tenderhearted about me." He also enjoyed finding time to read the poetry of Edwin Arlington Robinson, his favorite poet, for T.R. believed that "he certainly has a touch of genius in him." (Roosevelt appreciated Robinson's gifts so much that he found him a Trea-sury position that would allow the poet to work on his composi-tions.)[6] Within the government the president used Henry Cabot Lodge and Elihu Root as sounding boards. (Root had returned to the cabinet as secretary of state in July 1905.) And Roosevelt always enjoyed taking action in affairs of government, especially when he did not need congressional approval. Action supplied one of the best tonics to relieve frustration in the kinetic chief executive, and when he found freedom of action he was hap-piest. "Congress," he complained, "does from a third to a half of what I think is the minimum that it ought to do."[7] As com-mander in chief, while not free of congressional involvement, he had a good deal of latitude and used his authority to pur-sue matters of particular interest to him.

Mechanic in Chief

Rifles, swords, aircraft, submarines, artillery, battleships—military technology in general—fascinated Theodore Roosevelt. His boy-ish side came out when he handled a new weapon or witnessed the tools of war in action. He relished clambering around ships, discussing the merits of a particular design, or inspecting a new rifle, entrenching tool, or some other implement. There was, naturally, a serious side to Roosevelt's interest in military technology. He saw himself as promoting national preparedness. In an age of increasing mechanization, a nation could not fall behind in military technology for long and hope to sustain its influence in a competitive world. Although previous chief executives, such as Thomas Jefferson and Abraham Lincoln, had shown an interest in military technology, Roosevelt was the first president to draw the line so markedly between military technology and national power.

This interest in technology was a constant throughout Roosevelt's public career, but as commander in chief he wore three different hats when it came to such matters. One was the campaign hat of the Rough Riders. Roosevelt, especially early in his tenure, wanted to correct deficiencies that he had witnessed in Cuba. From time to time, as well, he would put on the working man's cap of the tinkerer or, more appropriately, the innovator. Roosevelt saw himself as the voice of a new generation of leadership. He deemed it his mission to push modern devices that he felt the previous generation, mostly Civil War veterans, was too conservative to embrace. Aircraft and submarines were the particular beneficiaries of Roosevelt's attention. Finally, he wore the top hat of the statesman or, better, the power politician. He wanted to ensure that the United States maintained technologies that would make it a respected player in the arena of power politics. In this capacity his attention gravitated the most toward his beloved battleships.[8]

Americans of T.R.'s generation shared his interest in technology. The nineteenth century was a time when gadgets were increasingly features of American life, especially for city dwellers like the Roosevelt family. Electric lighting, telephones, and a whole host of other devices were transforming the way that people lived. Roosevelt came of age with these products and saw them, like his fellow citizens, as evidence of the superiority of American political and economic institutions. For Roosevelt, technological leadership was synonymous with national fitness, a sign of the exceptional excellence of American thought and character. The importance that he attached to technology helps explain why, in spite of the burdens of his office, he spent so much time on technological questions.

Theodore Roosevelt was also a dabbler. The presidency provided him with the perfect opportunity to inject his opinion, try out new things, or meet leading talents in the country. This penchant for involvement stemmed from the confidence of a well-born man who, from boyhood, had grown used to meeting prominent people. Also, because of his uncommon intellect, Roosevelt believed that *he* had something to contribute on most matters. Moreover, he was a naturally inquisitive individual. Roosevelt derived great satisfaction from finding answers to questions, and he had many questions because of the numerous interests that fired his imagination, beyond even military matters. He surrounded himself with the literary lights of his day and was a patron of the arts, pushing for the creation of a national gallery of art. He also sponsored new designs for the coinage, and, most famously, there was his failed attempt to simplify American spelling in 1906. (He retreated from the effort to change spelling in official documents after becoming the object of much ridicule, but continued to pepper his personal correspondence with "thrus" and "althos.")[9] All in all, one of the most joyful features of the presidency for Roosevelt was that he possessed the opportunity to indulge his tendency to dabble.

In military affairs, if there was one area in which he felt particularly expert, then it was with the army. He based his expertise on the practical experience of having raised, trained, and fought a unit in 1898. When making recommendations after the war, he acted as if his four months of service were actual years in the army. Such familiarity had led to his suggestion soon after taking office about changing the color and fit of the army uniform and his concern about the size of the cavalry's spurs.[10]

Roosevelt, therefore, never completely doffed his cavalry uniform. And why should he? He had gained honor in 1898 and received intense personal gratification from his experiences in Cuba. As time passed and Roosevelt moved further from his Rough Rider years, he had less and less unfinished business from the war that he felt he needed to complete. In November 1901, however, he would expound at length to his German friend, Hermann Speck von Sternberg, about the proper use of cavalry and the right kind of weaponry for a cavalryman: "When it comes to actual fighting on horseback, I believe that normally the modern revolver in skillful hands is better than the saber or lance."[11]

Later, when he delved into technological issues that recalled his days in the military, his interest was sporadic and focused on devices with specific tactical applications. The Russo-Japanese War had led him to assign the army's general staff with the task of exploring the utility of swords, bayonets, and rifles in fighting at close quarters. Roosevelt had remained convinced of the rifle's usefulness but was interested in the practicality of a "short triangular bayonet." That implement, however, failed to meet stress tests.[12] At about the same time, the president displayed great interest in the army's development of entrenching tools. The siege warfare of the Russo-Japanese War likely inspired the project, and Roosevelt became enthusiastic when he heard of the work. He was not only closely following the contest in Asia, but he had also received a taste of life in the trenches outside Santiago in 1898. Roosevelt understood that soldiers needed equipment with which to dig in quickly if they were to survive on the modern battlefield. The main problem lay in making the shovels, picks, and other implements efficient, yet small and light. After samples of the tools came out, Roosevelt inspected them, found them "to be just right," and asked to keep them.

Gen. Adna R. Chaffee put off the eager chief executive, explaining that the Ordnance Department required the tools as models for large-scale production. He promised to send Roosevelt a pair as soon as a new set was struck.[13]

Digging tools were age-old, but a newer technology, and one of seemingly great potential for the future, had deeply impressed Roosevelt during the Cuba campaign, perhaps more than any other he saw in use. Late in his presidency this new instrument of warfare would again draw his attention. Machine guns had played a significant role in helping the American infantry take Spanish positions. Roosevelt had witnessed Gatling guns in action on the San Juan Heights. This early form of machine weapon was unwieldy. It consisted primarily of a cylinder of revolving barrels that the operators turned with a hand crank. A large carriage made the Gatling gun mobile, and a team of men would push it into battle. At Santiago Roosevelt saw four of these weapons in action. Lt. John Henry Parker commanded the Gatling gun battery, and he thrust them aggressively to the front to support the infantry. During the battle Roosevelt's men mistook, at first, the distinct drumming sound of the Gatlings for Spanish machine guns. But Roosevelt recalled that when he realized that they were, in fact, American weapons, "I . . . jumped to my feet, smiting my hand on my thigh, shouting along with exultation, 'It's the Gatlings, men, our Gatlings!'" The sound of the Gatlings, he claimed, "was the only sound which I ever heard my men cheer in battle." He sensed, then, the importance of this weapon and gave praise where it was due. "Parker," he observed, "deserved rather more credit than any other one man in the entire campaign." Roosevelt also developed a personal affinity for the lieutenant. Parker, for instance, administered the oath when Roosevelt received his colonel's commission, and T.R., in turn, wrote the introduction to Parker's book about his unit's work in Cuba.[14]

A decade following the Cuba expedition, Roosevelt weighed

in on a debate about the proper deployment of machine guns in battle. Machine-gun technology had only grown deadlier in the intervening ten years. As the *Army and Navy Journal* reported, the Maxim machine gun could produce a "leaden hail of 600 rifle bullets a minute." Army officers, however, were unsure about the best way to integrate machine-gun units into the fighting line. John Henry Parker, now a captain, advocated a separate machine-gun corps to promote expert use of the complicated weapon. War Department officials and members of the general staff favored incorporation of machine-gun detachments into existing cavalry and infantry outfits. They wanted to ensure the availability of machine guns to the largest number of units. The War Department seemed ready to rule against Parker when the enterprising captain took matters into his own hands. He bypassed official channels and presented his case directly to his old comrade in the White House.[15]

Roosevelt proved a receptive audience. He studied the issue in detail and then gave extensive instructions to the War Department. An October 1908 letter to Secretary of War Luke Wright, who assumed this post after William Howard Taft began his campaign to succeed Roosevelt, displayed the president's analytic powers and his ability to master technical problems. He would undertake this task, even though he was distracted with getting Taft elected. Roosevelt cut to the heart of both Parker's argument and the War Department's position and offered a middle way. He accepted the wisdom of attaching machine-gun troops to infantry and cavalry regiments and suggested that each battalion be equipped with two machine guns. The president was ever concerned about preparedness in case of a future war and recommended that a "large supply of machine guns and materiel should be secured and stored to meet the necessities of possible war." He was thinking about the expansion of forces if a flood of volunteers were ever needed. He also agreed to the organization of a "machine-gun troop in some regiment of cavalry, for experimental purposes." He did not, however, believe that much progress was possible without the help of expert officers, "whose special duty it is to supervise and work the companies up." He proposed to meet Parker's demands for specialists if Congress approved the necessary increase in officers. A bill was introduced to raise the number of officers so that some could devote themselves to machine-gun duty, but the legislation failed.[16]

Roosevelt may not have secured machine-gun specialists, but he could take satisfaction from having acted on a promising idea. In his mind his personal success was not always measured by the results. He could commend himself for simply acting, with having done what he saw as his duty and getting work started, although obtaining all that he wanted would have been the most rewarding. In the case of machine guns, he helped to end the debate and to begin practical tests, for that was "the best and quickest way of determining such modifications as ought to be made."[17] He would operate in a similar fashion in promoting two other technologies that showed much promise at the time and, like the machine gun, would realize a fuller potential for destruction.

Innovator in Chief

The headline suggested both alarm and wonder: "President Takes Plunge in Submarine, Remains below the Surface for Fifty-Five Minutes, Once 40 Feet under Water." In August 1905 Theodore Roosevelt had performed another exploit that captured the American imagination. While vacationing at Oyster Bay, Roosevelt decided to witness firsthand the operation of an emerging naval technology. The navy had dispatched the *Plunger* to Long Island Sound so that the president could observe it in action. He was supposed to view the vessel from the safety of the presidential yacht, the *Sylph*, but he could not resist the urge to ride aboard the craft. Two years previously at Annapolis, members of his cabinet had persuaded him not to take a ride in a submarine. His daughter Alice, though, had already experienced being underwater in the submarine *Moccasin* in September 1903, and not to be denied this time, Roosevelt stole off without informing his family or staff. A strong northeast wind roughened the water, but the president was determined.[18] After his voyage he not only called attention to himself and submarines but also worked to promote the submarine service as whole.

Roosevelt knew something of submarine technology before his ride. An earlier *Plunger* had been nearing completion shortly before he had resigned as assistant secretary in 1898.[19] His dive in 1905 made him enthusiastic for the devices. He reportedly "behaved like a delighted schoolboy over everything he saw" during an inspection of the vessel. The president "evinced particular interest in the torpedo mechanism," and he used the periscope to gain perspective on the experiments conducted by the crew. He was likely most thrilled when he took over the controls of the *Plunger* and when he witnessed a school of porpoises swim by a porthole while the boat rested below the surface. Upon his return Roosevelt expressed how impressed he was with the submarine and complimented its crew for their work.

The voyage was fun and interesting for T.R. It also represented a typical jaunt. He may have slipped away to board the *Plunger*, but Roosevelt certainly courted press coverage of the stunt. The dive to the bottom of Long Island Sound reinforced popular fascination with him, and it put him in the news at a time of the year when the federal government went into doldrums as officials escaped the summer heat of Washington DC.

The *Plunger* adventure also proved consequential for the submarine service. Roosevelt's trip highlighted the reliability of submarines and thereby helped allay concerns about the safety of the vessels. Although newspapers decried the president's risk taking, some news accounts repeated claims that the trip was as safe as a subway ride and noted the precautions taken to protect the commander in chief's well-being.[20] Roosevelt's playful day resulted, as well, in direct help for the men who operated the submarines. During his time with the submariners, he discovered that the navy discriminated against them. The Navy Department did not consider submariners to be on sea duty because they operated in coastal waters like Long Island Sound. Departmental officials resisted the argument that submariners, because of the nature of their business, incurred risks in coastal waters that other sailors on oceangoing vessels did not face. Sea duty brought pay and promotion benefits, and Roosevelt directed Secretary of the Navy Charles Bonaparte to correct the disparity and reward enlisted men in particular. He also ordered adequate quarters for officers serving on submarines, as they had none aboard or ashore.[21]

These measures allowed Roosevelt to play his cherished role of crusader. In this case he was doing more than promoting an innovative technology and the men who operated it. He was also waging battle against what he often termed "wooden thinking." As the most prominent representative of post–Civil War leadership, Roosevelt disparaged what he regarded as old-fashioned attitudes, which resulted in decisions being made simply because that was the way things had been done in the past. He associated such conservatism with age and considered it a reflection of encroaching dullness and caution rather than the boldness and cleverness that he regarded as signature features in any person of substance and influence. (Roosevelt had a hard time acknowledging that change might also bring upheaval and confusion.) With submarines T.R. proclaimed that certain "old style naval officers" in Washington "absolutely decline to recognize this fact [that submarines might be a useful supplement to the fleet] and hamper the development of the submarine boat in every way."[22] During his first term, four submarines had been authorized, but in his second term, after the *Plunger* trip, twenty more were ordered.[23]

The president's interest in submarines did not stop with the boats themselves but also extended to their principal weapon: the torpedo. Torpedoes had long been a part of the naval arsenal. Before the advent of the self-propelled torpedo, navies had lodged these implements into an opponent's hull through the use of a long spar. No matter the means of delivery, the torpedo offered the potential of a devastating strike because, if it worked properly, it could blow a hole in an enemy vessel beneath the waterline. The fact that battleships, destroyers, and other craft carried them, in addition to submarines, demonstrated the importance of the torpedo in naval thinking. Roosevelt had marveled at the torpedo mechanism of the *Plunger*, but three years after his voyage he worried about an advance in torpedo development. Lt. Cdr. Cleland Davis, working in the navy's Bureau of Equipment, had invented a torpedo that did not detonate until it penetrated the hull of a ship, and the president was aware of the destructive implications. After learning about trial runs of the new torpedo, Roosevelt expressed alarm. He felt that "this comes mighty near to revolutionizing naval warfare so far as torpedoes are concerned." The experimental Davis torpedo, he declared, "may prove to be a very dangerous implement of warfare," and, if that were indeed the case, then he believed that the United States should develop an effective response for its own vessels. Although the U.S. Navy had developed the weapon first, other powers could not be far behind in the production of similar technology. "We should at once take measures in the design of our new ships as well as in those building to provide adequate protection, if possible, against attack from the Davis torpedo." Roosevelt was particularly concerned that the design of new battleships incorporate a defense against the Davis torpedo. With the core of American naval power possibly at stake, the president was determined that the navy stay abreast of the latest developments.[24] Roosevelt's interest in torpedoes and submarines contained an irony. The improvement of these devices would come to threaten the dominance of the battleship—the instrument Roosevelt so treasured—in spite of the president's efforts to protect them.

Roosevelt did not only consider undersea warfare. He also turned his gaze skyward. In 1898, as assistant secretary of the navy, he had called attention to Prof. Samuel Langley's aviation experiments.[25] The War Department had already begun to explore the potential of Langley's work, so Roosevelt's urge to be the agent of innovation remained unsatisfied in this instance. Army officers had recognized the military advantages of aviation, and aeronautical experiments at the time were conducted with a focus on the military potential of aircraft. Such military funding of private researchers occurred in both the United States and Europe.[26] The War Department's interest in aviation deflected Roosevelt's attention, and soon more pressing affairs in 1898 consumed his time. He would not demonstrate concern about aviation again until well into his presidency and only then because the War Department's exploration of the potential of aircraft had lapsed.

A combination of circumstances helps to explain the inconsistent record of the War Department on aviation. The army had banked $50,000 on Professor Langley's flight experiments, and the government connection to the inventor's work was well known. The *Washington Post*, for example, informed readers of the military potential of Langley's craft with a headline that announced, "Government Backs Langley, the Professor's Airship Built as an Implement of War."[27] Langley also conducted his work in the public eye, with what he called an aerodrome—nicknamed the "Buzzard"—positioned on a houseboat in the Potomac River near Washington DC. As a result, expectations reached unrealistic levels as the professor prepared for a test in 1903. Langley tried to tamp down the inflated predictions, but to no avail. When the Buzzard failed to sustain flight but instead plowed twice into the mud of the Potomac, ridicule followed, and chastised War Department officials were reluctant to be connected to similar public humiliations. Members of Congress blasted the War Department for pouring money into Langley's folly and refused any more support for aviation development.[28]

The government cutoff of funds occurred at about the same time that Orville and Wilbur Wright flew their aircraft at Kitty Hawk, North Carolina. Their first flight occurred in December 1903, but the achievement went unheralded, especially in the United States, for about five years. The oversight was understandable. Unlike Langley, the Wrights preferred to conduct their experiments in remote settings, in part because of desirable environmental conditions, but also because they recognized much experimentation would be required before a practical aircraft could be produced, and they wanted to protect their ideas from competitors. Skepticism had risen, moreover, against the possibility of heavier-than-air flight after the Langley fiasco, and the Wrights' early attempts were short and open to contention about whether they had succeeded. Not surprisingly, when the Wright brothers offered their flyer to the War Department in 1905, the Board of Ordnance and Fortification rejected their proposal.[29]

Other influences were required to reignite military interest in aviation. The Aero Club of America, a private promotional group, formed in 1905 and championed the cause of aeronautical development. Club members decided that the best way to spur official interest was to bypass governmental bureaucracies and approach the man who embodied action for his generation and who had demonstrated impatience with bureaucratic foot-dragging. Roosevelt answered the club's request by making the War Department take a new look at aircraft. He paid for the investigation by dipping into funds from a discretionary appropriation for national defense. Capitol Hill had approved the money years earlier, so the president was able to bypass lawmakers.[30]

The War Department opened competitive bidding for three prototypes in December 1907. The Wrights won a contract and were the only ones to deliver a craft for flight trials at Fort Myer, Virginia, in September 1908. Orville Wright's early attempts were short and disappointing, but soon he broke world records for flight endurance. His exploits brought out the heads of army bureaus and three cabinet members: Secretary of War Luke Wright, Secretary of the Navy Victor Metcalf, and Secretary of Commerce and Labor Oscar Straus. The most optimistic predictions replaced skepticism about heavier-than-air flight. One forecast prophesied that the perfection of the airplane would relegate "the $8,000,000 battleship to the national junk heap."[31] These flights, along with similar ones that Wilbur was conducting in Europe, made the brothers truly famous, but more rational assessments about the implications of their accomplishment soon appeared. The *Washington Post* celebrated the Wrights' success as "among humanity's most remarkable achievements," yet the paper reminded readers that "the practical uses of the aeroplane, many confident prophets to the contrary notwithstanding, remain to be discovered."[32]

Where was Theodore Roosevelt during these exciting events? He was spending the warm months, as usual, at Sagamore Hill. Despite the distance from Washington, Roosevelt was reportedly following Orville Wright's exploits with great interest. He planned to visit the testing grounds upon his return later in September. Wright wanted to set a new world flight record to mark the president's visit. One reporter, well aware of Roosevelt's disdain for playing spectator, asked Wright if he would take the president into the air. Wright responded, "Well, I suppose I'd have to take him up. But I don't think I'd like to do it." The aviator explained that he would honor the president's wish, should it come, but he did not "think the chief executive of this nation should expose himself to unnecessary danger." Wright recalled Roosevelt's dive in the *Plunger* and said that T.R. should not have taken that risk.[33]

Roosevelt never had the chance to fly with Orville Wright. No matter the president's intentions, events intervened, proving that a golden age of flight had not yet dawned. Wright crashed a few days after he spoke about a possible presidential airplane ride. A propeller failure caused the mishap. The crash severely injured Wright and killed his passenger, Lt. Thomas Selfridge, who was regarded as one of the army's top aviation experts and, more important, was on the Army Aeronautical Board, for which Wright was conducting the flying tests. He had begged Wright for the ride, and the aviator had not felt as if he were in a position to refuse.[34]

The accident did not end aviation experiments. Observers recognized that the development of airplanes was hazardous and that accidents would occur.[35] Nevertheless, the growth of military aviation slowed in the United States until World War I. Aircraft lacked a major constituency, given the enduring peace and the weakness of neighboring nations. Even before the Wrights had presented their flyer for the army tests in September 1908, Congress had made clear that aviation was not a priority. Earlier in the year the House Committee on Military Affairs had rejected any more purchases of airplanes for the immediate future. The navy had taken a similar position in September 1907, when the general board rejected an aeronautical division for the Navy Department. The board claimed that the science of aviation was not advanced enough to be of concern.[36]

Roosevelt might have remained a driving force, but aviation was not a primary interest to him. His presidency was fast drawing to a close in the fall of 1908, and he most wanted to elect William Howard Taft as his successor in November. Moreover, airplanes remained a curiosity, and Roosevelt would rather put his trust in proven instruments of war instead of flimsy machines constructed of canvas and wood. He had, however, acted again as the innovator when he prompted War Department officials to take action on airplanes, and the tests at Fort Myer would finally bring full national attention to the Wrights. Although Orville Wright's crash set back the development of military aviation, work in that area would not stop. The advantages of a reliable flying machine were simply too evident. An American banker and aviation promoter put it well as he watched Wilbur Wright fly in France in 1908. Charles Flint, who was also the Wrights' financial representative, declared, "This machine will . . . revolutionize methods of fighting, both on land and sea. It can be used in lieu of light cavalry for scouting, can drop explosives on the deck of a battleship, and can carry dispatches across a hostile country."[37] Roosevelt's own family would join in that vision when the youngest son, Quentin, became an aviator during World War I. The Great War and the development of capable military aircraft, however, lay in the future. Roosevelt's first concern while commander in chief would be the development of the battle fleet as the first line of defense.

Big Guns for the Big Stick

"The strength of the navy rests primarily upon its battleships, and in building these battleships it is imperatively necessary . . . that they should be the very best of their kind." T.R. wrote those words in January 1907 and aimed them at a Congress that had become increasingly reluctant to authorize more battleship construction. This statement went to the heart of Theodore Roosevelt's naval policy and diplomacy. He needed battleships. Without them the United States could not be a major sea power, and America could not be a great nation unless it were a sea power. Roosevelt did believe in building other types of vessels. In fact, in the same message, he pronounced that "I thoroly believe in developing and building an adequate number of submarines; I believe in building torpedo-boat destroyers; there must be a few fast scouts, and, of course, various auxiliary vessels of different kinds."[38] Battleships, however, remained the crucial element, for they were the weapons that would decide the fate of the nation at sea. Additionally, they supplied a forceful prop to the foreign policy of the United States. But battleships also carried cultural significance. As products of the Industrial Revolution, they represented the might of a burgeoning American economy. Moreover, these seagoing fortresses were symbols of the American people's vitality and ability to perform in a competitive world. A mere quarter century before, wood and sails had been the order of the day in a U.S. Navy that lagged well behind others. Within a generation the United States had risen to become a leading naval power.[39] It was little surprise, then, that Theodore Roosevelt's interest in battleships bordered on the obsessive. They were the key to his foreign policy, to an American impact on the larger world, and to imperial involvements that, he believed, would strengthen the national character.

Roosevelt also fastened on battleships for the simple reason that they were a technology. More precisely, battleships were a complex technological system and an engineering accomplishment of the first order. These vessels provided the president with abundant opportunities to learn about ship design and construction. He sought detailed specifications, praising ideas that he liked and often suggesting improvements. For a busy chief executive, he displayed an impressive ability to learn technical information and recite the principles of ship design. William Sims, from his post as inspector of target practice, commented in 1905 that he found it hard to imagine "any other president asking for information concerning a technical subject."[40]

A voyage in 1906 abroad the newly commissioned battleship *Louisiana* excited the navalist and technological enthusiast in Theodore Roosevelt. Both as commander in chief and as assistant secretary of the navy, the president had seen large ships in action before. This time the experience was different. Roosevelt was traveling to Panama to witness the work being done on the Panama Canal. For the round trip, which included a stop in Puerto Rico on the return leg, he would be on the *Louisiana* for nearly two weeks. He reveled at the opportunity to see the latest in American naval technology in operation. The *Louisiana* was almost too small to contain him. He reported to his son Kermit that when he was not reading the works of John Milton and Tacitus, along with the German novel *Jörn Uhl,* he would "walk briskly up and down the deck." He explained that "I also spend a good deal of time on the forward bridge and sometimes on the aft bridge, and of course have gone over the ship to inspect it with the Captain." The pride in seeing first-hand what he had helped to create burst forth as he declared to Kermit, "It is a splendid thing to see one of these men-of-war, and it does really make one proud of one's country."[41]

Roosevelt inspected every nook of the *Louisiana.* He was no mere observer. For T.R. inspection meant personally perform-ing the work of the sailors. One of the crew of the *Louisiana* described Roosevelt's desire to learn as much as possible about the vessel and its crew. In a letter to his family, assistant electri-cian Walter Whitehead conveyed, "The President is going to eat his next meal with the crew. He is now going down in one of the firerooms to shovel coal for a while. He likes to do a little of everything. He is bound to find out everything for himself. It does not take him long to find out things." Roosevelt's hands-on method not only gained him firsthand knowledge and satisfied his appetite for action but also proved winning among the crew. Whitehead related that "if you would see him you would like him. He is no jollier, but an everyday man. He does not leave it to head officers; he goes right among the men." The president made such an impression that Whitehead declared that were Roosevelt to run again, "he certainly has made friends here."[42]

T.R.'s time on the *Louisiana* filled him with ideas for improv-ing vessels. Secretary of the Navy Bonaparte received an extensive list of recommendations shortly after the president's return to Washington in late November 1906. Roosevelt displayed the detailed level of his investigation when he began with directions to improve the "brasses"—the brass bearings—on new ships like the *Louisiana*. The chief engineer of the *Louisiana* had reported the premature wear of the bearings, and he relayed to the president that this problem was not limited to the *Louisiana*. Although the brasses represented an extremely technical matter, Roosevelt recognized how crucial they were to a ship's operation: "All of these ships [*Louisiana, West Virginia, Tennessee, Maryland*] had such trouble with the brasses as originally put in that it would have been a very dangerous, and possibly fatal, experiment, to have sent them . . . into active service against an enemy." He therefore ordered a "thoro investigation" of the matter to be conducted as soon as possible, and he wanted the results presented directly to him. Similarly, the president ordered a study to be done on the lubricating oils used on naval vessels, for he was not sure if they were the best. He was even willing to purchase lubricants from the Standard Oil Company, which he could "hardly be suspected of favoring" given his antitrust actions, if its oil was of superior quality. Roosevelt felt that he had firmer evidence that the navy had been sold inferior coal, for one time after coaling the *Louisiana* received a batch that "looked more like slate than coal." The difference in speed had been so noticeable that T.R. had decided to look into this problem himself, and he discovered, as with the brasses, that it was not an isolated incident. From his perspective "the Navy was being at least occasionally swindled by certain of the coal companies." Again, Roosevelt wanted Bonaparte to investigate the matter and report to him so that he could act. He was contemplating refusing to pay companies for poor coal or cutting off any dealings with them.[43]

Roosevelt's attention also fastened on the military features of the ship. In particular, he felt that the vessel was undergunned. The *Louisiana* carried a wide array of weaponry, featuring twelve-inch, eight-inch, seven-inch, and three-inch guns. Roosevelt believed that some of the calibers could have been more powerful. "I cannot help feeling," he wrote Secretary Bonaparte, "that it would have been far better to have substituted ten-inch guns for the eight and seven-inch guns . . . , and five-inch or four-inch guns for repelling torpedo boats, instead of three-inch guns."[44] The president's work in naval history surely informed his thinking, for he was well aware of the American tradition of building ships that were stouter and better armed than their foreign counterparts.[45] That had been true during the age of wood and sail, and, according to Roosevelt, the *Louisiana* did not meet that standard.

His comments about the ship's armament also reflected more modern concerns. Naval designers had debated the utility of the lower-caliber weapons, with some arguing that the biggest guns should be emphasized, to maximize offensive power, at the expense of smaller, more defensive weaponry. That debate was being resolved in the fall of 1906, when the British launched the all-big-gun *Dreadnought*. Roosevelt's comments about the armament of the *Louisiana* reflected his doubts about the value of loading battleships with lower-caliber guns. Indeed, he would conclude after much deliberation, that the U.S. Navy needed its own all-big-gun battleships.

In much of what he discussed about the *Louisiana*, Roosevelt acted as if he were reliving his year as assistant secretary of the navy. Perhaps the sight of the Cuban shore on his passage to Panama stirred memories from the late 1890s.[46] More likely, these detailed recommendations reflected the president's restless temperament, his insatiable curiosity, and his determination to build the best navy possible. The fact that he had extra time on his hands during his tour allowed him to indulge his interest in battleship design and technology. In making his recommendations on seemingly obscure details, he revealed an understanding about the nature of modern technology. As technology grew more complex, a breakdown in mundane, yet necessary, appliances such as the ball bearings could prove crippling, with potentially perilous consequences.

Roosevelt's ideas about the *Louisiana* amounted to little in the larger course of events. The newly commissioned battleship was already obsolete when Roosevelt sailed to Panama, and he would soon know that to be the case. In fact, all vessels like the *Louisiana* were out of date, for they had been superseded by the all-big-gun ship. Prior to the first sailing of Britain's *Dreadnought* on 1 October 1906, battleships were fitted with a mix of gun calibers: big guns (nine inches or more), medium-sized guns (five to eight inches), and smaller rapid-fire guns. Each gun size was to serve a different purpose in a naval engagement. The small rapid-fire weapons were to fight off swift-moving torpedo boats, while the medium-sized weapons would allow a ship to close on an opponent. The largest cannons supplied fire at the longest of ranges. All-big-gun ships maximized hitting power by dispensing with the medium-sized weapons to allow for ten or more of the biggest guns. The ships also grew in size to handle this large main battery, and bigger ships theoretically meant greater speed, thicker armor, better maneuverability, and longer endurance over the older mixed-caliber vessels.

The superiority of the all-big-gun ship may have been clear after the *Dreadnought*, the namesake for an entire new ship type, joined the battle line of the Royal Navy. The advantages of dreadnoughts were uncertain before 1906 and subject to a major debate within U.S. naval circles. Britain's navy was not the only service to consider these vessels. As early as 1902 Roosevelt contemplated a question surrounding the growing size of battleships. Alfred T. Mahan had written T.R. in October 1902. The writer wanted the president to consider a standard battleship design rather than pursue ever larger battleships with each authorization for new construction. Mahan argued that very little was gained with an increase in vessel size; numbers mattered instead. He quoted his *Lessons of the War with Spain* to support the point that "numbers therefore, mean increase of offensive power, other things remaining equal." In making his case, Mahan was not arguing against the all-big-gun ship, for the idea had not yet gained currency. He was instead drawing on history in an attempt to superimpose the Royal Navy's past on the American naval present. He compared a standard model battleship to the seventy-four-gun ship of the line that had helped Britain maintain dominance of the sea during the age of sail. The president considered Mahan's proposal but seemed disinclined to accept it. He ordered navy bureau chiefs to respond to the admiral's letter. They found, Roosevelt informed Mahan, that a significant increase in fighting power came with larger vessels: "There is in the American navy an increase of 50 per cent in offensive power for an increase of 25 per cent in tonnage."[47]

Roosevelt had not suddenly hit on the all-big-gun battleship in his reaction to Mahan. The mixed-caliber ship still ruled the waves in his mind. Roosevelt's note to Mahan did indicate why he would be amenable to the all-big-gun design once it was proposed. Bigger was better. It was only human nature to believe as much. That conclusion seemed especially true in Roosevelt's case because the president peppered his writing and speeches with words that stressed power, growth, and strength. More formidable battleships would also mean a more robust foreign policy and greater American prominence in the world. T.R.'s reaction to Mahan's proposal suggested, as well, that Roosevelt had little use for Mahan when it came to technological proposals.[48] He was content to let Mahan apply the lessons of history to popularize sea power. Such work would advance Roosevelt's own policies. The admiral appeared out of touch when he tried to use the history of the age of sail to propose ship designs in the fast-moving world of twentieth-century technology.

Serious consideration of the all-big-gun battleship began in America in 1903. That year Lt. Homer Poundstone proposed battleships that emphasized a main battery over all else.[49] Then during the summer, officers at the Naval War College debated the question of the all-big-gun ship, and in the fall the General Board of the U.S. Navy requested a preliminary design for such a vessel. Roosevelt entered the discussion in October 1904. He was already aware of Poundstone's ideas, which he endorsed, but the armament of the newly authorized *New Hampshire* was the matter of the moment. The *New Hampshire* was to be mixed caliber and weigh sixteen-thousand tons. It was to boast a battery of four twelve-inch guns, eight eight-inch guns, twelve seven-inch guns, and twenty three-pound guns. Roosevelt wanted to know if, instead of this multiplicity of weapons, "we ought to have on our battleships merely big twelve-inch guns and fourteen pounders, with nothing between." He already knew the answer of the Navy Department bureaucracy to this question because the multigun design of the *New Hampshire* was the work of the Board on Construction. Roosevelt wanted an outside voice, as was his habit, to provide a check on officials who, he felt, were too invested in the usual ways of doing business. As he so often did in naval affairs, the president turned to William Sims. Because Sims was a gunnery expert, with a record as a gadfly, he was a logical choice. His answer could have been foretold because of the fact that he *was* a gunnery expert and a friend and Annapolis classmate of Homer Poundstone. Sims gave a strong endorsement to the all-big-gun idea, his words characteristically hitting home as hard as the shots he directed as inspector of target practice.[50] The commander wrote that ships carrying twelve eleven-inch guns could "pierce the armor of any battleship in the world at long range."[51] Implicit in this statement was the message that if the United States failed to develop such ships, then American battleships might be the ones pierced by the shells of a navy that had adopted the all-big-gun ship.[52]

Roosevelt proposed that the Navy Department reconfigure the *New Hampshire* after receiving Sims's reply. The proposal met with a resolute chorus of "no." The Board on Construction, the Bureau of Construction, and the Bureau of Navigation all joined to say that there was no compelling reason to make a change and that recently produced American battleships were as powerful as anything contemplated in Europe. Sir William White, the designer of many Royal Navy battleships, lent assistance when he denounced the all-big-gun ship.[53] Faced with such strong opinions, Roosevelt acceded to the experts, and the *New Hampshire* remained a mixed-caliber vessel.

From 1904 to 1906 T.R. would be uncharacteristically indecisive on the all-big-gun ship question. His instinct inclined him to support the new design, but he was unwilling to push the proposition in the face of countervailing forces. Persistent pressure from the White House might have overcome reluctance in the Navy Department, and then the American navy, rather than the Royal Navy, may have introduced the all-big-gun vessel.[54] However, Roosevelt was rarely impulsive, especially when making policy decisions, even though critics painted him as wild and unpredictable. He would collect information, seek opposing views, and weigh the evidence before drawing a conclusion. On the question of the all-big-gun battleship he seemed to have particular trouble making up his mind. Even after the first American all-big-gun ship, the *Delaware*, was authorized in 1906, Roosevelt continued to have doubts.[55]

Why did indecision afflict Roosevelt in this matter? Powerful arguments supported both sides of the question. William Sims hammered the greater power of such vessels, but others argued that mixed-caliber ships could fire more quickly and accurately. They believed that naval engagements would be decided close in, where the larger number of medium and smaller-caliber guns would count for more. In short, Roosevelt was being asked to foresee how future naval battles would be fought. Understandably, he wanted as much information as possible before making a decision filled with such consequence. If the fog of war was thick, then, as historian Harold Winton has observed, the fog of peace could be even thicker in discerning the outlines of future conflicts.[56] The voices, moreover, that challenged the all-big-gun ship were formidable. Chief among them was Alfred T. Mahan. Roosevelt often disagreed with Mahan during his presidency, but he could never afford to ignore the admiral. Mahan wielded a mighty pen and, in the public mind, was *the* naval authority of the era. In June 1906 he would make an especially forceful case in favor of the mixed-caliber battleship that gave Roosevelt pause about the wisdom of the all-big-gun design. His evidence would come from the Russo-Japanese War of 1904–5. Mahan focused on Adm. Togo Heihachiro's victory over the Russian Baltic Fleet at Tsushima Strait in May 1905. Mahan argued that Togo decimated the Russian force because of superior choice of position, along with a greater rate of fire from the secondary batteries.[57]

On top of such arguments, Roosevelt also had to weigh the political task of making the case for all-big-gun ships to Capitol Hill. The request for a new type of ship seemed likely to spark controversy, especially with members who were anti-imperialist or concerned about a rising naval budget. Roosevelt needed the strongest possible case before going to Congress, which he did not yet have, especially after Mahan published his argument for continuing the mixed-caliber design.[58]

William S. Sims quelled any lingering doubt in Roosevelt's mind by countering Mahan and giving the president a stronger hand with which to deal with Congress. Roosevelt had asked Sims, Mahan, and the general board for another round of assessments regarding the all-big-gun ship in the summer of 1906. Sims supplied a twenty-six-page letter that proved conclusive. The letter supplied such a strong case on behalf of the all-big-gun ship that Roosevelt gave Sims permission to publish it. T.R.

told Sims, "I regard your article as convincing."[59] Once in the public record, the article provided a strong counterweight to Mahan's assessment of the Battle of Tsushima Strait. Sims's analysis punctured Mahan's case and even dented the older man's reputation. Sims proved that Mahan had based his case on faulty information and also showed that the admiral's assumptions about all-big-gun ships were misguided. In particular, Sims's countered Mahan's claims about the relative inaccuracy of the biggest guns. Sims deployed data to argue that bigger guns were actually more accurate than smaller calibers and that the Japanese victory at Tsushima would likely have been even more decisive if they had possessed all-big-gun ships.[60]

The appearance of the *Dreadnought* in 1906 also did much to settle the question. There was now an actual vessel that embodied the all-big-gun design. The new ship impressed from the day of its christening in February 1906. Cable traffic lit up around the world, for until that time the construction of the battle wagon had been shrouded in secrecy. The news of how quickly the hull had been assembled—four months after the laying of the keel—astounded officials and the public alike. The Washington reporter for the London *Times* noted how "the building and launching of the *Dreadnought* have aroused interest here which is both professional and political. Nobody is more interested than the President . . . to whom all things naval are of deep concern. That such a ship could have been built so quickly and so secretly astonishes naval experts." Once sea trials began in October 1906, the *Dreadnought* more than lived up to its promise. The superior size of the vessel meant that it could steam through heavy seas without problems, and the new turbine engines proved, according to Capt. Reginald Bacon, "markedly successful."[61] Firing of the big guns did not shake the decks to pieces, as some feared; rather, below decks the roar of the broadside was hardly noticed.[62] The implications of *Dreadnought* were clear: if other naval powers hoped to compete they had to build similar ships.

After the British stole a march on all the other navies, Theodore Roosevelt wanted dreadnoughts for the United States. His own words presented an obstacle in getting these vessels, and in sufficient numbers. Roosevelt had called a halt to continued expansion of the battleship fleet in his previous annual message. In December 1905 he had informed Congress that "it does not seem to be necessary, however, that the navy should—at least in the immediate future—be increased beyond the present number of units. What is now clearly necessary is to substitute efficient for inefficient units as the latter become worn out or as it becomes apparent that they are useless. Probably the result would be attained by adding a single battleship to our navy each year, the superseded or outworn vessels being laid up or broken up as they are thus replaced."[63] Roosevelt had inserted numerous qualifiers to leave himself room to maneuver: he talked about the "immediate future" and used words such as "probably." Yet the main message remained. Roosevelt was backing away from the great fleet expansion of his first term, when up to five battleships had been requested in a single year. An annual one-battleship replacement policy would instead take hold. Roosevelt would soon regret that he had ever delivered this pronouncement. He had made it shortly before the hull of the *Dreadnought* touched water and when mixed-caliber ships ruled the waves. His statement walled him in politically and gave his critics ammunition when he decided in 1907 to abandon the one-ship standard to build dreadnoughts in large enough numbers to preserve America's standing as a leading sea power.

So why did Roosevelt ever set the one-ship per year policy? The constraints that his statement imposed make the decision, in hindsight, certainly seem questionable. Even at the time, there were indications that he would have done better to leave himself a wider range of options than he did. After all, in 1904 the United States had begun designing the *Michigan* to emphasize big guns.[64] Roosevelt provided his best explanation for limiting battleship construction in a letter that he wrote to Leonard Wood in March 1905. He told Wood that the fleet had reached a size that put the United States "a good second to France and about on a par with Germany." T.R. claimed that he had wanted a minimum of forty armored vessels when he became president, and he felt that "I have now reached my mark" with twenty-eight battleships and twelve armored cruisers, either built or authorized. He also related to Wood that he had faced increasing difficulty in winning fleet increases with each passing year.[65] Indeed, that very year Roosevelt had grown alarmed when he heard from a reporter that the House of Representatives would not support a single new battleship, when he had asked for three. After a flurry of messages to Speaker Joseph Cannon and Rep. George Foss, head of the House Naval Affairs Committee, the president ultimately won two battleships for the next fiscal year.[66] In December 1905 he announced the one-ship-per-year idea likely because of this growing resistance to naval expenditures. The predictability of one ship per year was better than none, and the single battleship per annum would be less likely to incite congressional critics. Finally, Roosevelt relayed to Wood that he wanted to "rest" on naval expansion "while we bring up the personnel."[67] Naval construction had boomed under William McKinley and Roosevelt, but the navy was hard-pressed to recruit and train the men necessary to crew the new vessels. From 1899 to 1909 the number of sailors grew from 13,750 to 38,900, nearly tripling in size.[68] The president wanted to address the problem of personnel, but the launch of the *Dreadnought* would not afford him that luxury.

When Roosevelt stated the one-ship rule in December 1905, he likely felt that he had taken into account the need for flexibility in case of unforeseen events. His 1905 annual message, in fact, seemed to anticipate the coming of new ship designs when it described the substitution of "efficient for inefficient units" and "superseded" vessels. Indeed, one ship per year appeared adequate to keep the U.S. battle fleet at current strength and have it remain on a pace with foreign navies in terms of engineering. What T.R. did not anticipate was the speed at which Great Britain built the *Dreadnought*. At a time when battleships took years to assemble, the construction of the *Dreadnought* in one year overthrew notions about the rate at which the United States could afford to replace its older ships with new types. Two years after he issued the one-ship policy, and in a political atmosphere that had become stormy, Roosevelt would recant and appeal for more than one battleship per year.

As Theodore Roosevelt's presidency moved toward its final years, critics of the president would become emboldened and the political battles more bitter. Still, Roosevelt would continue to derive much pleasure from being president, and, as criticism strengthened, he especially enjoyed being commander in chief. That part of the presidential portfolio offered him considerable latitude. He could do much simply with direct orders, allowing him the immediate action that he craved.[69] Within military affairs his ability to consider, promote, and handle various technologies gave him great pleasure and represented one of the rewards of being president. He enjoyed handling entrenching instruments, suggesting modified designs for spurs, riding in submarines, and the like, but nothing made his heart soar like seeing and boarding battleships. Sixteen of these behemoths would be added to the navy under his watch, and their addition to the fleet represented one of his proudest accomplishments.

During his last years in the White House, he would use that battle fleet to both political and diplomatic advantage. Yet Roosevelt would find that he could not escape the fate of second-term presidents. Controversy followed controversy, and Roosevelt stood at the center of most. Some tumult, in fact, flowed from his use of his powers as commander in chief, and, perhaps most ironically, the military technology of which he was so interested and proud would prove to be at the center of one major dispute.

7

Battles without Blood

Theodore Roosevelt began 1909 with an annual New Year's Day ritual. He received both the general public and Washington officials at the White House. During the reception he reportedly shook 6,953 hands and still had the energy after hours on the greeting line to pick up and kiss his daughter Ethel and stage a mock round of boxing with sons Archie and Kermit. The atmosphere was festive, and the president was lighthearted.[1] Yet on that day of celebration, Roosevelt took time to dictate a letter to his recently elected successor, William Howard Taft. He was reacting to a bid by Taft's half-brother Charles to become a U.S. senator from Ohio and wanted to assure Taft that his opposition to Charles's campaign stemmed only from his desire to unify the Republican Party behind a candidate who could deny the incumbent, Joseph Foraker, another term. Foraker, a Republican, had emerged as a leading conservative foe, and Roosevelt, with only ill will for Foraker, referred to the senator's "unscrupulousness" and "infamy." The very day that he wrote to Taft, Roosevelt saw his wish granted, when an outmaneuvered Foraker withdrew from the Ohio race. He crowed two weeks later, that "I have gotten the men I went after, Foraker and Tillman."[2] (Sen. Benjamin Tillman of South Carolina was another antagonist.)

By 1909 the animosity between Roosevelt and certain members of Congress ran deeply. In Foraker's case the senator had opposed regulatory legislation and had a close relationship with

Standard Oil. Foraker had also challenged Roosevelt's authority as commander in chief after the president had summarily dismissed black soldiers at Brownsville, Texas, in 1906. The Ohioan had, additionally, dared to present himself as presidential timber in 1908 instead of deferring to Taft, Roosevelt's handpicked choice. The rancor between Foraker and Roosevelt was symptomatic of an increasingly poisonous political atmosphere by 1909. Roosevelt recognized that many on Capitol Hill wanted him to go. He informed Kermit that "Congress of course feels that I will never again have to be reckoned with and that it is safe to be ugly with me."[3] Roosevelt, ever righteous, ascribed base motives to his foes, while congressional opponents resented the president's broad interpretation of executive power. In his last annual message, T.R. had inflamed feelings by asking for the repeal of legislation that restricted the use of the Secret Service to protecting the president and investigating counterfeiters. Roosevelt claimed that "the restriction operates only to the advantage of the criminal, of the wrongdoer," and then in the next sentence suggested that members of Congress might be part of the criminal classes: "The chief argument in favor of the provision was that the Congressmen did not themselves wish to be investigated by Secret Service men." Senators and representatives denounced the president, and this controversy alone defied predictions that the time between Taft's election and nomination would be politically quiet. Roosevelt joked at how "the period of stagnation continues to rage with uninterrupted violence."[4]

In such an environment, opponents in business and on Capitol Hill counted the days until the president's departure on 4 March 1909. As much as he enjoyed holding power, Roosevelt may have done the same on occasion, as he had suffered a number of setbacks during his second term. He had received criticism after a stock market panic in 1907, attacks on his regulatory initiatives, and appeals from the public to reduce the level of political bickering in Washington. Even in that one area of executive authority that he prized so highly, being commander in chief, T.R. would see challenges to his authority and policies that threatened, at times, to undo his labors and his goal of a larger American destiny in the world.

Complications

"Is that strong enough?" Roosevelt fussed to journalist, and later his biographer, Joseph Bucklin Bishop. Political disturbances and financial troubles in the Caribbean nation of Santo Domingo (the Dominican Republic) distressed him. He was writing to Bishop in early 1904 and unhappy that he might have to take action. Roosevelt, as an apostle of civic duty, wanted the Dominicans to take responsibility for their own affairs. He vented to Bishop, "I have been hoping and praying for three months that the Santo Domingans would behave so that I would not have to act in any way. If I possibly can I want to do nothing to them. If it is absolutely necessary to do something, then I want to do as little as possible."[5] In the end, these words served as a preamble to the unveiling of his controversial corollary to the Monroe Doctrine in his annual message of 1904.[6] Disorder of any sort concerned Roosevelt. Political instability and debt in the Dominican Republic alarmed him, for he worried that the disarray might encourage European intervention. To forestall such a scenario, Roosevelt asserted an American police power in the Caribbean. This new policy meant that the United States would become a debt collector and an enforcer of order in Caribbean nations that could no longer meet their international financial obligations. By the time Roosevelt took the oath of office in his own right in 1905, he had placed the Dominicans under American protection and took over their customs houses.

Roosevelt's actions in Santo Domingo set a tone for his second administration. He was happy that his country had taken on the burdens of being a great power. His calls of the 1890s for

an increased American presence in the world, with the attendant benefits of assuming a higher duty, seemed to have been
answered. International involvement also redounded to his personal advantage. Roosevelt would add luster to his standing by
helping to broker a peace between Japan and Russia in 1905 and
by sending American delegates to the Algeciras Conference of
1906. That meeting helped settle a European dispute over influence in Morocco. In the case of the Portsmouth Treaty between
Japan and Russia, Roosevelt received the Nobel Peace Prize, an
honor that left him "profoundly moved and touched."[7] Even
as he enjoyed such recognition, he began to register some disappointment with the American people. Roosevelt had been
pleased in the aftermath of the Spanish-American War about
how many of his countrymen supported taking on imperial
responsibilities in the Philippines and the Caribbean. He realized as his second term advanced that the popular enthusiasm
for imperialism had faded.

Roosevelt lamented, in particular, the shifting public attitude toward the Philippines. He recalled that "in the excitement of the Spanish War people wanted to take the islands," but
by 1907 Americans believed that the islands "are of no value."
This change, he determined, cost the country, returning to a
familiar theme of national duty and honor: "It has been everything for the islands and everything for our own national character that we should have taken them and have administered
them with the really lofty and disinterested efficiency that has
been shown." "But," he went on, "it is impossible . . . to awaken
any public interest in favor of giving them tariff advantages; it
is very difficult to awaken any public interest in providing any
adequate defense of the islands." In short, Roosevelt was feeling the constraints of public opinion, even as he saw the complications and national risk from having assumed great power
responsibilities. For the Philippines, knowing that the country
would not "build the navy and erect the fortifications which

in my judgment it should," Roosevelt talked about the islands forming "our heel of Achilles" and about independence for the islands coming sooner than later.[8] Much of his second term, therefore, would be consumed with marrying American commitments to a realistic assessment of American military power and the limits of public tolerance for expansive policies. Roosevelt would be reluctant to add further obligations, such as in Santo Domingo, for fear of stretching public support and military capabilities too far. He would also work hard to maintain a consensus behind existing overseas interests.

Yet, given the increasingly stormy relationship with members of Congress and the thinness of public patience, managing the domestic politics of military and diplomatic affairs tested Roosevelt's talents. March 1906 brought with charges of massacre and atrocity in the Philippines. As governor of Moro Province, Leonard Wood ordered an assault against a group of restive Moro people in the southern part of the archipelago. Hundreds died, including women and children.[9] Charges flew immediately that the attack had been unnecessary. The Moros had resisted from a volcanic peak, Bud Dajo, so critics argued that a siege would have avoided the slaughter.[10] They also drew comparisons to the massacre of Native Americans at Wounded Knee in South Dakota in 1890. Roosevelt rose swiftly to his old friend's defense. After receiving Wood's version of events, the president responded, "This answer is entirely satisfactory." He went on to praise Wood's command for its "gallant and soldierly feat" and declared that Wood's men were "entitled to the heartiest admiration and praise of all those of their fellow-citizens."[11]

Roosevelt's statement did not end the criticism; rather, it served as an invitation to more. This was not 1902, when T.R. could dismiss accounts of American atrocities as the actions of a few hot-blooded men and avoid a sharp response. Then the Philippine Insurrection had seemed to be at a close, and years of continuing eruptions with the Moros had not yet occurred and thinned the patience of Americans for imperial projects. Members of Congress seized the opportunity to upbraid Roosevelt and blast Wood. One representative was appalled that the president would "attempt to defend such a monstrous outrage." Mississippi's John Sharp Williams threw perhaps the sharpest barbs with a reading of an altered version of "The Charge of the Light Brigade." Now titled "The Charge of the Wood Brigade," the poem made clear Williams's sentiments with lines such as "'Spare not a one,' he said; 'Shoot all six hundred!'"[12]

With Roosevelt as his defender, Wood would weather the storm. Indeed, he retained his recent appointment to command the Philippine Division.[13] The president nonetheless found such controversies harder to fend off in a political climate in which foes sensed a weakness imposed by the passage of time and Roosevelt's vow not to pursue another four years in the White House.

Brownsville

The criticism over the Bud Dajo assault would pale in comparison to the eruption over Roosevelt's handling of the Brownsville affair later in 1906. Charges that African American troops had shot up Brownsville, Texas, sparked a sequence of events that would reveal Roosevelt at his worst: he was arbitrary, inflexible, and unjust. He also gave in to base racial attitudes, angered black supporters, embarrassed himself publicly, and supplied ammunition to political foes. Roosevelt has been praised as an accomplished practitioner of the art of controversy, for he was adept at turning controversies to his political advantage. His conduct in the Brownsville case, however, showed the limits of his skill at turning disputes to his benefit. When his prerogatives as commander in chief, along with his sense of honor, were violated, his self-righteous streak took over and led to a self-inflicted political wound. More important, he denied justice to 167 soldiers when he summarily dismissed them from the service.

The Brownsville matter began in the summer of 1906, after the Twenty-Fifth U.S. Infantry had taken up residence at Fort Brown. The Twenty-Fifth was one of the army's colored units, and white citizens in nearby Brownsville were unhappy with its presence. Texas was part of the segregated South, and in the first years of the twentieth century racial separation had crystalized and the lynching of African Americans hit record numbers.[14] Upon their arrival in Brownsville, the soldiers of the Twenty-Fifth saw clearly the face of Brownsville racism. Local bars refused them service, and they were harassed and threatened in the street. Tensions reached a breaking point during the night of 13 August, when a group of between ten and twenty individuals shot up the town. The attackers killed one man and wounded a police officer. Was the assault the work of the troops or staged by others to cast blame on the soldiers? The townspeople gave their answer in a cable that pleaded for the immediate removal of the black troops from Fort Brown, claiming "our women and children are terrorized and our men are practically under constant alarm and watchfulness."[15]

This message played on the racial assumptions of the day, which were shared by the occupant of the White House. Roosevelt had garnered much favor with African American leaders by meeting with Booker T. Washington during his first months as president in 1901. He had also condemned, repeatedly, the practice of lynching. Yet the president did not transcend the basic attitudes of the day. He, of course, claimed the contrary when it came to executing the duties of the presidency. In the Brownsville case Roosevelt explained, "The action was precisely such as I should have taken had the soldiers guilty of the misconduct been white men instead of colored men."[16] Behind such pronouncements Roosevelt subscribed to the belief that black Americans belonged "to the most utterly undeveloped races of mankind" and were among the "inferior races."[17] Thus when it came to a question of bad behavior on the part of whites or blacks, he believed that blacks were more capable of criminal actions.

This assumption was hardly limited to the president. It ran throughout the army investigation of the Brownsville affair, which reinforced Roosevelt's own attitudes and influenced his decision to dismiss the troops in November 1906. During the incident the white officers at Fort Brown had called out the troops and found all present. Inspection of the soldiers' guns indicated that the weapons were clean and had not been fired. Nonetheless, army investigators assumed a conspiracy of silence on the part of the troops, fastening on the discovery of empty cartridges used by soldiers outside the walls of Fort Brown. The fact that spent army cartridges were readily available to civilian scavengers was not given much credence. After firing drills the unit had collected cartridges that could be recharged and had not secured them.[18] Instead, with the cartridges as evidence, and racial beliefs already indicting the troops, the inspector general of the army recommended that all the troops be dismissed if none would reveal the perpetrators. When no one came forward—perhaps because none of the soldiers had attacked the town—Roosevelt endorsed the inspector general's report and dismissed 167 troopers. They received not a hearing in a military court but summary justice instead.

This decision was one of the most unfortunate that Roosevelt made as president. Even if there had been a conspiracy of silence, then Roosevelt's summary action had denied the accused the full measure of military justice. Roosevelt would claim that "there has been the fullest and most exhaustive investigation." He did not, however, allow the procedures against the men to go further before ordering their dismissal. They were not accorded the formal opportunity of defense allowed in a court-martial. Roosevelt's action was hasty and ill-considered, and it reflected underlying racial bias. Roosevelt denied any prejudice on his part, yet his rush to judgment suggested otherwise.[19]

The violence in Brownsville had raised the specter of civil disorder for the president. He wanted a swift resolution lest a prolonged process of investigation and trial sparked more violence on the part of either whites or blacks. In an era when lynching was so prevalent, Roosevelt understood the incendiary nature of what had happened in Brownsville. The impulse to settle the matter, the fact that finding the troops' innocent would have provoked whites, and the prevailing racial attitudes of the time all combined to make for his summary decision. He worried additionally about order within the military itself. The finding of a "conspiracy of silence" disturbed him, as it challenged the maintenance of discipline. As he put it to Massachusetts governor Curtis Guild Jr., "When the discipline and honor of the American Army are at stake I shall never under any circumstances consider the political bearing of upholding that discipline and that honor."[20] The fact that Roosevelt had waited until after the November 1906 elections to announce the dismissal of the troops had opened him to charges of acting for political reasons and tarnished his claims that high-mindedness had informed his actions. He had apparently feared that an announcement before the midterm elections would adversely affect black Republican turnout at the polls.

Roosevelt's actions in discharging the soldiers of the Twenty-Fifth were certainly flawed and had brought justifiable questioning of his decision. His handling of the criticism in the Brownsville affair would turn a political controversy into a personal political swamp as 1906 turned into 1907. He would perceive attacks on his judgment in the Brownsville case as assaults on his authority as commander in chief and on the purity of his motives. Both were sensitive areas, and irritating them would provoke Roosevelt to hit back. He jealously guarded his prerogatives as head of the armed forces, perhaps more than any other part of his executive power. And questioning his character cut to the core of his self-identity as a moral crusader.

Joseph Foraker emerged as Roosevelt's adversary on Browns-ville. The Ohio senator challenged not only the president's executive authority in the Brownsville case but also Roosevelt's control over the Republican Party's electoral machinery. Foraker possessed a personality that seemed designed to clash directly with Roosevelt's own self-assuredness and militancy. In 1897 a *New York Times* editorial, which detailed Foraker's opposi-tion to political appointments made at the start of the McKin-ley administration, described Foraker's "incandescent state of mind," explaining that "he has been outraged to frenzy" by one particular appointment.[21] The strength of the senator's feelings on the Brownsville affair became apparent in Decem-ber 1906, when the president's annual message was to be read before the Senate. Traditionally, the annual message was the first item introduced, but Senator Foraker and Sen. Boies Penrose of Pennsylvania violated that precedent by submitting, first, res-olutions for an investigation into the dismissal of the troops at Brownsville. The press observed that these resolutions signaled an "immediate opening of hostilities between the Senate and the Executive."[22]

Indeed they did, for the president chose to respond directly to the resolution. The measure had formally been directed to Secretary of War Taft as a request for information, but Roos-evelt himself fired back. His blunt words would hardly soften feelings. In a message delivered on 19 December, Roosevelt immediately dismissed doubts about the culpability of the sol-diers, even though his reasoning was based on supposition. He claimed, for example, that the noncommissioned officers in the unit must have known about the rampage beforehand, as they were responsible for the gun racks. The culprits, he continued, could have fired their guns and gotten back to the barracks because of the two-and-a-half-block distance involved. Despite the president's assertions, the army inquiry had provided nei-ther proof of the noncommissioned officers' foreknowledge nor evidence of soldiers running back to the fort. Roosevelt apparently could not admit to the possibility of the soldiers' innocence. To do so not only would risk inflaming white opinion but would mean reversing himself after taking a stand. Instead, he asserted, "The townspeople were completely surprised by the unprovoked and murderous savagery of the attack. The soldiers were the aggressors from start to finish."[23] He argued that the soldiers were getting off lightly with dismissal, for "the punishment for mutineers and murderers such as those guilty of the Brownsville assault is death. . . . I would that it were possible for me to have punished the guilty men." As for the men who had served long and distinguished careers, Roosevelt informed his readers that they deserved the least sympathy, "for they are the very men upon whom we should be able especially to rely to prevent mutiny and murder."[24]

The president was overwrought and, rather than quiet matters, he had provided ammunition for Senator Foraker's next volley. Having his judgment questioned in a public forum had triggered Roosevelt's outburst, but a perception that his actions as commander in chief were being challenged arrested his political judgment further. In his answer to the congressional request, Roosevelt made a point of saying that it was within his right to dismiss the men summarily: "Be it remembered always that these men were all in the service of the United States under contracts of enlistment which by their terms and by statute were terminable by my direction as Commander in Chief of the Army."[25]

Senator Foraker leaped into this opening. On 20 December the Ohio senator rose to refute the president's claims. He identified weaknesses in the evidence against the discharged soldiers, describing one report as "only a lot of loose, unsworn statements, utterly flimsy, insufficient and unreliable in character." Taking direct aim at the president, Foraker challenged Roosevelt's contention that he had the authority to dismiss the soldiers. "Inasmuch as the men were charged with the crimes of murder, misprision of a felony and perjury," Foraker argued, "all of which they had denied under oath, they were entitled to a hearing before conviction and punishment."[26] In other words, the senator was claiming that Roosevelt had misconstrued and exceeded his authority as commander in chief. With the lines of dispute drawn, the stage had been set for a personal, public confrontation between senator and president. The display would serve only to diminish Roosevelt's stature.[27]

The spectacle would be a debate between a U.S. president and a U.S. senator. The Gridiron dinner of 26 January 1907 was the setting. Gridiron Club dinners had been a regular part of the Washington scene since 1885. At these affairs politicians and journalists engaged in an evening of good-natured jests. The occasion was intended "solely for fun and to make people forget 'shop' for one evening."[28] The 1907 Gridiron dinner would be dramatically different in tone. Speaker of the House Joseph Cannon captured the nature of the event when he reportedly quipped, "What in hell can I say about this mess?"[29]

The president of the United States was the chief disrupter. Roosevelt came to the dinner with little patience for gibes. Instead, when he rose to give remarks, it was Roosevelt the preacher militant who stood, and he was an irritated preacher at that. The object of his anger was the senior senator from Ohio. Roosevelt did not like the prospect of having his judgment on Brownsville second-guessed by senators in hearings that were soon to begin. As far as he was concerned, he had already settled the matter as commander in chief, and he declared that any Senate action was "academic." The authority for making such decisions was vested solely in him, he claimed, and no one else had the power to review his decision to dismiss the men.[30]

Because the president's comments, described as a "speech of biting sarcasm," had obviously been aimed at Foraker, the senator took the opportunity to respond. Although pale after the unexpected presidential assault, Foraker did not flinch as he "hurled back the gratuitous flings at himself and the Senate."[31] More precisely, Foraker lectured Roosevelt that what was occurring in the Senate was not academic, which the upcoming hearings would demonstrate. No discussion affecting the constitutional rights of all citizens, he argued, could be dismissed as merely theoretical. Foraker also blasted Roosevelt for discharging men without cause and thereby possibly violating the law. Roosevelt, contrary to his own view, Foraker railed, was not above the law.

The senator's remarks hit home, for it was clear to all that the president could barely restrain himself while the senator spoke. It was also apparent that the diners were on Foraker's side, for when he concluded many applauded and others rushed to congratulate him. According to reports, cheers continued for the senator well after a visibly angry Roosevelt jumped up to respond.[32] All decorum now gone, the president declared, "Some of those men were bloody butchers; they ought to be hung. . . . It is my business and the business of nobody else. It is not the business of Congress. . . . If they pass a resolution to reinstate these men, I will veto it; if they pass it over my veto, I will pay no attention to it. I welcome impeachment."[33] Following this rant, the spirit of the night completely spoiled, Roosevelt left quickly, and the Gridiron dinner broke up soon thereafter.

The confrontation between president and senator was the talk of Washington in the days that followed, and no account favored Roosevelt.[34] He was saved from complete embarrassment by a Gridiron tradition prohibiting the publication of exact remarks, but, as it was, much of what he said came out, and he had come across as both arrogant and embattled. Nothing could have served Foraker better. In fact, Roosevelt had weakened his case about his handling of the Brownsville affair just as the Senate was about to begin hearings. His ability to use controversy to good effect had broken down on this occasion. Deeply felt emotion had apparently undermined his political judgment. Roosevelt had acted in an environment in which his political foes were circling as his time as president had begun to wane. His natural inclination was to lash back, but he was, perhaps, especially vehement because his conduct as commander in chief, a role in which he had invested much feeling, had come into question. To him, being commander in chief was not just one of the duties of his office; it was very much part of his personal identity. In this role Roosevelt could be at his most vigorous, in a position to create action without the other restraints that often tied the president's hands. Now a senator whom he disdained was questioning his power and judgment as head of the armed forces, and this challenge triggered his most combative instincts.

Feelings aside, Foraker had Roosevelt at a disadvantage. The president had dismissed troops without allowing due process under the articles of war. Although Roosevelt announced after the heated Gridiron Club exchange that "I should absolutely disregard anything except my own convictions," he eventually proposed what he thought would be a face-saving expedient. Dismissed soldiers could be reinstated if they could prove their innocence. This measure would accomplish nothing for the discharged men, for they were being asked to prove a negative, as Sen. Charles Fulton, Republican of Oregon, pointed out. Foraker, supporting this view, claimed that the burden of proving guilt should rest with the government.[35] The matter basically dragged on in this manner through the remainder of Roosevelt's presidency. T.R. tried to find some way to put the issue to rest, while Senator Foraker fought to keep the matter alive.

The Brownsville affair would remain an open wound for Roosevelt, but not a mortal injury. It did not prevent the election of his chosen successor, William Howard Taft, who, by virtue of being Roosevelt's secretary of war, was automatically associated with the controversy. The affair did damage relations with African Americans. In Richmond, Virginia, the press reported

meetings among black residents to denounce President Roosevelt after the discharges were announced. News accounts also
relayed how "in several social clubs and other public places
portraits of the President have been taken down or turned
face to the wall. This is being done also in the homes of the
negroes."[36] In contrast, pictures of Senator Foraker were sell-
ing briskly. This upsetting of a traditional Republican Party
constituency did not, however, end up in a significant electoral shift, given the racial attitudes and discriminatory practices of the time and given the principal association of the
Democratic Party in the South with the disenfranchisement
of African Americans.

As a result, Roosevelt paid a heavier price for his conduct
in history than at the time. The major blemish to his historical
standing would come in later decades, after views on race had
shifted and after writers such as John Weaver and Ann Lane published treatments of the Brownsville affair in the early 1970s.[37]
Senator Foraker paid the immediate political penalty. Roosevelt
began to spurn his patronage requests and to support Rep. Theodore Burton for Foraker's Senate seat in the 1908 election. Presidential opposition and questionable ties to the Standard Oil
Company doomed Foraker. Accepting the inevitable, the senator acceded to Burton's candidacy.[38] The discharged soldiers
paid the highest price. A military commission was authorized to
examine the cases of the discharged men two days before Roosevelt left office in 1909. The soldiers would be allowed to testify, but, again, could win reenlistment only if they could prove
their innocence. Furthermore, the retired generals who composed the commission were likely to favor the president's position from the outset. As a result, the commission, after a year's
worth of hearings, refused to hear all the men who wished to
present their cases and seemed most inclined to entertain evidence that would incriminate, rather than exonerate, the soldiers. In the end, this commission found that soldiers had shot

up the town and stood by the discharges in all but fourteen cases. Justice would have to await different times.[39]

In 1972 the troopers were cleared of all charges. This righting of Roosevelt's wrong came too late to be of effective meaning to the men discharged, but it did correct the historical record and cast fresh attention on the twenty-sixth president's prejudices and his intemperate reaction when others challenged his personal sense of righteousness by preaching at him from higher moral ground.

Defects

The Brownsville affair and Senator Foraker aggravated Roosevelt, but they amounted to only one measure of trouble compared to what he would confront in the fall of 1907. In October a Wall Street panic began. Presidents have little actual leverage over the economy, and, being primarily political animals, few chief executives are prepared to deal with the intricacies of finance, production, and trade. Yet if the economy tumbles, they are likely to be a target of public ire, given their prominent position. Such was certainly the case with Roosevelt, who had displayed an inability to deal well with his personal finances. The panic of 1907 began out of an attempt to corner the copper market and soon led to the collapse of the venerable Knickerbocker Trust of New York. Knickerbocker's fall sent shock waves through the financial sector, and credit began to dry up.[40] Headlines tracked the mounting anxiety and reported how the great barons of capital, such as John D. Rockefeller, pledged, "to do my part to the full extent of my resources" to restore confidence.[41] Roosevelt, who had been hunting in Louisiana when the panic broke, offered a convenient target for blame. Echoing others, one critic declared, "It is a Roosevelt panic we have been having. A financial condition brought about by the Roosevelt policy. For two years under Roosevelt we have had a persistent policy of destruction."[42] The "policy of destruction" referred to trust-busting, which supposedly hurt the business climate. "Roosevelt panic" was a label that particularly struck at the president's popular standing.

Roosevelt, however, already had plans underway for an event that would generate favorable headlines. The feat for which he was preparing had never before been attempted in American naval history. Sixteen battleships were going to sail as a single force to the Pacific Ocean. Later Roosevelt would inform the public of an even more spectacular gesture. The fleet would return to the Atlantic via the long route. American sailors would enter the Pacific through the Strait of Magellan at the tip of South America, but they would get back to the United States only after an extended cruise around the world. Journalists greeted the news with lines that leaped off the page: "Score of Battleships Soon to Start for San Francisco" and "Monster Naval Display."[43] For Roosevelt the coming battleship cruise supplied a welcome distraction at a time when political and economic difficulties increasingly challenged him.

The cruise would serve several purposes. Militarily, Roosevelt had already been a good Mahanian by developing fleet formations. The new naval organization had now "reached the period when it is advisable to send the whole fleet on a practice cruise around the world," and for Roosevelt such a trial run was better in peace than in war: "The one thing that I won't run the risk of is to experiment for the first time in a matter of vital importance in time of war." War was very much on T.R.'s mind, and fear of an impending conflict did much to dictate the timing of the fleet cruise. Although the navy had been contemplating the exercise for nearly two years, strains in Japanese-American relations prompted Roosevelt to act. America at the turn of the twentieth century was a racially segregated nation, and African Americans were not the only group to suffer exclusion. When the San Francisco School Board mandated the segregation of Japanese, Chinese, and Korean students, the effect rippled across the

Pacific, and the Japanese erupted over the discrimination. Roosevelt tried to calm feelings but also wanted to impress Japan with American strength. He analyzed the situation succinctly for Henry Cabot Lodge in July 1907: "I shall continue to do everything I can by politeness and consideration to the Japs to offset the worse than criminal stupidity of the San Francisco mob. . . . I do not believe we shall have war; but it is no fault of the yellow press if we do not have it. The Japanese seem to have about the same proportion of prize jingo fools that we have."[44] Roosevelt's favorite African proverb guided his approach to handling the tension with Japan. He spoke softly with diplomacy designed to soothe and brandished a big stick of sixteen American battleships. Roosevelt was certain that the deployment would "have a pacific effect to show that it can be done."[45]

These objectives for the fleet cruise were the ones Roosevelt stated publicly. There were others that went unannounced. The dispatch of the battleships was a public relations event of the first order, a culmination of all the fleet reviews that Roosevelt had organized since he had been assistant secretary of the navy. He was ready to seize full political advantage. The cruise would help advance the cause of American sea power, for the public could see on display—and celebrated around the world—the result of years of investment. In addition, the cruise would publicize the need for the interoceanic canal in Panama. With the completion of the canal years away, the transit of the fleet around South America would remind the American public of the dash of the USS *Oregon* from the Pacific to Cuban waters during the Spanish-American War. As the London *Morning Post* predicted, "when the fleet reaches the Pacific the inhabitants of the East will begin to realize that it is very far off, and will become very anxious to see the Panama Canal completed. The West also lament the distance of the sea voyage separating it from the East, and will be eager to shorten it by opening the isthmus."[46]

Beyond such large-scale goals Roosevelt had a more immediate political purpose in mind. He did not state this objective outright, but it was obvious to all observers. The *Morning Post* discerned it soon after word arrived of the cruise: "Both the Eastern and Western populations will wish to have the battle ships on their own coast. Accordingly the East and West alike will be willing to vote the money for the construction of another eighteen battleships as well as for the Isthmian Canal."[47] The *Post's* numbers were high, but the paper's analysis was correct. Roosevelt wanted more battleships, especially because Great Britain's all-big-gun *Dreadnought* had made the ships on the world cruise obsolete. Roosevelt wanted Congress to spend more on dreadnoughts and, more important, to overthrow the one-ship-per-year replacement policy that he had announced in 1905. He was going to request the authorization of four battleships for the coming fiscal year. The public spectacle of a fleet cruise would give him ammunition to counter members of Congress wary of escalating naval costs.

If Roosevelt required any reminder that he faced an uphill struggle in breaking the one-ship policy, Sen. Eugene Hale of Maine, the strong-willed chair of the Senate Naval Affairs Committee, skeptic of imperial expansion and foe of Roosevelt's naval policy, refreshed the president's memory after the announcement of the battleship cruise. Hale was doubtful of the value of the deployment. He saw it as a ploy on the part of the General Board of the U.S. Navy to win more funding. As Hale put it, "The scheme had its birth with the general board of the navy, which for three or four years, in order to magnify the navy, exploited a war scare with Germany. When the people got tired of this they tried the same performance with Japan."[48]

Such statements by Hale, combined with a more private threat to deny funds for the additional coal that would be required, caused a round of presidential venting against the senator.[49] In his typical fashion Roosevelt labeled Hale, just like anyone who seriously opposed him, to be lacking in character and manliness. The president informed one confidant that Hale was an "arrant physical coward" and another that he was a "conscienceless voluptuary, and in his private affairs . . . he is as astute as he is unscrupulous."[50] Hale was anything but what the overheated Roosevelt had claimed. Rather, the editors of Roosevelt's own papers later described the senator as "stern, controlled, and honest"—hardly a conscienceless voluptuary.[51] As usual, Roosevelt's fulminations remained out of public view, and once a more sober frame of mind returned, he would have known that he had outmaneuvered Hale. The senator could not stop the naval spectacular unless he wanted to strand the battleship fleet on the West Coast. Hale had certainly perceived that the cruise was, in part, about securing more battleships, but there was little that he could do to halt it.[52]

For Roosevelt this victory over Hale must have been gratifying. Amid the eruptions between himself and his foes in Congress, the fact that his authority as commander in chief had not been clipped on the battleship deployment would have satisfied his need to act. More and more he seemed to confront restraints on his influence, yet in the naval realm that meant so much to him, he was going to be able to accomplish a political coup and a meaningful military and diplomatic exercise. Thus, Roosevelt's shock would be doubled when two trusted naval aides complicated his grand plan just after the battleship cruise commenced in December 1907.

The sixteen battleships of the Atlantic fleet passed Cape Henry, Virginia, at 11:25 a.m. on 16 December. The ships, carrying fourteen thousand sailors, began the first leg of the 14,394-mile journey to San Francisco "with a smooth sea and blue sky." Thousands lined the shore to cheer the ships on, waving flags and handkerchiefs.[53] All portents for the voyage seemed favorable. Roosevelt did not appear to want to let it go alone. The presidential yacht, *Mayflower*, stayed with the fleet after it reached the open sea, as if the commander in chief were tempted to accompany it to the Pacific.[54] Five days later he was in Washington when a sensational article appeared charging that the battleships that crowds had just applauded suffered from potentially devastating defects.

Henry Reuterdahl was a marine artist but also the American editor of *Jane's Fighting Ships.* When he wrote about battleships, his words commanded attention. In *McClure's Magazine* that December he dropped a bomb on Roosevelt's celebration of sea power. *McClure's Magazine* had already given voice to muckrakers with articles on the Standard Oil monopoly and other problems in early twentieth-century America. Reuterdahl's piece, "The Needs of Our Navy," would live up to that sensationalist heritage. He would charge that American battleships, the ones that had just departed for the Pacific, contained potentially fatal flaws in the placement of protective armor belts, the height of guns, the design of ammunition hoists and turrets, and the armor around secondary gun batteries. The article made all kinds of eye-catching statements, such as "the American navy is unprepared for war," "A fleet with Main Armor under Water," and "The Danger from Exploding Shells." In making these charges, Reuterdahl was obviously taking full advantage of the publicity accompanying the fleet cruise. His main purpose was to restart efforts to overhaul the Navy Department bureaucracy, on which he heaped responsibility for design defects in one class of ship after another. As Reuterdahl put it, "How is it possible that blunders of these proportions can be perpetuated? The answer to this is simply that no human being is responsible for this thing. It is done by a system—an organization so constituted that its very nature compels it to perpetuate mistakes."[55]

Reuterdahl's charges were not original with him, nor was the article particularly new. According to Sims biographer, Elting Morison, William S. Sims and Reuterdahl had spent much time together, and Sims had readily supplied a list of complaints about both American battleships and the Navy Department bureaucracy. Reuterdahl had summarized these arguments in draft form in 1904, but Sims was unwilling to see them published. By 1907 he was ready for them to be revealed, worried that reform had not yet come to the Navy Department and the end of Roosevelt's presidency was in sight. In good muckraking fashion Reuterdahl and Sims wanted to shock the public at a time when the battleship fleet was featured in the news. The public was a chief target, but so was the occupant of the White House.[56]

Roosevelt exploded when he heard of Reuterdahl's article. He wrote to Secretary of the Navy Victor Metcalf in early January 1908, and the tone of his letter suggested that he was barely able to contain his anger. He informed the secretary that

> There always are and always will be defects to correct both in the construction of ships and in the organization of the Department and in the actual drill of the fleet. It is well that these defects should be pointed out, but it is also well that they should be pointed out without hysterical exaggeration or malicious untruthfulness. . . . The officers of the navy who are guilty of such conduct deserve grave rebuke. They cast discredit upon the service and their conduct is deeply mortifying to every American who believes in the navy and is anxious to uphold its interest and honor.[57]

The outburst was vintage Roosevelt. He was upset, but the language was particularly strong because the officer in question, Sims, although favored by the president, had breached Roosevelt's sense of proper discipline at a particularly sensitive time. Not only was Roosevelt promoting the launch of the world cruise and fighting for the authorization of four more battleships, but the good order of the navy and his judgment had also recently been challenged by another naval officer. Rear Adm. Willard Brownson had been chief of the Bureau of Navigation in the Navy Department until just before the end of December 1907. At that time Admiral Brownson resigned rather than implement an order of the president. When Roosevelt had decided that a medical officer, rather than an officer of the line, should command the hospital ship *Relief*, Brownson determined that he no longer held the president's confidence and stepped down. The resignation soon became a matter of press speculation, especially as it revealed infighting among the Navy Department bureaus and raised questions about a presidential decision.[58] One admiral reportedly grumbled, "Think of a sawbones commanding a naval vessel!"[59] The *Washington Post* also charged that Roosevelt had favored the medical bureau because his family physician was Presley M. Rixey, the chief of the navy's Bureau of Medicine and Surgery.[60]

Given this environment, Roosevelt's anger at Sims was hardly surprising. The president had welcomed criticism of the navy in the past, but in private, not public. Indeed, Roosevelt would have naval officers to dinner and would then sometimes retire to his library for special conferences, which, according to Sims, "were free and open. He invited criticism. In fact, he distrusted those who did not criticise, even some of his own actions."[61]

Sims understood that he had crossed a line with the Reuterdahl article and that Roosevelt's continued support was crucial to his personal professional fortunes and ideas for naval reform. Navy regulations stated that officers were not to publish information about governmental actions on their own, and Sims received a letter from the Navy Department in February 1908 asking him what role, if any, he had played in the Reuterdahl piece. A case was evidently going to be made against him, and Sims needed the president at his side if he were to deflect charges of insubordination. Fortunately for him, Sims possessed natural advantages when it came to placating Roosevelt. He was the president's man in many ways. Sims's rise was a product of Roosevelt's campaign for naval improvement, and the two men shared a similar wit, crusader instinct, and sharp intellect. He was one of those individuals Roosevelt had inserted in high places to act as an ally. Moreover, Sims benefited from direct access to the president as his naval aide, and his standing was helped by the fact that he was married to Margaret Hitchcock, the daughter of the secretary of the interior.[62] He would play on all these factors to restore himself to favor.

After he received the Navy Department letter, Sims exploited his position to speak directly with the president. He knew just which chords to strike: he was forthright, he was humorous, and he played on the president's own history of stepping outside the rules for a worthy cause. According to Sims, he took the Navy Department letter to Roosevelt and asked, "What do you think of that, Mr. President?" According to Sims, Roosevelt replied, "What! . . . Haven't you been insubordinate?" At that moment Sims had the mental agility to turn Roosevelt around with one riposte. "There have been others. . . . What about the 'round-robin'?" With that one line Sims disarmed the president, who laughed at the recollection of his own conduct during the Cuba expedition. Sims had played well on Roosevelt's tendency to look for himself in others. How could he let punishment of Sims proceed when in the past he had gotten away with insubordinate conduct for a just cause? Roosevelt also did not want to lose a leading agent for naval reform, so he called for Secretary of the Navy Metcalf and instructed him to halt any action against Sims. He reminded the secretary that the Senate was investigating the Reuterdahl charges and that no witnesses in that probe were to face action.[63]

The Senate investigation would work to Roosevelt's advantage. It would allow him to turn a difficult situation into gain. His political astuteness, so badly absent during the Brownsville affair, was again evident when he defied public perceptions of his outspokenness. Theodore Roosevelt knew in this case to be quiet and practice the art of political silence.

Eugene Hale presided over the hearings. For Hale, the inquiry was intended to preserve the status quo in the navy. He was no friend of naval reformers like Sims and their agenda of installing a naval general staff. Rather, he treated the hearings as a means to reassure the public about the competence of the existing navy bureaus, the quality of ship design, and the unfounded nature of Reuterdahl's charges. Thus, the hearings were not a friendly forum for Sims and his supporters. The tone of the hearings was set on the first day, 25 February 1908, when the Senate Naval Affairs Committee called Rear Adm. George A. Converse to testify. Converse was the head of the navy's Board on Construction, and he defended the ship designs before a sympathetic audience. Upon adjournment for the day, Sen. George Perkins of California apologized to Converse and another officer, Rear Adm. Washington Capps, who was the chief constructor of the navy as head of the Bureau of Construction and Repair. Perkins offered, "We ought to apologize to you for calling upon you to refute such an article as this." Senator Hale followed immediately with "that's true. . . . It was written in such a vein that a layman could not understand how absurd the charges are."[64]

In that climate the cause of naval administrative reform stood no chance. The senators permitted no testimony on the problems of naval administration and allowed Rear Admiral Capps to cross-examine witnesses critical of present designs. When charges of a whitewash began to appear, the committee abruptly ended the hearings before public pressure forced it to consider administrative issues.[65]

Although Roosevelt would have been loath to admit it, events played out as well as he could have hoped. The public heard a defense about the quality of American battleship construction, even though the hearings were biased against naval reform. The Senate inquiry therefore served to tamp down that controversy. Hale and other members of Congress staved off Navy Department reform, a fight that Roosevelt did not desire at the time. The last thing he wanted was to anger senators when something he cared about much more deeply—additional battleships and breaking out of the one-ship-per-year policy—was soon coming up for a vote. Indeed, Roosevelt celebrated in April 1908 when Congress approved two of the four battleships that he had requested. Not that the fight had been easy, as he informed Henry White, the American ambassador to France: "I knew I would not get thru two . . . unless I made a violent fight for four." Indeed, Roosevelt had to threaten a veto of the bill to get the two-ship program. T.R. was particularly jubilant because Congress had agreed to break the one-ship policy. He exulted that "they [Congress] have now, as a result of the fight, announced as a steady policy that of building two ships a year—a great gain."[66] As a result, the United States could keep pace with other nations in the construction of dreadnoughts.

The cost had been the abandonment of Sims and other reformers. Roosevelt made a choice, and naval administrative reform was not at the top of his list and never would be when more battleships were at stake. Moreover, politically he could rally people behind such obvious symbols of national power as battleships, whereas too many interests were invested in maintaining the existing structure of the Navy Department. T.R. felt that he could not have both, so for him the natural choice was battleships. Where he especially let the reformers down was his silence toward them. He did not inform Sims and his fellow "insurgents," as they fashioned themselves, that a naval general staff would have to wait in line behind battleship authorizations. They were left to figure it out for themselves. One of Sims's close comrades in the reform camp, Cdr. Albert L. Key, discerned as much when he wrote in April 1908, "The thing I am disappointed in and practically hopeless about is the attitude of the President."[67]

In pushing changes to naval administration, the reformers had read their man only partly right. Theodore Roosevelt was their best hope for reform, but Roosevelt did not like their tactics: "I became convinced that Sims, Key, Winslow, and the other junior officers had greatly exaggerated the defects of which they complained."[68] His natural inclination was for change without disorder, and sensational pieces such as the Reuterdahl exposé offended his conservative instincts. As Elting Morison put it, Roosevelt "had excused the publication of Reuterdahl's article, but he never did approve of it."[69]

The president may have looked forward to building more all-big-gun battleships, but if he thought that the frustrated reformers would not disturb that process then he was fooling himself. By forgiving Sims the transgression of the Reuterdahl article, Roosevelt had provided a license for more reformer charges against the inefficient structure of the Navy Department. This time Sims and his allies worked within the navy and did not publish a muckraking article, but they struck against the new pride of the fleet, the dreadnoughts getting ready to take their place in the naval line. The Reuterdahl piece had criticized the older mixed-battery ships, but charges of defects in the newest of ships was bound to concern the president. Also such news could not remain in the confines of the Navy Department and would surely leak to the press. Commander Key initiated action when he informed the Navy Department of serious design flaws in the battleship *North Dakota*, which he had personally inspected at its construction site.[70] Key's critique did not provoke a response from the Navy Department, so William Sims took advantage of his access as presidential naval aide and laid the matter directly in Theodore Roosevelt's lap in June 1908.[71]

This time Sims and Key received a promising reaction from the White House. The criticism of the *North Dakota* unnerved Roosevelt. In saying that the earlier charges about battleship defects had been exaggerated, he also confessed that he been "left with the very uncomfortable feeling that there might be some real defects, and I want if possible to avoid any slip-up."[72] In other words, Roosevelt fretted that if defects had been possible in the design of the previous generation of battleships, then it was likely that the same process had produced flaws in the coming line of dreadnoughts. He would not tolerate similar problems with ships that were a symbol of his commitment to sea power. Also he could not afford another public controversy over design defects. The president therefore took the advice of Sims and ordered a conference at the Naval War College in Newport, Rhode Island, that would bring designers together with seagoing officers, and the general board of the navy, to render "an opinion as to whether any or all of these defects can be wholly or partially remedied, and particularly a recommendation as to all of the military characteristics which should be required in the battleships to be built in the immediate future."[73]

The calling of a conference, soon to be known as the Newport Conference, was by 1908 a typical action for Roosevelt. Already in his presidency T.R. had assembled commissions on public-land use, inland waterway improvements, and governmental operations.[74] These bodies joined diverse interests and experts, which not only supplied useful advice but also provided the political momentum needed to advance on matters where different groups competed. Roosevelt resorted to a similar approach with the navy. Ever sensitive to the impact of headlines and after the uproar over ship design of the past winter, he was going to anticipate any problems by taking early action. That way he could assure the public as to the quality of American ships and sustain support for a building program of two battleships per year.

The chance of a new eruption over design defects was indeed threatening even as the Newport Conference prepared to convene. On 21 July 1908, the day before the meeting opened, Henry Reuterdahl blasted the naval bureaus in a newspaper interview. The critic declared that the current officers in charge of ship construction had "learned modern man-of-warring in the old tin pot squadron" and "had little or no experience on board the present type of modern ships." Reuterdahl also predicted "the end of the entire bureau system." He concluded that in other countries, "if proof had been offered that millions . . . had been thoughtlessly and foolishly spent, official heads would have fallen."[75]

Reuterdahl may have established himself as a muckraking sensation, but in this case he was running directly counter to a masterful politician. Roosevelt knew well how to use his high office to generate publicity and shift attention from claims such as Reuterdahl's. He had determined earlier that he would put his stamp on the proceedings by opening them in person. But his mission was not to dismantle the Navy Department bureaucracy, as Reuterdahl wanted.[76] Rather, Roosevelt's goals were quite different. His public aim was to shore up confidence in his naval policies and in the competence of the Navy Department. In private he wanted to make sure that seagoing and bureau officers actually worked together to produce the best ships possible and reduce the unseemly bickering between them.

Roosevelt arrived at Newport at 9:45 a.m. on 22 July, after an eventful night sail from Oyster Bay. The *Mayflower* had run down a lumber schooner in foggy conditions and had to rescue the six-man crew. After a welcoming ceremony Roosevelt delivered his public address to the conference of officers and gave a "stirring appeal" for a large navy. Rousing as it may have been, the speech was filled with his usual platitudes about the need for a battleship navy and the ability to hit hard in case of war. Or, as Roosevelt put it, "No fight was ever won yet except by hitting, and the one unforgivable offense in any man is to hit soft."[77] Later, when he met with the conference without the press present, his tone became stern. Reportedly, he told the conference to fix any defects and to give more heed to the ideas of seagoing officers in battleship designs. He was serving notice that he would no longer tolerate the kind of intramural arguments and the pigeonholing of ideas that had been occurring.[78]

Roosevelt got one of the prizes that he craved from Newport. The calling of the conference itself, and his presence during the opening day, helped to allay concerns about the quality of American battleships. Rather than eye-catching stories about design flaws, the coverage of the first session and the days that followed built confidence in the actions being taken. For example, a story in the *Washington Post* in September 1908 noted how the president had approved plans, forwarded to him after his departure from Newport, about the newly authorized *Florida* and *Utah*. The paper perceived that Roosevelt, in approving these plans, had not been "deeply impressed with the arguments of the critics."[79] This perception would prove to be wrong. The sense conveyed to the public, however, was one of resolution: decisions had been made, and the president had taken action on any design issues. Full attention could now switch back to the progress of the world cruise.

Behind the pleasing public facade the Newport Conference did not prove particularly satisfactory to Roosevelt. By nature a conference was bound to produce compromises and not always the best ones. Roosevelt fumed in private about the dreadnought designs he had just approved. The conference had made minor corrections to the *North Dakota* but deemed it too far along to make major changes.[80] As for the *Utah* and *Florida*, Roosevelt felt that those ships could have been "much more formidable than will actually be the case," if the officials responsible for planning them had sought out earlier the ideas of "the younger officers of the type presented at the Newport Conference." He went on to complain that "the officials responsible for these ships seem to have limited themselves to the desire not to lag far behind other nations instead of doing what they ought to have done; that is tried to lead other nations." Yet despite believing that the navy suffered from "a certain woodenness of administration, to a lack of initiative and flexibility," Roosevelt was not about to reject the majority viewpoint from a conference he had called.[81]

By summoning experts and putting his personal stamp on their proceedings, he had boxed himself in and could only grumble about an imperfect result.[82]

The Newport Conference had also failed to bring anything more than a temporary truce between the bureaus and the reform party led by Sims. Reformers remained unhappy that the conference brought no momentum to their cause of departmental reform, and bureau officers still had to deal with the reformers' agitation.[83] Further controversy was inevitable and, from Roosevelt's point of view, would bring more distraction as he worked to get two more dreadnoughts authorized before he left office in March 1909.

Trouble came first from the bureau side of the table. The chief constructor of the navy, Rear Admiral Capps, took aim at the reformers in a speech to Naval Academy alumni in Chicago on 23 November 1908. Capps labeled the reformers "persons of no consequence" and used letters from Adm. George Dewey and other notables to bolster his case.[84] Roosevelt was not about to tolerate an unseemly back-and-forth between bureau advocates and reformers, so three days after Capps's speech he ordered a curtain of silence to descend on discussions of naval policy. He directed Secretary of the Navy Metcalf to issue an order "that under no circumstances is any officer to discuss before the public, or to give any information directly or indirectly concerning it, any question of naval policy" without first receiving permission from the secretary or the president. Any officer who disobeyed his order would "be held to account."[85] That order was still not enough, so when a second attack by Capps in his annual report for 1908 sent charges flying between the admiral and Sims's ally, Commander Key, Roosevelt showed what he meant by being "held to account." He condemned Capps's actions as "gravely reprehensible" and "grave misconduct," and he stripped the admiral of his duties as acting chief of the Bureau of Steam Engineering. Roosevelt also sent a message to the reformers, informing Key "that the backbiting, and attacks, and counterattacks . . . are to the last degree detrimental to the public service," and he threatened court-martial proceedings against both Capps and Key.[86]

Roosevelt had finally used his proverbial big stick to suppress the discord in the Navy Department. He likely did not do so earlier given the heat of publicity when the defects controversy had first ignited. To have acted against Sims, Key, and other reformers, or their bureau critics, would have invited further press scrutiny into the conduct of naval affairs just when Roosevelt was making a hard fight for four battleships. Also his affinity for Sims and Key restrained his hand as far as they were concerned. In the intervening year Roosevelt had gradually steered the reformer-bureau contest back into being an internal navy matter, which gave him a freer hand to deal with dissent. Thus, when it came to be a matter of good discipline and contravention of his orders, Roosevelt's instinct to act was aroused, and he moved swiftly to slap down Capps and Key. He took this measure to promote a larger goal on which he "had set my heart": the authorization of two more dreadnoughts.[87] The House approved on 22 January 1909. Passage in the Senate seemed likely, in spite of the poisonous relations with the White House, for Senator Hale conceded that with the world cruise "the whole country is convulsed with a fury and fever in favor of the navy."[88]

Although his priorities were set on securing more battleships, the president did not completely abandon faith with the advocates of Navy Department reform. His words to Key had been harsh, but Roosevelt wanted to go on record as at least having supported the overhaul of a department into which he had poured over $900 million.[89] If not a matter of top interest to him, retooling the naval bureaucracy was a matter of principle. He had stood for military preparation and for the Progressive ideal of greater efficiency, and he wanted the navy to have a general staff much as had been created for the army in 1903. It was also a matter of legacy. With his presidency coming to a close in March 1909, there was no chance Congress would act on naval administrative reform before then, but he wanted a template for change on the record. He could say he had tried, and he could leave the work to his handpicked successor.

In December 1908 he embraced a plan offered by his sixth, and final, secretary of the navy, Truman Newberry. The Newberry plan did not go far in changing the Navy Department, and Roosevelt's approval of it was provisional. In fact, he offered Newberry's plan as another tactical maneuver to quiet concerns over naval administration while he pushed his bill for battleship authorizations. The only upshot of this initiative was a conclave in January 1909 of former navy secretaries, retired senior officers, and active rear admirals. Formally labeled the Washington Naval Conference but later dubbed a "fine array of ancient mariners," this assembly merely endorsed Newberry's plan and adjourned.[90] Only after congressional passage of additional battleships did Roosevelt become serious and appoint a commission under former navy secretary William Moody. Acting with dispatch, because so little time remained in the president's term, the Moody Commission formulated a plan for a thorough overhaul of departmental organization. The Moody plan became the basis for an "aid" system of advisers during the Taft administration. (The word "aid" rather than "aide" was preferred by Taft's navy secretary, George von Lengerke Meyer.) Together with the general board of the navy, these aids served as a de facto general staff. Although Josephus Daniels, Woodrow Wilson's navy secretary, allowed the aid system to lapse, World War I forced Daniels to accept the creation of the Office of Chief of Naval Operations, which conducted fleet operations and prepared war plans.[91]

Roosevelt could not have foreseen any of these developments in early 1909. He had put change in motion, but it was too lit-

tle, too late. His interest in promoting a more modern government, and his ability to carry out bureaucratic change, extended
only so far. What he had accomplished mostly was to setup a
historical safety net. That is, if a major war erupted in the near
future and the existing system of naval administration broke
under the strain, Roosevelt could evade blame by pointing to
the Moody Commission as an example of his efforts to reform
the Navy Department.

Semper Fidelis?

If Roosevelt found that the naval reformer–naval bureau quarrel
was troublesome, then he would find that tampering with the
mission of the U.S. Marine Corps was even more daunting. Here
again he would tap into the wishes of the naval reformers that
so informed many of his decisions, and again he encountered
resistance to a proposed change. With the marines, he would
also be revisiting some unfinished business from the 1890s. The
result would be civil-military tension as the Marine Corps sought
to reverse the orders of its commander in chief and a defiant
Congress slapped down the president late in his administration.

Theodore Roosevelt had no love for the U.S. Marine Corps.
He would declare in November 1908, "They [the marines] have
augmented to themselves such importance, and their influence,
which they have gained by pandering to every political influence, has given them such an abnormal position for the size of
their corps that they have simply invited their own destruction.
I do not hesitate to say that they should be absorbed into the
army and no vestige of their organization should be allowed
to remain. They cannot get along with the navy, and as a separate command with the army the conditions would be intolerable."[92] This denunciation was again a private venting of feelings,
for he had erupted in front of his personal aide, Archie Butt.
Yet while these feelings did not necessarily govern Roosevelt's
actions, they did betray a deep-seated attitude toward the Marine

Corps, which ultimately helped to undermine a desired shift in the marines' mission.

Relations between sailors and marines had often been unhappy. Marines aboard ship had served as gun crews and provided landing parties, but they also offered security as ships' guards. This protective role dated from the early days of the navy when officers wanted protection from the foreign nationals who populated the crews of many vessels.[93] Naval reformer Lt. William F. Fullam argued in 1890 that the shipboard presence of marines lent itself to a penal colony atmosphere and hindered the navy's efforts to improve the training, education, and motivation of crews.[94] During his time as assistant secretary, Roosevelt absorbed this sentiment and apparently accepted it to the extent that he wished "to have both of these corps [the marines and Pay Corps] amalgamated with the line [of the navy]."[95] He had hoped to make that change as part of the personnel reform that he oversaw in the late 1890s but was unable to do so. As president, a chance to complete this unfinished business presented itself when the general board of the navy proposed a new mission for the Marine Corps.

Although it was not known at the time, the marines' seizure of Guantánamo Bay in 1898 pointed the way to the future of the corps. Robert W. Huntington's battalion had seized Guantánamo Bay as a staging area for operations in Cuba and as a consequence became, perhaps, the most celebrated unit of the Cuba campaign behind the Rough Riders. The expanded imperial commitments that resulted from the war with Spain indicated the desirability of having a force that could seize and defend anchorages for the fleet. Such a capability would allow the navy to be better able to project power into distant waters. From 1900 onward the general board struggled to turn this concept into reality. It wanted to obtain funding, men, and equipment for two expeditionary battalions, one for the Atlantic and one for Asiatic waters.[96] Roadblocks frustrated the board at every turn, with Congress, the naval bureaus, and the Marine Corps reluctant to lend support. Marine Corps headquarters remained wedded to the security mission, which had sustained the corps for a century, and many marines worried that separation from the fleet spelled the beginning of the end for the corps as a distinct service.[97]

Roosevelt involved himself in 1906. More accurately, the personnel law that Roosevelt had helped to author in the 1890s was revisited. Secretary of the Navy Charles Bonaparte reacted to complaints that personnel practices required officers "to become conversant with the many branches of the service." This measure had been intended to bridge the gap between line and engineering officers but had the effect of keeping "an officer from becoming an adept at any one thing."[98] As a result, Roosevelt authorized a new body to consider reforms. Truman Newberry, then the assistant secretary of the navy, was given charge of the new personnel board, which, in addition to studying personnel matters, was also going to consider "the organization, powers, or duties . . . of any bureau, or office . . . or of the commandant of the United States Marine Corps" as part of its duties.[99] This last item offered the possibility that the old project of amalgamating the Marine Corps to the naval line was about to be revived.

The Newberry Board's proposal never made it that far. Instead, its report was said to have "been lying quietly on the desk of the Secretary of the Navy since the day it was submitted."[100] Roosevelt's dislike of a recommendation to award staff officers with line titles represented the principal cause of failure, but the Marine Corps objected to provisions in the report as well. The marines' opposition foretold their reaction when Roosevelt determined two years later to act on his own authority to relieve the Marine Corps of its shipboard duties.

In early December 1908 the *Washington Post* announced, "The future of the marines has been definitely settled by President Roosevelt. He has decided that this branch of the ser-vice should be transferred to the infantry of the army."[101] An order to remove marines from sea duty had sparked this story, which would gradually propel a tide of resistance against the president. The order removing marines from ships fell in line with the wishes of naval reformers, who wanted to improve the atmosphere aboard ship and build an expeditionary force ready for swift deployment. Roosevelt, it seemed, was prepared to do more—the effective abolition of the Marine Corps as a military service. This intention went beyond anything proposed for the Marine Corps during the last episode of reform in the 1890s. Then Roosevelt had wanted the marines better integrated into the navy's ranks.

The earlier described outburst against the marines, the one that Archie Butt recorded, supplied the best insight into the president's thinking by late 1908. Roosevelt had gone beyond anything that the navy had wanted and, according to news reports, the army as well. "The army, navy, and marine corps," the *Washington Post* relayed, "are all stirred up over the report that the President will recommend that the marine corps be transferred to the army and merged with the infantry arm, and officers of all these services are pretty generally opposed to the proposition."[102] With opposition brewing at such a fundamen-tal level—navy and army support were essential for Roosevelt to succeed—the proposal seemed ill-considered at best. The pres-ident's impulse appeared grounded in his self-righteous streak, along with his identity as a government reformer. When he informed Butt that the marines had "simply invited their own destruction," Roosevelt revealed his feeling that the marines were no longer serving the public interest first because they had played politics too much.[103] If this loss of virtue alone was not enough to condemn them in Roosevelt's eyes, then the very existence of this service as a separate entity did. Politick-ing by marines to advance their own position represented an intolerable inefficiency to a man who had been a governmental reformer since the 1880s.

Leonard Wood apparently had an influence on Roosevelt's decision making. Army officers wanted ten more regiments of infantry, and the amalgamation of the Marine Corps would provide extra troops. No doubt this prospect confirmed for Roosevelt that his action was the right one. He could eliminate a troublesome entity and augment the army at the same time. Some army officers, however, were unsure that they liked the idea until they saw a detailed plan as to how the marines would be incorporated. General Wood was not among the reluctant. Rather, he was "known to be much taken with the President's new idea" and was working with the army's general staff on a scheme to add the marines. Wood, unlike his friend in the White House, did not see the complete end of a Marine Corps identity.[104] Still, his enthusiasm for transferring the corps to the army likely encouraged Roosevelt. Although Wood was thinking about the interests of the army, his intimacy with the president left a scent of the personal influence that Roosevelt so often decried when he saw it operating on others. He was quick to judge but reluctant to admit his own inconsistencies.

His strike against the marines would prove to be politically unrealistic and counterproductive. If he lacked strong support from the army and navy, then he was guaranteed to face determined resistance in Congress. There the Marine Corps had cultivated many friends, as Roosevelt himself acknowledged in his indictment of the marines. In the Senate, Eugene Hale opposed the measure, as did Francis Warren of Wyoming. The opposition of these two committee heads, with Hale heading up the Naval Affairs Committee and Warren the Military Affairs Committee, meant that legislation approving amalgamation would not reach the floor of the Senate.[105] Soon enough, the debate turned from legislation that would put the marines in the army to legislation that would restore them to service aboard ships.

By January 1909 moves were afoot in the House to tie the naval-appropriations bill to the return of the marines to sea duty, and by February 1909 the Senate, acting as a committee of the whole, approved an amendment to give the marines back their old duties. In essence, momentum built behind presenting the president with legislation that he could not refuse: if he wanted to secure other goals, including two battleships, then he had to accept the reversal of his orders.[106]

Roosevelt took the setback in relative stride. His time in office was expiring, and he did not regard the status of the marines as vital to the security of the nation. Battleships were, however, and he had gained two more. Still, he could not resist the urge to explain himself one more time. He wrote George Foss, chair of the House Naval Affairs Committee, that restoration of the marine guards was regrettable, albeit not particularly harmful. Roosevelt claimed that the marines' shipboard presence was detrimental and the removal had been made solely to bolster expeditionary battalions, but he thought the congressional action did damage by "creating the belief that the marines are kept aboard ship for nonmilitary reasons."[107]

He might have blamed Congress, but Roosevelt bore a good measure of responsibility for the reversal. In ordering two thousand marines to leave the fleet, T.R. had not attempted to build a consensus behind the directive. Instead, he seemed to regard this action as part of an exclusive portfolio as commander in chief. This view might have been technically accurate, but it was not politically realistic, given the marines' standing with Congress and in the national lore. Moreover, if his sole intention, as he stated to George Foss, was to build marine expeditionary battalions, then he had lost control of the debate by letting his wishes on amalgamation with the army be known. This apparent threat to the identity of the corps and its vital link to the navy was bound to generate full-scale opposition. The result was that the navy did not get the marine forces dedicated to expeditionary forces that it wanted to seize advance bases for the fleet, and much of that failure lay with Roosevelt's handling of the matter. When combined, his treasured notions regarding virtuous service, governmental efficiency, and the role of commander in chief had proved to be an unmanageable mix. After Roosevelt's departure, the advanced base force would develop, but progress was slow. Such a contingent began to emerge, but only because the general board and the secretary of the navy's office nurtured the concept behind it. In addition, the installation of more receptive commandants and the formation of an officers' lobby built key support from within the marines.[108]

All American presidents have had their share of setbacks. For those who served for more than four years, the reversals have tended to be more numerous during a second term. As able as Theodore Roosevelt was at projecting a public image and framing political debates, he could not escape that fate. The longer a chief executive serves, particularly as the term of office is about to expire, the harder it is for that person to remain a political force. Within the confines of that dynamic, Roosevelt managed to find some room to accomplish major military goals. He broke out of the one-battleship-per-year policy to keep the United States competitive in the race to build dreadnought-style battleships, and he dispatched the existing U.S. battle fleet on the world cruise. The building of the Panama Canal proceeded, and with these elements alone Roosevelt maintained the country on the great power trajectory that he had helped launch in the 1890s.

He might have achieved more, but Roosevelt could be his own worst enemy. Any perceived infringement on his power as commander in chief could make him intractable, even when a position that he took was ill-considered, as was the case in the Brownsville affair. His self-righteousness contributed to his stubbornness, for he tended to see opponents as morally lacking, which in turn inhibited compromise. He might, for example, have helped the drive for an advanced base force had he not felt the urge to act on the impulse to make the Marine Corps pay for what he saw as excessive politicking. At a time when he already had enough trouble with the more conservative element of the Republican Party and struggled with the financial panic of 1907, Roosevelt seemed to relish antagonizing his foes, even when controversy served no other purpose than personal satisfaction.

Like most leaders, Roosevelt was propelled, in large measure, by a desire to carve out a legacy. He wanted to establish precedents that his successors would find hard to reverse, especially when it came to an expansive role for the United States in the world. Thus much of his second term, in particular, was about completing a sound foundation for a great-power military establishment that would endure for the remainder of the twentieth century. His pursuit of that legacy is treated in the next chapter.

8

Looking beyond the White House

On 27 October 1908 Theodore Roosevelt celebrated his fiftieth birthday. He did so performing jumps on his horse Roswell, and he cleared all the hurdles attempted. Roswell, Roosevelt informed his daughter Alice, "is a fine old horse, and it is astonishing how well he jumps."[1] T.R. felt as if he had a number of jumps left in him as well. He complained periodically about weight gain and pain—particularly in the leg injured in the 1902 carriage wreck, but he continued to practice the strenuous life with his scramble walks and other activities.[2] Roosevelt also anticipated the Africa adventure that he planned to take upon exiting the White House, especially because son Kermit would join him on the journey. He drew great pleasure in making the various arrangements for the trip. Even as he looked forward to Africa, he became sentimental about his days in the White House, knowing that the time to leave was close. More and more his thoughts turned to the legacies he would leave once he became simply "Colonel Roosevelt."

Roosevelt derived satisfaction from the work he had undertaken since 1901. He believed that his signal achievement had been "to prevent the upgrowth in this country of . . . a plutocracy, a caste which regards power as exprest only in its basest and most brutal form, that of mere money." That, he told historian George Trevelyan on 1 January 1908, had been "my chief fight."[3] But he could point to more accomplishments. Roosevelt had expanded the role of the executive and given

unions better treatment from federal authorities, most notably in the anthracite coal strike of 1902. He had supported the
regulation of industry on behalf of consumers and railway cus-
tomers, and he had advanced the cause of conservation and
enforced antitrust legislation. Overseas he expanded the American role, with the assumption of police powers in the Caribbean, the construction of a canal in Panama, the deployment
of troops to Cuba, and the dousing of violent flare-ups in the
Philippines. Whether aboard or at home, all these efforts served
Roosevelt's quest to preserve American vitality and ensure that
the nation fulfilled its larger duties in the world. Among these
projects, his campaign to modernize the military establishment
and improve its readiness was part of the legacy he wanted to
leave for his successors.

In military matters Roosevelt had achieved much, but, as with
all the work of a president, many goals remained unfulfilled.
Most prized, he had added a total of sixteen battleships to the
fleet and increased the naval inventory in other ways, with six
cruisers, twenty destroyers, and twenty-four submarines authorized during his watch.[4] The navy had been reorganized to operate as a fleet, which the world cruise proved throughout 1908.
The army had also taken strides, with the advent of a general
staff and a dawning interest in aviation, among other things. Yet
for Roosevelt much work remained to be done. If he could not
reach all his objectives by the time he departed office, then he
would at least leave in place policies that his successors would be
hard-pressed to overturn and, he hoped, would want to build on.

Roosevelt's desire for a strong legacy went further than lay-
ing a foundation for progress in military affairs. It even went
beyond the hope that future generations would celebrate his
accomplishments. This work for a lasting legacy extended to
a more profound level. His first priority in his presidency, and
indeed over much of his life, was to elevate the moral quality
of America's public servants and, indeed, the larger citizenry.

When he wrote George Trevelyan in January 1908 about taking on plutocrats, he had lamented how the "typical American multimillionaire is an unlovely being, and scant is his share of the heirship of Washington and Lincoln, in the deeds of the men who in successive generations founded this Government, conquered this continent, and fought to finish a great war for union and for liberty."[5] Roosevelt wanted people to rise above themselves and to do public-spirited work. He projected the same ideal on the nation, for only by taking on larger responsibilities in the world, which served not only the national interest but also the larger world interest, would the United States meet the obligations required of a great power. The republic would endure, he felt, only with this assumption of a higher duty for the country and its citizens. Therefore, as his presidency neared its end, he continued to work on improving the quality of military officers, celebrating the nation's expanded role in the world, and leaving behind the means to project larger influence on world affairs.

An Officer of the Right Stripe

The quality of the officer corps concerned Roosevelt throughout his tenure. He had wanted to install a merit system of promotion, especially for the army, but that goal had remained out of reach. Well before his last months in office, Roosevelt understood that Congress was unlikely to grant his wish for a new promotion system. More than ever he wanted to place officers of his own choosing in higher command, and the time seemed especially right to advance an officer's case that had been deferred for several years. In short, John J. Pershing's moment had arrived.

John Pershing, although a captain, had become one of the best politically connected officers in the army by the time Roosevelt decided to promote him to brigadier general in 1906. Pershing knew the president of the United States, who had witnessed him in action in Cuba. Beyond that, Pershing had married into a politically powerful family. In January 1905 he married Helen Frances Warren, the daughter of Sen. Francis Warren, who became chair of the Senate Military Affairs Committee the following year. The Pershing-Warren wedding was one of the social events of 1905 in Washington DC. The president and Edith Roosevelt sat in the front row at the Church of the Epiphany, which was adorned with lilacs and white roses. Behind them was an array of guests that included Secretary of War William Howard Taft, numerous members of the Senate, diplomats, and top officers of the army.[6] Pershing's prominence and Senator Warren's influence would be needed to secure his promotion, for at this point in Roosevelt's presidency such a move would be controversial. It would be a controversy that Roosevelt welcomed.

In his earlier appointments Roosevelt had been seeding allies into the War Department bureaucracy and the top commands. By 1906 he was not thinking so much about men who would break down the "wooden" thinking in the top ranks. Rather, he was completing unfinished business because he had long wanted to promote Pershing, and he was making a statement with an eye toward the future. Pershing's record as a man of decisive action for his handling of the Moros in the Philippines still resonated, and he remained a man of the right stripe, in Roosevelt's view, for the top ranks of the army. His appointment to brigadier general, however, would be less about moving up a capable officer and more about Roosevelt demonstrating just what could have been done with merit promotions. He would elevate someone who could serve many years with a general's stars on his shoulders. Pershing was forty-six in 1906. The appointment, nonetheless, would trigger an outcry, far more than T.R. anticipated, and, because of that, would be among the last extraordinary promotions of Roosevelt's presidency.

If promoted, Pershing would jump over 862 officers. He would rise above so many because his permanent rank remained captain, and the highest temporary rank that he had ever held was major.[7] J. Franklin Bell actually had leaped more men during William McKinley's time. The main complaint instead was blatant favoritism. Pershing, after all, was married to the daughter of the senator in charge of the Military Affairs Committee. He also had been the president's military aide, and the two men had known each other for nearly a decade. It did not hurt Pershing's cause that Avery Andrews kept his name before the president, sometimes at Pershing's urging.[8] Roosevelt characteristically denounced the claims of partiality. Years later he reflected on the charges to Senator Warren and insisted that he had forgotten about Pershing's ties to the senator by the time of the promotion: "To promote a man *because* he marries a Senator's daughter would be an infamy; and to refuse him promotion for the same reason would be an equal infamy."[9]

Roosevelt's version betrayed a willfully selective memory, for it seemed unlikely that he could have forgotten the Pershing-Warren link only a year after he had attended the couple's wedding. Although no evidence exists of an arrangement between the president and the senator, it seems unlikely that Roosevelt would not have taken into account Warren's status in calculating the odds for winning approval of Pershing's promotion. The president seemed unwilling to admit, to both Warren and himself, that he was perfectly capable of going against his own principles about personal preferment when it suited his purpose. He would justify himself by claiming that his actions served the greater good, whether he was winning the assistant secretary's job in the 1890s or securing a general's stars for John Pershing in 1906. One result of this self-deception was that he blinded himself to the coming eruption over favoritism that would accompany such a promotion.

Roosevelt's unwillingness to admit, even privately, the appearance of preferential treatment recalled memories of his campaign two years before to make Leonard Wood a major general.

Although he could dismiss objections from Capitol Hill as being politically motivated, the divisions in the army that Pershing's nomination precipitated were striking and pointed to how much promotions perceived as political could affect morale and disturb civil-military relations. Within the officer corps, critics blasted the unfairness of the promotion and the president's interference in army affairs. One officer complained that Roosevelt lifted Pershing for no good reason and that such promotions were arbitrary and discouraging. Another informed Pershing that "the principle is bad . . . d—n bad," but he did not fault Pershing for accepting the promotion when offered. Also the bitter sentiment circulated that "it is better to have a Senator's wife for a mother-in-law than to have the best record in the United States Army."[10] Admittedly some officers, particularly junior ones, welcomed the promotion and hoped it signaled a decisive break with seniority. Capt. William C. Rivers congratulated Pershing, saying that the army needed generals who could "hustle" to make the rest of the service "hustle" as well. Another, Capt. Matthew C. Butler, wrote that he would be "glad when our Army is rid of some of the old fossils," as he was "tired of serving under men who have grown so old in the service that they are nothing short of 'block heads.'"[11]

Unhappiness over the promotion precipitated a scandal. Charges from anonymous sources, attributed later in the press to disgruntled army officers, surfaced soon after the promotion and threatened to undo Roosevelt's work. Pershing was charged with keeping a Filipino mistress during his tour in the Philippines and fathering two children by her. A sex scandal made for good newspaper sales and threatened to destroy Pershing's career. The administration claimed to have heard the charges before, investigated, and found them to be baseless. Pershing, taking no chances, gathered statements from fellow officers supporting his denials and even had the woman in question, and her husband, swear there was nothing to the story. Pershing's defense prevailed, and the charges faded away, but their existence pointed to the strength of feeling over the promotion.[12]

With Pershing, Roosevelt had succeeded in planting another younger officer in the higher ranks, but beyond that the promotion failed to change much. If the president had been hoping to make a point about rewarding merit, then that message was lost in the protests against favoritism. Roosevelt maintained that there had been no partiality, but appearances suggested otherwise. The result was that resistance would become so strong that not only were the president's hopes for a new system of promotion dead, but he would also be hard-pressed to win more promotions out of the normal line of advancement.

Roosevelt offered just two more merit promotions during the remainder of his presidency. Both officers had qualifications that made their elevation acceptable to the Senate, but even then the process of confirmation was slow. James B. Aleshire could claim expertise in the quartermaster corps. At the time of his promotion in July 1907, he was fifty years old, a major, and the assistant to the quartermaster general, Brig. Gen. Charles F. Humphrey, who was retiring. Aleshire possessed more than technical knowledge to commend him to the president. He had also proven himself capable in the field. The new quartermaster general had served in Cuba and the Philippines, and he had been on the march to Peking during the Boxer Rebellion. Aleshire's case was also helped by the fact that he enjoyed a reputation in the army as an excellent judge of horses. That skill remained important in an army that still moved mainly by foot and hoof, and it could not have hurt Aleshire's case with a president who prized horses and a daily ride.[13] The other nominee, whom Roosevelt judged a "fine fellow," also had a special circumstance working to his advantage. At the time of his promotion in October 1907, William Wotherspoon was the acting president of the Army War College. Wotherspoon was also older, fifty-six at the time, and a lieutenant colonel, so his climb to brigadier general was shorter.[14] Despite such factors, the Senate Military Affairs Committee delayed confirmation of the promotions after complaints occurred again about moving officers out of their regular turn. Eventually, the Senate did confirm Aleshire and Wotherspoon, but these were the last two unusual promotions that Roosevelt made. In 1908 he nominated only colonels for advancement.[15]

Over the course of his presidency, Roosevelt did succeed in jumping eight men to brigadier general from junior positions as low as captain. He also promoted thirty-one others who were more senior at the time of promotion and who would serve at least a few years as general before retirement. Among the eight who leaped the most in rank, all made notable contributions. John Pershing would become the most famous as leader of the American Expeditionary Forces during World War I, and he would retire as a "General of the Armies" in 1924. Tasker Bliss would also achieve prominence in World War I as the U.S. military representative to the Allied Supreme War Council. After the hostilities he served as a delegate to the Versailles Peace Conference. Both James Aleshire as quartermaster general and William Crozier as chief of ordnance provided long service. Crozier remained head of his bureau into World War I, and Aleshire served on the Council of National Defense during that conflict, having retired as quartermaster in 1916. After helping to design the army's general staff, William Carter ended his career as commander of the Second Division in Hawaii in 1915, but he was recalled to active duty in 1917 to help with the mobilization. He served until 1918. Thomas Barry commanded the army of occupation in Cuba after troops reentered that country in 1906. Barry's service there won him promotion to major general in 1908, and he went on to become superintendent of the Military Academy and commander of American forces in the Philippines and China. Albert Mills presided over the Military Academy until 1906, later served as president of the Army War

College, and then held a command in the Philippines. He had just worked out plans for mobilization of the militia as head of the Division of Militia in the War Department when pneumonia claimed him in September 1916. Lastly, William Wotherspoon, one of Roosevelt's final appointments, moved into the general staff after his time at the Army War College, first as an assistant to the chief of staff and then, briefly, as chief himself in 1914.[16]

These officers served well, but problems occurred with their long service. "Roosevelt men" were placed in the top ranks, and there they would remain. In other words, by installing a new crop of top commanders, the president created his own "Roosevelt hump," which mimicked in miniature the Civil War hump of officers that had stalled promotions in the first place. Inevitably, the same dry rot that T.R. sought to combat would occur in some cases, as younger men were again forced to wait for their elders to retire. Crozier and Aleshire seemed most out of touch as mobilization for a possible conflict began in 1916. Historian Paul Koistinen, a student of the economic mobilization for World War I, has described Crozier's and Aleshire's performances during congressional hearings over the National Defense Act of 1916 in damning tones: "Chief of Ordnance William Crozier appeared to have some narrow awareness of modern military problems; Quartermaster James B. Aleshire lacked even that."[17] Crozier fared just as poorly in the eyes of military historian Edward M. Coffman, who characterized the ordnance chief as an "officer who firmly believed that his technicians should dictate to the combat troops what weapons they should use," and not the other way around.[18] With his move to the Council of National Defense in 1916, Aleshire would not serve as quartermaster during the Great War, and Crozier would be removed as head of ordnance during the struggle. Officers such as Pershing and Bliss counterbalanced men who were no longer able to meet the demands placed on them, and such shortcomings illustrated Roosevelt's case for an improved promotion system.

The weeding out of officers beyond their prime was not unique to the United States during World War I. European militaries went through that process earlier after the outbreak of hostilities. For example, during the critical month of August 1914, when the Germans attacked to the west and France's drive eastward hit a buzz saw of German defenses, the French military relieved one army commander, three corps commanders, and thirty-six commanders of divisions. These dismissals occurred not only because of reverses at the hands of the Germans but also because of simple mistakes on the part of the commanders themselves.[19] Similarly for the United States, General Pershing freely relieved colonels and generals who he felt were not up to the rigors of commanding in wartime.[20] Although the American performance was far from trouble free, such actions did accelerate the mobilization of forces to France, which ultimately would number in the millions. This record helped redeem the performance of 1898.

Living the Strenuous Life

Roosevelt may have been unable to reform the promotion system, but he would find another path to boost vitality. He would impose a physical test on army and navy officers. This action appealed to T.R. in multiple ways. He could use his own powers and not have to consult Congress. A physical test also satisfied his belief that all men, and even more so military officers, should embrace some form of vigorous living. In Roosevelt's mind a physical requirement would make manifest his program for improving the body and fostering manly virtues. Society could only benefit, and the military would become more effective.

Roosevelt began to raise physical standards in the spring of 1907. He started at the lowest level by ordering new physical qualifications for cadets at the Military Academy. The minimum height went from sixty-four to sixty-five inches, and acceptable chest measurements were increased as well. This change went unchallenged, but the imposition of a physical test on commissioned officers sparked a different reaction.[21]

For officers Roosevelt imposed a fitness requirement that recalled his days as a Rough Rider. He wrote to Secretary of War Taft, "As I have personally observed some field officers who were physically unable to ride even a few miles at an increased gait, and as I deem it essential that the field officers of the line of the army should be at all times physically fit . . . I desire that you give the necessary directions to have the physical condition of all officers of the line . . . actually tested."[22] He mandated that officers be able to pass a horsemanship test in which they needed to ride a total of fifteen miles, some at a trot, some at a gallop, and some at a walk. This first test did little to achieve the president's goals, but it did do much to inspire ridicule. After twenty-eight "fat Colonels" took the test in October 1907, the *New York Times* headlined "Rotund Colonels Ride to Triumph" and went on to describe how "the only casualties were two pairs of split riding breeches and the defection of two newspaper men." The paper also reported that one officer was tempted to believe that the test would be postponed when he woke to a driving rain, but he quickly roused himself with the thought that "if Roosevelt hears that the ride was called off on account of rain he will get out of the canebrakes to-day and be here day after to-morrow to take us out himself." After the ease of this first test, which nobody failed, some believed that Roosevelt would raise the requirements. They knew their commander in chief well.[23]

The president established a tougher test in December 1907. He ordered that field officers be able to ride thirty miles per day over three consecutive days. One new feature of the test required that the exercise would occur under the conditions of a forced march. That is, the test would not be entirely on horseback. At certain points officers would need to leave the saddle and trot alongside their horse.[24] This task was no longer a "gentle jaunt," and it provoked sharp criticism, except from junior officers. Younger men liked the idea because they hoped that it would speed their prospects for promotion by pushing senior officers to retire.

Older officers, however, said that the president had "gone horse mad," which indicated not just distaste for the test, and the president, but also concern that the emphasis on horsemanship was not appropriate for all branches of the service. Cavalrymen should be able to take and pass such a test, but many questioned why seacoast artillerymen or engineers should have to meet such a requirement. This complaint about Roosevelt being "horse mad" perhaps also reflected resentment over the apparent presidential preference for cavalry.[25] Officers were additionally angry about the indignity of the test. They felt humiliated when children would jeer at them as they passed and the press would ridicule their efforts. They also knew of, and resented, the comments that subordinate officers were making about the state of their physical fitness. The tests, moreover, were expensive, as officers often had to travel to take them, and some felt they proved nothing. As one officer put it, "the ability to ride any given distance is certainly no distinguishing mark of a soldier. There is not a cowboy in our land that cannot ride further and faster than the average army officer." He suggested that if riding were the essential quality, then "abolish West Point and select our future commanders from our cow punchers."[26]

Such complaints had an effect. Public support rallied around endangered officers, especially for engineers involved in civilworks projects. For example, New Yorkers did not want to lose the services of Col. William L. Marshall. The colonel was reportedly a "very stout man," but he was "in fine health" and responsible for reclamation work being done on Governors Island in New York Harbor. The army did make an accommodation for the coast artillerymen, who never rode horses. They received the option of a fifty-mile hike. This test, too, had to be completed in three days.[27] Such modifications did not silence critics, for officers continued to complain about the arbitrary nature of the tests and how no allowances were made for age or for men stationed in the tropics, who faced the rigors of the exam in a stressful climate.[28]

The loudest reaction came from another service altogether. Roosevelt decided that navy officers should also pass a physical test. Just as with the coast artillerymen, he gave sailors a choice: they could ride or walk, or they could take advantage of a third option, a bicycle. For men used to sailing the seas, and not tramping in the dirt or riding, the order caused anxiety and injury. The *New York Times* recorded how accidents injured several naval officers as they prepared to ride horses and bicycles. Even the majority who decided in favor of walking did not escape harm. William Sims recorded that naval officers suffered blistered feet and lost toenails and succumbed to other afflictions during the first tests. As a result, after William Howard Taft took over from Roosevelt in 1909, naval officers were particularly hopeful that the physical test might be modified.[29]

Roosevelt had anticipated that eventuality before he departed office. He was determined that the fitness tests remain, and he reacted to press and military criticism in a characteristic fashion. The president determined to complete the navy riding test himself, and in one day, not three. He hoped to attract popular attention, shame critics into silence, and thereby make the test harder to abandon.

On 13 January 1909 a party of four departed the White House at 3:40 a.m. The group consisted of the president; his military aide Capt. Archie Butt; the surgeon general of the navy, Adm. Presley M. Rixey; and naval surgeon Cary T. Grayson. Their goal was to ride to Warrenton, Virginia, and back on the same day. Fresh mounts were provided along the route, and the president, reportedly, "was a hard man to follow," as he kept the group on a strict schedule. The group took rest periods of only ten minutes, except at Warrenton, where they dined on soup and roast beef. Telephone messages had preceded the men, and a crowd of about a thousand turned out hoping to see the president. Rather than resting after dinner, he went outside to a burst of applause, and then he commenced politicking, shaking hands and telling the townspeople how much he was enjoying the day. The return trip did not commence until after 5:00 p.m.[30]

Roosevelt's return was not as pleasant as the ride to Warrenton. At Centreville, Virginia, a winter storm began to rage, so in blinding sleet and snow the riders had to navigate treacherous roads in the dark. T.R. arrived at the White House at 8:10 p.m., "covered with mud and ice from the brim of his Rough Rider hat to the tips of his riding boots." In spite of the long hours in the saddle and the miserable weather, he sprang from his horse as if having just taken a ride in the park and declared, with a wide grin, that the journey "was bully." Altogether, the trip had covered ninety-eight miles of the Virginia countryside.[31]

The next day Roosevelt told callers that he felt "fit as a fiddle," and Admiral Rixey, after seeing the president, said he was "none the worse for his arduous trip."[32] Although Roosevelt's condition could not have been better, the impact on his fitness policy was harder to measure. The physical tests lasted beyond Roosevelt's presidency, but officers continued to resent the test, and many resisted the physical fitness routines that would keep them healthy. Many reportedly viewed the requirement merely as something to get by each year so that they did not have to worry about it for another twelve months. Thus, it failed to inspire officers to embrace rigorous exercise with the same zeal as the president. The navy was the first service to give way.[33] In 1911 the navy test became less demanding but increased in frequency. Officers would walk twenty-five miles in two days every three months, with lighter standards at tropical stations. The following year the naval test became a monthly walk of ten miles in one day because the Taft administration wanted to encourage year-round physical training. Later the test was abandoned altogether.[34] The War Department held steady for a longer time. The navy's example inspired a study of less rigorous but more frequent testing. The army, however, left Roosevelt's test ride untouched until spring 1917, when the demands of wartime compelled its abandonment.

In the end, Roosevelt's physical test did not have the desired effect. The fitness standard inspired neither a change in behavior nor a rush to retirement by unfit or older officers. Annual retirements because of the test amounted to less than a handful. In June 1909 the *Army and Navy Journal* reported that the fitness requirement had not yet caused a single officer to retire from the navy, and five years later the *Journal* estimated that the test eliminated only one to two officers each year. Preliminary medical examinations caught more, but such checkups could continue without a required physical test.[35]

The Architecture of Empire

Compelling individuals or institutions to change traditional practices can be a hard task. The fact that Roosevelt attempted to do so with physical standards demonstrated his boundless confidence in his judgment as to what was morally and practically right. In fact, in Roosevelt's mind the moral imperative became particularly strong the more that he perceived a practical benefit for military effectiveness. Given institutional and individual resistance, forcing a change in physical fitness standards was hard. He could, though, leave another legacy that would be much greater, tangible, and help make the imperial presence of the United States felt for decades to come. Roosevelt would help to engineer an overseas military-base structure that remained an enduring part of the American military and diplomatic architecture for the twentieth century and beyond.

If William McKinley had presided over the acquisition of an overseas empire, then it became Roosevelt's task to protect it.

This work, if accomplished, would be much more enduring than physical fitness requirements, for bases, once established, could not be swept away at the stroke of a pen. Such installations would be a symbol of the expanded American presence and, in a real way, part of United States' overseas interests. Bases would allow American ships to refuel and repair in distant locations such as the Philippines or the eastern Caribbean, and they would facilitate peak performance against an enemy in those waters. Their development was essential in Roosevelt's mind, for without them his foreign and naval policies would not work. The process of deciding where to locate bases and begin work on them was neither quick nor easy. The question over bases would span the length of Roosevelt's presidency and would generate tension between the army and navy and between the commander in chief and his principal military advisers. By Roosevelt's last two years in office, recommendations were reversed, confusion occurred, and the president experienced a crisis in confidence about the military advice that he was receiving.

The General Board of the U.S. Navy first confronted the task of where to place overseas bases immediately after the United States acquired an overseas empire. This problem of locating and then developing overseas bases would vex the general board from its inception through the end of Roosevelt's presidency. At first, when the afterglow of imperial conquest was still running high, the general board thought that the navy required numerous overseas bases. These facilities were to be scattered throughout the Caribbean, Central America, the western Pacific, and East Asia.[36] Resources and strategic reality soon dictated another approach. The board recognized that the navy could not support or protect an extended network of facilities, so, instead, board members settled for one major base in the Caribbean and one in the Pacific, with provisions also made to protect an isthmian canal.[37]

The decision about the location of the chief U.S. base in the

Caribbean occurred without much debate. General board members picked Guantánamo Bay in southeastern Cuba, and Roosevelt accepted their judgment and approved a lease in October 1903. An option was retained on Bahía Honda in northwestern Cuba, in case the navy wanted to build a coaling station there.[38] Guantánamo Bay made good geographic and strategic sense. The bay could admit large ships, was easily defended, and was impossible for an enemy to obstruct. It also overlooked the Windward Passage, the main avenue of trade through the Caribbean, and thus guarded the approaches to an isthmian canal. The location would enable naval operations as far as the eastern coast of Central America and the northern reaches of South America.[39]

Diplomatically, establishing a base in Cuba presented few problems to the Roosevelt administration. For the Cubans, it was a different matter. They were realizing some of their gravest concerns about the Americans since the United States had arrived in 1898. The Cubans did not want to surrender the land, but their new constitution contained provisions, engineered by the United States and adopted as a result of American insistence, that stipulated the right of the United States to establish bases on the island.[40] Roosevelt had reminded Secretary of State John Hay of those provisions a year before the navy settled on Guantánamo Bay: "Would it not be just as well to let the Cubans know at once and definitely that . . . the naval stations are to be ceded and in the near future? There is no intention of placing a naval station at Havana or at Santiago; but the question itself is not a matter open to discussion by the Cubans. It is already contained in their constitution, and no discussion concerning it will be entertained."[41] Roosevelt did concede something to the Cubans' national pride in avoiding sites such as Havana or Santiago, but overall his manner was high-handed.

The president might have discounted the Cubans, but in the case of the site of a Pacific base, he would reproach his own officer corps. Early in Roosevelt's tenure, his military advisers had determined the best location for a base in the western Pacific. The general board of the navy had endorsed Olongapo, which lay along Subic Bay in the Philippines. In December 1903 the Joint Army-Navy Board, which had been created to help coordinate policy between the two services, ratified the choice. For the navy Olongapo had much to offer as a location. Subic Bay lay sixty miles from Manila, the key to the island of Luzon, and Luzon was the key to the entire Philippine archipelago. At Olongapo the navy could intercept a seaborne enemy on the way to attack the capital. Narrow channels made the bay defensible, and its big harbor, which could accommodate the largest ships, was well protected from storms and ideally suited for a dockyard. Fresh-water supplies and satisfactory hygienic conditions made the location even more attractive.[42] The joint board left no doubt about its preference for Subic Bay. In a report to Congress, the joint board, which was presided over by Adm. George Dewey, stated "that Manila is not, but that Subig Bay is, suited for a naval base and station, and of all the harbors in the archipelago it is the best for the purpose."[43]

This clear endorsement led Roosevelt to campaign hard for funds to fortify the Subic Bay site. In February 1904 he informed Rep. Theodore Burton that expansionist policies in the Pacific and East Asia hinged on a naval station at Subic Bay. "If we are to have a naval station in the Philippines; if we are to have a fleet in Asiatic waters, or to exert the slightest influence in eastern Asia where our people hope to find a market, then it is of the highest importance that we have a naval station in the Philippines at Subig Bay." If not, Roosevelt declared, "then we should be manly enough to say that we intend to abandon the Philippines at once."[44] Later in 1904, the president indicated that he believed that the question of a base in the Philippines was settled. There could be no doubt about the president's view, for in forwarding a report of the general board to Leonard Wood,

Roosevelt affirmed, "I agree with this report." He went on to assert that "the question as to choosing between Subig Bay and Manila has been gone over with great care, and while I did not of course take part in the discussions among the military and naval officers, which finally induced them with practically una-nimity to decide upon Subig Bay, I agree entirely with the deci-sion to which they came."[45]

Roosevelt's letter to Wood had come about after his friend had made a case for Manila being the principal military focus in the Philippines. Wood had been persuasive enough in lay-ing out that Manila was the key to the islands that he had sown doubt in Roosevelt's mind. Because of those doubts, Roosevelt had turned the question over to the general board again, and it was in response to that request that he had heard unequiv-ocally from Admiral Dewey that Subic Bay was far superior to Manila Bay. In fact, Dewey had claimed that if Manila were the place then the Americans risked being bottled up just as he had sealed in the Spaniards in 1898.[46]

A few years later, therefore, Roosevelt's temper was under-standable when his military advisers reversed themselves. The joint board abandoned its unbending stance on Subic Bay and recommended in 1907 that Manila receive emphasis instead. It did so because of the Japanese siege and capture of Port Arthur in 1904–5. Army opinion held that Subic Bay was sim-ilar in configuration to Port Arthur and equally vulnerable to land attack. The army lacked sufficient forces to protect both Subic Bay and Manila from a land assault, and therefore it rec-ommended that defenses must focus on Manila, the ultimate prize at stake in any assault on the Philippines. As the capital, Manila needed to be held if the United States were to main-tain its political hold, but Manila and Subic Bay were too far distant for mutual support.[47]

Roosevelt exploded. He had gone to Congress repeatedly for funds for Subic Bay, and now his military advisers said that was "all wrong." The result was a "humiliating experience," and "Congress," he admitted, "has a right to complain of the Executive Department in this matter." Roosevelt lamented to Secretary of the Navy Victor Metcalf that the Subic Bay episode had inflicted great harm to congressional confidence in the president's top uniformed advisers: "This year a great many Senators and Congressmen have said to me that they disbelieved in the general staff for either the army or the navy because of the curious attitude of the Joint Board in this Philippine defense matter."[48]

Roosevelt joined members of Congress in having doubts about his military advisers. The difficulty was easily identified. Members of the different services were not really talking to one another, despite the creation of a body such as the joint board to coordinate between the army and navy. Roosevelt found this maddening because he was not receiving the best considered advice, nor was Congress. As a layman, he noted sternly, he had the "right to assume" that the recommendations he was receiving were the "best under actual conditions." Instead, he suspected that the navy had not truly consulted the army before endorsing Subic Bay. "No naval officer," he informed Secretary Metcalf, "has a right to advise the fortification of Subig Bay without putting in the most careful proviso that the advice is only to be considered in case the military authorities report the scheme as satisfactory."[49]

Roosevelt also wondered about the true depth of study devoted to the matter, asking if "this was ever made a general staff study" and "whether the successive and widely varying conclusions reached are due to original and careful study by the members of the general boards and joint boards or whether they have resulted from the perfunctory ratification of the views of some subordinate officer." No matter the case, Roosevelt believed there was a problem that needed to be resolved. His query indicated that he understood all too well how bureaucracies worked, with senior members often relying too heavily on the work of their juniors. He also demonstrated that he was not just going to leave any investigation to the military but would take an active part, for he wished to see any reports that might have been produced by staff officers regarding a Pacific base.[50] In short, he wanted an accounting.

The president's critique identified a number of flaws in any advisory system. Boards and committees have often relied on a few members to get the actual work done, and what would later be called "group think" can take hold and lead to recommendations that have not adequately incorporated alternatives. Indeed, in the case of Subic Bay or Manila, one officer did have undue influence, but he was not junior in rank. Adm. George Dewey fixed on Subic Bay for its naval features, and, because he was the chair of the joint board, his was the dominant voice, sidelining doubts about that location. Roosevelt was right that the navy and army were not really communicating, in spite of the joint board. The services had different perspectives in their views about the defense of American interests in the Pacific. Army officers focused on the protection of bases, especially because they knew that they might be under attack from an enemy for three to four months before the main elements of the navy could arrive from the Atlantic to relieve them. Navy officers, being good Mahanians, concentrated on offense and using the waters of the Pacific to take the war to the enemy. They did not want geographic positions to unduly dictate their strategy.[51]

In all, Roosevelt was taking on a problem without an easy remedy, the breaking down of parochial views and practices. The joint board had been an attempt at bringing coordination, but the quest for "jointness" would remain a pursuit for the remainder of the twentieth century. The creation of the Joint Chiefs of Staff, as part of the making of a national security establishment in 1947, was one example, and later reforms would follow. For Roosevelt time was too short in his presidency for a further revamping of the military structure, so beyond his lecture and demand for materials no meaningful action occurred.

The retreat from Subic Bay, while embarrassing to the administration, did have a positive strategic impact. The Philippines as a whole was rejected as a site. Instead, Pearl Harbor in the Hawaiian Islands became the choice for a major Pacific base. The harbor was large, protected on land by mountains, and close to Honolulu. Work had to be done on the harbor entrances to accommodate naval needs, but the strategic position of Pearl Harbor overcame any engineering concerns. A Hawaiian base would allow the United States to dominate the mid-Pacific, and from this central location the navy could project power to many other places. Also, the strategic location commended itself because it was not at the end of a long line of supply or close to a potential rival like Japan, and it would also help to shield the West Coast of the United States. As the *Washington Post* put it, Hawaii was "the Crossroad of the Pacific."[52]

This optimistic assessment assumed the presence of the battle fleet, but that force would not be stationed in the Pacific in the foreseeable future. Absent a war in the Pacific, the battleships would remain in the Atlantic, given the presence of potential rivals, chiefly Germany; the vital urban and economic centers of the East Coast; and American interests in the Western Hemisphere. Even after the completion of the Panama Canal, a transfer to the Pacific would take time. Thus, no matter the location of a base, the strategic dilemma remained. The United States could not protect its Pacific possessions adequately without the battle fleet, and that fleet resided in other waters. Roosevelt understood the problem but was unable to solve it at the time. A truly two-ocean navy was an obvious answer but remained a dream, given the absence of political will to construct a force of that scale.[53]

Nonetheless, the navy required a major base if it were to operate at a distance in the Pacific, and Roosevelt demanded that the development of Pearl Harbor be done correctly. He wanted no more embarrassments or more reasons for critics to question the military advisory system. Thus, he ordered "careful consideration given to . . . the defense of Hawaii by both army and navy and a report made . . . thereon."[54] This new report would be part of a multifaceted approach for securing funding. The world cruise of the battle fleet, which served to publicize so many aspects of naval affairs, also assisted the effort. The visit of the sixteen battleships in July 1908 pointed out the inadequacy of existing facilities at Honolulu. One observer reported that "there was no room for all the ships inside" and that it was an "open roadstead." The ships also "could not coal off Honolulu with comfort," and four ships had to go seventy miles to Maui to fuel. Roosevelt also worked closely with members of Congress to speed appropriations for harbor development. When Republican representative Arthur Bates of Pennsylvania proposed a three-million dollar appropriation to begin work on Pearl Harbor, Roosevelt invited him to the White House to show support. The *Washington Post* speculated that talk of war between Japan and the United States had inspired the bill and the meeting, for the paper felt the proposal was really an administration measure. Certainly concerns over tensions with Japan did not harm the bill's prospects, and in 1908 nearly a million dollars was appropriated for the project. More was to come, for by the end of the year the Navy Department announced plans to build the world's largest dry dock at Pearl Harbor.[55]

The decisions made about a Pacific base would have a far-reaching effect. Roosevelt could not know it at the time, but the choice of Pearl Harbor would significantly shape the course of the Pacific War in the 1940s. That conflict first came to the United States at Pearl Harbor, the Philippines, and other Pacific outposts. Although Japanese aircraft mauled American forces at Pearl Harbor in December 1941, Hawaii remained secure throughout the war, whereas the Philippines were much more exposed and fell to Japan. From the Hawaiian Islands, the United States had a forward outpost that became the staging area for much of the Pacific war effort.

Cruising the World

While Roosevelt wrestled with the problem of establishing overseas bases in 1907 and 1908, the centerpiece of his naval policy, the battle fleet, continued to circumnavigate the globe. After departing Hawaii in late July 1908, the fleet made calls in New Zealand, Australia, Japan, China, and the Philippines from August through November. Then the ships made for the Indian Ocean and Suez in December, before wending their way home via the Mediterranean Sea in early 1909. The entire voyage lasted sixteen months.[56]

Roosevelt followed the fleet's progress with characteristic interest. For example, he thanked the chief of the Bureau of Navigation, Rear Adm. John E. Pillsbury, in October 1908 for forwarding two messages from Rear Adm. Charles Sperry, who was in command of the battle fleet. In praising the work of Sperry, the president also lauded the performance of the sailors in a rifle-shooting exercise, and he had questions and comments that conveyed his usual concern for detail whenever the navy was involved: "Who do you think was responsible for those stories about the misconduct of the fleet? I suppose the utmost care will be taken to see that coal is already at Colombo. What was the hitch in New Zealand?" To his satisfaction, the refueling of the fleet in Ceylon (Sri Lanka) would go smoothly, and any problems caused in New Zealand were forgotten after the tremendous reception that the fleet received there and in Australia.[57]

Roosevelt devoted special attention to the visit to Japan. Tensions between the United States and Japan had risen following the Russo-Japanese War. The peace treaty that Roosevelt had brokered was unpopular in Japan, and then the decision of the San Francisco School Board in 1906 to segregate Asian students led to further outrage. Therefore, when Roosevelt announced the transfer of the battle fleet from the Atlantic to the Pacific, there were predictions that Japan would see the move as a threat. Years later, in his autobiography, Roosevelt claimed that he doubted at the time the Japanese would treat the dispatch of the fleet as a hostile gesture. "Japan knew my sincere friendship and admiration for her and realized that we could not as a Nation have any intention of attacking her." Further, he said that if his estimation was wrong, then "it would have been proof positive that we were going to be attacked anyhow, and that in such event it would have been an enormous gain to have the three months' preliminary preparation which enabled the fleet to start perfectly equipped."[58]

The Japanese turned out to be models of diplomacy and politeness, and the visit struck just the right tone between the two peoples. Afterward, Roosevelt wrote to Admiral Sperry and praised his own judgment: "I anticipated good in every way from the voyage of the fleet; but it has far more than come up to my anticipations." He also confided to his friend Arthur Hamilton Lee, who had been the British military attaché in Cuba in 1898, that "my policy of constant friendliness and courtesy toward Japan, *coupled with sending the fleet around the world*, has borne good results!"[59]

Along with diplomatic benefits, the technical performance of the fleet delighted Roosevelt. He proclaimed to British author Sydney Brooks in December 1908 that "at this moment our battle fleet is doing what no other similar fleet of a like size has ever done—that is circumnavigating the globe—and is also at this moment in far more efficient battle trim, from the stand point of battle tactics and even from the standpoint of gunnery, than when it started out a year ago."[60] The fleet doubtlessly did hone tactical and gunnery skills owing to the numerous exercises conducted during the journey, and engineers learned how to maximize the endurance of their ships for long-distance voyages.[61]

The president was especially pleased with the performance of the small ships—torpedo boat destroyers—for he had overridden senior navy commanders to send them. He recounted how shortly before the fleet embarked he had observed target practice off Provincetown, Massachusetts, and afterward had dined with two lieutenants who commanded torpedo boat destroyers. They urged the president to reconsider the idea of sending only large ships, insisting that the smaller vessels could withstand the voyage. Roosevelt claimed that he changed his mind on the spot because "I was only too glad to accept the word of the men who were to do the job."[62] This account appeared in his autobiography years after the fact, but even if it exaggerated Roosevelt's change of heart, the episode still reflected his penchant for rewarding boldness, whether in fact or rhetorically.

Naturally, when the fleet returned to Hampton Roads, Roosevelt was going to be there. The moment was going to be his, and it would be a fitting capstone to his presidency. He had built up the fleet, changed its formation, improved its gunnery, and showcased it before the world. Soon there would be an interoceanic canal to speed its transit from the Atlantic to the Pacific. A centerpiece of his foreign policy was to be assembled in one place for all to see. It was time for him to celebrate.

Much of Washington was traveling to Hampton Roads to join in the festivities. Secretary of the Navy Truman Newberry, two hundred members of Congress, and other officials planned to greet the fleet, along with wives, daughters, and sisters—"not a few of whom, unable to resist the allurement of the hour, have canceled dates at home." Steamboats to Virginia were crowded, as were railcars, as people flooded south. Prominent members of Congress engaged a special car, and for the president of the American National Bank, I. H. Lynn, the steamer *Queen Anne* was carrying a party of thirty. Many of these dignitaries planned to attend a Navy League dinner on the night after the fleet returned, although the president would not be among them. He would arrive on the presidential yacht *May-flower* on 21 February, amid many private craft contending for a view of the returning fleet.[63]

The morning of 22 February 1909 dawned so overcast that it was hard to determine where sea ended and sky began. But the clouds could not depress Theodore Roosevelt's spirit that day. At 10:00 a.m. the first masts appeared on the horizon, and soon the *Connecticut* appeared, with a line of more battleships in tow. Roosevelt was at the center of the spectacle that followed. Each ship delivered a twenty-one-gun salute to the president, and another twenty-one to George Washington, whose birthday was being observed. As the ships passed the *Mayflower*, officers on each bridge appeared with white gloved hands raised in salute, and sailors in dress blues lined the starboard side of their ships. Roosevelt lifted his hat in response. Once the naval parade was concluded, he boarded the four flagships of each fleet division to greet the officers and men. On the *Connecticut* he nearly suffered a mishap. Roosevelt climbed up five feet to the base of the aft twelve-inch gun turret and almost lost his footing on a hydrant that he was using to make his ascent. He recovered, and the crew cheered "lustily." He drew more shouts with prepared remarks, which he peppered with frequent asides. The men particularly embraced his comments on their gunnery skills, and the fact that they were part of the first battle fleet to circle the globe. "Other nations may follow," announced the president, "but they have got to go behind." After his remarks and when Roosevelt was about to be piped off the ship to continue his round of visits, the assembled gave him three cheers, to which he responded, "If there were enough of me, I would cheer for you."[64]

Roosevelt sailed for Washington DC at 5:15 p.m., after the ships took their place at anchor in two rows. The ceremonies may have concluded, but the impact of the cruise continued. Roosevelt had secured his two battleships in 1909, and William

Howard Taft worked to sustain the building of two battleships per year, although he succeeded at that goal only for the first half of his presidency. During the last two years, Congress found the size of the battleship force sufficient and authorized only one battleship each year.[65] Culturally, the image of the fleet itself—ships colored buff and white and moving from port to port—would endure in the public mind. This voyage supplied an iconic moment for American sea power. Nevertheless, the navy had plans for the ships upon their return. The peacetime color scheme of buff and white was abandoned in favor of the permanent use of wartime colors—a symbol of readiness. The ships of the world cruise would be repainted gray, and the ornamentation on their bows was removed.[66]

The shift to the gray color scheme as Roosevelt retired from the White House signified a more significant change than just an alteration of hue—a transformation more far-reaching than could possibly be recognized at the time. It symbolized a change in warfare and the culture surrounding the conduct of war that would soon grip the world during the Great War and remain after that cataclysm. If readiness was the goal in painting the ships gray, then increasingly a premium would be placed on a permanent state of mobilization as the twentieth century passed. The alteration also foreshadowed the passing of romantic conceptions of modern warfare, notions that World War I would banish. Roosevelt subscribed to romanticized ideas of war, whether they involved his boyhood impressions of the Civil War, his depiction of his service in 1898, or the martial values that he conveyed to his offspring. For good reason, biographer H. W. Brands dubbed him "The Last Romantic."[67] The dispatch of the fleet on the world cruise fit within that ethos. Granted, the cruise served diplomatic, political, and military purposes, but the image of ornamented ships with white hulls and buff-colored superstructures slicing through the seas and visiting lands still deemed exotic by Americans left a deep sentimental impression in the popular mind. The conclusion of the cruise symbolized the end of the founding era of the new steel navy. Gray was the color of industry, of mechanization. This somber color signaled the descent into a harsher age.

The Adventurous Life of Colonel Roosevelt

Adventure beckoned to Theodore Roosevelt after he left the White House in March 1909. As a young man, he had envied his younger brother Elliott's trips to far-off lands. Roosevelt would now have his chance. In 1909 and 1910 he would safari in sub-Saharan Africa with Kermit and then tour Egypt and Europe, where he was feted throughout the continent. He also accepted his Nobel Prize belatedly and represented President Taft at the funeral of King Edward VII. In Africa he collected thousands of specimens for the Smithsonian Institution, zoos, and natural history museums, and in Egypt and Europe he delivered numerous speeches and met many heads of state, before a triumphal return to the United States in June 1910.[68] Retirement was never in the offing, and Roosevelt soon plunged back into politics to save the Progressive causes that he had championed and to reclaim the power that he coveted. The result was a break with William Howard Taft, whom Roosevelt felt had proved too conservative. He attempted to take the Republican nomination in 1912 and, failing that, made an ill-fated attempt to win as the Progressive Party candidate. That effort split the vote between Taft and T.R. and helped put Democrat Woodrow Wilson into the White House. In the ensuing years Wilson would become the last great political foe of the old Rough Rider.

To nurse his political wounds after the bruising fight of 1912, Roosevelt decided on another great adventure, the chance to be a true explorer in the Amazonian jungle. Along with Kermit he would be part of an expedition to chart the Rio Dúvida in Brazil in 1913–14. The Roosevelts would be going into uncharted territory, and the experience nearly killed the ex-president.

T.R. would reinjure the leg that had been hurt in the streetcar accident, and soon a high-fever and delirium invalided him for much of the journey. When the expedition emerged in April 1914, Roosevelt had lost fifty pounds, and his health never fully recovered.[69] He would also return to a world in which Europe was about to erupt into war.

Military affairs remained an abiding interest amid the swirl of events. T.R. signaled as much with his preference to be known as "Colonel Roosevelt," a nod to the triumphs of 1898 and a way of staying connected to exploits that had validated him personally and elevated him politically. One of his last letters as president in March 1909 demonstrated the continuing significance that military matters would play in his post-executive life. He wrote to William Howard Taft, "under no circumstances divide the battleship fleet between the Atlantic and Pacific Oceans prior to the finishing of the Panama Canal." Roosevelt recalled pressures to do just that when he sent the fleet on the world cruise, but he implored Taft to resist such sentiment. He also cautioned the incoming president that the Russians' decision to divide their fleet between the Pacific and the Baltic had been the most important factor in their defeat by Japan. By contrast, "the entire Japanese force was always used to smash some fraction of the Russian force." Roosevelt sent a copy of this parting advice to Alfred Thayer Mahan to assure the admiral that a fundamental tenet of sea power was being passed from one administration to the next.[70]

Familiar patterns would guide Roosevelt's involvement with military matters. New technologies, for example, continued to intrigue him. In August 1911 he asked Gen. William Wotherspoon, who was going to meet Kaiser Wilhelm, to inform him "what they are doing about aviation in Germany," as well as what efforts the Japanese had made to develop aircraft.[71] He had demonstrated this interest in flying in a literal fashion the previous year when he had been the first person who had held the presidency to take flight. The colonel was riding the campaign circuit in 1910, championing candidates in congressional races. He was in Missouri that October to help the Progressive ticket when he visited an aviation exposition near Saint Louis. Pilot Arch Hoxsey invited the ex-president to take a flight, as the flying conditions were ideal. Roosevelt accepted and scrambled aboard the craft. Within minutes, fifteen thousand spectators were treated to the sight of Theodore Roosevelt, wearing flying cap and goggles, buzzing by a hundred feet above the ground and waving enthusiastically. After landing, Roosevelt exclaimed about the flight, "It was great! First class! It was the finest experience I have ever had. I wish I could stay up for an hour, but I haven't the time this afternoon."[72]

More than keeping abreast of technological developments, Roosevelt wanted to jump into a fight—as he had in 1898—if ever the chance occurred again. Trouble in Mexico offered the possibility, just as it had after a border incident in 1886, when Roosevelt had first pronounced his dream of raising a unit of rough riders.[73] In 1911 a revolution ended the decades-long rule of Porfirio Díaz. Roosevelt contacted President Taft in March 1911 to explore the option of raising a division of volunteers, in case big trouble erupted over Mexico. He hoped that war would not occur and also stated his disinclination to be involved in an intervention that would require merely the policing of Mexican affairs. Roosevelt saw such work as "peculiarly irksome and disagreeable and profitless police duty." No glory could come from such service. Rather, he sought action only in a "serious war," a conflict in which a big power such as Japan backed Mexico. Then, he wanted "to raise a division of cavalry, such as the regiment that I commanded in Cuba." He had in mind the men who would command brigades and regiments and claimed that he would fill the division with westerners and southerners, along with a few from the east—much like he had in the war with Spain. Roosevelt acknowledged that the possibility of such a conflict was remote, and, indeed, President Taft was reluctant to intervene in Mexico. Still, he did promise to honor Roosevelt's request should hostilities start.[74]

Events in Mexico over the next several years continued to stir Roosevelt's desire for action. The Mexican Revolution spun from one upheaval to the next: from the removal of the Díaz regime, to the short-lived presidency of Francisco Madero, to Madero's bloody overthrow by Gen. Victoriano Huerta, and to Huerta's removal and factional warfare. Because of the common frontier, Mexico fell within the American sphere of interest. Roosevelt felt that Mexico was to the United States what Paraguay was to Brazil, Argentina, and Chile, or, in short, "Mexico is *our* Paraguay."[75] Turmoil in Mexico was a concern, but attacks on American citizens that grew out of the violence raised cries for intervention. The worst tensions came in early 1916, after troops under northern revolutionary leader Francisco Villa shot eighteen American mining engineers and then crossed the border and raided Columbus, New Mexico, killing seventeen Americans. In response the Wilson administration dispatched a punitive expedition under General Pershing to hunt down the elusive Villa.[76] Even more trouble with Mexico looked likely, and if it came to major hostilities, Roosevelt wanted to be a part of it.

In early July 1916 he wrote to Secretary of War Newton D. Baker, requesting permission to raise a division. Much like he had for Taft, Roosevelt sketched out his ideas for the configuration of the unit, which would be primarily infantry, but mounted soldiers would be heavily represented. One brigade, he proposed, would be cavalry, and one—but possibly two—of the brigades would be mounted infantry. The emphasis on mounted soldiers demonstrated again Roosevelt's partiality toward for cavalry but also likely reflected a belief that mobility would be essential for operating in Mexico and that horses still provided the best way for moving across the long distances there. In a nod to more recent military developments, Roosevelt proposed to equip the division with a motorcycle regiment, and he also wanted an aviation squadron.[77]

The degree to which Roosevelt had been thinking about commanding again became clear in the personnel arrangements for his proposed division. Regular army officers would be assigned using the formula of one to every thousand men. In the event of war he would produce a list of the specific officers that he would like to serve on his staff and in the field, down to the rank of major. Roosevelt also informed the secretary that he had already "made conditional offers to various civilians whom I would desire to have as Divisional Quartermaster General, as Colonels, Lieutenant Colonels, and Majors; and to a very few whom I would desire to have as captains or lieutenants." These men were selected, he claimed, on their perceived ability to raise troops and then to command them.[78] Implicit here was that each man had the moral fiber for service and leadership.

Roosevelt would not get his chance for action in Mexico. Pershing's expedition was enough involvement for Secretary Baker and President Wilson, and mounting tensions with the Mexican government of Venustiano Carranza, the futility of capturing Villa, and concern about Germany persuaded them to end the intervention in February 1917. For T.R. the episode would turn out to be a preview of his actions a year later, after war had been declared against Germany. He would dust off his plans for a division and again lobby the administration for a command. The Mexican affair also provided him with an opportunity to criticize Woodrow Wilson's leadership, which he would only amplify when it came to Wilson's conduct of relations with Germany and, later, his wartime leadership. In the case of Mexico he blasted Wilson for failing to prepare for war—stating at one point that "it looks as if Wilson would drift stern foremost into war with Mexico, without having made a particle of preparation for it." More important, he found Wilson to be lacking in character. Roosevelt believed that Wilson pursued a policy toward Mexico that was "neither Peace nor War" just to help him win the 1916 presidential election.[79] Even more damning, Roosevelt put Wilson in league with the presidents that he disdained the most for their weak stewardship: "This creature," he wrote, "is not of the Jackson, but the Jefferson and Buchanan type."[80]

The flare-up with Mexico also reinforced for Roosevelt the deficiencies of the National Guard. In June 1916 President Wilson called up the entire National Guard and sent it to the Mexican border. Over 130,000 men were involved. The Villa raid provided the pretext for Wilson's order, but, according to historian John K. Mahon, he apparently dispatched the guard chiefly to see how well it could mobilize. Generously put, the results were uneven. Many men were physically unfit, others did not show up, and still others were excused because of family responsibilities. Still, over 110,000 arrived at the border within two weeks, and most men served about nine months there.[81] For Roosevelt the episode proved again the weaknesses of the guard and supplied ammunition to attack Wilson. "The National Guard," he wrote, "cannot be properly trained, and probably of two thirds of the men who go, over one half have people depending upon them, and they are themselves depending upon jobs." He decried the call-up as a shabby political move on the part of Wilson, contending that the mobilization "has simply been wicked." The families of the guardsmen suffered in service of a policy, he felt, that was "neither Peace nor War" but that would help Wilson win reelection.[82]

By 1916 most everything associated with Woodrow Wilson was poisonous to Theodore Roosevelt. His feeling against Wilson involved much more than the handling of affairs with Mexico. The former Princeton professor had claimed the presidency in 1912, thanks in large part to the fissure in Republican ranks. No matter his own role in Wilson's elevation, Roosevelt wanted to reclaim the power of the presidency. Not only did Wilson hold the position that Roosevelt craved, but he had also pushed through a sweeping reform program. In Roosevelt's opinion, however, this academic lacked the strength of character of a true national leader. "Wilson," Roosevelt wrote to Rudyard Kipling, "is a scholarly, acrid pacifist of much ability and few scruples." Moreover, Wilson had made bad appointments, in Roosevelt's view. Secretary of State William Jennings Bryan was "the most ridiculous creature that we have ever had in a high public office in this country," and Secretary of the Navy Josephus Daniels was also a "ridiculous figure."[83] Then war broke out in Europe, and Woodrow Wilson, this unworthy leader in Roosevelt's jaundiced view, was in office. Roosevelt believed himself to be a man of destiny, with the experience and character to stand at the helm during a great world crisis. The Great War was meant for him, and he would make it his last crusade, as he sought to push the country to prepare militarily, lobbied to lead forces himself, and strove to vanquish his number one political enemy.

9

The Last Crusade

In early November 1918 an exhausted Germany agreed to an armistice. The Great War had ended. Far from the fighting and bedridden by a body that could no longer sustain the strenuous life, Theodore Roosevelt was contemplating death with honor. He was not thinking of himself, but of Germany's emperor, Wilhelm II. The kaiser had abdicated, and Roosevelt expressed contempt for Wilhelm's exit. The former German emperor "was not even a valorous barbarian." He had skulked off with his six sons, "saving their own worthless carcasses at the end, leaving their women, like their honor, behind them."[1] Roosevelt thought that if he had been in the kaiser's place he would have taken his sons and charged an Allied strongpoint for honor's sake, hoping for a quick death.[2]

Since the outbreak of fighting in 1914, Roosevelt had answered a new call to arms. Even without the power of the White House, he felt that he had the duty, the experience, the prominence, and, above all, the courage to help steer the United States on the correct course through the stormy seas of the European war. He would work hard to push military preparedness and training, and not just because such measures were a practical thing to do. Preparedness was the sign of a nation stepping up to its responsibilities, and readiness would weld the stern stuff of soldiering into the body politic. When the United States joined the fighting in 1917, Roosevelt offered up his own body to the cause. Denied that chance, he saw his sons off to war. T.R. became instead a crusader for the war effort, and he battled against Woodrow Wilson, a man whom he considered wholly unfit to govern.

Preparedness

The European conflict would come to consume Roosevelt's attention. German ambitions had long worried the colonel. Even before the war broke out, he had felt that German aggressiveness could be restrained only with French and British military readiness. In 1911 Roosevelt claimed that German war plans contained "as possible courses of action, flank marches through both Belgium and Switzerland." Only the threat of war by the other great powers, he felt, kept them from violating the treaties guarding Belgian and Swiss sovereignty.[3] The events of August 1914 would prove Roosevelt partially right, when Germany ignored Belgium's neutrality to strike at France. From then on he would push for American military preparedness and a muscular foreign policy regarding the war in Europe.

As he had in the past, Theodore Roosevelt viewed military preparation as an expression of national vigor and moral fitness. A ready army and navy demonstrated that the United States was willing to defend its interests and act in a world that could only benefit from the responsible exercise of American power. Roosevelt maintained a similar vision for those citizens who volunteered to serve the public good. These were people who had entered "the contest" and wanted to do something worthwhile for their community, state, and country.[4] This time around, unlike the lead-up to the war with Spain, Roosevelt looked beyond the traditional mustering of volunteers at the outbreak of war. Rather, he promoted a system of constant military training that would provide more than just an influx of ready manpower; it would also benefit the national character in an age of industry and cities. In short, his campaign for military readiness in the run-up to American intervention in the Great War was another way for him to extend his Progressive ideals, using military means as the conduit. The effort would also make him feel as if he were in the arena again, answering the summons of the trumpet.

Within months after the European order shattered, Roosevelt laid out the military, moral, and civic imperative behind preparedness. All aspects of readiness intertwined into a single intellectual framework. He wrote a series of *New York Times* articles on the war in Europe, and in "Preparedness without Militarism" echoed old themes about service in pushing for the adoption of universal military training in the United States. Based on the Swiss system, Roosevelt's proposal envisioned having boys begin military drill during their last years of high school. Upon graduation, trainees would spend four months in the army, and then, for eight to ten days each year, citizens would renew their training. This system appealed to the old Rough Rider because it would teach men "how to take care of themselves," unlike the "drill hall and parade ground" so often used for National Guard experience. Civilians who had been exposed to hard living and discipline would emerge as better people with a strengthened sense of civic responsibility—just the type of citizen needed in a rapidly growing urban and industrial society. Such training would also allow the United States to "render to righteousness" in the world. To do this, the country would need to be able to "back righteousness with force, to put might back of right."[5] Here it all was, married into a single vision, Roosevelt's civic, martial, moral, and Progressive political agenda for an emerging American century.

If universal military training was Roosevelt's ideal, then the Plattsburg idea represented its practical expression, the best that could be obtained at the time. The Plattsburg idea stemmed from the efforts of Leonard Wood to create a national military reserve. As army chief of staff in 1912, Wood had promoted a federal reserve force, but the resulting legislation proved ineffective. By 1914 the reserve consisted of only sixteen enlisted men.[6] Plattsburg represented Wood's route to creating a pool of men with some military training. By 1914, no longer army chief of staff, Wood was commander of the Department of the East for the army, and he used Plattsburgh Barracks to offer military training to public-spirited college students and business executives. Participants would spend several weeks learning military basics and experiencing rigorous discipline and exercise, and they would pay for the privilege to do so. According to the Plattsburgh *Press-Republican*, the camp had expanded to the point that eight thousand to ten thousand men attended during the summer of 1916.[7]

Participants indeed got a taste of the rigors of military living. Campers in June 1916 undertook a weeklong hike to the Canadian border, during which they carried their guns and thirty-seven-pound packs and slept in pup tents. They marched and conducted maneuvers amid a deluge, with more rain forecast.[8] In September a group of trainees again withstood an exercise during which they "emerged from the fray drenched to the skin."[9] This type of harsh experience was just the sort that Theodore Roosevelt embraced. The trainees were enduring physical and mental stress in service to a larger civic purpose, and as a result they would become better citizens, who could be of future use to their country. As a result, Roosevelt enthusiastically supported the Plattsburg camps.

The colonel visited the Plattsburg encampment during the first summer of training there. On 25 August 1915 T.R. came dressed in what approximated campaign gear: "tan riding suit, military leather leggings, and a cream fedora hat." He toured the tent city; watched members of the businessmen's regiment work out problems; ate camp food for lunch; watched artillery, cavalry, and engineering exercises; and saw the entire force pass in review. Late in the day, as the sun was setting, he showed that he was in full fighting trim in a speech delivered before an assembly of campers, regular army, and civilians that numbered over five thousand. His remarks, in part, echoed themes that he had sounded since the 1890s. He celebrated the civic virtue being demonstrated, as he praised the regulars there "as the highest type of American," and he also recognized the businessmen campers, telling them, "You have done your duty. In doing it, you have added to your value as citizens." Also, just as in the 1890s, he returned to the idea that America was in danger of becoming weak, if "professional pacifists" had their way. In other words, he warned that such "people are seeking to Chinafy this country." Newer themes also appeared in the speech, principally Roosevelt's call for universal military training, for he declared, "Camps like this are schools of civic virtue, as well as of military efficiency. They should be universal and obligatory for all our young men. Every man worth his salt will wish to come to them."[10]

Roosevelt planned to do more than just praise the trainees. He used the speech to warn against the broader dangers threatening the country. One menace was "professional German-Americans" who had worked to corrupt American institutions and who were "against America doing its international duties." Another peril was an attitude by which "we have treated elocution as a substitute for action." For thirteen months Roosevelt complained, the United States had "played an ignoble part among the nations." The country had allowed the weak to be attacked and had "seen our own men, women, and children murdered on the high seas" without taking action, a reference to Wilson's statement about being too proud to fight after the sinking of the passenger liner *Lusitania* in 1915. In other words, Roosevelt was using his Plattsburg platform to take a swipe at the Wilson administration. If there was any question about his intention to provoke controversy, he put those doubts to rest with a remark that he made just before departing the camp that evening. Roosevelt reacted to a comment frequently made that people must stand by the president. "I heartily subscribe to this," he said, "on condition and only on condition that it is followed by the statement so long as the President stands by the country."[11] For Roosevelt, Wilson had failed to uphold American honor through too much talking and too little action.

Roosevelt's recipe for generating attention through controversy worked again. Coverage of the Plattsburg speech made front-page news, with headlines that highlighted his criticism of President Wilson's policies. The *New York Times*, for example, led with "If President Is Wrong, Citizens Should Show Him His Duty"; "Impatient of Eloquence"; and "Criticises Failure to Strengthen Defense—Flays Pacifists and Hyphenated Germans."[12] All these lines captured the message and tone of Roosevelt's remarks just as he hoped would happen. As he confided on 2 September to his son Archie, "The Administration took ferocious umbrage; and ever since my speech I have been in an intricate row. But I am extremely glad I spoke. It was worth while to have one man state the things that ought to be stated."[13] Indeed, Roosevelt immediately plunged into an exchange with Secretary of War Lindley Garrison on the efforts to prepare the nation for war. Roosevelt's denunciation of the Wilson administration did not sit well in Washington, and T.R. claimed that he had "gone to the limit of my vocabulary in an endeavor to make such pleas just as strong as words would make them."[14]

Roosevelt relished the back-and-forth with the administration, but part of the price for advancing his views was a reprimand for Leonard Wood. Immediately after the speech, Secretary Garrison released the text of a telegram that he had sent to Wood warning that no further political addresses should be allowed. He informed Wood that "it is difficult to conceive of anything which could have a more detrimental effect on the real value of this experiment than such an incident."[15] In other words, Garrison validated the training occurring at the camp but did not want Plattsburg, or any other training site, to be a platform for policy pronouncements, certainly not ones critical of the

Wilson administration. He surmised Wood's involvement with the Plattsburg speech—not a hard conclusion to reach given Roosevelt's and Wood's mutual affinity. T.R., in fact, admitted Wood's complicity to Archie, but under the strictest confidence. Days after the affair he confided not only that he "made the speech . . . at Wood's request" but that Wood had reviewed the address prior to delivery.[16] Roosevelt wanted to shield his old comrade from being charged with collaboration, knowing that, if found out, Wood would face more severe consequences than a public reprimand from the secretary of war.

The Wilson administration, bearing the responsibility of power, was not about to be rushed into a large-scale prepared-ness program. Only in 1916, amid the pressures of his reelection campaign, did the president embrace military reform and preparedness legislation. The National Defense Act did not bring the universal military training program that Roosevelt wanted, nor did the measure provide for a full-blown readiness program. The law did map out a structure for expanding the army to 175,000 and for growing the National Guard to 400,000 as the first federal reserve force. Lawmakers also provided for reserve officer training at camps such as Plattsburg and at universities. The measure helped to insulate Wilson from charges of letting American defense languish. The defense act, however, was carefully couched so that it could not be seen as the first step toward American intervention in the war.[17] Wilson, after all, was running as the man had who kept America out of war.

The steps toward preparedness were not enough for T.R., but he could take personal pleasure from the fact that three of his four sons underwent Plattsburg training. Ted, Archie, and Quentin participated. Kermit could not, but surely would have, except that he was working in South America for a branch of City National Bank.[18] Quentin received a certificate stating "that he had done good work and that with more age and experience he would make an excellent Second Lieutenant." Ted performed well also, and he earned a promotion to sergeant at the camp. The performance of his third son, Archie, excited Roosevelt the most. Archie's evaluation, T. R. recorded, "read in the highest terms, stating that he was fit to be Captain in a volunteer regiment now." In fact, at the camp Archie performed so well that he was made a second lieutenant and stayed two weeks after the end of a student camp to work with business executives. "Rather to my delight"—his father's pride bursting through—"he was put over Ted!"[19]

Their participation affected Roosevelt deeply. The boys' Plattsburg training meant that he had passed on his principles to the next generation. He took their embrace of martial values as more than a sign that he had succeeded as a father, for their willingness to serve also signaled to him that the virtues he so treasured would remain strong in twentieth-century America. His sons were examples of a public spiritedness that he hoped would penetrate the broader citizenry. Furthermore, their training really helped to make Plattsburg a Roosevelt family project and gave meaning to Roosevelt's words about preparedness. Indeed, more than just training was involved for the Roosevelts. Eldest son Ted had been instrumental in getting the program off the ground in 1915. Ted was on the committee that worked with Leonard Wood to develop the initial four-week camp and to bring in participants. He informed Kermit that his brother would be surprised "to find out how many of the men we know have been aroused and are willing to go; about twenty two have signified their assent so far."[20]

The Plattsburg experience grew into a significant phenomenon before the manpower demands of World War I swallowed up the training program. In 1915 summer camps brought in almost three thousand participants, and during the following year there were ten camps across the country that drilled a total of ten thousand trainees. Although the camps were held at various locations each year, the public associated the training drive with the Plattsburg encampment, and hence the effort became known as the Plattsburg movement.[21] The spirit of Plattsburg continued after the Great War with Citizens' Military Training Camps, conducted by the army until World War II.[22]

Rough Rider Dismounted

If Roosevelt believed that the civilian volunteers training in 1915 and 1916 demonstrated the spirit demanded of right-minded Americans, then he felt that Woodrow Wilson began to redeem the nation's honor only in April 1917, when he asked for a declaration of war against the imperial German government. "I care nothing for his [Wilson's] future, and nothing for my own. But I care immensely for this country, and I wish to have it a land of which my grandchildren will be proud to be citizens." In saying this Roosevelt also viewed Wilson's decision to go to war as a justification of his own position, and he made sure to feed his views to a journalist, in this case John Callan O'Laughlin, a trusted Roosevelt man. Although by trade a newspaper correspondent, O'Laughlin had served briefly as assistant secretary of state under Roosevelt and had been a delegate to the Progressive convention in 1912. He would later publish the *Army and Navy Journal.* Roosevelt informed O'Laughlin in April 1917 that all previous criticism would "drift into oblivion, if he [Wilson] will now go into the war with all his heart, and with single-minded patriotism serve this country."[23]

But Roosevelt could not so easily stop his criticism of Wilson. In the same letter to O'Laughlin, he wrote a postscript that decried "the folly of the Administration's war proposals." He was particularly upset that the Wilson administration was going to use a draft to preclude the recruitment of volunteer units. Roosevelt wanted volunteer outfits along the lines of 1898. He desired such units, in part, because they were what he knew. Raising these formations would also give expression to the civic-mindedness he had preached, and they would allow him the chance to reach again for glory in uniform. Conscription, he felt, should be used "to reach people who ought *not* to be exempt from service; but it is nonsense to use it to prevent men from serving."[24]

The fighting in Europe offered new crusades, adventure, and, possibly, glorious death. If Roosevelt felt that American intervention justified his preparedness efforts and prewar criticism of the Wilson administration, then his next campaign was to persuade the government to allow him to raise troops, lead them into battle, and make volunteers the foremost way of raising mass numbers. The latter goal, he hoped, would lead one day to a system of universal training to provide a more ready reserve for the nation. He would be frustrated on every count. Roosevelt would have to content himself with viewing the war from the sidelines. He would have to experience the fighting through the eyes of the next generation—his sons—and busy himself with scrutinizing the Wilson administration's conduct of the war.

The colonel began his campaign to raise a volunteer unit well before the declaration of war. His effort fit a pattern dating to the 1880s. Whenever he had seen the possibility of conflict on the horizon, he had discussed raising an outfit to fight. He had done as much whether the trouble was on the Mexican border in the 1880s, was with Spain in the 1890s, or involved Mexican revolutionaries in the 1910s. In the case of Germany, he confessed his ambitions to old friends. In November 1916 he responded to an invitation from Arthur Hamilton Lee to visit England. Lee had served as the British military attaché during the war with Spain, had witnessed the Rough Riders in action, and then had served in the British embassy in Washington.[25] Roosevelt declined but explained that he would make the journey on just one condition: "I would like to visit the Front at the head of an American Division of 12 Regiments like my Rough Riders—but not otherwise."[26] With war clouds darkening in mid-February 1917, he wrote to Jean Jules Jusserand, the longtime French ambassador to the United States and regular companion on his scrambles through Rock Creek Park, that in the event of war between America and Germany, "I should be profoundly unhappy unless I got into the fighting line, and I believe I should raise a division of 20,000 men." Roosevelt went on to predict "that in six months I could get this division ready for the trenches," and "that I would not be a political general, and that I would expect no favors of any kind, except the great favor of being sent to the front."[27] In making this last assertion, Roosevelt was willfully denying that his very presence would be a political statement and that back in 1898 he had tugged political strings when necessary.

Roosevelt's campaign for a command extended beyond his network of friends. Indeed, he had already made a formal appeal for a volunteer unit by the time he had written Jusserand. He wrote Secretary of War Newton D. Baker on 2 February 1917, just days after Germany announced resumption of unrestricted submarine warfare. Roosevelt wanted to remind Baker that he had already filed an application for permission to raise a division and that, in case war looked likely, he be notified immediately. Edith and he were planning a trip to Jamaica, and Roosevelt wished to know whether or not he should sail. As in 1898, he did not want anything to interfere with his chance for action. Roosevelt also revealed to Baker that he had been planning for the eventuality: "I have prepared the skeleton outline of what I have desired the Division to be, and what men I should recommend to the Department, for brigade and regimental commanders, Chief of Staff, Chief Surgeon, Quartermaster general, etc. etc. etc." He also signaled that he intended to rely on the men who had been involved in the preparedness movement or, as he put it, the "men earning their living in the active business of life."[28]

The colonel of 1917 was trying to follow the path of 1898. Roosevelt had seen the rewards from being the first to jump into action during the war with Spain. His alacrity, then, had not only gotten him to Cuba with the first troops but had satisfied his drive to prove himself in battle and had made him into a national political figure. In the Great War compulsion again drove him to prove that he was not a mere armchair jingo. The desire for action was a constant, as was the need to put in practice the gospel of civic duty that he preached.

Roosevelt quickly made apparent how much he wanted a command. The Allies needed men, and he believed that he could provide them. He claimed that he could prepare a division for France within sixty days.[29] On 7 February, five days after his first letter to Secretary Baker, he wrote Baker again to tell him that he had cancelled the Jamaican trip and to remind the secretary that he would like to raise a division and would "strain every nerve to have it ready for efficient action at the earliest moment." In fact, to demonstrate how swiftly he was prepared to move, Roosevelt requested that Baker assign him "Captain Frank McCoy, of the regular army, as my divisional Chief of Staff, with the rank of Colonel." More than that, he wondered if McCoy might be "permitted now to come on and see me here, so that I may immediately go over with him all the questions that it is possible to go over at this time, in connection with raising the division?" McCoy, as it turned out, was in Mexico, even if Baker had been willing to grant the request.[30]

Roosevelt's blood was up, and Newton Baker understood that the Rough Rider presented a problem for the Wilson administration. The colonel's blasts against Wilson's leadership had proved irksome. Now his enthusiasm for a volunteer division threatened to undo plans to raise a mass army systematically. Roosevelt was the one person who might be able to create overwhelming political pressure for old-style volunteer units. Volunteer formations along the lines raised for the Spanish-American War and the Civil War would be a magnet for manpower and could disrupt plans to raise a national force in a more controlled fashion through selective service. With this system the army and National Guard were the only options for enlistment. Men could volunteer for either, and then the draft would fill any gaps in those services. In actual operation, selective service would spur enlistments, as many men chose to avoid the dictates of being conscripted.[31] Beyond the potential disruption of mobilization plans, the notion of Roosevelt fighting in France raised another issue for the Wilson administration. Just as he had in 1898, if not more so, the ex-president would likely be the object of a media frenzy, and, if somehow he did not attract such attention, he would find ways to generate publicity. The Wilson administration did not want to provide such a platform to Roosevelt, nor see him divert attention from the administration's war leadership. Secretary Baker had to find a way to put off Roosevelt without seeming to mistreat the colonel.

From the first Baker tried to dampen Roosevelt's enthusiasm. He pointed out that no additional forces could be raised without congressional authorization and that there were no funds available for such a project. He also informed Roosevelt that the type of volunteer force that the colonel wanted was not part of the planning for this war: "A plan for a very much larger army than the force suggested in your telegram has been prepared for the action of Congress whenever required. Militia officers of high rank will naturally be incorporated with their commands, but the general officers for all volunteer forces are to be drawn from the regular army."[32] Baker's last line made clear that an inspired amateur such as Roosevelt would not be awarded a general's stars.

Pushing hard, however, had gotten Roosevelt to where he was in public life. His had been one of the first units sent to Cuba because he had seized the initiative and employed contacts to expedite the equipping and training of the Rough Riders. Why should 1917 be any different? His response to Baker suggested that he was not to be denied, along with a rising impatience with the secretary of war. Roosevelt told the secretary that he understood that much more than a division would be required. He had proposed his division "for immediate use in the first expeditionary force sent over." Moreover, Roosevelt objected to Baker's insinuation that he was not qualified for high command: "In reference to your concluding sentence, I wish respectfully to point out that I am a retired Commander-in-Chief of the United States Army, and eligible to any position of command over American troops to which I may be appointed." He reminded Baker that he had ended up the campaign in Cuba in command of a brigade.[33]

Sensing that Roosevelt was on the brink of a fresh break with the administration, Secretary Baker tried a new tactic. He met with Roosevelt in Washington and attempted to divert him toward other ways to serve the war effort. The colonel could use his political standing to help win passage of a draft and a war loan. Indeed, Roosevelt contacted members of Congress to support such measures, but his visit with Baker seemed only to encourage him to pursue his first object, a military command.[34] His desire for a command was so strong that he could not admit the truth: the administration was not going to grant a repeat of the Rough Riders.

Roosevelt's time in Washington also included a meeting with President Wilson. T.R. and the president met around midday on 10 April. By all accounts Wilson received Roosevelt with courtesy, and the colonel heard much that he liked from the president. He greeted Wilson's call for war with enthusiasm and "heartily backed" the administration's proposal for conscription. From this measure Roosevelt hoped that "the principle of universal obligatory training and service" would become a permanent national policy. He also used the occasion to push for volunteer formations, claiming that a force of draftees and one of volunteers would be mutually beneficial to the war effort: "The army to be raised on the plan of obligatory service . . . will in all probability not be available for use for at least a year. My proposal is to supplement this by legislation which will permit the raising of whatever number of volunteers is now necessary." Further, this call for volunteers would exclude classes of men who might be subject to conscription and thus would "represent a pure addition to our military strength." The fact that volunteer forces—"composed of men who otherwise would not be used at all"—might not consist of the best military material did not seem to matter to Roosevelt. Martial ardor and a desire to serve would override any shortcomings. Wilson listened but, not surprisingly, was noncommittal.[35]

Roosevelt anticipated that his health and physical fitness might serve as a barrier to securing an officer's commission, perhaps as a result of Baker having seen him in person. His weight remained a problem, arthritis was crippling him, and he had never fully recovered from his trip through the Brazilian jungle. Roosevelt met the issue of his health head-on, by claiming that the very physical fitness standards he had established did not apply to the position he sought. He was so determined to secure a command that not only did he brazenly discount his own physical test, claiming that his main job would be "enlisting the best type of fighting men, and putting into them the spirit which will enable me to get the best possible results out of them in the actual fight," but he also compared himself to German field marshal Paul von Hindenburg. "Hindenberg [sic]," Roosevelt noted, "was of course a retired officer, who had been for four years on the retired list, and who could not physically have passed an examination."[36] Yet Hindenburg, while older, was the Germans' top commander.

Roosevelt refused to take the hint, even after meeting with President Wilson and Newton Baker. The secretary's patience ended on 13 April. He did not mince words and informed Roosevelt that he had "reached some conclusions which I think, in frankness, I ought to indicate to you." Baker cited the Army War College Division of the general staff, stating that there would be no rash deployments to Europe. An expedition was to be dispatched only after adequate training had occurred. He stressed that purely military considerations informed his decisions and that Roosevelt could find other, nonmilitary ways to contribute. Finally, Baker made clear that there were to be no amateurs in the top-most ranks. He wanted the best, most experienced officers, men "who have devoted their lives exclusively to the study and pursuit of military matters and have made a professional study of the recent changes in the art of war."[37]

Roosevelt's response to Baker was fifteen pages long. In saying that he wanted only the "ablest and most experienced professional military man in our country" in command of any expeditionary force, with others serving who had "actual military experience," Baker devalued not just Roosevelt's crowning moment in Cuba but the Rough Rider's concept of officership.[38] Roosevelt preferred "Colonel" as his postpresidential title for a reason. The adventure of 1898 was a key part of his identity. Further, although he appreciated the importance of military training and experience, he still felt that good character was the essential ingredient for command and that he had the requisite virtues in abundance.

Baker also irritated Roosevelt when he stated that all available officers in the regulars and the National Guard would be used for preparing troops for action. Baker's assigning the National Guard to an equal place with the standing army was bound to provoke a reaction. Roosevelt's disdain for the guard had not tempered since his presidency. The guard remained, in his mind, an institution that was fundamentally broken. Roosevelt recalled the attempt to mobilize the National Guard along the southern border during 1916. He characterized the experience as a fiasco and informed Baker that the plan to use guardsmen as trainers was "completely divorced from sound military policy."[39] Such contemptuous sentiments could hardly win favor from a War Department that had overseen the deployment.

Roosevelt was hardly alone in his opinion of the guard. The press also criticized the guardsmen's performance, and the army chief of staff, Maj. Gen. Hugh Scott, claimed that the guard was unready for service and needed additional months of training. Roosevelt's hostility, however, was obvious. He could not reject quickly enough an offer from Gov. Charles Whitman to commission him as a general in the New York guard in May 1917. His opinion was set even before the governor made the offer, for the guard, apart from any defects, might not go overseas to the action that Roosevelt craved. "In my opinion nothing can be done through the New York National Guard. The men I want won't enlist if I can't tell them that I intend to go abroad, and expect to be sent abroad. I am not engaged in enlisting home guards."[40] All in all, he did not view the guard as a truly military organization.

Nothing was going to help his case with the Wilson administration, but Roosevelt kept pressing. He continued to deride the guard—fit only for "purely state duty"—and to push the concept of a volunteer unit. Even after Baker informed him on 11 May 1917 that his decision against a volunteer unit was final, Roosevelt persisted. He appealed to President Wilson once more, and Wilson turned down him again. The president claimed he did so regretfully and assured Roosevelt that the decision was "based entirely upon imperative considerations of public policy and not upon personal or private choice."[41] More likely, some combination of those factors affected Wilson's decision.

Roosevelt was going to sit out the war. The Wilson administration had sent signals for weeks that the Rough Riders would not rise again. Their old colonel just could not admit that reality, hence his lengthy letters, elaborate plans, and personal visits to promote a volunteer force. He was eager again for war, just as he had been in the 1890s. This time, however, the war, his political position, and the man—now aged beyond his years—were different.

Roosevelt did claim one salutary effect coming out of his campaign. The administration decided in May 1917 to send over an American army division as soon as possible to lift Allied spirits and to begin an American contribution in the trenches. Roosevelt embraced the analysis of the *Brooklyn Daily Eagle*, which claimed that the "Roosevelt agitation," along with Allied pressure, had led to the deployment. Roosevelt also took pleasure from the fact that one of the men he had promoted over hundreds of others during his presidency, John J. Pershing, would lead the American expeditionary force. In Pershing he had a connection in a high place, and, as he so often did, he attempted to use that relationship for personal advantage.[42]

Pershing would arrive in Paris on 13 June 1917. For Roosevelt the immediate task was getting his sons there as soon as possible. If he could not go, then the younger generation would represent the Roosevelt name. Taking advantage of his ties to Pershing, he wrote soon after the general's selection to lead the American expedition to France. Roosevelt "very heartily" congratulated Pershing and then asked for a place for his sons Ted and Archie with Pershing's force. He highlighted their Plattsburg training, stressing how Ted was a major and Archie a captain. Roosevelt believed that they were qualified to go as officers, "even if only as second lieutenants." What he, and they, most wanted was action: "But they are keenly desirous to see service; and if they serve under you at the front, and are not killed, they will be far better able to instruct the draft army next fall, or next winter, or whenever they are sent home." Roosevelt noted how the president had limited officers in the expedition to regulars, and if this rule was to be applied strictly, then he hoped that "my two sons . . . may serve under you as enlisted men." Roosevelt also noted how both Ted and Archie spoke French, which he felt might qualify them further. Not one to rebuff Roosevelt, Pershing responded that he would ask for both Ted and Archie to serve on his staff at their reserve ranks.[43]

No matter their status, Roosevelt wanted his sons to be at the front. Even more, he wished for them to have the test of combat that he had faced. War remained for him more than a physical trial and demonstration of manliness. Conflict was a forge that would harden one's character so that only the best qualities remained: courage of conviction, devotion to bettering oneself and one's society, and a rejection of all that was base. These virtues represented the ultimate benefits of being "in the arena." This calling was not to be just for Ted and Archie. Roosevelt also arranged for his second son, Kermit, to join British forces in Mesopotamia, and the youngest, Quentin, to become part of the fledgling Army Air Service.[44] No matter where or how they served, all four wanted to get into the action, a trait instilled in them by their father.

Roosevelt, therefore, lived the war through his sons. He took great pride in their work as soldiers and saw them as examples of the values that he wanted all Americans to embrace. They mirrored his eagerness to be in the thick of the fighting. In June 1917 Kermit expressed his concern that Ted and Archie were going overseas before him: "I've never been behind before, and don't like to begin." He acknowledged, though, that for his father, "it's a thousand times harder, of course," to be left behind.[45] Such a wish for action was just what Roosevelt wanted to see, and he repeatedly praised his sons from his perch at Sagamore Hill. He was thrilled in August 1917 to learn that Ted was given command of a battalion in a regular army regiment and that all four boys, along with his son-in-law Richard Derby, were going into action. He told Ted, "You have the fighting tradition! I am overjoyed that you four have your chance, whatever the cost." Later that month he again told Ted of his pride and his own regret at missing out on a much bigger conflict than the Spanish-American War: "I am *very* proud of you—and of all my boys. And my only personal consolation is that I was in the only war I had a chance at, even altho it was only a small one."[46]

From afar Roosevelt continued to prod his sons. To Archie he expressed pleasure in early September 1917 that both he and Ted had "at once got into the line." To Quentin he confessed his disappointment at not being able to be with him in France. While the boys were exposed to danger, he was "at home in do-nothing ease and safety." However, that feeling, he confessed, had been replaced by the "immense pride" he had in Quen-tin and his three brothers: "all of *you* children, have by your deeds justified *my* words!!"[47] After all, he told Archie later that month, upon learning that his third son had declined a staff position, "We are fighting men; it is in the line that we can do our work to best advantage."[48]

The proud father was particularly pleased when he learned of his sons' exploits at the front. Kermit was the first to see fighting, serving with British forces in Mesopotamia. There he took part in combat around Baghdad, under the leadership of British general Frederick Maude, who, T.R. learned, had been "much pleased" with Kermit's work.[49] Then in March 1918 Roosevelt received word that Archie had earned the French Croix de Guerre in combat action, although he had suffered, according to early reports, wounds to the leg and a broken arm. The "excitement about Archie," Roosevelt told Quentin, occurred under "dra-matic circumstances," which thrilled the colonel. The wounds he characterized as slight.[50] His pride, though, burst all bounds when he informed Georges Clemenceau, the French prime min-ister, about Archie being awarded the Croix de Guerre: "I am prouder of his having received it than of my having been Pres-ident!"[51] Then Quentin's turn came. He had his first taste of aerial combat on the western front, as the German offensive of 1918 began to slow. In July Roosevelt learned that Quentin had downed an enemy aircraft in action near Château-Thierry. T.R. rejoiced, "We are immensely excited over the press reports of Quentin's feat." After all, Quentin "now had his crowded hour," a time that took his father back to the moment when he had stood the ultimate test at the San Juan Heights. Nothing more mattered, for Quentin had "his day of honor and triumph."[52] "The last of the 'lion's brood' had been bloodied!" Roosevelt wrote to Kermit on 13 July 1918.[53]

Quentin's victory, indeed, made for a stirring tale. His air battle consisted of single combat and had all the features that gave air warfare in World War I a romantic cast, restoring a sense of individual glory amid the mass slaughter. This was just the kind of war his father had pictured as a child, and it was the image of conflict that he had passed on to his sons. Quentin had been part of a flight of four airplanes flying north of Château-Thierry. The flyers were eight miles over German lines when they became separated in a cloud. Emerging, Quentin saw three other aircraft and, assuming they were his companions, dropped to their rear. Then he realized his error. The other aircraft had German markings. He sent fifty tracers into the nearest German airplane and sent it spinning. The other two Germans attacked, but Quentin evaded them and returned safely to base, without a mark on himself or his airplane.[54] Such accomplishments made for legends about knights of the air, but covered a grim reality. The war in the air had its own type of attrition, as a pilot's life expectancy was very brief.

That truth would claim Quentin within days of his victory and bring home to his father the true costs of war. On 14 July Quentin was in a patrol of ten aircraft surveying the American lines. A half hour into their flight they reportedly encountered eight members of the German unit made famous by Baron Manfred von Richthofen, the Flying Circus. Air-to-air combat ensued, and then the Americans pursued the retreating Germans into enemy airspace. After the Americans turned for home, they noticed that two of their number were absent. One had made a forced landing, but Lieutenant Roosevelt's plane was missing. There was some hope that he may have survived, as no one had seen his plane go down. On 17 July his parents learned that he was missing, and then on 20 July the German government announced his death. The Germans gave him a military funeral. On 9 August American airmen located his grave. Quentin had been in action for five weeks and fought in three air battles before his fatal encounter of 14 July.[55]

In public and with his family, the colonel put on a brave face. He honored Quentin as a paragon of the values he had preached for so long. To Kermit, he extolled his youngest, proclaiming, "No man could have died in finer or more gallant fashion." Although Roosevelt confessed his sorrow and lamented "that the young should die," he still declared "how infinitely better death is than life purchased on unworthy terms."[56] To James Bryce, the former British ambassador to the United States, Roosevelt summed up Quentin's death and the deaths of so many others in even loftier tones: "But they have died with high honor, and not in vain; for it is they, and those like them, who have saved the soul of the world."[57]

In private Roosevelt was in anguish. The personal loss was great. At Sagamore Hill the staff there would hear him say "Poor Qunikins" when Roosevelt thought he was alone.[58] Daughter Ethel reported that her mother came to terms with the loss sooner than her father, who appeared "far more unreconciled and more bitter." Ethel thought that for T.R. "it is particularly hard having the youngest go—and he had so much before him."[59] Historian H. W. Brands has suggested that Quentin's death hastened Roosevelt's own demise.[60] By the fall of 1918, he was in and out of the hospital, aged beyond his sixty years. The infections that had plagued him since the Amazon and the streetcar collision of 1902 were the likely culprits. His doctors treated him for inflammatory rheumatism, but whatever the cause Roosevelt was virtually immobile by the fall of 1918. If that were not enough of a blow to his spirit, Quentin's death sapped his zest for life.

The death of his youngest also may have triggered a profound personal crisis. Roosevelt had steadfastly maintained his notions of valor. Quentin's death caused him to question those ideas, even if it did not shatter them entirely. About ten days after hearing the reports from France, while he was still in the early stages of grief, he admitted that "to feel that one has inspired a boy to conduct that has resulted in his death, has a pretty serious side for a father." Yet he would not surrender to his doubts, for his next thought raced back to his old principles: "and at the same time I would not have cared for my boys and they would not have cared for me if our relations had not been just along that line."[61] His was a mind being pulled between two poles. One still held romantic conceptions of battle, but the other now experienced the cost of war and what life was like for those left at home. The strain was bound to wear at him.[62]

Although Quentin's life was the highest price that the Roosevelt family paid in the Great War, the conflict exacted a toll on two other sons. Ted was gassed and shot in the leg in the summer of 1918. He would be away from the front until just before the armistice in November.[63] Archie's wounds turned out to be much worse than T.R. had originally thought. The wounds to Archie's arms and legs were enough to have him sent back to America for recovery. With Archie, however, the wounds were more than physical. His sister Ethel expressed in September 1918, upon his return home, her surprise that he was doing so well, as "he wrote such desperate letters that I was terribly frightened about him." Although Archie remained "weak and ill," she reported to Kermit that "he is normal." Psychological wounds apparently remained. Ethel noted nearly a month later how hard it was to go to the apartment of Archie and his wife, Gracie, noting that they were "entirely different from any of us & quite detached."[64]

For her father's part, he did acknowledge the severity of Archie's physical wounds once he learned more about them, and he understood that Archie would recover more quickly if he came home rather than "spend months of pain and idleness in Paris."[65] Once Archie was back in the family fold, Roosevelt described his wounds in glowing terms: "Of our four hawks one has come home, broke-winged, but his soul as high as ever."[66] He did not acknowledge the trauma to Archie that Ethel had perceived. Rather, for the colonel, Archie was "completely reconciled to coming back, and is very happy, and really seems his natural old self."[67] Roosevelt's impression of his son may have been correct or perhaps involved an element of denial. Archie may well have put on a brave face to shield his condition. For Roosevelt to have confronted the additional cost of war, so soon after Quentin's death, might have been too much to ask.

Politics provided Roosevelt with a diversion from his personal grief and gave him a battle that he could fight. After President Wilson had denied his request to raise volunteer units, T.R. resumed his attacks against the administration. He would not declare a truce as far as Wilson was concerned. Before the American entry into the fighting, Roosevelt had railed against the lack of preparedness. Now he blamed the lag in American mobilization on the administration's prewar policies and the president's failure to embrace volunteer formations. Equally unpardonable was Wilson's dilatory behavior in mobilizing shipping to expedite the transport of war goods to the fighting front. Roosevelt also heaped scorn on individuals associated with Wilson and the war effort. Bainbridge Colby, of the United States Shipping Board, had "not a qualification for the place," and Walter Lippmann and Felix Frankfurter were unfit as assistants to the secretary of war. In sum, such men were more of Wilson's "ridiculous creatures." Later the colonel found Wilson's war aims, the Fourteen Points, to be unacceptable. The only acceptable condition for peace with Germany was unconditional surrender. To negotiate a peace on the basis of the Fourteen Points "would represent not the unconditional surrender of Germany but the conditional surrender of the United States." Roosevelt declared, "Let us dictate peace by the hammering guns and not chat about peace to the accompaniment of the clicking of typewriters."[68]

Policy differences aside, the fact that Wilson held power and he did not was a principal reason for Roosevelt's antagonism. Woodrow Wilson was commander in chief at a momentous time, and Roosevelt considered himself the much better man to direct a war. Two months after the United States declared war, and soon after Wilson denied T.R.'s ambition to raise troops, Roosevelt resumed his criticism of the president's character. He described Wilson as "merely a rhetorician, vindictive and yet not physically brave." The colonel would also denounce Wilson as hypocritical, cynical, and unpatriotic, believing that the chief executive acted only in his political self-interest and not the best interest of the country. For Roosevelt prime evidence was in the president's 1916 campaign slogan: "He kept us out of war." Wilson, he believed, "had no convictions in the matter." The campaign slogan was a clever one and secured a second term for Wilson, but Roosevelt claimed that a larger disservice to the country had been done. Rather than build public support for a necessary intervention, which T.R. believed should have resulted after the sinking of the *Lusitania*, Wilson had misled the public and then pivoted a few months later to take the country into war. The result, Roosevelt believed, was confusion and a nation morally and materially unprepared for battle.[69]

As the 1918 congressional elections approached, Roosevelt saw a prime role for himself. He could help heal the remaining wounds that he had inflicted on the Republican Party in 1912, position himself as a possible candidate for president in 1920, and strike a blow against Woodrow Wilson by breaking the Democratic hold on both houses of Congress. Roosevelt worked throughout the fall of 1918 for Republican candidates, and then in October Wilson made the election personal when he asked the public for a vote of confidence via the November races. The president needed a renewed Democratic majority if voters "wish me to continue to be your unembarrassed spokes-man in affairs at home and abroad."[70]

Roosevelt was eager to see Wilson embarrassed when votes were cast on 5 November. On 28 October 1918 the colonel went to Carnegie Hall in New York City and blasted the president. The receptive crowd of Republicans heard an energized Roos-evelt deliver what one newspaper headlined as a "Rabid Polit-ical Speech." Indeed, Wilson's recent appeal for a Democratic result was the perfect ammunition for Roosevelt. T.R. charac-terized as "veriest nonsense" the idea that "failure to return a Democratic Congress this fall would be interpreted by the Allies and Germany as being a repudiation of the war aims of this country." Rather, Roosevelt proclaimed, "what we need is an American Congress, a Congress of straight-out Americans and not a Congress of rubber stamps." He went on to condemn the Wilson administration's war leadership, partisanship, and inefficiency. Roosevelt also called for repudiation of the Four-teen Points. "Good Americans should regard them with suspi-cion," he believed, because Germany and German sympathizers in America had embraced them, especially "Germanized Social-ists" and "Bolshevists of every grade."[71]

Roosevelt traveled with Edith on 5 November to the Oyster Bay blacksmith shop, the local polling place, to cast his vote. As he left, the colonel expressed his desire for a Republican tri-umph. He got his wish. The Republicans won a strong majority in the House of Representatives and a slim margin, but a major-ity nonetheless, in the Senate.[72] Roosevelt had long wanted to beat Woodrow Wilson and took credit for the "stinging rebuke." He savored that Wilson had made the election a vote of con-fidence and lost. In working for the Republican victory, Roo-sevelt believed that he "was able to render substantial service to the allies" in keeping Wilson from negotiating a peace with Germany, "which would put him personally on a pinnacle of glory" but would "double-cross the allies." That is, Roosevelt believed he had saved the Allies from a peace that would be far too favorable to Germany.[73]

He would not have long to enjoy the victory. His health was failing fast. On 11 November, the day of the armistice, he was taken back to the hospital for a lengthy stay. High fevers, inflammatory rheumatism, and symptoms of pulmonary embolism plagued him. He left the hospital to return to Sagamore Hill at Christmas but remained weak, virtually an invalid.[74] Death came quietly as he slept in the early morning of 6 January 1919. An embolism had quieted the strenuous life of Theodore Roosevelt.

Conclusion

Even as his health failed, Theodore Roosevelt considered a run for the presidency in 1920. He saw the election as another call to duty. Rejecting an appeal to run for New York governor in 1918, he told his sister Corinne, "I have only one fight left in me, and I think I should reserve my strength in case I am needed in 1920."[1] Had he lived and had all the political pieces somehow aligned, Roosevelt would have been in an interesting place as president in the 1920s. One wonders what pronouncements he might have aimed at the cultural developments of that decade. Would his Progressive impulses have found resonance in the political environment of post–Great War America? And in what direction would he guide foreign and military policies as leader of a nation that remained unsure about its role as a major power? Roosevelt's personal appeal might have won him the White House, but the idea that Americans loved the man, if not his policies, might have been true by the 1920s, making him more than ever a man who had lived beyond his time.

In diplomatic and military affairs, the level of international engagement that Theodore Roosevelt wanted, while notably different from Woodrow Wilson's internationalist vision, seemed unlikely to find broad favor among a public disillusioned by the experience of World War I. Roosevelt derided Wilson's internationalism as unrealistic and self-serving, but he did not completely dismiss proposals such as the League of Nations. He stated in late 1918 that "I am for such a League," but with provisions. T.R. did not think that much could be expected from it, and he did not want it to "interfere with some such system . . . of universal obligatory training for all our young men."[2] With his support, and that of Henry Cabot Lodge, the Senate may have approved the Treaty of Versailles. Roosevelt's aspiration for an even closer alignment with Great Britain was more dubious. He claimed to Rudyard Kipling in November 1918 that he was "willing now to go into any kind of close agreement with the British Empire," including a possible "mutual guarantee based on a defensive alliance."[3] This proposed "entanglement" would likely have been a dead letter given the postwar political climate, even if it were Theodore Roosevelt who advocated the idea. Also in the realm of the unlikely would be Roosevelt catering to postwar impulses to cut back on armaments, especially the world's navies. The Washington Naval Conference of 1921–22 trimmed sixty-six capital ships from naval inventories. It is hard to conceive of Theodore Roosevelt agreeing to pare a considerable number of vessels from the U.S. fleet, much less host the conference in the first place. Yet Americans cheered Secretary of State Charles Evans Hughes's dramatic cuts when he proposed them in November 1921.[4]

Roosevelt had been a true turn-of-the-century man, and at the height of his powers he had helped the U.S. government, and the military specifically, become more effective institutions. He could be labeled a modernizer, and if he represented a bridge between older and newer, then by the time of his death America had crossed much of the span to a modern society and culture. A fundamental tension between traditional and modern continued to exist in society, but at the time of Roosevelt's death the country was on the cusp of more liberal social behavior, the jazz age, a consumer-products boom, and so much more. Although Roosevelt possessed abundant curiosity, loved learning, and enjoyed new gadgets, the heightened sexuality of the

1920s and emergence of the "New Woman" would likely have distressed him, and he would have worried about Americans becoming too obsessed with material pursuits. The preacher militant in him likely would have again summoned Americans to do, in his opinion, better.

Roosevelt may have embraced the industry, cities, and technology of modern America, but he remained a Victorian to the end of his days. He viewed people in moral terms and judged them along such lines. For one of his favorite soldiers, John Pershing, he heaped praise, labeling Pershing's actions as "brilliant" and "admirable."[5] He expressed, by contrast, dislike of Woodrow Wilson in the strongest terms. Wilson was the "cold-blooded, selfish, and tricky creature now at the head of the nation, who does *not* give a rap for the country."[6] Such views validated Roosevelt's personal political outlook and granted him a license to act on his own ideas and on his own behalf because *he* would be serving a higher calling. His sense of purpose had led him to personal and political success in life but had also spawned some of his greatest controversies.

Roosevelt's father, the idolized Theodore Senior, had instilled the call to higher duty, and T.R.'s romanticized view of war pressed deeper that sense of obligation. Roosevelt constantly measured himself in civic life against the standard of his father and, in military affairs, drew inspiration from his Confederate uncles. To his credit Roosevelt sought to "do better" throughout his life, whether he was trying to build his body as a boy, weed out corruption, or risk danger in war or the jungle. He sought the same for the nation, as he promoted new administrative systems, worked to install men of his own type in positions of authority, and urged Americans, in general, to serve their country, states, and communities. He certainly succeeded with his own offspring, as all of his children participated in public life in various ways.

Roosevelt could look back with pride on all that he had done when he turned sixty in October 1918. He told Kermit that he was "glad to be sixty, for it somehow gives me the right to be titularly as old as I feel," and he hoped Kermit would have the same happiness that he had experienced.[7] Indeed, beyond enjoying a large family and a growing brood of grandchildren, Roosevelt could review a long list of accomplishments. During his presidency he had set precedents in the conservation of natural resources and business regulation. He extended the reach of the presidency and expanded the United States' international role. The construction of the Panama Canal was a particular point of pride, as was the continued expansion of the U.S. Navy, which together were part of an integrated foreign and military policy. Roosevelt understood that he had a secure place in history.

In military matters he had armed the country for a new century. Roosevelt did not succeed in all that he set out to do, but he did expand greatly on a foundation of military modernization laid in the late nineteenth century, and he advanced technology, personnel policy, and training for twentieth-century missions. He accomplished more with the navy, with the adoption of a true fleet formation and the addition of sixteen battleships.[8] The fleet remained unbalanced, as Roosevelt failed to win approval of enough smaller vessels, and finding crew members for new ships remained a challenge, but the enlarging of the navy was still an important achievement. He also promoted the move to the powerful dreadnought-style of battleship and took an interest in submarine technology. Efforts to reform the administration of the Navy Department, however, were cast aside in favor of expanding the battleship force.

The army received less attention but also underwent significant change. Roosevelt could rely on trusted lieutenants Elihu Root and William Howard Taft for stewardship over the War Department. The creation of a general staff, small as it was at the time, provided a starting point for a more modern command system. Militia reform legislation put the National Guard on the path to more federal involvement in training and supply. Roosevelt was not a fan of the guard, but being a practical politician he realized that abolition of the guard was not a possibility and that limited reform was the most that he could manage at the time. His administration also encouraged larger unit maneuvers and a more professional and physically fit officer corps. The attempt to seed younger officers in top commands grew from his inability to secure reform of the promotion system, and his physical fitness requirements also had flaws but pointed the army in the right direction.

Roosevelt was a shrewd politician. He would never have gotten far if he were not. The securing of the Republican nomination in 1904 demonstrated his mastery of party machinery, and his ability to shepherd significant measures through Congress showed his ability to work with the legislature. Roosevelt created trouble for himself when his self-righteous streak took over his better judgment. He was an effective leader because he had core principles that informed the goals he wanted to accomplish. Compromise was often required as a political tactic to achieve a higher legislative and moral end. T.R. recognized that politics was the art of the possible, but there were times, especially when he saw his presidential position challenged, that he would not back off from a stand. His actions in the Brownsville affair represented the most notorious case of such behavior. Roosevelt refused to yield ground even after his order seemed increasingly unjust, and he grew intemperate at the challenges to his judgment and authority. In other areas his physical fitness test for officers was arbitrary, and his proposal to abolish the Marine Corps proved counterproductive. Both grew out of a sense that there was a moral failing that he needed to address. The maintenance of a small Marine Corps seemed inefficient, but, more important, the corps had sinned through excessive self-promotion. As for physical standards, poor conditioning reflected a grave personal flaw in Roosevelt's mind, and he denied complaints that the physical test was unfair. His stubbornness in such situations diminished his standing and needlessly subtracted from the objective that he was seeking to obtain.

Roosevelt would make controversial stands to advance what he deemed a greater good, especially when he felt it was the only way to achieve results. He could do so because his status as commander in chief granted a certain liberty of action. His promotion of younger officers to high command was one example. Roosevelt could not secure legislation for wholesale personnel reform, but he could win individual votes in the Senate to install younger officers—and allies—in top posts. Over time, passed-over officers and their partisans slowed this practice, but Roosevelt did install several men who would take the army to war in 1917.

Less irritating was Roosevelt's tendency to dabble in areas of personal interest, and his fascination with military technology often expedited change. He took advantage of being president to gain access to a variety of projects. He could indulge the boyish side of his personality, whether he was poking around the inner workings of a battleship, handling a new set of entrenching tools, or taking the controls of a submarine. In these ventures he did more than satisfy himself. He promoted emergent technologies. The adoption of the all-big-gun battleship kept the United States in line with developments in the other major naval powers, even though it meant even larger naval budgets. Ironically, he also played a significant role in advancing the technologies that would one day be the undoing of the battleship. After his submarine trip Roosevelt recognized the contributions of submarine crews, thereby making service in these vessels more attractive and helping to ensure the continued development of subsurface technology. He had also maintained an interest in aviation since his service as assistant secretary of the navy. During his presidency the War Department would begin to pursue the development of these frail craft, which became a tormentor of battleships during World War II.

Roosevelt could not foresee how the aircraft and submarines of his day would evolve. He was more farsighted in establishing overseas military bases to project power and protect interests. Later conflicts, chiefly World War II and the Cold War, would make that overseas architecture very elaborate, but the principles that guided Roosevelt endured. Although the needs of coal-fired vessels were different from those of diesel and nuclear-powered ships, advanced stations remained necessary, crews needed rest and replacement, and ships required refit. Moreover, forward bases provided the intangible quality of presence that assisted national foreign policy. Pearl Harbor and Guantánamo Bay remained bases, and the naval station at Subic Bay grew into a major installation, especially during the Vietnam War.[9] Moreover, Roosevelt's dispatch of the battle fleet on the world cruise forecast the fleets and the task forces used in more recent times to project American power.

Capable forces and a robust foreign policy were of one piece, but Roosevelt had an additional agenda in pushing these things. Moral concerns were his primary interest, and Roosevelt fretted about the moral well-being of the nation. During his lifetime he had witnessed the emergence of an economic giant with cities that teemed in the millions. He worried that rapid urbanization and industrialization brought with it a Faustian bargain: the degradation of the national soul. As one who subscribed to the importance of the frontier experience in building a virtuous character, Roosevelt feared that moral decay would take hold. There would be fewer opportunities for rough living in which people could develop physical power and demonstrate courage and independence—hence Roosevelt's passion for conserving nature and his desire that the nation take on imperial duties. His support for Universal Military Training and the

Plattsburg movement stemmed equally from concerns about preparedness and giving young men discipline and an outlet for national service. Universal Military Training would not be adopted during his lifetime or thereafter, although a military draft would be used in both world wars and during the Cold War. The Plattsburg idea has found continued life in the Reserve Officers Training Corps.

Roosevelt's martial spirit would live on in his children. His three surviving sons—Ted, Kermit, and Archie—continued to exhibit their father's dash and eagerness to see battle when the next world war erupted. Doing the most to live up to his name, Ted served as assistant secretary of the navy after World War I, governor of the Philippines, and governor of Puerto Rico. He sought active duty again in 1941. Commissioned a colonel, he became a brigadier general in 1942 and participated in the invasions of North Africa and Sicily. His hour of glory came in the Normandy landings of 6 June 1944. When his unit landed nearly a mile off target at Utah Beach, Roosevelt personally led his men inland and got them on track, exposing himself all the while to German fire. Ted received the Medal of Honor for this action. Death soon claimed him, but not in battle. He collapsed and died from a heart condition about a month later.[10]

Kermit tried to repeat his Great War experience by using family ties to join British forces in the spring of 1940. He lasted until early 1941. His nemesis was liquor. Reminiscent of his uncle Elliott, he had taken to drink and a mistress, and his alcoholism would only grow worse during World War II. The family used connections to get him a commission in the U.S. Army, but his body, so ravaged by excess, could not tolerate even light service. In June 1943, stationed in Alaska, he picked up a gun and committed suicide.[11]

Archie had endured severe physical and psychological wounds in World War I, but he again wanted to be part of the fight in World War II. Family influence also won him a commission. He

served in the South Pacific, demonstrating once more the Rooseveltian proclivity for taking risks. His luck ran out when he
was wounded and again declared, as in World War I, 100 percent disabled. Unlike his older brothers, Archie would survive
the war and died at age eighty-five in 1979.[12]

Roosevelt lived on in other ways, too. Daughter Ethel dedicated herself to preserving his memory, and Alice, the eldest
child, remained a fixture in Washington DC until her death
in 1980. Even though T.R. died in 1919, reminders of the man
and his work dot the American landscape. His visage on Mount
Rushmore remains the most obvious example, but a national
park, historic sites, a memorial, and a Utah city—among other
things—bear his name. The U.S. military, particularly the navy,
has also continued to honor the former commander in chief.
Three ships have borne his name. The first was a troop transport in World War I. A ballistic submarine, far from the tiny
Plunger of Roosevelt's time, had his name from 1961 to 1982.
Since 1986 a *Nimitz*-class aircraft carrier (CVN-71) has carried
on his legacy. Known in the fleet as "Rough Rider," the *Theodore
Roosevelt* has participated in several actions, including Operations Desert Shield and Desert Storm in 1991.[13] This ship was a
fitting tribute, for it helped carry the navy from the century that
Roosevelt began into the twenty-first. Supplanting battleships
as the queen of naval battle, aircraft carriers have been a powerful way for the United States to exert influence. Such vessels
are a natural extension of the work that Theodore Roosevelt
began as he sought to prepare the military, and the American
nation, for the challenges of his time.

NOTES

Introduction

1. Trask, *War with Spain*, 240–45; Roosevelt, *Rough Riders*, 117–26.

2. Theodore Roosevelt to Henry Cabot Lodge, 19 July 1898, in Morison, *Letters*, 2:853.

3. Roosevelt, *Rough Riders*, 117–18, 126–34, 136, 138–39.

4. Roosevelt to William Sturgis Bigelow, 29 March 1898, in Morison, *Letters*, 2:803.

5. Roosevelt, *Autobiography*, 7.

6. Hoganson, *Fighting for American Manhood*; Bederman, *Manliness and Civilization*.

7. Roosevelt to Lodge, 10 July 1898, 19 July 1898, in Morison, *Letters*, 2:851–52.

8. E. Morris, *Rise of Theodore Roosevelt*, 665–66, 686, 738.

9. See, for example, Berman, *Lyndon Johnson's War*; Larrabee, *Commander in Chief*; and Williams, *Lincoln and His Generals*.

10. Roosevelt to Georges Clemenceau, 6 June 1917, Correspondence and Compositions, MS Am 1540, TRCH.

11. Dalton, *Theodore Roosevelt*, 6–7; see also Brands, *T.R.*

12. Brands, *T.R.*, x.

13. Roosevelt, *American Ideals*, in Hagedorn, *Works*, 13:197.

14. Dalton, *Theodore Roosevelt*, 9.

15. Cooper, *Pivotal Decades*, 36.

16. Burton, *Learned Presidency*.

17. Wiebe, *Search for Order*; Skowronek, *New American State*.

18. Dyer, *Idea of Race*, 31–32.

19. Roosevelt to Frederick Jackson Turner, 10 February 1894, in Morison, *Letters*, 1:363.

20. McCoy, *Elusive Republic*, 70.

21. Roosevelt to Turner, 4 November 1896, in Morison, *Letters*, 1:564.

1. Beginnings

1. Robinson, *My Brother Theodore Roosevelt*, 206–7.

2. For example, see Bederman, *Manliness and Civilization*; Collin, *Culture, Diplomacy, and Expansion*; Hoganson, *Fighting for American Manhood*; and Watts, *Rough Rider*.

3. Dalton, *Theodore Roosevelt*, 17–19; McCullough, *Mornings on Horseback*, 182–83.

4. Dalton, *Theodore Roosevelt*, 27.

5. Roosevelt, *Autobiography*, 11.

6. McCullough, *Mornings on Horseback*, 71–76.

7. Roosevelt, qtd. in E. Morris, *Rise of Theodore Roosevelt*, 40.

8. Roosevelt, *Autobiography*, 11.

9. Theodore Roosevelt to Josephine Shaw Lowell, 20 February 1900, in Morison, *Letters*, 2:1193.

10. E. Morris, *Rise of Theodore Roosevelt*, 40, 44, 49, 53–55, 60.

11. Dalton, *Theodore Roosevelt*, 52.

12. Roosevelt to Henry Cabot Lodge, 29 April 1896, in Morison, *Letters*, 1:536.

13. Roosevelt, qtd. in Gardner, *Departing Glory*, 326.

14. "The Late Mr. Roosevelt," *New York Times*, 13 February 1878, 2.

15. Roosevelt, *Naval War of 1812*, in Hagedorn, *Works*, vol. 6.

16. Lance C. Buhl, "Maintaining 'An American Navy,' 1865–1889," in Hagan, *In Peace and War*, 147–48.

17. Roosevelt, *Naval War of 1812*, in Hagedorn, *Works*, 6:xxiv, 360–72; Burton, *Learned Presidency*, 47–48.

18. Roosevelt, *Naval War of 1812*, in Hagedorn, *Works*, 6:xxiv; Burton, *Learned Presidency*, 48.

19. Roosevelt, *Naval War of 1812*, in Hagedorn, *Works*, 6:365.

20. Mahon, *History of the Militia*, 113, 116–18.

21. Roosevelt, *Strenuous Life*, in Hagedorn, *Works*, 13:564.

22. Headquarters, Eighth Regiment, National Guard of New York to Roosevelt, letter fragment, 24 August 1883, MS Am 1454, TRCH.

23. Roosevelt to Lt. T. W. Young, 16 April 1883, 1858–1919 Correspondence and Compositions, MS Am 1540, TRCH.

24. Address before the New York State National Guard Association, 8 February 1900, MS Am 1454.50 (137), TRCH.

25. E. Morris, *Rise of Theodore Roosevelt*, 305.

26. E. Morris, *Rise of Theodore Roosevelt*, 197–98; Address, 8 February 1900, MS Am 1454.50 (137), TRCH.

27. Roosevelt to Anna Roosevelt, 17 June 1884, in Morison, *Letters*, 1:73.

28. Roosevelt to Anna Roosevelt, 16 April 1887, in Morison, *Letters*, 1:126–27.

29. *New York Star*, qtd. in Kimmel, "Born to Run," in Kimmel, *Politics of Manhood*, 134; Watts, *Rough Rider*, 126.

30. Address, 8 February 1900, MS Am 1454.50 (137), TRCH.

31. Roosevelt to Lodge, 10 August 1886, 25 May 1898, in Morison, *Letters*, 1:108, 2:833.

32. Roosevelt, *Rough Riders*, 17.

33. Turk, *Ambiguous Relationship*, 14.

34. Roosevelt, *Autobiography*, 114–20, 124–25; E. Morris, *Rise of Theodore Roosevelt*, 323–27.

35. Roosevelt, *American Problems*, in Hagedorn, *Works*, 16:250.

36. Roosevelt to Lodge, 20 April 1887, in Morison, *Letters*, 1:127.

37. Roosevelt to Anna Roosevelt, 8 July 1888, in Morison, *Letters*, 1:142.

38. Roosevelt to Henry C. Merwin, 18 December 1894, in Morison, *Letters*, 1:412–17; Blum, *Republican Roosevelt*, 3.

39. Roosevelt, *American Ideals*, in Hagedorn, *Works*, 13:259.

40. Roosevelt, *Autobiography*, 210.

41. Roosevelt to William Strong, 17 April 1897, in Morison, *Letters*, 1:595.

42. Vandiver, *Black Jack*, 1:161–62; Andrews, *My Friend and Classmate*, 52–54; Roosevelt, *Winning of the West*, in Hagedorn, *Works*, vol. 9; see especially pages 323–24, 330–31, 340–41, and 345–46 for Roosevelt's plaudits to Anthony Wayne and the army in pacifying the Old Northwest.

43. Millett, "Roosevelt and His Generals"; Roosevelt to William S. Cowles, 11 February 1896, in Morison, *Letters*, 1:512.

44. Roosevelt to W. S. Cowles, 11 February 1896, in Morison, *Letters*, 1:512; Roosevelt to Francis V. Greene, 15 September 1897, 13 January 1898, in Morison, *Letters*, 1:679, 758–59; Roosevelt to Lodge, 21 July 1899, in Morison, *Letters*, 2:1037; Malone and Johnson, *Dictionary of American Biography*, 7:565–66. The quote is from Roosevelt to John Hay, 1 July 1899, in Morison, *Letters*, 2:1025.

45. Roosevelt to Anna Roosevelt, 4 July 1895, in Morison, *Letters*, 1:464.

46. Spector, *Professors of War*, 1.

47. Stephen B. Luce to Roosevelt, 13 February 1888, series 1, roll 1, TRLC.

48. Turk, *Ambiguous Relationship*, 15; Luce-Roosevelt Correspondence, roll 19, SLLC.

49. Roosevelt to Alfred Thayer Mahan, 12 May 1890, in Morison, *Letters*, 1:221.

50. Roosevelt, *Literary Essays*, in Hagedorn, *Works*, 12:264, 273, 280.

51. Roosevelt to Mahan, 1 May 1893, in Morison, *Letters*, 1:315 and note 2.

52. Mahan to Roosevelt, 18 March 1893, 26 March 1893, in Seager and Maguire, *Letters and Papers*, 2:98–99, 100–101; Roosevelt to Mahan, 1 May 1893, in Morison, *Letters*, 1:315.

53. Mahan to Hilary Herbert, 25 January 1894, in Seager and Maguire, *Letters and Papers*, 2:212–15.

54. Spector, *Professors of War*, 54–55; Nicolosi, "Stephen B. Luce," 121.

55. Burton, *Learned Presidency*, 48; Turk, *Ambiguous Relationship*, 1–2, 15–20, 37, 106.

56. Roosevelt to Anna Roosevelt, 4 July 1895, in Morison, *Letters*, 1:464–65; Roosevelt to W. S. Cowles, 22 December 1895, 11 February 1896, 20 June 1896, in Morison, *Letters*, 1:501, 512, 544; E. Morris, *Rise of Theodore Roosevelt*, 540.

57. Roosevelt to Anna Roosevelt, 4 July 1895, in Morison, *Letters*, 1:464; Roosevelt to W. S. Cowles, 25 April 1898, in Morison, *Letters*, 2:821.

58. Dalton, *Theodore Roosevelt*, 139.

59. Roosevelt, *American Ideals*, in Hagedorn, *Works*, 13:28.

60. Roosevelt to Bellamy Storer, 10 August 1896, in Morison, *Letters*, 1:556; Roosevelt to Maria Longworth Storer, 5 December 1896, in Morison, *Letters*, 1:569; Roosevelt to M. Storer, 16 September 1901, series 1, roll 19, TRLC; E. Morris, *Rise of Theodore Roosevelt*, 512, 538–44.

61. Roosevelt to M. Storer, 20 October 1895, in Morison, *Letters*, 1:495.

62. McCullough, *Mornings on Horseback*, 144–45.

63. E. Morris, *Rise of Theodore Roosevelt*, 429–31, 437–38.

64. Roosevelt to Anna Roosevelt, 29 July 1894, in Morison, *Letters*, 1:392.

65. E. Morris, *Rise of Theodore Roosevelt*, 474.

66. Roosevelt, *American Ideals*, in Hagedorn, *Works*, 13:15.

67. Roosevelt to George F. Becker, in Morison, *Letters*, 2:1068.

68. Roosevelt to Lodge, 29 April 1896, in Morison, *Letters*, 1:535–36; Roosevelt to Cecil Arthur Spring Rice, 2 December 1899, in Morison, *Letters*, 2:1104; Roosevelt, *American Ideals*, in Hagedorn, *Works*, 13:9, 17, 246–47, 253, 259–60.

69. Roosevelt to Lodge, 29 April 1896, in Morison, *Letters*, 1:536; Roosevelt to Spring Rice, 2 December 1899, in Morison, *Letters*, 2:1104.

70. Roosevelt to Becker, in Morison, *Letters*, 2:1068.

71. Roosevelt, *American Ideals*, in Hagedorn, *Works*, 13:242, 246–47, 253–54, 258; Hofstadter, *Social Darwinism*, 188–89.

72. Roosevelt, *American Ideals*, in Hagedorn, *Works*, 13:253–54, 260.

73. Roosevelt to Spring Rice, 2 December 1899, in Morison, *Letters*, 2:1104.

2. In the Arena

1. Theodore Roosevelt to Thomas Lounsbury, 2 March 1897, in Morison, *Letters*, 1:583.

2. Roosevelt to Anna Roosevelt Cowles, 21 February 1897, in Morison, *Letters*, 1:582.

3. E. Morris, *Rise of Theodore Roosevelt*, 543–44, 555.

4. "Mr. Roosevelt Is Chosen," *New York Times*, 7 April 1897, 1.

5. Roosevelt to A. R. Cowles, 21 February 1897, in Morison, *Letters*, 1:583; Roosevelt to William E. Mantius, 20 April 1897, in Morison, *Letters*, 1:599.

6. Roosevelt to Bowman Hendry McCalla, 19 April 1897, in Morison, *Letters*, 1:599.

7. Roosevelt to Cecil Arthur Spring Rice, 28 April 1897, in Morison, *Letters*, 1:604.

8. Roosevelt to William McKinley, 26 April 1897, in Morison, *Letters*, 1:602–3; Roosevelt to John Davis Long, 26 April 1897, in Morison, *Letters*, 1:603–4.

9. Roosevelt to Spring Rice, 29 May 1897, in Morison, *Letters*, 1:618. See also Roosevelt to Spring Rice, 28 April 1897, in Morison, *Letters*, 1:604.

10. Roosevelt to Long, 18 September 1897, in Morison, *Letters*, 1:682; Roosevelt to William Eaton Chandler, 26 October 1897, in Morison, *Letters*, 1:700–701.

11. Roosevelt to Chandler, 23 September 1897, 30 October 1897, in Morison, *Letters*, 1:688, 701.

12. Roosevelt to Long, 18 September 1897, in Morison, *Letters*, 1:682; Roosevelt to Chandler, 26 October 1897, in Morison, *Letters*, 1:700–701.

13. Roosevelt to Long, 4 September 1897, in Morison, *Letters*, 1:668.

14. Roosevelt to Alfred T. Mahan, 3 May 1897, in Morison, *Letters*, 1:607.

15. Morison, *Admiral Sims*, 4.

16. "President Honors Sims," *New York Times*, 29 September 1936, 27.

17. Roosevelt to William S. Sims, 24 November 1897; Sims to Roosevelt, 6 December 1897, both in folder 1, box 96, WSLC; Morison, *Admiral Sims*, 48–50.

18. Roosevelt, *American Ideals*, in Hagedorn, *Works*, 13:186–87.

19. Roosevelt and Lodge, *Hero Tales*, in Hagedorn, *Works*, 10:148.

20. McCullough, *Mornings on Horseback*, 175–79.

21. Karsten, *Naval Aristocracy*, 65–69.

22. Roosevelt to Ira N. Hollis, 24 September 1897, 3 November 1897, in Morison, *Letters*, 1:688, 706; Roosevelt to Edwin L. Godkin, 5 January 1898, in Morison, *Letters*, 1:951–52; Ronald Spector, "The Triumph of Professional Ideology: The U.S. Navy in the 1890s," in Hagan, *In Peace and War*, 183–84.

23. Hunter Davis to Stephen B. Luce, 21 March 1898, roll 9, box 10, SLLC.

24. Thomas Selfridge to Long, 19 November 1897, in Allen, *Papers of John D. Long*, 34–36.

25. Karsten, *Naval Aristocracy*, 63.

26. Roosevelt, *American Ideals*, in Hagedorn, *Works*, 13:187–88.

27. Dana M. Wegner, "The Union Navy, 1861–1865," in Hagan, *In Peace and War*, 107–8; Karsten, *Naval Aristocracy*, 280.

28. Karsten, *Naval Aristocracy*, 285–86.

29. "Promotion Based on Merit," *Washington Post*, 7 December 1897, 4.

30. Karsten, *Naval Aristocracy*, 284.

31. "Promotion Based on Merit."

32. Roosevelt to Long, 30 December 1897, in Morison, *Letters*, 1:750; Roosevelt to Godkin, 5 January 1898, in Morison, *Letters*, 1:751–52; Spector, "Professional Ideology," in Hagan, *In Peace and War*, 183–84; Paullin, *History of Naval Administration*, 457–64.

33. Roosevelt to F. Dibble, 17 January 1899, in Morison, *Letters*, 2:915.

34. Bailey, *Diplomatic History*, 415–18; Roosevelt, *American Ideals*, in Hagedorn, *Works*, 13:196.

35. Roosevelt to Chandler, 27 September 1897, in Morison, *Letters*, 1:691. Roosevelt reported similar sentiments to Secretary Long, in Roosevelt to Long, 20 September 1897, in Morison, *Letters*, 1:684. In an 1899 letter to Chandler, Roosevelt revised his assessment of Howell and called him a "man of great character and force." See Roosevelt to Chandler, 19 October 1899, in Morison, *Letters*, 2:1086.

36. Roosevelt to Chandler, 19 October 1899, in Morison, *Letters*, 2:1086; Roosevelt to Dibble, 17 January 1899, in Morison, *Letters*, 2:915.

37. Roosevelt to William F. Fullam, 28 June 1897, in Morison, *Letters*, 1:633.

38. Trask, *War with Spain*, 80.

39. Long, qtd. in, Trask, *War with Spain*, 79.

40. Roosevelt to Long, 16 February 1898, in Morison, *Letters*, 1:773.

41. Spector, *Professors of War*, 88–111.

42. Roosevelt, *Autobiography*, 215.

43. Trask, *War with Spain*, 81.

44. Roosevelt to Alexander Lambert, 1 April 1898, in Morison, *Letters*, 1:808.

45. Roosevelt to Henry Cabot Lodge, 21 September 1897, in Morison, *Letters*, 1:685–86; Roosevelt to William W. Kimball, 19 November 1897, in Morison, *Letters*, 1:717; Roosevelt to Long, 14 January 1898, in Morison, *Letters*, 1:759–63; Roosevelt to Mahan, 14 March 1898, in Morison, *Letters*, 1:793.

46. Mahan to Roosevelt, 1 May 1897, in Seager and Maguire, *Letters and Papers*, 2:506.

47. Roosevelt to Spring Rice, 19 November 1900, in Morison, *Letters*, 1:1423; Roosevelt to Hermann Speck von Sternberg, 19 November 1900, in Morison, *Letters*, 1:1428.

48. Roosevelt to Lodge, 21 September 1897, in Morison, *Letters*, 1:685.

49. Roosevelt to Caspar Frederick Goodrich, 28 May 1897, 16 June 1897, in Morison, *Letters*, 1:617–18, 626.

50. Turk, *Ambiguous Relationship*, 31–32.

51. Roosevelt, *American Ideals*, in Hagedorn, *Works*, 13:189.

52. Roosevelt to Bellamy Storer, 26 September 1897, in Morison, *Letters*, 1:691; Roosevelt to Mahan, 9 June 1897, in Morison, *Letters*, 1:622.

53. Roosevelt to Long, 30 September 1897, in Morison, *Letters*, 1:695–96.

54. "Roosevelt on Hand Early," *New York Times*, 14 May 1897, 3.

55. Roosevelt to Lodge, 11 September 1897, in Morison, *Letters*, 1:673; Roosevelt to Henry C. Taylor, 24 May 1897, in Morison, *Letters*, 1:617.

56. O'Connell, *Sacred Vessels*.

57. "Admiral Sicard's Fleet," *New York Times*, 8 September 1897, 5.

58. Roosevelt to Paul Dana, 16 August 1897, in Morison, *Letters*, 1:652; Roosevelt to Jacob Riis, 2 September 1897, in Morison, *Letters*, 1:666.

59. "Guns Boomed at Sea," *Washington Post*, 10 September 1897, 7; "Admiral Sicard's Fleet," 5.

60. Roosevelt to Frederic Remington, 15 September 1897, in Morison, *Letters*, 1:680.

61. Roosevelt to Lodge, 11 September 1897, in Morison, *Letters*, 1:673; Roosevelt to Montgomery Sicard, 29 November 1897, in Morison, *Letters*, 1:720.

62. Roosevelt also took an active interest in gunnery practice, which involved techniques that were extremely dependent on technological capabilities. Roosevelt to Long, 22 June 1897, 23 June 1897, in Morison, *Letters*, 1:630, 631; Roosevelt to William Laird Clowes, 3 August 1897, in Morison, *Letters*, 1:637; Roosevelt to Long, 4 September 1897, in Morison, *Letters*, 1:668; Roosevelt to Arent Crowninshield, 24 November 1897, in Morison, *Letters*, 1:720; Roosevelt to Sims, 24 November 1897; Sims to Roosevelt, 6 December 1897, both in folder 1, box 96, WSLC; Roosevelt to Long, 4 Janu-

ary 1898, in Allen, *Papers of John D. Long*, 40–41; William H. Emory to Frederick Rodgers, 17 January 1898; Rodgers to Roosevelt, 21 January 1898, both in file 5936-10, GRND.

63. Steve Graham, "Samuel Pierpont Langley (1834–1906)," 3 May 2000, http://earthobservatory.nasa.gov/Features/Langley/.

64. Roosevelt to Long, 25 March 1898, 30 March 1898, in Morison, *Letters*, 1:799, 2:806.

65. Roosevelt, *American Ideals*, in Hagedorn, *Works*, 13:198.

66. Roosevelt to Long, 6 May 1898, in Morison, *Letters*, 2:825.

67. Roosevelt to A. R. Cowles, 19 November 1897, in Morison, *Letters*, 1:718.

68. Bailey, *Diplomatic History*, 451–52, 455.

69. Roosevelt to C. Whitney Tillinghast, 9 March 1898, in Morison, *Letters*, 1:792.

70. Roosevelt to Tillinghast, 24 December 1897, 13 January 1898, 25 February 1898, in Morison, *Letters*, 1:748, 758, 784.

71. Roosevelt to Fullam, 28 June 1897, in Morison, *Letters*, 1:633.

72. Roosevelt to Philemon Tecumseh Sherman, 15 November 1897, in Morison, *Letters*, 1:716.

73. Roosevelt to Douglas Robinson, 6 March 1898, MS Am 1540, TRCH.

74. Roosevelt to D. Robinson, 30 March 1898, in Morison, *Letters*, 2:805.

75. Roosevelt to D. Robinson, 30 March 1898, in Morison, *Letters*, 2:805.

76. Roosevelt to William S. Cowles, 29 March 1898, in Morison, *Letters*, 2:803.

77. Roosevelt to D. Robinson, 6 March 1898, MS Am 1540, TRCH.

78. Roosevelt to Corinne Roosevelt Robinson, 13 March 1898, MS Am 1540, TRCH.

79. Roosevelt to Lambert, 29 March 1898, in Morison, *Letters*, 1:804; Roosevelt to W. S. Cowles, 29 March 1898, in Morison, *Letters*, 2:803.

80. Roosevelt to Long, 16 February 1898, 18 February 1898, 19 February 1898, in Morison, *Letters*, 1:773–74, 775–79, 779–81; Roosevelt to Benjamin Franklin Tracy, 18 April 1898, in Morison, *Letters*, 2:818.

81. Roosevelt to Charles Henry Davis, 9 March 1898, in Morison, *Letters*, 1:791

82. Roosevelt, *Autobiography*, 219.

83. Trask, *War with Spain*, 81.

84. Trask, *War with Spain*, 81.

85. "Our Warships at Hongkong," *New York Times*, 2 March 1898, 1; "Spaniards Much Alarmed," *New York Times*, 4 March 1898, 1.

86. Roosevelt to Brooks Adams, 21 March 1898, in Morison, *Letters*, 1:798.

87. Roosevelt to Kimball, 19 November 1897, in Morison, *Letters*, 1:717.

88. Trask, *War with Spain*, 52–56.

89. Roosevelt to D. Robinson, 2 April 1898, in Morison, *Letters*, 2:809.

90. Roosevelt to William Sturgis Bigelow, 29 March 1898, in Morison, *Letters*, 2:802.

91. Spector, "Professional Ideology," in Hagan, *In Peace and War*, 182.

92. Roosevelt to Bigelow, 29 March 1898, in Morison, *Letters*, 2:803.

93. Roosevelt to William Astor Chanler, 21 April 1898, in Morison, *Letters*, 2:819.

94. Roosevelt, *Autobiography*, 223.

95. J. Lane, *Armed Progressive*, 14–15, 26; E. Morris, *Rise of Theodore Roosevelt*, 577.

96. Roosevelt to Augustus Peabody Gardner, 1 December 1897, in Morison, *Letters*, 1:723.

97. Roosevelt, *Autobiography*, 223.

98. Roosevelt, *Autobiography*, 222.

99. Roosevelt, *Rough Riders*, 4; Roosevelt and Lodge, *Men of Action*, in Hagedorn, *Works*, 11:248–58.

100. Roosevelt, *Rough Riders*, 3–4.

101. Roosevelt, *American Ideals*, in Hagedorn, *Works*, 13:197.

102. Roosevelt, *American Ideals*, in Hagedorn, *Works*, 13:189.

103. Roosevelt, *Rough Riders*, 47.

104. Roosevelt, *Autobiography*, 224, 231.

105. Roosevelt to Brooks Brothers, 2 May 1898, in Morison, *Letters*, 2:822.

106. Roosevelt to Lodge, 19 May 1898, in Morison, *Letters*, 2:831.

107. Roosevelt to Robley D. Evans, 20 April 1898, in Morison, *Letters*, 2:818.

108. Roosevelt, *Pocket Diary*, entries for 16 and 17 April 1898.

109. Roosevelt, *Autobiography*, 228–29, 230; Roosevelt to Lodge, 12 June 1898, in Morison, *Letters*, 2:842

110. Roosevelt, *Rough Riders*, 46–53.

111. Roosevelt, *Pocket Diary*, entry for 3 June 1898.

112. Roosevelt to Lodge, 12 June 1898, in Morison, *Letters*, 2:840–43.

113. Roosevelt to Lodge, 10 June 1898, in Morison, *Letters*, 2:837; Roosevelt to Lodge, 10 June 1898, in Morison, *Letters*, 2:837–38; Roosevelt to Lodge, 12 June 1898, in Morison, *Letters*, 2:840–43.

114. Roosevelt to Lodge, 19 July 1898, in Morison, *Letters*, 2:851–52; Roosevelt to D. Robinson, 19 July 1898, in Morison, *Letters*, 2:855

115. Roosevelt to Lodge, 19 July 1898, in Morison, *Letters*, 2:851–52.

116. Roosevelt to Lodge, 19 July 1898, in Morison, *Letters*, 2:851–53; Roosevelt to D. Robinson, 19 July 1898, in Morison, *Letters*, 2:855.

117. Roosevelt to Lodge, 31 July 1898, in Morison, *Letters*, 2:863.

118. Cosmas, *Army for Empire*, 1–5, 74–75, 87–89, 102; William R. Roberts, "Reform and Revitalization, 1890–1903," in Hagan and Roberts, *Against All Enemies*, 204; Millett and Maslowski, *For the Common Defense*, 299.

119. Trask, *War with Spain*, 180.

120. Roosevelt to Lodge, 5 July 1898, 7 July 1898, in Morison, *Letters*, 2:849, 2:850.

121. Roosevelt to Lodge, 3 July 1898, 7 July 1898, 10 July 1898, in Morison, *Letters*, 2:846, 850.

122. Trask, *War with Spain*, 180.

123. Roosevelt to Lodge, 7 July 1898, in Morison, *Letters*, 2:850.

124. Roosevelt to Lodge, 10 July 1898, in Morison, *Letters*, 2:850–51; Millett and Maslowski, *For the Common Defense*, 295–97.

125. Millett and Maslowski, *For the Common Defense*, 296; Trask, *War with Spain*, 220–24.

126. Roosevelt to Lodge, 19 July 1898, 3 July 1898, in Morison, *Letters*, 2:846, 852.

127. Millett and Maslowski, *For the Common Defense*, 297–98.

128. Roosevelt to Lodge, 19 July 1898, in Morison, *Letters*, 2:853; Roosevelt to C. Robinson, 19 July 1898, 2:856; Roosevelt to D. Robinson, 27 July 1898, in Morison, *Letters*, 2:860.

129. "Losses in 114 Days' War," *New York Times*, 3.

130. Roosevelt, *Rough Riders*, 135, 152, 169.

131. Dalton, *Theodore Roosevelt*, 173.

132. Roosevelt to Lodge, 10 July 1898, in Morison, *Letters*, 2:851.

133. Roosevelt to Lodge, 31 July 1898, in Morison, *Letters*, 2:861–63; Roosevelt to William R. Shafter, 3 August 1898, in Morison, *Letters*, 2:864.

134. Cosmas, *Army for Empire*, 257.

135. Roosevelt to Lodge, 31 July 1898, in Morison, *Letters*, 2:861–63; Roosevelt to Shafter, 3 August 1898, in Morison, *Letters*, 2:864–65.

136. Roosevelt to Shafter, 3 August 1898, in Morison, *Letters*, 2:865–66; Roosevelt, *Rough Riders*, 210–11; E. Morris, *Rise of Theodore Roosevelt*, 659–60.

137. Cosmas, *Army for Empire*, 258; E. Morris, *Rise of Theodore Roosevelt*, 660, 703.

138. "The Rough Riders Land at Montauk," *New York Times*, 16 August 1898, 1.

139. "More Troops for Montauk," 11 August 1898, *New York Times*, 2.

140. Trask, *War with Spain*, 435.

141. E. Morris, *Rise of Theodore Roosevelt*, 686.

142. "Chart 5," in Morison, *Letters*, 2:1456–57.

143. Address before the New York State National Guard Association, 8 February 1900, MS Am 1454.50 (137), TRCH.

144. Roosevelt, *Autobiography*, 234, 235.

145. Roosevelt to Russell A. Alger, 23 July 1898, in Morison, *Letters*, 2:859–60, 860n; Roosevelt to Charles Eliot, 23 August 1898, in Morison, *Letters*, 2:869.

146. Roosevelt to Lodge, 4 November 1898, in Morison, *Letters*, 2:887.

147. "The 71st Regiment Inquiry," *New York Times*, 6 January 1899, 5.

148. Roosevelt to Lodge, 31 July 1898, in Morison, *Letters*, 2:863.

149. "71st Officers on Trial," *New York Times*, 21 April 1899, 1.

150. Roosevelt to William Conant Church, 8 May 1899, in Morison, *Letters*, 2:1003.

151. "The 71st Court Martial," *New York Times*, 1 February 1899, 3.

152. Roosevelt to Thomas C. Platt, 8 May 1899, in Morison, *Letters*, 2:1006 and note 4.

153. "Major Smith's Demand: He Wants to Be Restored to Duty," *New York Times*, 23 May 1899, 2.

154. Roosevelt to Philip Reade, 16 April 1900, in Morison, *Letters*, 2:1262–63.

155. Roosevelt to William H. H. Llewellyn, 8 May 1900, in Morison, *Letters*, 2:1294–95.

156. Kathleen Dalton has interpreted Roosevelt's mental state in the days after the battle in the same way. See *Theodore Roosevelt*, 174.

157. Roosevelt to Newton D. Baker, 8 May 1917, Correspondence of Theodore Roosevelt and Secretary of War Newton D. Baker, fMS Am 1454.16, TRCH.

158. Roosevelt to William Henry Harrison Webster, 16 April 1900, in Morison, *Letters*, 2:1264.

159. Roosevelt to Edward M. Hoffman, 30 April 1900, in Morison, *Letters*, 2:1278–79.

160. "Major Andrews Chosen," *New York Times*, 29 December 1898, 3.

161. Roosevelt to William Cary Sanger, 27 January 1900, in Morison, *Letters*, 2:1142.

162. Mahon, *History of the Militia*, 138–39; Sanger, *Report on the Reserve*.

163. Roosevelt to Platt, 7 February 1900, in Morison, *Letters*, 2:1174.

3. The New Hand on the Helm

1. "President's Landau Struck by a Car," 4 September 1902, *New York Times*, 1; "The President at Sea Girt Camp," *New York Times*, 25 July 1902, 2.

2. "Defense of the Soldiers," 3 September 1902, *New York Times*, 3.

3. "Defense of the Soldiers."

4. "President Roosevelt has Many Callers," 22 September 1901, *New York Times*, 7.

5. Alice Roosevelt, qtd. in MacMillan, *War That Ended Peace*, 20.

6. Cooper, *Warrior and the Priest*, 70; Dalton, *Theodore Roosevelt*, 212–13.

7. Theodore Roosevelt to Kermit Roosevelt, 15 October 1904, in Morison, *Letters*, 4:984; Roosevelt to Edwin B. Haskell, 10 December 1904, in Morison, *Letters*, 4:1063

8. Roosevelt to K. Roosevelt, 15 October 1904, in Morison, *Letters*, 4:984.

9. Roosevelt to E. Haskell, 10 December 1904, in Morison, *Letters*, 4:1063–64; Dalton, *Theodore Roosevelt*, 212; Ponder, "Publicity," 547; Chambers, *Tyranny of Change*, 143–44; Cooper, *Warrior and the Priest*, 70; William Loeb to Robert Shaw Oliver, 29 November 1904, file 8018, series 60, box 51, SWOF.

10. Roosevelt to K. Roosevelt, 26 October 1904, in Morison, *Letters*, 4:993–94.

11. Laski, *American Presidency*, 144–45, 148; Ponder, "Publicity," 547.

12. Roosevelt to Arthur Hamilton Lee, 25 July 1900, in Morison, *Letters*, 2:1363.

13. "Lesson of Antietam," *Washington Post*, 18 September 1903, 3.

14. "Speeches of the Day" and "Sherman Unveiled," *Washington Post*, 16 October 1903, 4, 1.

15. "Fleet's Array a Grand Sight," 4 September 1906, *New York Times*, 1–2; "Destroyers Crash at Naval Review," *New York Times*, 18 August 1903, 1; Henry C. Taylor to George Dewey, 27 June 1903, folder 1, box 13, GDLC; Roosevelt to

Dewey, 1 August 1903, folder 1, box 16, GDLC; *Army and Navy Journal*, 15 August 1903, 1257; Memorandum to the President, 24 March 1904, vol. 12, WMLC.

16. Roosevelt to Elihu Root, 4 September 1906, in Morison, *Letters*, 5:394.

17. Roosevelt to Root, 4 September 1906, in Morison, *Letters*, 5:394.

18. "Fleet's Array a Grand Sight."

19. "President at Sea Girt Camp."

20. Dewey to Charles Dickinson, 28 October 1903, folder 3, box 16, GDLC.

21. Henry H. Boyce to Dewey, 24 July 1903, folder 5, box 15, GDLC; Roosevelt to Benjamin F. Tracy, 19 March 1903, series 1, roll 33, TRLC; Rappaport, *Navy League*, 5–6, 8; J. W. Miller to Truman H. Newberry, 18 August 1906, file 19678-2; Newberry to J. Miller, 21 August 1906, file 19678-3, both in GRND.

22. "Andrew Carnegie's Plea for Peace," 7 April 1907, *New York Times*, SM1.

23. John W. Foster to Dewey, 9 January 1904, folder 1, box 17, GDLC; Letter from Mrs. Donald McLean, 14 April 1907, folder 4, box 25, GDLC; "Thirty Reasons Why Our Navy Should Not Be Enlarged," and "President Roosevelt Accepts the Honorary Presidency of the Practical Peace League and Espouses Its Program for Peace," in *Publications of Peace Societies*, 17, 64–65; Roosevelt to Andrew Carnegie, 6 September 1906, in Morison, *Letters*, 5:398; Leopold, *Elihu Root*, 99.

24. Roosevelt to Carl Schurz, 8 September 1905, in Morison, *Letters*, 5:16.

25. Roosevelt to Cecil Arthur Spring Rice, 1 July 1907, in Morison, *Letters*, 5:699.

26. "Mr. Hoar Demands an Inquiry," *Baltimore Sun*, 28 January 1902, 4.

27. "Concentration Camps for the Filipinos," *Baltimore Sun*, 19 December 1901, 4.

28. "Tales of the Water Cure," *Baltimore Sun*, 19 April 1902, 2.

29. Linn, *Philippine War*, 310–11, 313–19.

30. "Smith's Cruel Order," *Washington Post*, 20 April 1902, 4; "Waller Asked Vengeance," *Baltimore Sun*, 1 April 1902, 2.

31. "Gen. Smith Punished," *Baltimore Sun*, 17 July 1902, 2; "Major Glenn Found Guilty," *Baltimore Sun*, 23 July 1902, 2; Linn, *Philippine War*, 319.

32. "Charged with Crimes," *Baltimore Sun*, 28 July 1902, 8.

33. "Root Defends Army," *Baltimore Sun*, 20 February 1902, 2.

34. "Mr. Lodge's Defense," *Baltimore Sun*, 6 May 1902, 2; Jones, *Honor in the Dust*, 318–20.

35. "Plans Western Trip," *Washington Post*, 30 May 1902, 3.

36. "The Army in the Philippines," *New York Times*, 31 May 1902, 8.

37. Roosevelt to William Cary Sanger, 8 October 1901, in Morison, *Letters*, 3:163.

38. Roosevelt to Root, 2 October 1902, in Morison, *Letters*, 3:335.

39. Roosevelt to Hermann Speck von Sternberg, 19 May 1900, in Morison, *Letters*, 2:1303; Roosevelt to Root, 25 July 1900, 12 July 1902, in Morison, *Letters*, 2:1360, 3:291; Roosevelt to Root, 27 December 1902, folder 7, box 162, ERLC. Lt. Gen. Nelson Miles's views on uniform reform are contained in two

letters to Secretary of War Root. See entries for 22 February 1902 and 16 July 1902, microform no. M-857, roll 15, vol. 38, ARHQ.

40. Park Benjamin to Stephen B. Luce, 25 April 1905, roll 11, box 12, SLLC; Luce to Dewey [memorandum], 25 March 1905, roll 11, box 12, SLLC; William J. Barnette to Luce, 15 February 1906, roll 11, box 12, SLLC (for the comment on "cold mush," see Barnette to Luce, 19 May 1905, roll 11, box 12, SLLC); "Henry Clay Taylor, U.S. Navy," folder 19, box 1, HTLC; Paul T. Heffron, "Paul Morton: 1 July 1904–30 June 1905," in Coletta, *American Secretaries*, 1:469–70, 472; Heffron, "Secretary Moody," 31–33; "Report of the Secretary of the Navy" (1905), in *Navy Department*, 3–4; "Report of the Secretary of the Navy" (1906), in *Navy Department*, 5–6; Rumble, "Rectitude and Reform," 202–3, 216–19.

41. Roosevelt, *Naval War of 1812*, in Hagedorn, *Works*, 6:365.

42. Roosevelt to Theodore E. Burton, 23 February 1904, in Morison, *Letters*, 4:736.

43. Roosevelt to William Eaton Chandler, 2 November 1901, in Morison, *Letters*, 3:186.

44. Theodore Roosevelt, "Why the Nation Needs an Effective Navy," in Roosevelt, *American Problems*, in Hagedorn, *Works*, 16:250.

45. Roosevelt, *Autobiography*, 124–25.

46. Roosevelt to Henry Cabot Lodge, 27 March 1901, in Morison, *Letters*, 3:31–32.

47. Roosevelt to Chandler, 2 November 1901, in Morison, *Letters*, 3:186.

48. Theodore Roosevelt, "First Annual Message," in Roosevelt, *State Papers*, in Hagedorn, *Works*, 15:122.

49. E. Morris, "Matter of Extreme Urgency," 77.

50. "Mississippi II (Battleship No. 23)," *Navy History and Heritage Command*, 4 September 2016, www.history.navy.mil/research/histories/ship-histories /danfs/m/mississippi-ii.html.

51. "U.S.S. Connecticut Ready for Launching," 18 September 1904, *New York Times*, 8.

52. E. Morris, "Matter of Extreme Urgency," 76.

53. Roosevelt to George von Lengerke Meyer, 12 April 1901, in Morison, *Letters*, 3:52.

54. Roosevelt to Spring Rice, 13 May 1905, in Morison, *Letters*, 4:1178. Roosevelt, of course, wrote this letter long after the Venezuelan crisis had passed, but it seemed to reflect the impressions that he had gathered of the Kaiser, in part, as a result of that episode.

55. E. Morris, "Matter of Extreme Urgency," 80, 83–84; Hendrix, *Theodore Roosevelt's Naval Diplomacy*, 25–53.

56. Hagan, *This People's Navy*, 142, 203.

57. Reckner, *White Fleet*, 61; Taylor to Dewey, 2 December 1903, folder 4, box 13, GDLC; Taylor to Luce, 5 December 1903, roll 10, box 11, SLLC; Luce to Taylor, 7 December 1903, roll 10, box 11, SLLC; Taylor to Luce, 9 Decem-

ber 1903, roll 10, box 11, SLLC; "Report of the Chief of the Bureau of Navigation" (1902, 1903), in *Navy Department*, 414, 466.

58. Costello, "Planning for War," 159–60; Reckner, *White Fleet*, 7, 61; E. Miller, *War Plan Orange*, 87–90.

59. Roosevelt, "Third Annual Message," in Roosevelt, *State Papers*, in Hagedorn, *Works*, 15:201. Related comments in other annual messages are found on the following pages of the *State Papers*: (Second) 157, (Fourth) 261, (Fifth) 310–11, (Sixth) 405, (Seventh) 473–74, (Eighth) 544.

60. Roosevelt to William Howard Taft, 3 March 1909, in Morison, *Letters*, 6:1543.

61. Alfred T. Mahan to Roosevelt, 10 January 1907, in Seager and Maguire, *Letters and Papers*, 3:202.

62. Roosevelt to Mahan, 12 January 1907, in Morison, *Letters*, 5:550–51; Roosevelt to Newberry, 6 August 1907, 10 August 1907, in Morison, *Letters*, 5:743–44, 745; General Board of the Navy to the Secretary of the Navy, 15 August 1907, letterbook 5, box 2, GBNA.

63. Turk, *Ambiguous Relationship*.

64. Roosevelt to Thomas C. Platt, 28 June 1902, in Morison, *Letters*, 3:283.

65. Taylor to the Secretary of the Navy, 3 July 1902; H. Wood to Commander in Chief of the European Squadron, 3 July 1902; Taylor to French Ensor Chadwick, 8 July 1902; Dewey to the Chief of the Bureau of Equipment, 17 July 1902; Dewey to the Secretary of the Navy, 17 July 1902; Dewey to the Secretary of the Navy, 22 July 1902, all in letterbook 2, box 1, GBNA; "Self-Reliance Taught by the Naval Manoeuvres," 30 November 1902, *New York Times*, 27.

66. Memorandum from Secretary of the Navy William Moody to Taylor, 24 July 1902, folder 12, box 13, GDLC.

67. Roosevelt to Platt, 28 June 1902, in Morison, *Letters*, 3:283.

68. Roosevelt to Matthew Quay, 27 October 1902, in Morison, *Letters*, 3:368–69.

69. "Admiral Dewey to Go to Sea," 15 June 1902, *New York Times*, 1; "Admiral Dewey Sails," 2 December 1902, *New York Times*; E. Morris, "Matter of Extreme Urgency," 78; Bailey, *Diplomatic History*, 469–70.

70. Roosevelt to Dewey, 14 June 1902, in Morison, *Letters*, 3:275.

71. Journal of the Commander in Chief, 6 January 1903, box 2, GDLC, 87, 91.

72. Morison, *Admiral Sims*, 49–50.

73. Roosevelt to Charles A. Boutelle, 21 August 1897, in Morison, *Letters*, 1:656; Roosevelt to William S. Cowles, 25 August 1897, in Morison, *Letters*, 1:658–59.

74. Roosevelt to William Sturgis Bigelow, 29 October 1897, in Morison, *Letters*, 1:702.

75. Roosevelt to Arent Crowninshield, 24 November 1897, in Morison, *Letters*, 1:720; Roosevelt to John D. Long, 4 January 1898, in Allen, *Papers of John D. Long*, 40; Roosevelt to William S. Sims, 24 November 1897, folder 1, box 96, WSLC; Sims to Roosevelt, 6 December 1897, folder 1, box 96, WSLC.

76. Roosevelt to Long, 4 January 1898, in Allen, *Papers of John D. Long*, 40; Roosevelt to Crowninshield, 24 November 1897, in Morison, *Letters*, 1:720.

77. Roosevelt to Paul Morton, 24 September 1904, in Morison, *Letters*, 4:952.

78. Roosevelt to Morton, 24 September 1904, in Morison, *Letters*, 4:952.

79. Trask, *War with Spain*, 104, 265–66.

80. Sims to Roosevelt, 16 November 1901, folder 1, box 96, WSLC.

81. Sims's letter to Roosevelt is quoted in full in Morison, *Admiral Sims*, 102–4.

82. Morison, *Admiral Sims*, 102–4.

83. Roosevelt to Sims, 27 December 1901, in Morison, *Letters*, 3:212.

84. Morison, *Admiral Sims*, 5.

85. Roosevelt to W. S. Cowles, 12 December 1901, in Morison, *Letters*, 3:206–7; Roosevelt to Taylor, 27 December 1901, in Morison, *Letters*, 3:212.

86. Morison, *Admiral Sims*, 107.

87. O'Neil's comments on Sims's charges are contained in a report dated 22 April 1902 and housed in folder 1, box 96, WSLC.

88. Taylor to Roosevelt, 1 January 1902, series 1, roll 23, TRLC.

89. Sims to Roosevelt, 11 March 1902, folder 1, box 96, WSLC.

90. Roosevelt to Taylor, 22 April 1902, in Morison, *Letters*, 3:253–54.

91. Roosevelt to Taft, 21 August 1907, in Morison, *Letters*, 5:760. Roosevelt was recollecting in this letter.

92. Roosevelt to Taylor, 22 April 1902, in Morison, *Letters*, 3:253–54.

93. Morison, *Admiral Sims*, 126–28, 245, 249.

94. Roosevelt to William Henry Moody, 6 March 1903, in Morison, *Letters*, 3:441.

95. Roosevelt, qtd. in Morison, *Admiral Sims*, 137.

96. Morison, *Admiral Sims*, 136–37.

97. Morison, *Admiral Sims*, 237.

98. "Admiral Taylor Is Dead," 27 July 1904, *New York Times*, 1.

99. Roosevelt to Charles H. Darling, 14 March 1903, in Morison, *Letters*, 3:446.

100. Roosevelt to Taylor, 15 September 1903, in Morison, *Letters*, 3:601–2. The quotation is from Roosevelt to Moody, 21 April 1904, in Morison, *Letters*, 4:776.

101. Roosevelt to Taylor, 15 September 1903, in Morison, *Letters*, 3:601–2; Roosevelt to Moody, 21 April 1904, in Morison, *Letters*, 4:776; Roosevelt to Sims, 13 October 1906, 23 October 1907, in Morison, *Letters*, 5:455, 821.

102. Memorandum for the Secretary of the Navy, 24 March 1904, vol. 12, WMLC; Roosevelt to Lawrence Fraser Abbott, 14 March 1904, in Morison, *Letters*, 4:751–52; Roosevelt to Sims, 7 July 1906, in Morison, *Letters*, 5:333–34; Roosevelt to Taft, 28 September 1906, in Morison, *Letters*, 5:433; Roosevelt to Charles J. Bonaparte, 28 November 1906, in Morison, *Letters*, 5:515.

103. "The President's Journey," 6 August 1902, *New York Times*, 8. The quotation is from "President Watches Mayflower's Practice," 7 August 1902, *New York Times*, 3.

104. "President Watches Mayflower's Practice."

105. Roosevelt to Moody, 4 August 1902, in Morison, *Letters*, 3:308.

106. "President Watches Mayflower's Practice."

107. Roosevelt to Moody, 12 May 1903, in Morison, *Letters*, 3:475.

108. Roosevelt to Albert Gleaves, 7 August 1902, in Morison, *Letters*, 3:310.

109. "Disaster Shocks Washington," 14 April 1904, *New York Times*, 1; "Missouri Turret Explosion; 29 Die," in *New York Times*, 14 April 1904, 1; "Report of the Chief of the Bureau of Navigation" (1904), in *Navy Department*, 527.

110. "Disaster Shocks Washington."

111. Morison, *Admiral Sims*, 138–41.

112. B. Belknap to Sims, 15 April 1904, folder 1, box 96, WSLC.

113. Roosevelt to Moody, 10 May 1904, in Morison, *Letters*, 4:793–94; Morison, *Admiral Sims*, 141.

114. Roosevelt to Taft, 21 August 1907, in Morison, *Letters*, 5:760.

115. Roosevelt to Moody, 4 August 1902, in Morison, *Letters*, 3:308.

116. Roosevelt to Taft, 21 August 1907, in Morison, *Letters*, 5:760.

4. Arms and the Men

1. "The President's Journey," 6 August 1902, *New York Times*, 8.

2. Abbott, *Letters of Archie Butt*, 71.

3. Theodore Roosevelt to Leonard Wood, 4 June 1904, in Morison, *Letters*, 4:820–21; Roosevelt to Kermit Roosevelt, 5 March 1904, in Morison, *Letters*, 4:744; Roosevelt to Michael Joseph Donovan, 13 December 1904, in Morison, *Letters*, 4:1065.

4. Roosevelt to K. Roosevelt, 4 December 1902, 17 January 1903, in Morison, *Letters*, 3:389, 406; Roosevelt to Theodore Roosevelt Jr., 20 January 1903, in Morison, *Letters*, 3:408; Dalton, *Theodore Roosevelt*, 235–36.

5. Butt, *Letters*, 121–22.

6. Butt, *Letters*, 120.

7. Roosevelt, *American Problems*, in Hagedorn, *Works*, 16:20.

8. McCoy, *Elusive Republic*, 70.

9. Roosevelt to William Moody, 21 September 1907, in Morison, *Letters*, 5:802–3.

10. Roosevelt to Henry Cabot Lodge, 23 September 1901, in Morison, *Letters*, 3:150.

11. Roosevelt to Wood, 4 June 1904, in Morison, *Letters*, 4:820.

12. *Times*, 5; William Crozier to Roosevelt, October 1899, file 6251, series 60, box 50, SWOF; "Report of the Secretary of War" (1899), in *War Department*, 3–4.

13. "Report of the Secretary of War" (1899), in *War Department*, 48.

14. William R. Roberts, "Reform and Revitalization, 1890–1903," in Hagan and Roberts, *Against All Enemies*, 201; Peter Karsten, "Armed Progressives: The Military Reorganizes for the American Century," in Israel, *Building the Organizational Society*, 199, 217; Weigley, *Towards an American Army*, 139; Abrahamson, *America Arms*, 4–5, 7; Andrews, *My Friend and Classmate*, 47–48.

15. "Report of the Secretary of War" (1899), in *War Department*, 3–4.

16. Millett, "Roosevelt and His Generals," 4–5; U.S. Congress, Committee on Military Affairs, *Nomination of Leonard Wood*, 21, 523.

17. Millett, "Roosevelt and His Generals," 4–5; J. Lane, *Armed Progressive*, 86, 116–17; *Webster's American Military Biographies*, 29, 132–33; Funston, *Memories of Two Wars*, 426; Grenville Dodge to Wood, 9 November 1903, folder 3, box 32, LWLC; Samuel B. M. Young to Russell A. Alger, 29 December 1903, folder 4, box 32, LWLC.

18. Roosevelt, *Pocket Diary*, entry for 17 April 1898; Dunne, *Mr. Dooley on Ivrything*, 4.

19. Millett, "Roosevelt and His Generals," 4–5; S. Young to Alger, 29 December 1903, folder 4, box 32, LWLC.

20. Wooster, *Nelson A. Miles*, 251.

21. "General Frank Bell," *Army and Navy Journal*, 16 February 1901, 607.

22. Millett, "Roosevelt and His Generals," 5; J. Lane, *Armed Progressive*, 86, 116–17; *Webster's American Military Biographies*, 29, 132–33; Funston, *Memories of Two Wars*, 426; S. Young to Alger, 29 December 1903, folder 4, box 32, LWLC; Dodge to Wood, 9 November 1903, folder 3, box 32, LWLC.

23. Roosevelt to Oliver Wendell Holmes, 5 December 1904, in Morison, *Letters*, 4:1059–60.

24. Roosevelt, *State Papers*, in Hagedorn, *Works*, 15:123.

25. Roosevelt, *State Papers*, in Hagedorn, *Works*, 15:123–24; E. Morris, *Theodore Rex*, 70–77.

26. E. Morris, *Theodore Rex*, 65, 77.

27. Roosevelt, "Eighth Annual Message," in Roosevelt, *State Papers*, in Hagedorn, *Works*, 15:544. Related comments in other annual messages are found on the following pages of the *State Papers*: (Second) 157, (Third) 199–200, (Fourth) 262, (Fifth) 307–08, (Sixth) 406, (Seventh) 470, 474–76.

28. "The New Chief of the General Staff," 7 October 1917, *New York Times*, 74.

29. Palmer, *Bliss, Peacemaker*, 77–79; Heitman, *Historical Register*, 225, 228; S. Young to Alger, 29 December 1903, folder 4, box 32, LWLC; Wood to Roosevelt, 4 January 1902, series 1, roll 23, TRLC; List of Ages, folder 3, box 281, JPLC; John J. Pershing to Burkett, 21 November 1903, folder 3, box 281, JPLC; Child, *Register of Graduates*, 296; J. Clark, *Preparing for War*, 197–98.

30. "Major General Corbin," 2 March 1900, *New York Times*, 6.

31. Wood to B. K. Roberts, 8 September 1903, folder 4, box 32, LWLC; Millett, "Roosevelt and His Generals," 7; Lists of promotion of line and staff officers to general officers, 13 April 1909, file 10343, series 5, box 107, WDGS.

32. "Seven Moro Forts Taken: Twenty-Five of the Enemy Killed, While American Loss Is Nil," 23 September 1902, *Washington Post*, 3; "May Be a Brigadier," 23 May 1903, *Washington Post*, 4.

33. Roosevelt to Daniel S. Lamont, 14 July 1903, in Morison, *Letters*, 3:517.

34. Roosevelt to Oswald Garrison Villard, 25 July 1903, 3:531.

35. Roosevelt, *State Papers*, in Hagedorn, *Works*, 15:200.

36. Memorandum from Henry C. Corbin, 8 July 1903, file 514783, series 25, AGOF; Elihu Root to Roosevelt, 16 July 1903, file 938273, series 25, AGOF; Roosevelt to Villard, 17 July 1903, folder 14, box 162, ERLC; Roosevelt to Root, 17 July 1903, in Morison, *Letters*, 3:519; Roosevelt to Villard, 25 July 1903, in Morison, *Letters*, 3:513; S. Young to Alger, 29 December 1903, folder 4, box 32, LWLC; Millett, "Roosevelt and His Generals," 8; George W. Davis to the Secretary of War, 10 March 1906, microform no. M-1395, file 3849, ACP 1886, AGOF.

37. Roosevelt to Thomas H. Barry, 20 July 1903, in Morison, *Letters*, 3:521–22.

38. S. Miller, *Benevolent Assimilation*, 196–97; Roosevelt, *State Papers*, in Hagedorn, *Works*, 15:123; Roosevelt to Pershing, 12 December 1898, folder 13, box 177, JPLC; Col. James Kerr, general staff memorandum, 8 May 1906, subject file "General Officers," box 15, series 3, WDGS; Office of the Chief of Staff memorandum, 1913, file 10196, series 5, box 106, WDGS.

39. Roosevelt to Hermann Speck von Sternberg, 18 March 1901, in Morison, *Letters*, 3:22.

40. "Censure of General Miles," 22 December 1901, *New York Times*, 1; Wooster, *Nelson A. Miles*, 251–52.

41. U.S. Congress, Committee on Military Affairs, *Efficiency of the Army*, 34; Wooster, *Nelson A. Miles*, 242.

42. "Day of Glory for West Point," 12 June 1902, *New York Times*, 1–2.

43. Roosevelt to Lodge, 3 September 1903, in Morison, *Letters*, 3:587.

44. U.S. Congress, Committee on Military Affairs, *Nomination of Leonard Wood*, 21.

45. Deere, "Here Come the Yankees," 732–34, 737–38; Lasch, "Anti-Imperialists," 323; Leuchtenburg, "Progressivism and Imperialism," 488; Smith, *Henry M. Teller*, 217–21, 228.

46. Dalton, *Theodore Roosevelt*, 203.

47. U.S. Congress, Committee on Military Affairs, *Nomination of Leonard Wood*, 18–21.

48. Estes G. Rathbone to Root, 19 March 1903, with enclosure, folder 5, box 32, LWLC; Wood to John O. Skinner, 7 January 1903, folder 1, box 33, LWLC; Richard P. Hallowell to Wood, 13 November 1903, folder 2, box 32, LWLC; George H. Burton to Wood, 14 November 1903, folder 4, box 33, LWLC; Wood to Root, 21 March 1903, folder 6, box 32, LWLC; T. S. Wylly to Wood, 2 December 1903, folder 4, box 33, LWLC; Chauncy Baker to Wood, 16 September 1903, folder 3, box 32, LWLC; F. Steinhart to Wood, 20 December 1903, folder 3, box 32, LWLC; Letter to S. Young, 18 December 1903, folder 5, box 33, LWLC; Tasker Bliss to Mrs. Leonard Wood, 19 March 1904, folder 1, box 34, LWLC; Letter from Root, 23 March 1903, folder 6, box 32, LWLC; U.S. Congress, Committee on Military Affairs, *Nomination of Leonard Wood*, 3–4; J. Lane, *Armed Progressive*, 97–98, 125–26.

49. Roosevelt to Wood, 12 September 1903, in Morison, *Letters*, 3:598.

50. Roosevelt to Root, 21 July 1903, folder 14, box 162, ERLC.

51. Roosevelt to Wood, 1 August 1903, folder 7, box 32, LWLC.

52. Roosevelt to Wood, 1 August 1903, 12 September 1903, folder 7, box 32, LWLC; Roosevelt to Wood, 12 December 1903, folder 6, box 32, LWLC; Roosevelt to Villard, 17 July 1903, folder 14, box 162, ERLC; Roosevelt to Wood, 8 June 1904, in Morison, *Letters*, 4:827.

53. Untitled manuscript, ca. 1912, folder 3, box 1, WCLC.

54. Roosevelt to Wood, 26 August 1903, folder 7, box 32, LWLC.

55. Roosevelt to Wood, 8 June 1904, in Morison, *Letters*, 4:827; Alger to Wood, 17 December 1903, folder 4, box 33, LWLC; Alger to Wood, 19 March 1904, folder 3, box 34, LWLC; Record of Senate vote, 58th Cong., 2nd sess., folder 1, box 1, FALC; McCallum, *Leonard Wood*, 211.

56. Roosevelt to Wood, 8 June 1904, in Morison, *Letters*, 4:827.

57. Roosevelt, *Rough Riders*, 125, 135.

58. "Day of Glory."

59. Roosevelt to William McKinley, 30 December 1900, file 354545, series 25, AGOF; Memorandum to Supply Division, 1 July 1902, file 107590 AGO 1898, series 25, AGOF; Roosevelt to Villard, 25 July 1903, in Morison, *Letters*, 3:531; Roosevelt to Wood, 8 June 1904, in Morison, *Letters*, 4:827; Millett, "Roosevelt and His Generals," 8; "The Case of Col. Mills," 26 March 1904, *New York Times*, 8.

60. Roosevelt to McKinley, 30 December 1900, file 354545, series 25, AGOF; Memorandum to Supply Division, 1 July 1902, file 107590, AGO 1898, series 25, AGOF; Roosevelt to Villard, 25 July 1903, in Morison, *Letters*, 3:531; Roosevelt to Wood, 8 June 1904, in Morison, *Letters*, 4:827; Millett, "Roosevelt and His Generals," 8.

61. *Army and Navy Journal*, 16 April 1904, 867.

62. *Army and Navy Journal*, 26 March 1904, 779; 23 April 1904, 887; 30 April 1904, 922; 7 May 1904, 951.

63. A. L. Mills to Frederick Ainsworth, Military Secretary, 7 May 1904, file 526630, series 25, AGOF; Mills to Ainsworth, Military Secretary, 29 December 1904, file 958332, series 25, AGOF; *Army and Navy Journal*, 17 December 1904, 403.

64. Roosevelt to Wood, 8 June 1904, 4 June 1904, 8 June 1904, in Morison, *Letters*, 4:827, 820, 827.

65. Millett, "Roosevelt and His Generals," 11–12.

66. Roosevelt to Wood, 8 June 1904, in Morison, *Letters*, 4:827.

67. "Army Appropriation Bill," *Army and Navy Journal*, 23 April 1904, 894–95; *Army and Navy Journal*, 30 April 1904, 911; *Army and Navy Journal*, 18 June 1904, 1105.

68. Millett, "Roosevelt and His Generals," 8–9.

69. Dalton, *Theodore Roosevelt*, 202.

70. Mahon, *History of the Militia*, 139; J. Clark, *Preparing for War*, 192.

71. Roosevelt to John Hay, 1 July 1899, in Morison, *Letters*, 2:1024–28; Roosevelt to Lodge, 21 July 1899, in Morison, *Letters*, 2:1038–39.

72. Roberts, "Reform and Revitalization," in Hagan and Roberts, *Against All Enemies*, 207–15.

73. Doubler, *Civilian in Peace*, 143; Mahon, *History of the Militia*, 139; J. Clark, *Preparing for War*, 193.

74. Doubler, *Civilian in Peace*, 143–44; Mahon, *History of the Militia*, 139–40; "Infringement," in "Militia Bill in Senate," 16 December 1902, *New York Times*, 8.

75. "The Militia Bill," 23 January 1903, *New York Times*, 8.

76. "The President at Sea Girt Camp," *New York Times*, 25 July 1902.

77. Roosevelt, "Second Annual Message," in Roosevelt, *State Papers*, in Hagedorn, *Works*, 15:157.

78. "President at Sea Girt Camp."

79. Roosevelt to Newton D. Baker, 22 April 1917, Correspondence of Theodore Roosevelt and Secretary of War N. Baker, fMS Am 1454.16, TRCH.

80. "Report of the Secretary of War" (1902), in *War Department*, 40–41; Adna R. Chaffee to the Secretary of War, 16 January 1904, subject files "Maneuvers," series 3, box 22, WDGS.

81. Weigley, *Towards an American Army*, 137; Abrahamson, *America Arms*, 4, 45–46, 87.

82. Weigley, *United States Army*, 318.

83. "Report of the Secretary of War" (1899), in *War Department*, 48.

84. Roosevelt, "First Annual Message," in Roosevelt, *State Papers*, in Hagedorn, *Works*, 15:122.

85. Roosevelt to Gerald Kitson, 4 May 1901, in Morison, *Letters*, 3:70.

86. Roosevelt, *State Papers*, in Hagedorn, *Works*, 15:118–19, 123.

87. Roosevelt to Kitson, 4 May 1901, in Morison, *Letters*, 3:70.

88. Sheridan, *Personal Memoirs*, 358–453; Miles, *Serving the Republic*, 262–66; Moten, "Delafield Commission," 177–79.

89. Roosevelt to Root, 15 March 1902, in Morison, *Letters*, 3:243; Roosevelt to Speck von Sternberg, 19 July 1902, in Morison, *Letters*, 3:297; Robert Shaw Oliver to Chaffee, 29 July 1905, subject files "French Maneuvers," series 3, box 14, WDGS; Memorandum for the Military Secretary, 22 June 1906, subject files "German Maneuvers," series 3, box 15, WDGS; Corbin to Barry, 11 June 1907, file 1129860, series 25, box 4481, AGOF; Root to William Howard Taft, 27 November 1905, microform no. M-1395, file 2118, ACP 1894, AGOF.

90. "Discusses Army and Navy," 24 September 1902, *New York Times*, 2.

91. Roosevelt, *State Papers*, in Hagedorn, *Works*, 15:156.

92. Memorandum for the Chief of Staff from Arthur L. Wagner, 25 July 1904, subject files "Maneuvers," series 3, box 21, WDGS; Chaffee to the Secretary of War, 16 January 1904, subject files "Maneuvers," series 3, box 22, WDGS; "Report of the Secretary of War" (1903), in *War Department*, 26–27.

93. "Report of the Secretary of War" (1904), in *War Department*, 30, 36–37; "Report of the Secretary of War" (1905), in *War Department*, 30–32; "Report of the Secretary of War" (1906), in *War Department*, 46–48; Nenninger, "Army Enters the Twentieth Century," in Hagan and Roberts, *Against All Enemies*, 221.

94. "Discusses Army and Navy."

95. Nenninger, "Twentieth Century," in *Against All Enemies*, 221–22; J. Clark, *Preparing for War*, 205.

96. Roosevelt to the Secretary of War, with attached note from Chaffee, 1 February 1904, subject files "Maneuvers," series 3, box 22, WDGS.

97. Rules for army and navy maneuvers, 1902, series 1, roll 29, TRLC; "Report of the Secretary of War" (1902), in *War Department*, 25; *Army and Navy Journal*, 27 September 1902, 76.

98. "Navy Tries to Run Past Newport Forts," 6 September 1902, *New York Times*, 1.

99. Roosevelt to Chaffee, 3 July 1905, in Morison, *Letters*, 4:1260–62.

100. Chaffee to Roosevelt, 15 August 1905, subject files, "Expeditionary Force," series 3, box 14, WDGS; Roosevelt, *State Papers*, in Hagedorn, *Works*, 15:307, 408 ; Millett, "General Staff," 114.

101. Roosevelt to S. Young, 8 August 1903, in Morison, *Letters*, 3:546.

102. Roosevelt to Chaffee, 3 July 1905, in Morison, *Letters*, 4:1260–62; Roosevelt, *State Papers*, in Hagedorn, *Works*, 15:262, 307, 407.

103. "Discusses Army and Navy."

5. The Institutions of Command

1. "Cuba in Throes of Rebellion," 24 August 1906, *Washington Post*, 1.

2. Millett, *Politics of Intervention*, 48–53, 59–60.

3. Theodore Roosevelt to George Otto Trevelyan, 9 September 1906, in Morison, *Letters*, 5:401.

4. "Cuba in Throes of Rebellion."

5. Skowronek, *New American State*; Wiebe, *Search for Order*.

6. Roosevelt to James Wilson, 25 July 1899, in Morison, *Letters*, 2:1041; Roosevelt to George F. Becker, 6 September 1899, in Morison, *Letters*, 2:1067; Roosevelt to John Hay, 6 December 1899, in Morison, *Letters*, 2:1105.

7. Upton, *Military Policy*.

8. "Report of the Secretary of War" (1899), in *War Department*, 45–49.

9. Bryan, qtd. in *Thinkexist.com*, 5 May 2005, http://en.thinkexist.com /quotation/behold_a_republic_standing_erect_while_empires/329920.html.

10. "Canned Beef Killed a Cat," 17 January 1899, *New York Times*, 1; Roosevelt to George Davis, 28 February 1899, in Morison, *Letters*, 2:952; Trask, *War with Spain*, 484–85; Millett and Maslowski, *For the Common Defense*, 303.

11. Roosevelt to William A. Wadsworth, 7 April 1898, in Morison, *Letters*, 2:814; Trask, *War with Spain*, 88–89.

12. Roosevelt, "First Annual Message" and "Second Annual Message," in *State Papers*, in Hagedorn, *Works*, 15:123, 157.

13. On Elihu Root's lobbying effort, see, for example, the "Report of the Secretary of War" (1902), in *War Department*, 42–49. In the *North American Review* for October 1902, William Carter published "A General Staff for the Army," 558–65.

14. Root to Roosevelt, 5 January 1903, series 1, roll 32, TRLC.

15. War Department General Staff, 1907–17, file 10171, series 5, box 105, WDGS; Hewes, *From Root to McNamara*, x.

16. Roosevelt to Root, 7 March 1902, in Morison, *Letters*, 3:241; Roosevelt to Oswald Garrison Villard, 22 March 1902, in Morison, *Letters*, 3:247; Nelson Miles to Root, 17 February 1902, series 1, roll 24, TRLC; Roosevelt to Root, 18 February 1902, 7 March 1902, 19 March 1902, folder 6, box 162, ERLC.

17. "War Department's Breach with the Senate," 23 April 1902, *New York Times*, 1.

18. Roosevelt to Villard, 22 March 1902, in Morison, *Letters*, 3:247.

19. U.S. Congress, *Congressional Record*, 57th Cong., 2nd sess. (1903), 36:502–8, 1502, 1633; J. Clark, *Preparing for War*, 194.

20. Records of the Committee on Department Methods and the President's Commission on Economy and Efficiency, 1905–13, RG 51, DMPC; Forrest McDonald, "The American Presidency: Has It Helped Us to Form a More Perfect Union?" Heritage Lecture 498, Heritage Foundation, 11 March 1994, www.heritage.org/political-process/report/the-american-presidency-has-it-helped-us-form-more-perfect-union.

21. U.S. Congress, *Congressional Record*, 57th Cong., 1st sess. (1902), 35:502; Draft of General Orders for 14 August 1903, file 495145, series 25, box 3493, AGOF; Benjamin Alvord, memorandum, 16 June 1904, folder 10, box 279, JPLC; William R. Roberts, "Reform and Revitalization, 1890–1903," in Hagan and Roberts, *Against All Enemies*, 214; Millett and Maslowski, *For the Common Defense*, 311.

22. U.S. Congress, *Congressional Record*, 57th Cong., 2nd sess. (1903), 36:502; Draft of General Orders for 14 August 1903, file 495145, series 25, box 3493, AGOF.

23. Albert L. Key to Roosevelt, 14 April 1908, series 1, roll 82, TRLC.

24. Roosevelt, *Rough Riders*, 62, 81–84; Roosevelt to Samuel Baldwin Marks Young, 18 September 1899, in Morison, *Letters*, 2:1075–76; Roosevelt to William McKinley, 29 January 1900, Morison, *Letters*, 2:1150–51.

25. Statement of the Military Service of Major General Samuel Baldwin Marks Young, file 1324, ACP 1881, series 25, AGOF; General Orders No. 7, 9 January 1904, file 1324, ACP 1881, series 25, AGOF.

26. Adna R. Chaffee, letters received by the Appointment, Commission, and Personal Branch, 1871–94, microform no. M-1395, file 2118, ACP 1894, AGOF; Adjutant General's Office, *Official Army Register*, 5, 6; Karnow, *In Our Image*, 187–93; William Howard Taft to Roosevelt, 13 September 1902, series 1, roll 29, TRLC.

27. Adna R. Chaffee to the Adjutant General of the Army, 18 February 1904, series 1, roll 41, TRLC; Chaffee to William Loeb, 7 October 1904, series 1, roll 42, TRLC; Chaffee to the Secretary of War, 23 March 1904, series 1, roll 43, TRLC; Chaffee to Taft, 29 March 1904, series 1, roll 43, TRLC; Chaffee to William Loeb Jr., 17 January 1905, 6 March 1905, series 1, rolls 52, 53, TRLC; Chaffee to Taft, 21 July 1905, series 1, roll 57, TRLC.

28. Parker, *Old Army*, 373.

29. Henry C. Corbin to Taft, 12 August 1905, folder 12, box 1, HCLC.

30. Taft to Mrs. H. C. Corbin, 9 June 1905, folder 6, box 1, HCLC; Taft to H. Corbin, 17 June 1905, folder 12, box 1, HCLC; Loeb to Joseph B. Foraker, 24 June 1905, folder 9, box 1, HCLC; H. Corbin, 12 August 1905, folder 12, box 1, HCLC; William S. Seekeudon to H. Corbin, 5 September 1905, folder 3, box 1-A, HCLC; Taft to H. Corbin, 1 December 1905, folder 12, box 1, HCLC; Fred W. Carpenter to the Military Secretary, 1 February 1906, file 1096335, series 25, AGOF; Raines, "Bell and Military Reform," 1–2.

31. Foraker to Roosevelt, folder 9, box 1, HCLC; John McCook to H. Corbin, 8 February 1906, folder 11, box 1, HCLC; Raines, "Bell and Military Reform," 1; "New Chief of Staff Will Be General Bell," *New York Times*, 2 February 1906, 6.

32. "New Chief of Staff"; J. Clark, *Preparing for War*, 207, 210–12.

33. Young to Root, 11 December 1903, series 1, roll 39, TRLC; Arthur MacArthur to Young, 13 December 1903, series 1, roll 39, TRLC; Roosevelt to Taft, 7 March 1904, in Morison, *Letters*, 4:744; Young, *General's General*, 305–6, 308, 310–12.

34. Newspaper clipping, *Leavenworth Star*, 2 February 1906, file 1101199, series 25, AGOF; Meixsel, "United States Army Policy," 66; Raines, "Bell and Military Reform," 3–5; Roosevelt to Wilson, 4 August 1897, in Morison, *Letters*, 1:638; Roosevelt to John D. Long, 26 August 1897, in Morison, *Letters*, 1:662.

35. J. Clark, *Preparing for War*, 241.

36. Memorandum for Secretary, General Staff, from Thaddeus Jones, 5 September 1907, file 14192, series 60, box 61, SWOF; Subject files "Cook Wagon," series 3, box 10, WDGS; Nenninger, "Army Enters the Twentieth Century," in Hagan and Roberts, *Against All Enemies*, 223–24.

37. William H. Carter to Root, 30 October 1903, subject file "General Staff," series 3, box 16, WDGS; War Department Orders, 30 December 1903, subject file "Chief of Staff," series 3, box 9, WDGS; Young, circular letter, 1 September 1903, subject files "General Staff," series 3, box 15, WDGS; Weigley, *United States Army*, 323.

38. Roosevelt to William Cary Sanger, 8 October 1901, in Morison, *Letters*, 3:163; Roosevelt to Root, 2 October 1902, in Morison, *Letters*, 3:335.

39. Roosevelt to Young, 8 August 1903, in Morison, *Letters*, 3:546.

40. Roosevelt to Taft, 4 January 1905, in Morison, *Letters*, 4:1090–91; Report of Special Committee of the General Staff, pt. 2, 25 January 1905, Subject files "Sword, The," series 3, box 29, WDGS.

41. Roosevelt to Taft, 4 January 1905, in Morison, *Letters*, 4:1090–91.

42. Report of Special Committee of the General Staff, pt. 2, 25 January 1905, Subject files "Sword, The," series 3, box 29, WDGS; Memorandum for the Secretary of War, 4 April 1905, Subject files "Rifle, Model of 1903," box 26, series 3, WDGS.

43. Subject files, "Flag U.S.," box 14, series 3, WDGS.

44. Subject files "Wham, Joseph, W.," box 31, series 3, WDGS.

45. Roosevelt to Chaffee, 3 July 1905, in Morison, *Letters*, 4:1260–62.

46. Roosevelt to Chaffee, 3 July 1905, in Morison, *Letters*, 4:1260–62.

47. Roosevelt, *American Ideals*, in Hagedorn, *Works*, 13:183.

48. Subject files "Army War College," box 3B, series 3, WDGS; Subject files, "Transportation of Troops by Rail in Time of War," box 30, series 3, WDGS; Millett, "General Staff," 114; Hewes, *From Root to McNamara*, 12.

49. Roosevelt to Taft, 11 January 1906, in Morison, *Letters*, 5:132–33.

50. Millett, "General Staff," 114. For the full story of the second military intervention, see Millett, *Politics of Intervention*.

51. Millett, "General Staff," 114–15; Taft to Roosevelt, 15 and 16 September 1906, roll 488, WTLC; Roosevelt to Chaffee, 3 July 1905, in Morison, *Letters*, 4:1260–62; Subject file, "Expeditionary Force," series 3, box 14, WDGS.

52. Roosevelt to Trevelyan, 9 September 1906, in Morison, *Letters*, 5:401.

53. Millett, "General Staff," 115–16.

54. Millett, "General Staff," 117–18.

55. Millett, "General Staff," 117–19; Roosevelt to James Franklin Bell, 1 September 1906, in Morison, *Letters*, 5:391.

56. Roosevelt, *State Papers*, in Hagedorn, *Works*, 15:408.

57. Millett, "General Staff," 118.

58. Nenninger, "Twentieth Century," in Hagan and Roberts, *Against All Enemies*, 226–27; Weigley, *United States Army*, 332–33; Weigley, *Towards an American Army*, 175.

59. Bell to Roosevelt, 18 July 1907, series 1, roll 75, TRLC; Bell to William Howard Taft, 7 February 1908, series 1, roll 80, TRLC; William W. Wotherspoon to Bell, 2 July 1908, series 1, roll 83, TRLC.

60. Roosevelt to Bell, 8 January 1907, series 2, roll 344, TRLC; Loeb Jr., to Bell, 23 December 1907, series 2, roll 347, TRLC.

61. Roosevelt to Emily T. Carow, 16 August 1903, in Bishop, *Letters to His Children*, 54.

62. Spector, *Professors of War*, 14, 47, 64, 88–95; "Henry C. Taylor, U.S. Navy," folder 10, box 1, HTLC.

63. George Belknap's comments are contained in Belknap to the Secretary of the Navy, 24 May 1891, box 1, HTLC.

64. Costello, "Planning for War," 16–17.

65. Spector, *Professors of War*, 136; Henry C. Taylor to Long, 30 January 1900, in Allen, *Papers of John D. Long*, 305–6; Taylor to Long, 14 February 1900, in Allen, *Papers of John D. Long*, 311–12.

66. "A Naval General Staff," *Boston Herald*, 23 March 1900. Ronald Spector points out Taylor's ignorance of business practice by referring to Henry Varnum Poor's study of the board of directors of a number of railroads. Poor concluded that the boards hindered rather than helped because of the ignorance and incompetence of the board members. Spector, *Professors of War*, 134, 136–37. The following article sprang from Taylor's memorandum to the Secretary Long: Taylor, "Memorandum on General Staff," 442.

67. "A Naval Staff," *Boston Herald*, 23 March 1900.

68. Taylor to George Dewey, 22 June 1901, folder 1, box 13, GDLC.

69. Taylor took a very long view regarding general staff reform. He stressed that "the Germans took fifty years to perfect their General Staff; we will not probably achieve it in less than twenty-five years." See "Memorandum on General Staff," 441.

70. "Secretary Long to Quit," *New York Times*, 8 March 1902, 1; *Encyclopædia Britannica* digital ed., s.v. "Moody, William."

71. Alfred T. Mahan to Roosevelt, 7 September 1903, in in Seager and Maguire, *Letters and Papers*, 3:73–74; Roosevelt to Taylor, 15 September 1903, in Morison, *Letters*, 3:601–2.

72. Roosevelt, "Third Annual Message," in *State Papers*, in Hagedorn, *Works*, 15:201.

73. Roosevelt to Taylor, 15 September 1903, in Morison, *Letters*, 3:601–2.

74. Roosevelt to Root, 16 February 1904, in Morison, *Letters*, 4:731.

75. George Kibbe Turner, "Our Navy on the Land," *McClure's Magazine* 32 (February 1909): 398.

76. Turner, "Navy on the Land," 398, 400–401; U.S. Congress, *Congressional Record*, 60th Cong., 1st sess. (1908), 42:559; Albion, "Naval Affairs Committees," 1233; Sprout and Sprout, *Naval Power*, 297.

77. "The White House Dinner," *New York Times*, 25 February 1902, 1; "The Nation's Problems," *New York Times*, 28 August 1902, 1.

78. "To See Naval Evolutions with Secretary Moody," *New York Times*, 8 August 1902, 3; "Secretary Moody Hurt," *New York Times*, 13 January 1903, 1.

79. "Increase in the Navy," *New York Times*, 27 February 1903, 3.

80. U.S. Congress, Committee on Naval Affairs, *Hearings on H.R. 15403*, 912; Heffron, "Secretary Moody," 47.

81. U.S. Congress, Committee on Naval Affairs, *Hearings on H.R. 15403*, 920–22, 945.

82. U.S. Congress, Committee on Naval Affairs, *Hearings on H.R. 15403*, 927, 935, 946–47, 954–56, 962–65, 981.

83. The quotes are from Roosevelt to Paul Morton, 25 July 1904, in Morison, *Letters*, 4:847; see also "Assistant Secretary Hackett to Retire," *New York Times*, 19 October 1901, 8.

84. Roosevelt to Morton, 25 July 1904, in Morison, *Letters*, 4:848.

85. "To Succeed Darling," *New York Times*, 24 March, 1905, 3; "Charles H. Darling Retires," *New York Times*, 1 November 1905, 5.

86. "Admiral Taylor Is Dead," 27 July 1904, *New York Times*.

87. Roosevelt to Morton, 25 July 1904, in Morison, *Letters*, 4:848, 847.

88. "Morton's 'Mistake,'" *New York Times*, 23 January 1905, 6.

89. Churchill, qtd. in Massie, *Castles of Steel*, 19–20.

6. In the Fullness of It All

1. Theodore Roosevelt to Kermit Roosevelt, 10 November 1904, in Morison, *Letters*, 4:1024.

2. "Roosevelt Hero of Brilliant Day," *New York Times*, 5 March 1905, 1.

3. "Inaugural Ball in Fairy Garden, *New York Times*, 5 March 1905, 4.

4. Roosevelt to Robert B. Roosevelt, 6 March 1905, in Morison, *Letters*, 4:1131.

5. Roosevelt to K. Roosevelt, 4 December 1902, 10 January 1909, in Morison, *Letters*, 3:389, 6:1472; Roosevelt to William Kent, 4 February 1909, in Morison, *Letters*, 6:1504; Roosevelt to Philander C. Knox, 8 February 1909, in Morison, *Letters*, 6:1512.

6. Roosevelt to Theodore Roosevelt Jr., 19 November 1905, in Morison, *Letters*, 5:82; Roosevelt to K. Roosevelt, 5 December 1906, in Morison, *Letters*, 5:521; Roosevelt to Edwin Arlington Robinson, 27 March 1905, in Morison, *Letters*, 4:1145.

7. Roosevelt to Leonard Wood, 9 March 1905, in Morison, *Letters*, 4:1136.

8. Oyos, "Implements of War."

9. Gatewood, *Art of Controversy*, 213–20.

10. Roosevelt to William Cary Sanger, 8 October 1901, in Morison, *Letters*, 3:163.

11. Roosevelt to Hermann Speck von Sternberg, 9 November 1901, in Morison, *Letters*, 3:192.

12. Roosevelt to William Howard Taft, 4 January 1905, in Morison, *Letters*, 4:1090–91; Roosevelt to Adna R. Chaffee, 3 July 1905, in Morison, *Letters*, 4:1260–61; Report of Special Committee of the General Staff, pt. 2, 25 January 1905, subject files "Sword, The," series 3, box 29; Memorandum for the Secretary of War, 4 April 1905, subject files, "Rifle, Model of 1903," series 3, box 26, WDGS.

13. Capt. Joseph T. Dickman to Brig. Gen. Tasker H. Bliss, 17 May 1905; Lt. Gen. Chaffee to Secretary of War Taft, 23 May 1905; William Loeb, Jr. to Taft, 23 May 1905; Fred W. Carpenter to Loeb Jr., 24 May 1905; all in subject files "Intrenching Tools," series 3, box 17, WDGS.

14. Roosevelt, *Rough Riders*, 135–36, 165; Armstrong, *Bullets and Bureaucrats*, 101,112–13, 120; Parker, *Gatling Gun Detachment.*

15. "The Machine Gun Companies," *Army and Navy Journal*, 31 October 1908, 225; Armstrong, *Bullets and Bureaucrats*, 160–63.

16. Roosevelt to Luke Wright, 26 October 1908, in Morison, *Letters*, 6:1319–20; Armstrong, *Bullets and Bureaucrats*, 163–64.

17. Roosevelt to Wright, 26 October 1908, in Morison, *Letters*, 6:1319–20.

18. "President Takes Plunge in Submarine, Remains below the Surface for Fifty-Five Minutes, Once 40 Feet under Water," *New York Times*, 26 August 1905, 1–2; "Miss Roosevelt in a Submarine Boat," *New York Times*, 11 September 1903, 6.

19. "Five Vessels Almost Ready," *New York Times*, 27 April 1898, 1.

20. "President Takes Plunge"; "Our Submerged President," *New York Times*, 27 August 1905, 6; "President under Sea; Nation Is Appalled," *New York Journal*, 26 August 1905, 3; *Army and Navy Journal*, 2 September 1905, 16.

21. Roosevelt to Charles J. Bonaparte, 28 August 1905, in Morison, *Letters*, 4:1324–25; Bonaparte to Roosevelt, 3 October 1905, file 20652, GRND.

22. Roosevelt to Bonaparte, 28 August 1905, in Morison, *Letters*, 4:1324–25.

23. Naval Building Programs, 1902–15, in Morison, *Letters*, 6:1516.

24. The quotes are from Roosevelt to William Sheffield Cowles, 25 August 1908, in Morison, *Letters*, 6:1197; Roosevelt to Victor Howard Metcalf, 8 October 1908, in Morison, *Letters*, 6:1278; "President Takes Plunge."

25. Roosevelt to John D. Long, 25 March 1898, 30 March 1898, in Morison, *Letters*, 1:799, 2:806.

26. Mackersey, *Wright Brothers*, 241–44, 246–49.

27. "Government Backs Langley, the Professor's Airship Built as an Implement of War," *Washington Post*, 24 July 1903, 4.

28. Mackersey, *Wright Brothers*, 205–7, 247; Johnson Hagood, "Down the Big Road," JHMI, 104–6; Gross, "George Owen Squier," 284–85.

29. Mackersey, *Wright Brothers*, 205–7, 215, 230–31, 233, 247, 246–49.

30. Hagood, "Down the Big Road," JHMI, 104–6; Gross, "George Owen Squier," 284–85.

31. Mackersey, *Wright Brothers*, 367–69, Gross, "George Owen Squier," 286; *Army and Navy Journal*, 28 December 1907, 433; *Army and Navy Journal*, 15 February 1908, 628; *Army and Navy Journal*, 12 September 1908, 42–43; "Wright Flies over an Hour," *New York Times*, 10 September 1908, 1–2; "Wright Out for a New Record!," *New York Journal*, 10 September 1908, 1–2; "In Air More Than Hour, Wright Makes Record," *Washington Post*, 10 September 1908, 1. The quotation is from "Battleships to Be No More Than Junk When Planes Fight," *New York Journal*, 17 September 1908, 3.

32. "After Wright Ship," *Washington Post*, 7 September 1908, 1. The quotation is from "Conquest of the Air," *Washington Post*, 12 September 1908, 6.

33. "Fears Risk in Flight," *Washington Post*, 15 September 1908, 1.

34. "Airship Falls, Lieut. Selfridge Killed, Wright Hurt," *Washington Post*, 18 September 1908, 1.

35. "The Aeroplane Catastrophe," *Washington Post*, 19 September 1908, 6.

36. Gross, "George Owen Squier," 286–87; *Army and Navy Journal*, 15 February 1908, 628; *Army and Navy Journal*, 19 September 1908, 70–71; Report of the General Board, 26 September 1907, letterbook 5, box 2, GBNA.

37. "After Wright Ship."

38. Roosevelt to George E. Foss, 11 January 1907, in Morison, *Letters*, 5:545.

39. Oyos, "Implements of War," 644–45; O'Connell, *Sacred Vessels*, 83–86.

40. William S. Sims, notation on correspondence file, 1905, folder 4, box 96, WSLC; Oyos, "Implements of War," 648–49.

41. Roosevelt to K. Roosevelt, November 1906, in Morison, *Letters*, 5:495.

42. "Roosevelt as Stoker in Hold of Warship, *New York Times*, 14 November 1906, 1.

43. Roosevelt to Bonaparte, 28 November 1906, in Morison, *Letters*, 5:511–13.

44. Roosevelt to Bonaparte, 12 November 1906, in Morison, *Letters*, 5:496.

45. Roosevelt, *Naval War of 1812*, in Hagedorn, *Works*, 6:43, 367; Oyos, "Implements of War," 645.

46. Roosevelt to K. Roosevelt, November 1906, in Morison, *Letters*, 5:495.

47. Alfred T. Mahan to Roosevelt, 16 October 1902, in Seager and Maguire, *Letters and Papers*, 3:38–39; Roosevelt to Mahan, 25 October 1902, in Morison, *Letters*, 3:368.

48. Turk, *Ambiguous Relationship*.

49. McBride, *Technological Change*, 66.

50. Roosevelt to Sims, 5 October 1904, in Morison, *Letters*, 4:973, 973n; Morison, *Admiral Sims*, 17.

51. Sims to Roosevelt, 6 October 1904, file 18711, GRND.

52. Oyos, "Implements of War," 646.

53. Morison, *Admiral Sims*, 162–63.

54. Oyos, "Implements of War," 648.

55. Morison, *Admiral Sims*, 163.

56. Winton, "Scorecards on Military Effectiveness," 726.

57. Morison, *Admiral Sims*, 164–66.

58. Oyos, "Implements of War," 647.

59. Roosevelt to Sims, 27 September 1906, in Morison, *Letters*, 5:427.

60. Morison, *Admiral Sims*, 168–70.

61. London *Times*, qtd. in Massie, *Dreadnought*, 480, 482.

62. Massie, *Dreadnought*, 482.

63. Roosevelt, "Fifth Annual Message," in *State Papers*, in Hagedorn, *Works*, 15:309.

64. McBride, *Technological Change*, 68–69, 71.

65. Roosevelt to Wood, 9 March 1905, in Morison, *Letters*, 4:1136.

66. Roosevelt to Joseph Cannon, 27 December 1904, 13 January 1905, in Morison, *Letters*, 4:1080–81, 1101; Roosevelt to Foss, 10 January 1905, 13 January 1905, in Morison, *Letters*, 4:1097, 1101–2.

67. Roosevelt to Wood, 9 March 1905, 4:1136.

68. Harrod, *Manning the New Navy*, 5.

69. Roosevelt to Wood, 9 March 1905, in Morison, *Letters*, 4:1136.

7. Battles without Blood

1. "White House Gay," *Washington Post*, 2 January 1909, 1.

2. Theodore Roosevelt to Kermit Roosevelt, 14 January 1909, in Morison, *Letters*, 6:1475–76; Roosevelt to William Howard Taft, 1 January 1909, in Morison, *Letters*, 6:1454–56.

3. Roosevelt to K. Roosevelt, 14 January 1909, in Morison, *Letters*, 6:1475.

4. Roosevelt, "Eighth Annual Message," in *State Papers*, in Hagedorn, *Works*, 15:528; Roosevelt to K. Roosevelt, 10 January 1909, in Morison, *Letters*, 6:1473; Dalton, *Theodore Roosevelt*, 342.

5. Roosevelt to Joseph B. Bishop, 23 February 1904, in Morison, *Letters*, 4:734.

6. Roosevelt, "Fourth Annual Message," in *State Papers*, in Hagedorn, *Works*, 15:256–57.

7. Roosevelt to Jørgen Løvland, 10 December 1905, in Morison, *Letters*, 5:524.

8. Roosevelt to Taft, 21 August 1907, in Morison, *Letters*, 5:761–62.

9. Linn, *Guardians of Empire*, 39.

10. "Fine, Cables Johnston, Answering Roosevelt," *New York Times*, 12 March 1906, 6.

11. "No Wanton Slaughter of Moros, *New York Times*, 15 March 1906, 1.

12. "Wood's Battle Called Murder in Congress," *New York Times*, 16 March 1906, 1.

13. Linn, *Guardians of Empire*, 39.

14. Dyer, *Idea of Race*, 102; Dalton, *Theodore Roosevelt*, 321.

15. E. Morris, *Theodore Rex*, 453.

16. Roosevelt to Curtis Guild Jr., 7 November 1906, in Morison, *Letters*, 5:489.

17. Roosevelt to Harry Hamilton Johnston, 11 July 1908, in Morison, *Letters*, 6:1126.

18. Weaver, *Brownsville Raid*, 181.

19. Roosevelt to Guild Jr., 7 November 1906, in Morison, *Letters*, 5:490, 489.

20. Roosevelt to Guild Jr., 7 November 1906, in Morison, *Letters*, 5:489.

21. "Foraker," *New York Times*, 15 April 1897, 6.

22. "Congress and the President," *New York Times*, 4 December 1906, 8.

23. "Roosevelt Defends Dismissal of Troops," *New York Times*, 20 December 1906, 5.

24. "Defends Dismissal of Troops."

25. "Defends Dismissal of Troops."

26. Foraker, *Notes of a Busy Life*, 243, 239.

27. Lembeck, *Taking on Theodore Roosevelt*, 240–53.

28. "Show Motley King," *Washington Post*, 27 January 1907, 2; the quotation is from "War of the Strong," *Washington Post*, 29 January 1907, 1.

29. Cannon, qtd. in Weaver, *Brownsville Raid*, 142.

30. Joseph B. Foraker to Joseph B. Foraker Jr., 29 January 1907, in Foraker, *Notes of a Busy Life*, 250–51.

31. "War of the Strong."

32. "Cheers for Foraker," *Washington Post*, 29 January 1907, 1.

33. Roosevelt, qtd. in Dalton, *Theodore Roosevelt*, 322; A. Lane, *Brownsville Affair*, 147–48.

34. Lembeck, *Taking on Theodore Roosevelt*, 273–83.

35. Weaver, *Brownsville Raid*, 184–86.

36. "Denounce the President," *New York Times*, 13 December 1906, 1.

37. Weaver, *Brownsville Raid*; A. Lane, *Brownsville Affair*.

38. Lembeck, *Taking on Theodore Roosevelt*, 327–32, 364–69, 371–72.

39. Weaver, *Brownsville Raid*, 224–25, 247–48.

40. E. Morris, *Theodore Rex*, 497–99; Donald, *Lion in the White House*, 203–5.

41. "Cortelyou Puts in $25,000,000," *New York Times*, 24 October 1907, 1.

42. "Chance to Win with a Democrat, *New York Times*, 14 November 1907, 5.

43. "Fleet to Pacific, Metcalf Says: Score of Battleships Soon to Start for San Francisco; Monster Naval Display," *Washington Post*, 5 July 1907, 1.

44. Roosevelt to Henry Cabot Lodge, 10 July 1907, in Morison, *Letters*, 5:709–10; Dalton, *Theodore Roosevelt*, 287.

45. Roosevelt to Elihu Root, 13 July 1907, in Morison, *Letters*, 5:717.

46. "Fleet Will Aid Canal," special cable to the *Washington Post* from the London *Morning Post*, 6 July 1907, 2.

47. "Fleet Will Aid Canal."

48. "Japanese Are for Peace," *Washington Post*, 13 July 1907, 2.

49. Reckner, *White Fleet*, 12.

50. Roosevelt to Charles J. Bonaparte, 13 July 1907, in Morison, *Letters*, 5:716; Roosevelt to Root, 13 July 1907, in Morison, *Letters*, 5:717.

51. Editors' note, number 2, in Morison, *Letters*, 5:717.

52. Reckner, *White Fleet*, 12.

53. "Battleships Pass Capes," *Washington Post*, 17 December 1907, 9.

54. Reckner, *White Fleet*, 24.

55. Henry Reuterdahl, "The Needs of Our Navy," *McClure's Magazine* 30 (January 1908): 251–56, 260.

56. Morison, *Admiral Sims*, 182–84.

57. Roosevelt to Victor Howard Metcalf, 2 January 1908, in Morison, *Letters*, 6:892.

58. Reckner, *White Fleet*, 66–67.

59. "Navy Men Take Sides," *Washington Post*, 26 December 1907, 2.

60. "Rixey Close to President," *Washington Post*, 26 December 1907, 2.

61. William S. Sims, note attached to letter from Sims to Roosevelt, 22 September 1904, folder 1, box 96, WSLC.

62. Navy Department to Captain Sims, 15 February 1908, folder 7, box 96, WSLC; Morison, *Admiral Sims*, 148–49, 178, 184.

63. William S. Sims, "Roosevelt and the Navy," pt. 2, *McClure's Magazine* 54, no. 10 (1922): 62.

64. "Ships Not Faulty," *Washington Post*, 26 February 1908, 1.

65. U.S. Congress, Committee on Naval Affairs, *Hearings on the Bill*; "Sims Causes Strife by Criticising Navy," *New York Times*, 3 March 1908, 2; U.S. Congress, Committee on Naval Affairs, *Report concerning Alleged Defects*.

66. Roosevelt to Henry White, 27 April 1908, in Morison, *Letters*, 6:1017–18.

67. Key, qtd. in Morison, *Admiral Sims*, 199.

68. Roosevelt to Truman Newberry, 1 July 1908, in Morison, *Letters*, 6:1102.

69. Morison, *Admiral Sims*, 200.

70. Albert L. Key to Metcalf, 9 June 1908, series 1, roll 83, TRLC.

71. Sims to Roosevelt, 23 June 1908, series 1, roll 83, TRLC; Roosevelt to Metcalf, 30 June 1908, in Morison, *Letters*, 6:1101

72. Roosevelt to Newberry, 1 July 1908, in Morison, *Letters*, 6:1102.

73. Roosevelt to Metcalf, 30 June 1908, in Morison, *Letters*, 6:1101.

74. Gould, *Presidency of Theodore Roosevelt*, 112, 204, 220–22.

75. "Attacks Navy Chiefs," *Washington Post*, 22 July 1908, 4.

76. "Attacks Navy Chiefs."

77. "Navy to Hit Needed," *Washington Post*, 23 July 1908, 1.

78. Roosevelt to John Merrell, 6 July 1908, in Morison, *Letters*, 6:1108.

79. "President Approves Plans," *Washington Post*, 1 September 1908, 7; "Debate on Battleships," *Washington Post*, 2 September 1908, 2.

80. Morison, *Admiral Sims*, 207.

81. Roosevelt to Newberry, 28 August 1908, in Morison, *Letters*, 6:1199.

82. Morison, *Admiral Sims*, 211.

83. Morison, *Admiral Sims*, 208.

84. Capps, qtd. in the note to Roosevelt to Metcalf, 26 November 1908, in Morison, *Letters*, 6:1383.

85. Roosevelt to Metcalf, 26 November 1908, in Morison, *Letters*, 6:1383.

86. *Report of the Bureau of Construction*, 470; Roosevelt to Newberry, 29 December 1908, 2 January 1909, in Morison, *Letters*, 6:1453–54, 1456; Roosevelt to Key, 8 January 1909, in Morison, *Letters*, 6:1469–71; Roosevelt to Newberry, 8 January 1909, in Morison, *Letters*, 6:1471–72.

87. Roosevelt to K. Roosevelt, 23 January 1909, in Morison, *Letters*, 6:1481.

88. U.S. Congress, *Congressional Record*, 60th Cong., 2nd sess. (1909), 43:2380.

89. Gould, *Presidency of Theodore Roosevelt*, 267.

90. U.S. Congress, Committee on Naval Affairs, *Reorganization of the Navy Department*, 862; Roosevelt to Newberry, in Morison, *Letters*, 6:1456–57. The quotation is from Benjamin, "Reorganization," 1385.

91. U.S. Congress, Committee on Naval Affairs, *Proposed Reorganization*, 34–35; "Report of the Secretary of the Navy" (1910), in *Navy Department*, 5–7; Paolo E. Coletta, "Josephus Daniels: 5 March 1913–5 March 1921," in Coletta, *American Secretaries*, 2:537–39, 544; Ray, "Bureaus Go on Forever," 53; Hooper, *Navy Department*, 14–15.

92. Roosevelt, qtd. in Archie Butt to Clara Butt, 19 November 1908, in Abbott, *Letters of Archie Butt*, 184–85.

93. Millett, *Semper Fidelis*; John Lejeune to Augustine Lejeune, 19 February 1899, roll 1, JLLC.

94. Millett, *Semper Fidelis*, 123, 128; For reactions to Fullam's viewpoint, see Stephen B. Luce to William F. Fullam, 24 November 1890; Henry Glass to Fullam, 7 December 1890; William C. Wise to Fullam, 18 April 1896; Charles H. Davis to Fullam, 22 April 1896; Benjamin H. Buckingham to Fullam, 20 April 1896; all in folder 1, box 1, WFLC.

95. Roosevelt to Eugene Hale, 5 January 1898, in Morison, *Letters*, 1:752.

96. Adm. George Dewey to the Secretary of the Navy, 6 October 1900, letterbook 1, box 1, GBNA; Dewey to the Secretary of the Navy, 3 August 1906, letterbook 4, box 1, GBNA; John D. Long to Roosevelt, 11 January 1902, series 1, roll 24, TRLC.

97. Dewey to the Secretary of the Navy, 6 October 1900, 1 November 1901; General Board to the Secretary of the Navy, 1 November 1901, all in letterbook 1, box 1, GBNA; Memorandum from the General Board, 17 September 1903;

Dewey to the Secretary of the Navy, 26 September 1903; memorandum from Dewey, 29 December 1903, all in letterbook 2, box 1, GBNA; Dewey to the Secretary of the Navy, 20 February 1904, 3 February 1905; General Board to the Secretary of the Navy, 21 June 1905, all in letterbook 3, box 1, GBNA; Dewey to the Secretary of the Navy, 16 February 1906, 3 August 1906, 13 August 1906, all in letterbook 4, box 1, GBNA; Dewey to the Secretary of the Navy, 17 June 1907, 26 September 1907, both in letterbook 5, box 2, GBNA; Costello, "Planning for War," 120–21; Millett, *Semper Fidelis*, 137.

98. "Alter Navy Personnel Act," *Washington Post*, 8 August 1906, 7.

99. "New Army Board Named," *Washington Post*, 17 August 1906, 6; Roosevelt to Joseph Cannon, 24 January 1907, 5:563–64.

100. "United States Navy," *Washington Post*, 20 January 1907, E2.

101. "Army and Navy Gossip," *Washington Post*, 6 December 1908, E2.

102. "Army to Get Marines," *Washington Post*, 4 December 1908, 1.

103. Roosevelt, qtd. in A. Butt to C. Butt, 19 November 1908, Abbott, *Letters of Archie Butt*, 184–85.

104. "Army to Get Marines."

105. "Army and Navy Gossip," 13 December 1908, E2.

106. U.S. Congress, Committee on Naval Affairs, House Subcommittee on Naval Academy and Marine Corps, *U.S. Marine Corps*, hearings, 7–15 January 1909, 438–39, 448–49, 469, 481–82, 578, 586, 588, 591, 605, 609, 612, 619–39; Millett, *Semper Fidelis*, 141–43.

107. Roosevelt to George E. Foss, 18 February 1909, in Morison, *Letters*, 6:1525.

108. Millett, *Semper Fidelis*, 275–77.

8. Looking beyond the White House

1. Theodore Roosevelt to Alice Roosevelt Longworth, 28 October 1908, in Morison, *Letters*, 6:1322.

2. Roosevelt to Kermit Roosevelt, 20 October 1908, in Morison, *Letters*, 6:1303.

3. Roosevelt to George Otto Trevelyan, 1 January 1908, in Morison, *Letters*, 6:882–83.

4. "Naval Building Programs, 1902–1915," in Morison, *Letters*, 6:1516.

5. Roosevelt to Trevelyan, 1 January 1908, in Morison, *Letters*, 6:882–83.

6. "Wedded at Epiphany," *Washington Post*, 27 January 1905, 7.

7. James H. Canfield to Frank L. Stetson, 25 January 1895, microform no. M-1395, file 3849, ACP 1886, AGOF; "Pershing's Big Jump," news clipping; "He Deserved Promotion," *Syracuse Herald*, 17 September 1906, both in folder 4, box 281, JPLC.

8. Leonard Wood to the U.S. Army Adjutant General, 30 July 1898; Orders No. 60, 24 October 1903; William Loeb to Elihu Root, 25 November 1903, all in microform no. M-1395, file 3849, ACP 1886, AGOF; Avery Andrews to Charles Nagel, 23 October 1903; Andrews to Roosevelt, 16 November 1903;

Roosevelt to Andrews to Roosevelt, 17 November 1903; Canfield to John J. Pershing, 9 December 1903; Recommendations for Brigadier General; Pershing to Elmer J. Burkett, 21 November 1903, all in folder 3, box 281, JPLC; Burkett to Roosevelt, 1 December 1903, microform no. M-1395, file 3849, ACP 1886, AGOF; Smythe, *Guerrilla Warrior*, 52–59; Pershing to Wood, 8 September 1903, folder 4, box 32, LWLC.

9. Smythe, *Guerrilla Warrior*, 118; "Brigadier General Pershing," *Atlanta Constitution*, 17 September 1906, folder 4, box 281, JPLC; "The Pershing Incident," *Baltimore Evening Star*, 30 May 1912, folder 7, box 281, JPLC; Roosevelt to Francis Warren, 19 November 1910, folder 13, box 177, JPLC.

10. George G. Dorsett to Frederick Ainsworth, 30 November 1907, file 1309504, series 25, AGOF; Letcher Hardeman to Pershing, 17 September 1906, folder 4, box 281, JPLC; "General Pershing," *New York Times*, 23 December 1906, 6.

11. William C. Rivers to Pershing, 29 September 1906; Matthew C. Butler to Pershing, 21 September 1906, both in folder 4, box 281, JPLC.

12. William H. Bean to William Cary Sanger, 25 October 1902, microform no. M-1395, file 3849, ACP 1886, AGOF; Smythe, *Guerrilla Warrior*, 126–32; "Pershing's Life Clean, Senator Warren Says," *New York Times*, 21 December 1906, 7; Lacey, *Pershing*, 55–56.

13. "Humphrey Is Retired," *Washington Post*, 2 July 1907, 5.

14. Roosevelt to James Franklin Bell, 13 July 1907, in Morison, *Letters*, 5:715; Bell, *Commanding Generals*, 106.

15. "Army Nominations Help Up," *Washington Post*, 6 December 1907, 4; Record of Service, 16 July 1912, folder 3, box 1, WCLC; Millett, "Roosevelt and His Generals," 11.

16. "Major General James B. Aleshire, 23rd Quartermaster General, July 1907–September 1916," *US Army Quartermaster Foundation*, accessed 3 July 2017, http://old.qmfound.com/MG_James_Aleshire.htm; "Tasker Howard Bliss: General, United States Army, *Arlington National Cemetery Website*, accessed 3 July 2017, www.arlingtoncemetery.net/thbliss.htm; "William Giles Harding Carter: Major General, United States Army," *Arlington National Cemetery Website*, accessed 3 July 2017, www.arlingtoncemetery.net/whcarter.htm; "William Crozier: Major General, United States Army," *Arlington National Cemetery Website*, accessed 3 July 2017, www.arlingtoncemetery.net/wcrozier.htm; "General A. L. Mills, Ill 12 Hours, Dies," *New York Times*, 19 September 1916, 11; "General T. H. Barry Dies in Washington," *New York Times*, 31 December 1919, 7; Bell, *Commanding Generals*, 106.

17. Koistinen, *Mobilizing for Modern War*, 153.

18. Coffman, *War to End All Wars*, 32.

19. Beckett, *Great War*, 55–56.

20. Coffman, *Regulars*, 208.

21. "One Inch Is Added to Cadets' Stature," *New York Times*, 26 May 1907, 2.

22. Roosevelt, qtd. in "One Inch Is Added."

23. "Rotund Colonels Ride to Triumph," 9 October 1907, *New York Times*, 10.

24. "President Orders More Riding Tests," *New York Times*, 6 December 1907, 6.

25. "Army Rides Cost $15,000," *New York Times*, 26 November 1907, 5; "Army Officers Alarmed," *New York Times*, 5 December 1907, 1; "More Riding Tests, 6; "Captains Glad at 90-Mile Riding Test," *New York Times*, 6;

26. "Officers Criticise Army Test Ride," *New York Times*, 27 April 1908, 13.

27. "Want Marshall Retained," *New York Times*, 25 November 1907, 5; "50-Mile Walk Next for Army Officers," *New York Times*, 9 August 1908, 9.

28. "Officers Criticise Army Test Ride."

29. "Waiting for Taft to Drop Navy Tests," *New York Times*, 18 April 1909, 8; William S. Sims, notes on letter to Roosevelt, 16 November 1908, folder 7, box 97, WSLC; "Naval Physical Test," clipping, *Army and Navy Register*, 17 January 1914; Sims, comment on letter of 25 January 1916, both in folder 4, box 82, WSLC.

30. "98-mile Ride Bully, President Declares," *New York Times*, 14 January 1909, 1.

31. "98-mile Ride Bully."

32. "Roosevelt Not Weary," *New York Times*, 15 January 1909, 1.

33. Sims, memorandum to Roosevelt, 27 November 1908, folder 7, box 97, WSLC; *Army and Navy Journal*, 14 August 1909, 1415; 24 December 1910, 470, 490; 19 June 1915, 1337.

34. *Army and Navy Journal*, 24 December 1910, 490; 4 November 1911, 285; Sims, notes on letter to Roosevelt, 16 November 1908, folder 7, box 97, WSLC.

35. *Army and Navy Journal*, 26 June 1909, 1223; 27 June 1914, 1367.

36. Lt. Cdr. Edmund B. Underwood to Adm. George Dewey, 28 May 1901; Report of the General Board, 25 June 1901; Minutes of General Board meeting, September 1901, all in folder 1, box 56, GDLC; Dewey to the Secretary of the Navy, ca. 1–27 June 1903, folder 4, box 15, GDLC.

37. Spencer Miller to Dewey, 17 September 1902, folder 1, box 14, GDLC; Dewey to S. Miller, 24 September 1902, folder 1, box 14, GDLC; Dewey to the Secretary of the Navy, 29 September 1904, letterbook 3, box 1, GBNA; Dewey to the Secretary of the Navy, 20 December 1907, letterbook 5, box 2, GBNA; Costello, "Planning for War," 185, 188.

38. Lease to the United States by the Government of Cuba, February 1903, file 13948-65, GRND.

39. Dewey to the Secretary of the Navy, 1 February 1905, GB 406, letterbook 3, box 1, GBNA.

40. "Cuba Offers Naval Station," *New York Times*, 8 November 1903, 4.

41. Roosevelt to John Hay, 23 October 1902, in Morison, *Letters*, 3:367.

42. Dewey to the Secretary of the Navy, 15 June 1903, letterbook 2, box 1, GBNA; Dewey to Roosevelt, 4 August 1904, letterbook 3, box 1, GBNA; Dewey to the Secretary of the Navy, ca. 1–27 June 1903, folder 4, box 15, GDLC; Dewey to the Secretary of the Navy, 5 March 1908, file 13669, GRND.

43. Report of joint board, qtd. in "Forts for Subig Bay," *Washington Post*, 5 January 1904, 5; Dewey to Roosevelt, 4 August 1904, letterbook 3, box 1, GBNA.

44. Roosevelt to Theodore Burton, 23 February 1904, in Morison, *Letters*, 4:737.

45. Roosevelt to Wood, 5 August 1904, in Morison, *Letters*, 4:881.

46. Dewey to Roosevelt, 4 August 1904, letterbook 3, box 1, GBNA.

47. Major General Bell to the Secretary of War, 21 December 1907, file 398406, series 25, AGOF; Dewey to the Secretary of the Navy, 5 March 1908, file 13669, GRND; Linn, *Guardians of Empire*, 83–84.

48. Roosevelt to William Howard Taft, 11 February 1908, file 13669, GRND; Roosevelt to Victor Howard Metcalf, 11 February 1908, in Morison, *Letters*, 6:937–39.

49. Roosevelt to Metcalf, 11 February 1908, in Morison, *Letters*, 6:937–39.

50. Roosevelt to Metcalf, 11 February 1908, in Morison, *Letters*, 6:937–39.

51. Linn, *Guardians of Empire*, 83, 86–90.

52. "In Pearl Harbor with Our Fleet," *Washington Post*, 16 August 1908, SM1.

53. Braisted, *United States Navy*, 3–8.

54. Roosevelt to Metcalf, 11 February 1908, in Morison, *Letters*, 6:938.

55. "Pearl Harbor"; "Favors Hawaiian Base," *Washington Post*, 3 March 1908, 2; "Plans of Big Dock Drawn," *Washington Post*, 19 December 1908, 4; Linn, *Guardians of Empire*, 87.

56. Reckner, *White Fleet*, 88–90, 93–99, 110–22, 138, 141–54; Roosevelt, *Autobiography*, 572–73.

57. Roosevelt to John E. Pillsbury, 23 October 1908, in Morison, *Letters*, 6:1314–15 and notes 1, 2.

58. Roosevelt, *Autobiography*, 564.

59. Roosevelt to Charles S. Sperry, 5 December 1908, in Morison, *Letters*, 6:1411–12; Roosevelt to Arthur Hamilton Lee, 20 December 1908, in Morison, *Letters*, 6:1432.

60. Roosevelt to Sydney Brooks, 28 December 1908, in Morison, *Letters*, 6:1444.

61. Reckner, *White Fleet*, 87, 90, 138.

62. Roosevelt, *Autobiography*, 566–67.

63. "Exodus to the Roads: Washington, Official and Social, Goes to Greet Fleet," *Washington Post*, 21 February 1909.

64. "Only after Battle Such a Home-Coming," *Washington Post* 23 February 23 1909, 1; "Praises His Men: Admiral Sperry Gives Them Their Full Share of Credit," *Sun* (Baltimore), 23 February 1909, 2.

65. "Praises His Men"; "Large Sum for Navy," *Washington Post*, 17 January 1909, 2; Baer, *One Hundred Years*, 48.

66. "Only after Battle."

67. Brands, *T.R.*, 811–15.

68. Dalton, *Theodore Roosevelt*, 358–63.

69. Dalton, *Theodore Roosevelt*, 427–39; Millard, *River of Doubt*.

70. Roosevelt to Taft, 3 March 1909, in Morison, *Letters*, 6:1543; Roosevelt to Alfred Thayer Mahan, 3 March 1909, in Morison, *Letters*, 6:1543.

71. Roosevelt to William W. Wotherspoon, 8 August 1911, 7:320.

72. Roosevelt, qtd. in Gardner, *Departing Glory*, 193; "The Week in the World," *University Missourian*, 16 October 1910, 5.

73. Roosevelt to Henry Cabot Lodge, 10 August 1886, in Morison, *Letters*, 1:108.

74. Roosevelt to Taft, 14 March 1911, in Morison, *Letters*, 7:243–44.

75. Roosevelt to Albert Fall, 26 February 1915, in Morison, *Letters*, 8:905–6.

76. O'Toole, *When Trumpets Call*, 299; U.S. Congress, Committee on Foreign Relations, *Investigation of Mexican Affairs*, 348.

77. Roosevelt to Newton D. Baker, 6 July 1916, in Morison, *Letters*, 8:1087.

78. Roosevelt to Baker, 6 July 1916, in Morison, *Letters*, 8:1087–88.

79. Roosevelt to Julian Street, 3 July 1916, in Morison, *Letters*, 8:1085–86.

80. Roosevelt to Lodge, 3 July 1916, in Morison, *Letters*, 8:1087.

81. Mahon, *History of the Militia*, 151–52; Doubler, *Civilian in Peace*, 159–62.

82. Roosevelt to Street, 3 July 1916, in Morison, *Letters*, 8:1085–86

83. Roosevelt to Rudyard Kipling, 4 November 1914, in Morison, *Letters*, 8:830; Roosevelt to Munro Smith, 24 March 1915, in Morison, *Letters*, 8:912–13.

9. The Last Crusade

1. Theodore Roosevelt to Arthur Hamilton Lee, 19 November 1918, in Morison, *Letters*, 8:396–97.

2. O'Toole, *When Trumpets Call*, 400–401.

3. Roosevelt to Henry Cabot Lodge, 12 September 1911, in Morison, *Letters*, 7:343.

4. Roosevelt, *American Ideals*, in Hagedorn, *Works*, 13:28–34. Roosevelt was writing in this specific instance in the context of political reform during the late 1890s, but the sentiment he conveyed had a universal cast.

5. Theodore Roosevelt, "Preparedness without Militarism," *New York Times*, 15 November 1914, SM5.

6. Mahon, *History of the Militia*, 142–43; Millett and Maslowski, *For the Common Defense*, 330–31.

7. Jeff Myers, "Plattsburgh Idea Helped the U.S. Prepare for World War II," *Press-Republican*, 26 September 1999.

8. "Rookies Off Today on All-Week Hike," *New York Times*, 26 June 1916, 5.

9. "Rookies Fight Battle in Steady Downpour," *New York Times*, 5 September 1916, 4.

10. "T.R. Talks at Plattsburg," *New York Times*, 26 August 1915, 1.

11. "T.R. Talks at Plattsburg."

12. "T.R. Talks at Plattsburg."

13. Roosevelt to Archibald Roosevelt, 2 September 1915, in Morison, *Letters*, 8:965.

14. "Roosevelt Calls Wilson Policy Weak and Timid," *New York Times*, 29 August 1915, 1.

15. "Col. Roosevelt Chased by Some Washington Hornets," *Wall Street Journal*, 27 August 1915, 6.

16. Roosevelt to Archibald Roosevelt, 2 September 1915, in Morison, *Letters*, 2 8:965.

17. Millett and Maslowski, *For the Common Defense*, 341–42.

18. Roosevelt to Lee, 6 August 1915, in Morison, *Letters*, 8:960; Renehan, *Lion's Pride*, 108; O'Toole, *When Trumpets Call*, 270; Roosevelt Jr. to Kermit Roosevelt, 29 May 1915, folder: Roosevelt, Theodore, Jr. (Brother) 1898–1918, box 15, KRLC.

19. Roosevelt to K. Roosevelt, 28 August 1915, in Morison, *Letters*, 8:962–63.

20. Theodore Roosevelt Jr. to K. Roosevelt, 29 May 1915, folder: Roosevelt, Theodore, Jr. (Brother) 1898–1918, box 15, KRLC.

21. Millett and Maslowski, *For the Common Defense*, 340–41.

22. Kington, *Forgotten Summers*.

23. Roosevelt to John Callan O'Laughlin, 13 April 1917, in Morison, *Letters*, 8:1173–74.

24. Roosevelt to O'Laughlin, 13 April 1917, in Morison, *Letters*, 8:1173–74.

25. Roosevelt to Corinne Roosevelt Robinson, 7 June 1898, in Morison, *Letters*, 2:836; Roosevelt to Lodge, 10 June 1898, in Morison, *Letters*, 2:838.

26. Roosevelt to Lee, 10 November 1916, in Morison, *Letters*, 8:1124–25.

27. Roosevelt to Jules Jusserand, 16 February 1917, in Morison, *Letters*, 8:1152; Beale, *World Power*, 26–27.

28. Roosevelt to Newton D. Baker, 2 February 1917, Correspondence of Theodore Roosevelt and Secretary of War Newton D. Baker by Theodore Roosevelt, fMS Am 1454.16, TRCH.

29. E. Morris, *Colonel Roosevelt*, 487–88, 493; "Colonel Is Hopeful after Wilson Visit," *New York Times*, 12 April 1917, 8.

30. Roosevelt to Baker, 7 February 1917, 19 March 1917, Roosevelt-Baker Correspondence, fMS Am 1454.16, TRCH.

31. Weigley, *United States Army*, 354, 356–57.

32. Baker to Roosevelt, 20 March 1917, Roosevelt-Baker Correspondence, fMS Am 1454.16, TRCH.

33. Roosevelt to Baker, 23 March 1917, Roosevelt-Baker Correspondence, fMS Am 1454.16, TRCH.

34. Baker to Roosevelt, 26 March 1917; Roosevelt to Baker, 12 April 1917, Roosevelt-Baker Correspondence, fMS Am 1454.16, TRCH.

35. "Colonel Is Hopeful."

36. Roosevelt to Baker, 12 April 1917, Roosevelt-Baker Correspondence, fMS Am 1454.16, TRCH.

37. Baker to Roosevelt, 13 April 1917, Roosevelt-Baker Correspondence, fMS Am 1454.16, TRCH.

38. Baker to Roosevelt, 13 April 1917, Roosevelt-Baker Correspondence, fMS Am 1454.16, TRCH.

39. Roosevelt to Baker, 22 April 1917, Roosevelt-Baker Correspondence, fMS Am 1454.16, TRCH.

40. Roosevelt to Joseph Medill McCormick, 25 April 1917, in Morison, *Letters*, 8:1184–85.

41. Roosevelt to Baker, 8 May 1917; Baker to Roosevelt, 11 May 1917; Roosevelt to Woodrow Wilson, telegram, 18 May 1917; Wilson to Roosevelt, telegram, 19 May 1917, all in Roosevelt-Baker Correspondence, fMS Am 1454.16, TRCH.

42. "2,600 U.S. Marines Going to France under Pershing," *Brooklyn Daily Eagle*, 19 May 1917, 1; Roosevelt to John J. Pershing, 20 May 1917, in Morison, *Letters*, 8:1192–93 and note 2; Roosevelt to Charles J. Bonaparte, 25 May 1917, in Morison, *Letters*, 8:1194–97 and note 2.

43. Roosevelt to Pershing, 20 May 1917, in Morison, *Letters*, 8:1192–94 and note 3.

44. Roosevelt to Lee, 18 June 1917, in Morison, *Letters*, 8:1201; Roosevelt to David Lloyd George, 20 June 1917, folder: Roosevelt, Theodore (Father) Copies of Letters to Kermit from TR, 1917–18, box 15, KRLC.

45. K. Roosevelt to Roosevelt, 19 June 1917, folder: Roosevelt, Theodore (Father), 1898–1918, box 15, KRLC.

46. Roosevelt to Roosevelt Jr., 9 August 1917, 22 August 1917, in Morison, *Letters*, 8:1221–22, 1226–27.

47. Roosevelt to Archibald Roosevelt, 1 September 1917, in Morison, *Letters*, 8:1231–32; Roosevelt to Quentin Roosevelt, 1 September 1917, 1232, 1234.

48. Roosevelt to Archibald Roosevelt, 19 September 1917, in Morison, *Letters*, 8:1241.

49. Roosevelt to K. Roosevelt, 29 November 1917, in Morison, *Letters*, 8:1257.

50. Roosevelt to Archibald Roosevelt, 13 March 1918, in Morison, *Letters*, 8:1300; Roosevelt to Q. Roosevelt, 17 March 1918, in Morison, *Letters*, 8:1301–2.

51. Roosevelt to Georges Clemenceau, 22 March 1918, in Morison, *Letters*, 8:1303.

52. Roosevelt to K. Roosevelt, 20 June 1918, in Morison, *Letters*, 8:1339; Roosevelt to Ethel Roosevelt Derby, 12 July 1918, in Morison, *Letters*, 8:1351.

53. Roosevelt to K. Roosevelt, 13 July 1918, folder: Roosevelt, Theodore (Father) Copies of Letters to Kermit from TR, 1917–18, box 15, KRLC.

54. "Quentin Roosevelt Win Aerial Fight," *New York Times*, 11 July 1918, 3; "Companions Tell of Quentin's Fight," *New York Times*, 19 July 1918, 13.

55. "Companions Tell"; "Quentin Roosevelt's Grave Found," *Wall Street Journal*, 9 August 1918, 5; Roosevelt to George V, 22 July 1918, in Morison, *Letters*, 8:1353.

56. Roosevelt to K. Roosevelt, 21 July 1918, folder: Roosevelt, Theodore (Father) Copies of Letters to Kermit from TR, 1917–18, box 15, KRLC.

57. Roosevelt to James Bryce, 7 August 1918, in Morison, *Letters*, 8:1358.

58. Roosevelt, qtd. in Brands, *T.R.*, 802.

59. Derby to K. Roosevelt, 25 August 1918, folder: Family Correspondence, Derby, Ethel Roosevelt, 1918–24, box 4, KRLC.

60. Brands, *T.R.*, 802–4, 810–11.

61. Roosevelt to Mary L. Brown, 26 July 1918, in Morison, *Letters*, 8:1355.

62. Brands, *T.R.*, 799.

63. Roosevelt to George V, 22 July 1918, in Morison, *Letters*, 8:1353; Roosevelt to Roosevelt Jr., 10 November 1918, in Morison, *Letters*, 8:1390.

64. Derby to K. Roosevelt, 15 September 1918, folder: Family Correspondence, Derby, Ethel Roosevelt, 1918–24, box 4, KRLC; Derby to Belle Willard Roosevelt, 5 October 1918, folder: Family Correspondence, Derby, Ethel Roosevelt, 1918–24, box 4, KRLC.

65. Roosevelt to Henry Bordeaux, 27 May 1918, in Morison, *Letters*, 8:1336; Roosevelt to B. Roosevelt, 11 August 1918, in Morison, *Letters*, 8:1360.

66. Roosevelt to B. Roosevelt and K. Roosevelt, 8 September 1918, folder: Roosevelt, Theodore (Father) Copies of Letters to Kermit from TR, 1917–18, box 15, KRLC.

67. Roosevelt to Lee, 8 September 1918, in Morison, *Letters*, 8:1368.

68. Roosevelt to Lodge, 15 August 1917, 24 October 1918, in Morison, *Letters*, 8:1222–23, 1380.

69. Roosevelt to William Allen White, 3 August 1917, in Morison, *Letters*, 8:1216–17.

70. "President Asks for Vote of Confidence," *Wall Street Journal*, 26 October 1918, 8.

71. "Roosevelt Takes Stump, Delivers Rabid Political Speech before New York Republicans," *Baltimore Sun*, 29 October 1918, 5.

72. "Roosevelts Cast Votes," *New York Times*, 6 November 1918; "Senate Majority Two, Possibly Four," *New York Times*, 8 November 1918, 24.

73. Roosevelt to Roosevelt Jr., 10 November 1918, in Morison, *Letters*, 8:1390; Roosevelt to Lee, 19 November 1918, in Morison, *Letters*, 8:1396–97.

74. E. Morris, *Colonel Roosevelt*, 545–50.

Conclusion

1. Robinson, *My Brother Theodore Roosevelt*, 346.

2. Theodore Roosevelt to James Bryce, 19 November 1918, in Morison, *Letters*, 8:1400.

3. Roosevelt to Rudyard Kipling, 30 November 1918, in Morison, *Letters*, 8:1408–9.

4. Bailey, *Diplomatic History*, 639–40.

5. Roosevelt to John J. Pershing, 6 June 1916, 19 August 1918, in Morison, *Letters*, 8:1050–51, 1363.

6. Roosevelt to Charles Sumner Bird, 2 November 1918, in Morison, *Letters*, 8:1388.

7. Roosevelt to Kermit Roosevelt, 27 October 1918, in Morison, *Letters*, 8:1382.

8. Roosevelt to Henry L. Stimson, 10 February 1909, in Morison, *Letters*, 8:1516.

9. Ralph Jennings, "U.S. Navy Edges Back to Subic Bay in the Philippines—Under New Rules," *Christian Science Monitor*, 12 November 2015; Manuel Mogato, "Philippines Offers Eight Bases to U.S. under New Military Deal," *Reuters*, 13 January 2016; "They're Baaack: U.S. Navy Returns to Philippines' Subic Bay Amid China Fears," 13 November 2015, *Sputnik*.

10. Renehan, *Lion's Pride*, 226, 232–35, 237–39.

11. Renehan, *Lion's Pride*, 229–32.

12. Renehan, *Lion's Pride*, 232–33, 244.

13. Commander, Naval Air Forces, uss *Theodore Roosevelt*, "Traditions," www.public.navy.mil/AIRFOR/cvn71/Pages/TRADITIONS.aspx; "uss *Theodore Roosevelt*: cvn 71," *U.S. Carriers*, www.uscarriers.net/cvn71history.htm; "Deployments of uss *Theodore Roosevelt*," *Navy Site*, navysite.de/cvn/cvn71deploy.htm, all accessed 20 August 2017.

BIBLIOGRAPHY

Archival and Manuscript Materials

AGOF   Office of the Adjutant General. Record Group 94. National Archives and Records Administration, Washington DC.

ARHQ   Records of the Headquarters of the Army. Record Group 108. National Archives and Records Administration, Washington DC.

DMPC   Records of the Committee on Department Methods and the President's Commission on Economy and Efficiency. Record Group 51. Office of Management and Budget. National Archives and Records Administration, Washington, DC.

ERLC   Elihu Root Papers. Manuscript Division. Library of Congress, Washington DC.

FALC   Frederick Ainsworth Papers. Manuscript Division. Library of Congress, Washington DC.

GBNA   General Records of the Navy Department. Record Group 80. Records of the General Board of the Navy. National Archives and Records Administration, Washington DC.

GDLC   George Dewey Papers. Manuscript Division. Library of Congress, Washington DC.

GRND   General Records of the Navy Department. Record Group 80. General Correspondence, 1897–1915. Office of the Secretary of the Navy. National Archives and Records Administration, Washington DC.

HCLC   Henry C. Corbin Papers. Manuscript Division. Library of Congress, Washington DC.

HTLC   Henry C. Taylor Papers. Manuscript Division. Library of Congress, Washington DC.

JHMI   Johnson Hagood Papers. U.S. Army Military History Institute, Carlisle Barracks PA.

JLLC   John Lejeune Papers. Microfilm edition. Manuscript Division. Library of Congress, Washington DC.

JPLC   John Pershing Papers. Manuscript Division. Library of Congress, Washington DC.

KRLC   Kermit Roosevelt and Belle Roosevelt Papers. Manuscript Division. Library of Congress, Washington DC.

LWLC   Leonard Wood Papers. Manuscript Division. Library of Congress, Washington DC.

SLLC   Stephen B. Luce Papers. Microfilm edition. Manuscript Division. Library of Congress, Washington DC.

SWOF   Office of the Secretary of War. Record Group 107. National Archives and Records Administration, Washington DC.

TRCH   Theodore Roosevelt Collection. Houghton Library. Harvard University, Cambridge MA.

TRLC   Theodore Roosevelt Papers. Microfilm edition. Manuscript Division. Library of Congress, Washington DC.

WCLC   William Harding Carter Papers. Manuscript Division. Library of Congress, Washington DC.

WDGS   War Department General and Special Staff. Record Group 165. National Archives and Records Administration, Washington DC.

WFLC   William F. Fullam Papers. Manuscript Division. Library of Congress, Washington DC.

WMLC   William H. Moody Papers. Manuscript Division. Library of Congress, Washington DC.

WSLC   William S. Sims Papers. Manuscript Division. Library of Congress, Washington DC.

WTLC   William Howard Taft Papers. Microfilm edition. Manuscript Division. Library of Congress, Washington DC.

Published Works

Abbott, Lawrence R., ed. *The Letters of Archie Butt.* Garden City: Doubleday, Page, 1925.

Abrahamson, James L. *America Arms for a New Century: The Making of a Great Military Power.* New York: Free Press, 1981.

Adjutant General's Office. *Official Army Register, 1904.* 58th Cong., 2nd sess., 1904, War Dept. Doc. No. 218.

Albion, Robert G. "The Naval Affairs Committee, 1816–1947." *United States Naval Institute Proceedings* 78 (1952): 1227–37.

Allen, Gardner Weld. *Papers of John D. Long.* Vol. 78. Massachusetts Historical Society Collections. Norwood MA: Plimpton, 1939.

Andrews, Avery Delano. *My Friend and Classmate John J. Pershing, with Notes from My War Diary.* Harrisburg PA: Military Service, 1939.

Annual Reports of the Navy Department. Washington DC: Government Printing Office, 1902, 1903, 1904, 1905, 1906, 1910.

Annual Reports of the War Department. Washington DC: Government Printing Office, 1899, 1902, 1903, 1904, 1905, 1906.

Armstrong, David A. *Bullets and Bureaucrats: The Machine Gun and the United States Army, 1861–1916.* Westport CT: Greenwood, 1982.

Baer, George W. *One Hundred Years of Sea Power: The U.S. Navy, 1890–1990.* Stanford: Stanford University Press, 1994.

Bailey, Thomas A. *A Diplomatic History of the American People.* 9th ed. Englewood Cliffs NJ: Prentice Hall, 1974.

Beale, Howard K. *Theodore Roosevelt and the Rise of America to World Power.* New York: Collier Books, 1973.

Beckett, Ian F. W. *The Great War: 1914–1918.* Harlow, England: Pearson Education, 2001.

Bederman, Gail. *Manliness and Civilization: A Cultural History of Gender and Race in the United States, 1880–1917.* Chicago: University of Chicago Press, 1995.

Bell, William Gardner. *Commanding Generals and Chiefs of Staff: Portraits and Biographical Sketches.* Washington DC: Government Printing Office, 2005.

Benjamin, Park. "The Reorganization of the Navy Department," *Independent* 67 (December 1909): 1384–87.

Berman, Larry. *Lyndon Johnson's War: The Road to Stalemate in Vietnam.* New York: Norton, 1989.

Bishop, Joseph B. *Theodore Roosevelt and His Time.* New York: Scribner's Sons, 1920.

———. *Theodore Roosevelt's Letters to His Children.* New York: Scribner's Sons, 1923.

Blum, John M. *The Republican Roosevelt.* Cambridge MA: Harvard University Press, 1954.

Blumenson, Martin. *The Patton Papers, 1885–1940.* Vol. 1. Boston: Houghton-Mifflin, 1972.

Braisted, William R. *The United States Navy in the Pacific, 1909–1922.* Austin: University of Texas Press, 1971.

Brands, H. W. *T.R.: The Last Romantic.* New York: Basic Books, 1997.

Bruce, Robert. *Lincoln and the Tools of War.* New York: Bobbs-Merrill, 1956.

Burton, David H. *The Learned Presidency: Theodore Roosevelt, William Howard Taft, Woodrow Wilson.* London: Associated University Presses, 1988.

Carter, William H. *The American Army.* Indianapolis: Bobbs-Merrill, 1915.

———. "A General Staff for the Army." *North American Review* 175 (October 1902): 558–65.

Challener, Richard D. *Admirals, Generals, and American Foreign Policy, 1898–1914.* Princeton: Princeton University Press, 1973.

Chambers, John Whiteclay, II. *The Tyranny of Change: America in the Progressive Era, 1900–1917.* New York: St. Martin's Press, 1980.

Chessman, G. Wallace, *Theodore Roosevelt and the Politics of Power.* Boston: Little, Brown, 1969.

Child, Paul W., ed. *Register of Graduates and Former Cadets of the United States Military Academy.* West Point NY: Association of Graduates, USMA, 1990.

Clark, Champ. *My Quarter Century of American Politics.* Vol. 1. New York: Harper and Brothers, 1920.

Clark, J. P. *Preparing for War: The Emergence of the Modern U.S. Army, 1815–1917.* Cambridge MA: Harvard University Press, 2017.

Clary, David A. *Fortress America: Corps of Engineers, Hampton Roads, United States Coastal Defense.* Charlottesville: University Press of Virginia, 1990.

Coffman, Edward M. *The Old Army: A Portrait of the American Army in Peacetime, 1784–1898.* Oxford: Oxford University Press, 1986.

———. *The Regulars: The American Army, 1898–1941.* Cambridge: Belknap, 2004.

———. *The War to End All Wars: The American Military Experience in World War I.* Madison: University of Wisconsin Press, 1986.

Coletta, Paolo E. *American Secretaries of the Navy, 1775–1972.* 2 vols. Annapolis MD: Naval Institute Press, 1980.

Collin, Richard H. *Theodore Roosevelt, Culture, Diplomacy, and Expansion.* Baton Rouge: Louisiana State University Press, 1985.

———. *Theodore Roosevelt's Caribbean: The Panama Canal, the Monroe Doctrine, and the Latin American Context.* Baton Rouge: Louisiana State University Press, 1990.

Cooper, John Milton, Jr. *Pivotal Decades: The United States, 1900–1920.* New York: Norton, 1990.

———. *The Warrior and the Priest: Woodrow Wilson and Theodore Roosevelt.* Cambridge MA: Belknap, 1983.

Corwin, Edward S. *The President: Office and Powers, 1787–1948.* 3rd ed. New York: New York University Press, 1948.

Cosmas, Graham A. *An Army for Empire: The United States Army in the Spanish-American War.* Columbia: University of Missouri Press, 1971.

———. "Military Reform after the Spanish-American War: The Army Reorganization Fight of 1898–1899." *Military Affairs* 35 (1971): 12–18.

Costello, Daniel J. "Planning for War: A History of the General Board of the Navy, 1900–1914." PhD diss., Fletcher School of Law and Diplomacy, 1968.

Crunden, Robert. *Ministers of Reform: The Progressives' Achievement in American Civilization, 1889–1920.* New York: Basic Books, 1982.

Cutright, Paul R. *Theodore Roosevelt: The Making of a Conservationist.* Urbana: University of Illinois Press, 1985.

Dalton, Kathleen. *Theodore Roosevelt: A Strenuous Life.* New York: Knopf, 2002.

Danbom, David B. *"The World of Hope": Progressives and the Struggle for an Ethical Public Life.* Philadelphia: Temple University Press, 1987.

Deere, Carmen D. "Here Come the Yankees! The Rise and Decline of United States Colonies in Cuba, 1898–1930." *Hispanic American Historical Review* 78, no. 4 (1998): 729–65.

Dennett, Tyler. *Roosevelt and the Russo-Japanese War.* New York: Doubleday, Page, 1925.

Department of War, Office of the Judge Advocate General. *The Military Laws of the United States.* 1901. 4th ed. Washington DC: Government Printing Office, 1911.

Donald, Aida D. *Lion in the White House: A Life of Theodore Roosevelt.* New York: Basic Books, 2007.

Doubler, Michael D. *Civilian in Peace, Soldier in War: The Army National Guard, 1636–2000.* Lawrence: University Press of Kansas, 2003.

Dunne, Peter Finley. *Mr. Dooley on Ivrything and Ivrybody.* New York: Dover, 1963.

Dyer, Thomas G. *Theodore Roosevelt and the Idea of Race.* Baton Rouge: Louisiana State University Press, 1980.

"Evils of Our Naval Bureaucracy." *Literary Digest* 37 (1908): 875–76.

Foraker, Joseph B. *Notes of a Busy Life.* Vol. 2. Cincinnati: Stewart and Kidd, 1916.

Funston, Frederick. *Memories of Two Wars: Cuban and Philippine Experiences.* London: Constable, 1911.

Gardner, Joseph L. *Departing Glory: Theodore Roosevelt as Ex-President.* New York: Scribner's Sons, 1973.

Gates, John M. *Schoolbooks and Krags: The United States Army in the Philippines, 1898–1902.* Westport CT: Greenwood, 1973.

Gatewood, Willard. *Theodore Roosevelt and the Art of Controversy: Episodes of the White House Years.* Baton Rouge: Louisiana State University Press, 1970.

Gould, Lewis. *The Presidency of Theodore Roosevelt.* Lawrence: University Press of Kansas, 1991.

———. *The Presidency of William McKinley.* Lawrence: Regents Press of Kansas, 1980.

Greene, Fred. "The Military View of American National Policy, 1904–1940." *American Historical Review* 66 (1960): 354–77.

Gross, Charles J. "George Owen Squier and the Origins of American Military Aviation." *Journal of Military History* 54 (July 1990): 281–305.

Habakkuk, H. J. *American and British Technology in the Nineteenth Century: The Search for Labour-Saving Inventions.* Cambridge: Cambridge University Press, 1962.

Hagan, Kenneth J., ed. *In Peace and War: Interpretations of American Naval History, 1775–1984.* 2nd ed. Westport CT: Greenwood, 1984.

———. *The People's Navy: The Making of American Sea Power.* New York: Free Press, 1991.

Hagan, Kenneth J., and William R. Roberts, eds. *Against All Enemies, Interpretations of American Military History from Colonial Times to the Present.* Westport CT: Greenwood, 1986.

Hagedorn, Hermann, ed. *The Works of Theodore Roosevelt, National Edition.* 20 vols. New York: Scribner's Sons, 1926.

Harbaugh, William H. *The Life and Times of Theodore Roosevelt.* Rev. ed. New York: Oxford University Press, 1975.

Harrod, Frederick S. *Manning the New Navy: The Development of a Modern Naval Enlisted Force, 1899–1940.* Westport CT: Greenwood, 1978.

Hatch, Carl E. *The Big Stick and the Congressional Gavel: A Study of Theodore Roosevelt's Relations with His Last Congress, 1907–1909.* New York: Pageant, 1967.

Heffron, Paul T. "Secretary Moody and Naval Administrative Reform: 1902–1904." *American Neptune* 29 (January 1969): 30–48.

Heitman, Francis B. *Historical Register and Dictionary of the U.S. Army, 1789–1903*. 1903. Reprint, Washington DC: Government Printing Office, 1965.

Hendrix, Henry J. *Theodore Roosevelt's Naval Diplomacy: The U.S. Navy and the Birth of the American Century*. Annapolis MD: Naval Institute Press, 2009.

Herwig, Holger. *Politics of Frustration: The United States in German Naval Planning, 1889–1941*. Boston: Little, Brown, 1976.

Hewes, James. *From Root to McNamara: Army Organization and Administration, 1900–1963*. Washington DC: Center of Military History, 1975.

———. "The United States Army General Staff, 1900–1917." *Military Affairs* 38 (1974): 67–72.

Hofstadter, Richard. *Social Darwinism in American Thought*. Rev. ed. Boston: Beacon, 1955.

Hoganson, Kristin L. *Fighting for American Manhood: How Gender Politics Provoked the Spanish-American and Philippine-American Wars*. New Haven CT: Yale University Press, 1998.

Hooper, Edwin B. *The Navy Department: Evolution and Fragmentation*. Washington DC: Naval Historical Foundation, 1978.

Israel, Jerry, ed. *Building the Organizational Society*. New York: Free Press, 1972.

Jones, Gregg. *Honor in the Dust: Theodore Roosevelt, War in the Philippines, and the Rise and Fall of America's Imperial Dream*. New York: Penguin, 2012.

Karnow, Stanley. *In Our Image: America's Empire in the Philippines*. New York: Random House, 1989.

Karsten, Peter. *The Naval Aristocracy: The Golden Age of Annapolis and the Emergence of Modern American Navalism*. New York: Free Press, 1972.

Kimmel, Michael S. "'Born to Run': Nineteenth-Century Fantasies of Masculine Retreat and Recreation (or the Historical Rust on Iron John)." In *The Politics of Manhood: Profeminist Men Respond to the Mythopoetic Men's Movement (and the Mythopoetic Leaders Answer)*, edited by Michael S. Kimmel, 115–50. Philadelphia: Temple University Press, 1995.

Kington, Donald M. *Forgotten Summers: The Story of the Citizens' Military Training Camps, 1921–1940*. San Francisco: Two Decades, 1995.

Koenig, Louis. *The Chief Executive*. 4th ed. New York: Harcourt, Brace, Jovanich, 1981.

Koistinen, Paul A. C. *Mobilizing for Modern War: The Political Economy of American Warfare: 1865–1919*. Lawrence: University Press of Kansas, 1997.

Lacey, Jim. *Pershing: Lessons in Leadership*. New York: Palgrave MacMillan, 2008.

Lane, Ann J. *The Brownsville Affair: National Crisis and Black Reaction*. Port Washington NY: Kennikat, 1971.

Lane, Jack C. *Armed Progressive: General Leonard Wood*. San Rafael CA: Presidio, 1978.

Larrabee, Eric. *Commander in Chief: Franklin Delano Roosevelt, His Lieutenants, and Their War*. New York: Simon and Schuster, 1987.

Lasch, Christopher. "The Anti-Imperialists, the Philippines, and the Inequality of Man." *Journal of Southern History* 24, no. 3 (1958): 319–31.

Laski, Harold J. *The American Presidency: An Interpretation.* 2nd ed. New Brunswick NJ: Transaction Books, 1980.

Leddy, Edward F. *Magnum Force Lobby: The National Rifle Association Fights Gun Control.* Lanham MD: University Press of America, 1987.

Lembeck, Harry. *Taking on Theodore Roosevelt: How One Senator Defied the President on Brownsville and Shook American Politics.* Amherst NY: Prometheus Books, 2015.

Leopold, Richard W. *Elihu Root and the Conservative Tradition.* Boston: Little, Brown, 1954.

Leuchtenburg, William. "Progressivism and Imperialism: The Progressive Movement and American Foreign Policy, 1898–1916." *Mississippi Valley Historical Review* 39, no. 3 (1952): 483–504.

Linn, Brian M. *Guardians of Empire: The U.S. Army and the Pacific, 1902–1940.* Chapel Hill: University of North Carolina Press, 1997.

———. *The Philippine War, 1899–1902.* Lawrence: University Press of Kansas, 2000.

———. *The U.S. Army and Counterinsurgency in the Philippine War, 1899–1902.* Chapel Hill: University of North Carolina Press, 1989.

Livermore, Seward. "The American Navy as a Factor in World Politics, 1903–1913." *American Historical Review* 63 (1958): 863–79.

———. "Theodore Roosevelt, the American Navy, and the Venezuelan Crisis of 1902–1903." *American Historical Review* 41 (April 1946): 452–71.

Mackersey, Ian. *The Wright Brothers: The Remarkable Story of the Aviation Pioneers Who Changed the World.* London: Time Warner Paperbacks, 2003.

MacMillan, Margaret. *The War That Ended Peace: The Road to 1914.* New York: Random House, 2013.

Mahan, Alfred T. "Reflections, Historic and Other, Suggested by the Battle of the Sea of Japan." *United States Naval Institute Proceedings* 32 (June 1906): 447–71.

Mahon, John K. *History of the Militia and the National Guard.* New York: Macmillan, 1983.

Malone, Dumas, and Allen Johnson, eds. *Dictionary of American Biography.* 20 vols. New York: Scribner's Sons, 1937.

Marcus, Alan I., and Howard P. Segal. *Technology in America: A Brief History.* New York: Harcourt Brace Jovanovich, 1989.

Massie, Robert K. *Castles of Steel: Britain, Germany, and the Winning of the Great War at Sea.* New York: Random House, 2003.

———. *Dreadnought: Britain, Germany, and the Coming of the Great War.* New York: Ballantine Books, 1991.

McBride, William M. *Technological Change and the United States Navy, 1865–1945.* Baltimore: Johns Hopkins University Press, 2000.

McCallum, Jack. *Leonard Wood: Rough Rider, Surgeon, Architect of American Imperialism.* New York: New York University Press, 2006.

McCoy, Drew R. *The Elusive Republic: Political Economy in Jeffersonian America.* Williamsburg VA: Institute of Early American History and Culture, 1980.

McCullough, David. *Mornings on Horseback.* New York: Touchstone, 1981.

McDonough, Judith R. "William Henry Moody." PhD diss., Auburn University, 1983.

Meixsel, Richard. "United States Army Policy in the Philippine Islands, 1902–1922." Master's thesis, University of Georgia, 1988.

Miles, Nelson. *Serving the Republic: Memoirs of the Civil and Military Life of Nelson A. Miles.* New York: Harper and Brothers, 1911.

Millard, Candice. *The River of Doubt: Theodore Roosevelt's Darkest Journey.* New York: Random House, 2006.

Miller, Edward S. *War Plan Orange: The U.S. Strategy to Defeat Japan, 1987–1945.* Annapolis MD: Naval Institute Press, 1991.

Miller, Stuart C. *"Benevolent Assimilation": The American Conquest of the Philippines, 1899–1903.* New Haven CT: Yale University Press, 1982.

Millett, Allan R. "The General Staff and the Cuban Intervention of 1906." *Military Affairs* 32 (Fall 1967): 113–19.

———. "Military Professionalism and Officership in America." A Mershon Center Briefing Paper. Columbus: Mershon Center, 1977.

———. *The Politics of Intervention: The Military Occupation of Cuba, 1906–1909.* Columbus: Ohio State University Press, 1968.

———. *Semper Fidelis: The History of the United States Marine Corps.* New York: Macmillan, 1980.

———. "Theodore Roosevelt and His Generals, the Politics of Promotion to Brigadier General in the United States Army, 1901–1909." Inaugural lecture notes, Ohio State University, Columbus, April 1974.

Millett, Allan R., and Peter Maslowski, *For the Common Defense: A Military History of the United States of America.* 2nd ed. New York: Free Press, 1994.

Morison, Elting. *Admiral Sims and the Modern American Navy.* 1942. Reprint, New York: Russell and Russell, 1968.

———, ed. *The Letters of Theodore Roosevelt.* 8 vols. Cambridge MA: Harvard University Press, 1951–52.

Morris, Edmund. *Colonel Roosevelt.* New York: Random House, 2010.

———. "'A Matter of Extreme Urgency,' Theodore Roosevelt, Wilhelm II, and the Venezuela Crisis of 1902: United States–Germany Conflict over Alleged German Expansionistic Efforts in Latin America." *Naval War College Review* 55 (Spring 2002): 73–85.

———. *The Rise of Theodore Roosevelt.* New York: Coward, McCann, and Geoghegan, 1979.

———. *Theodore Rex.* New York: Random House, 2001.

Morris, Richard Knowles. *John P. Holland, 1841–1914: Inventor of the Modern Submarine.* Annapolis MD: Naval Institute Press, 1966.

Morris, Sylvia Jukes. *Edith Kermit Roosevelt.* New York: Vintage Books, 1980.

Moten, Matthew. "The Delafield Commission and the American Military Profession." PhD diss., Rice University, 1996.

Mowry, George E. *The Era of Theodore Roosevelt and the Birth of Modern America, 1900–1912*. New York: Harper and Row, 1958.

"The Navy and Its Critics." *Literary Digest* 36, no. 1 (1908): 1–3.

Neu, Charles E. *An Uncertain Friendship: Theodore Roosevelt and Japan, 1906–1909*. Cambridge MA: Harvard University Press, 1967.

Nicolosi, Anthony S. "The Navy, Newport and Stephen B. Luce." *Naval War College Review* 37 (September–October 1984): 121.

O'Connell, Robert L. *Sacred Vessels: The Cult of the Battleship and the Rise of the U.S. Navy*. New York: Oxford University Press, 1991.

O'Gara, Gordon C. *Theodore Roosevelt and the Rise of the Modern Navy*. Princeton: Princeton University Press, 1943.

O'Neill, William L. *The Progressive Years: America Comes of Age*. New York: Dodd, Mead, 1975.

O'Toole, Patricia. *When Trumpets Call: Theodore Roosevelt after the White House*. New York: Simon and Shuster, 2005.

Oyos, Matthew M. "Theodore Roosevelt and the Implements of War." *Journal of Military History* 60, no. 4 (1996): 631–55.

Palmer, Frederick. *Bliss, Peacemaker: The Life and Letters of General Tasker Howard Bliss*. New York: Dodd, Mead, 1934.

Parker, James. *History of the Gatling Gun Detachment Fifth Corps, at Santiago, with a Few Unvarnished Truths concerning That Expedition*. Kansas City MO: Hudson-Kimberly, 1898.

———. *The Old Army: Memories, 1872–1918*. Philadelphia: Dorrance, 1929.

Paullin, Charles Oscar. *Paullin's History of Naval Administration, 1775–1911*. Annapolis MD: Naval Institute Press, 1968.

Ponder, Stephen. "'Publicity in the Interest of the People': Theodore Roosevelt's Conservation Crusade." *Presidential Studies Quarterly* 20 (Summer 1990): 547–55.

Pringle, Henry F. *Theodore Roosevelt: A Biography*. New York: Harcourt, Brace, 1931.

Publications of Peace Societies. Columbus: Ohio State University Library, n.d.

Pursell, Carroll, Jr. *Technology in America: A History of Individuals and Ideas*. 2nd ed. Cambridge: MIT Press, 1990.

Raines, Edgar F., Jr. "Major General J. Franklin Bell and Military Reform: The Chief of Staff Years, 1906–10." PhD diss., University of Wisconsin, 1976.

Ranson, Edward. "Nelson A. Miles as Commanding General, 1895–1903." *Military Affairs* 29 (Winter 1965–66): 194–200.

Rappaport, Armin. *The Navy League of the United States*. Detroit: Wayne State University Press, 1962.

Ray, Thomas. "The Bureaus Go on Forever." *United States Naval Institute Proceedings* 94 (January 1968): 50–63.

Reckner, James R. *Teddy Roosevelt's Great White Fleet*. Annapolis MD: Naval Institute Press, 1988.

Renehan, Edward J. *The Lion's Pride: Theodore Roosevelt and His Family in Peace and War.* New York: Oxford University Press, 1998.

Report of the Bureau of Construction and Repair to the Secretary of the Navy, 1908. Washington DC: Government Printing Office, 1908.

Report of the Personnel Board, Appointed by the Secretary of the Navy, August 16, 1906. Washington DC: Government Printing Office, 1906.

Robinson, Corinne Roosevelt. *My Brother Theodore Roosevelt.* New York: Scribner's Sons, 1921.

Roosevelt, Theodore. *American Ideals.* In Hagedorn, *Works,* vol. 13.

———. *American Problems.* In Hagedorn, *Works,* vol. 16.

———. *An Autobiography.* 1913. Reprint, New York: Da Capo, 1985.

———. *Literary Essays.* In Hagedorn, *Works,* vol. 12.

———. "The Naval Policy of America as Outlined in Messages of the Presidents of the United States, from the Beginning to the Present Day." *United States Naval Institute Proceedings* 23 (1897): 509–21.

———. *Naval War of 1812.* In Hagedorn, *Works,* vol. 6.

———. *Pocket Diary, 1898: Theodore Roosevelt's Private Account of the War with Spain,* edited by Wallace Finley Dailey. Cambridge MA: Harvard University, 1998.

———. *The Rough Riders.* New York: Scribner, 1902. Reprint, New York: Da Capo, 1990.

———. *State Papers as Governor and President, 1899–1909.* In Hagedorn, *Works,* vol. 15.

———. *The Strenuous Life.* In Hagedorn, *Works,* vol. 13.

———. *The Winning of the West.* In Hagedorn, *Works,* vols. 8, 9.

Roosevelt, Theodore, and Henry Cabot Lodge. *Hero Tales from American History.* In Hagedorn, *Works,* vol. 10.

———. *Men of Action.* In Hagedorn, *Works,* vol. 11.

Rumble, Walker. "Rectitude and Reform: Charles J. Bonaparte and the Politics of Gentility 1851–1921." PhD diss., University of Maryland, 1971.

Runcie, James E. "American Misgovernment of Cuba." *North American Review* 170 (February 1900): 284–94.

Sanger, William C. *Report on the Reserve and Auxiliary Forces of England and the Militia of Switzerland: Prepared for President McKinley and Secretary of War Root.* Washington DC: Government Printing Office, 1903.

Seager, Robert, Jr., and Doris D. Maguire, eds. *Letters and Papers of Alfred Thayer Mahan.* 3 vols. Annapolis MD: Naval Institute Press, 1975.

Sheridan, Philip H. *Personal Memoirs of P. H. Sheridan.* Vol. 2. New York: Webster, 1888.

Sims, William S. "The Inherent Tactical Qualities of All-Big-Gun, One-Caliber Battleships of High Speed, Large Displacement and Gun Power." *United States Naval Institute Proceedings* 32 (1906): 1337–66.

Skowronek, Stephen. *Building a New American State: The Expansion of National Administrative Capabilities, 1877–1920.* Cambridge: Cambridge University Press, 1982.

Smith, Duane A. *Henry M. Teller: Colorado's Grand Old Man.* Boulder: University Press of Colorado, 2002.

Smythe, Donald. *Guerrilla Warrior: The Early Life of John J. Pershing.* New York: Scribner's Sons, 1973.

Spector, Ronald. *Professors of War, the Naval War College and the Development of the Naval Profession.* Newport RI: Naval War College Press, 1977.

Sprout, Harold, and Margaret Sprout. *The Rise of American Naval Power, 1776–1918.* 2nd ed. Princeton: Princeton University Press, 1967.

Stillson, Albert C. "The Development and Maintenance of the American Naval Establishment, 1901–1909." PhD diss., Columbia University, 1959.

———. "Military Policy without Political Guidance: Theodore Roosevelt's Navy." *Military Affairs* 25 (1961): 18–31.

Taylor, Henry C. "Memorandum on General Staff for the U.S. Navy." *United States Naval Institute Proceedings* 26 (1900): 441–48.

Trask, David F. *The War with Spain in 1898.* New York: Macmillan, 1981.

Turk, Richard W. *The Ambiguous Relationship: Theodore Roosevelt and Alfred T. Mahan.* Westport CT: Greenwood, 1987.

Upton, Emory. *The Military Policy of the United States from 1775.* Washington DC: Government Printing Office, 1904.

U.S. Congress. *Congressional Record.* 57th Cong., 1st sess.; 57th Cong., 2nd sess.; 60th Cong., 1st sess.; 60th Cong., 2nd sess. Washington DC: Government Printing Office, 1902, 1903, 1908, 1909.

———. *Report of the Commission Appointed by the President to Investigate the Conduct of the War Department in the War with Spain.* 8 vols. 56th Cong., 1st sess., S. Doc. No. 221. Washington DC: Government Printing Office, 1900.

U.S. Congress, Committee on Foreign Relations. *Investigation of Mexican Affairs, Preliminary Report and Hearings.* 66th Cong., 2nd sess., S. Doc. No. 285. Washington DC: Government Printing Office, 1920.

U.S. Congress, Committee on Military Affairs. *Efficiency of the Army.* Hearings. 57th Cong., 1st sess., S. Doc. No. 3917. Washington DC: Government Printing Office, 1902.

———. *Establishment of a General Staff Corps in the Army.* 57th Cong., 2nd sess., S. Doc. No. 6332. Washington DC: Government Printing Office, 1902.

———. *Hearings on the Nomination of Leonard Wood to Be Major General.* 58th Cong., 2nd sess., Exec. Doc. C. Washington DC: Government Printing Office, 1904.

U.S. Congress, Committee on Naval Affairs. *Certain Needs of the Navy.* 60th Cong., 2nd sess., S. Doc. No. 740. Washington DC: Government Printing Office, 1909.

———. *Final Report of the Commission on Naval Reorganization.* 60th Cong., 2nd sess., S. Doc. No. 743. Washington DC: Government Printing Office, 1909.

———. *Hearings on H.R. 15403, for a General Board.* 58th Cong., 2nd sess., H.R. Rep. No. 164. Washington DC: Government Printing Office, 1904.

———. *Hearings on the Bill (S. 3335) to Increase the Efficiency of the Personnel of the Navy and Marine Corps of the United States.* 60th Cong., 1st sess., No. 1. Washington DC: Government Printing Office, 1908.

———. *Hearings on the Proposed Reorganization of the Navy Department.* 61st Cong, 2nd sess. Vol. 48 (Senate Library). Washington DC: Government Printing Office, 1910.

———. *Members of Chi Alpha Ministerial Society of the City of New York Protesting against the Further Multiplication of Battle Ships in the United States Navy.* 60th Cong., 1st sess., S. Doc. No. 210. Washington DC: Government Printing Office, 1908.

———. *Memorial of Sundry Citizens of New York City Remonstrating against Authorizing Construction of Four New Battle Ships.* 60th Cong., 1st sess., S. Doc. No. 378. Washington DC: Government Printing Office, 1908.

———. *Methods of Conducting Business and Departmental Changes in the Navy Department.* 60th Cong., 2nd sess., S. Doc. No. 693. Washington DC: Government Printing Office, 1909.

———. *Naval Appropriation Bill H.R. 20471.* 60th Cong., 1st sess., H.R. Rep. No. 1398. Washington DC: Government Printing Office, 1908.

———. *Personnel of the Navy.* 59th Cong., 2nd sess., H.R. hearings embodied in S. Doc. No. 142. Washington DC: Government Printing Office, 1906.

———. *Reorganization of the Navy Department, February 4, 1909.* Vol. 47. No. 60. (Senate Library). Washington DC: Government Printing Office, 1909.

———. *Report concerning Alleged Defects of Naval Vessels.* 60th Cong., 1st sess., S. Doc. No. 297. Washington DC: Government Printing Office, 1908.

———. *Statement in Refutation of Alleged Defects of Naval Vessels.* 60th Cong., 1st sess., S. Doc. No. 298. Washington DC: Government Printing Office, 1908.

U.S. Congress, Committee on Naval Affairs, House Subcommittee on Naval Academy and Marine Corps. *Status of the U.S. Marine Corps.* 60th Cong., 2nd sess. Washington DC: Government Printing Office, 1909.

Vandiver, Frank E. *Black Jack: The Life and Times of John J. Pershing.* 2 vols. College Station: Texas A&M University Press, 1977.

Watson, James E. *As I Knew Them: Memoirs of James E. Watson.* New York: Bobbs-Merrill, 1936.

Watts, Sarah. *Rough Rider in the White House: Theodore Roosevelt and the Politics of Desire.* Chicago: University of Chicago Press, 2003.

Weaver, John D. *The Brownsville Raid.* New York: Norton, 1970.

Webster's American Military Biographies. Springfield MA: Merriam, 1978.

Weigley, Russell. *History of the United States Army.* 2nd ed. Bloomington: Indiana University Press, 1984.

————. *Towards an American Army: Military Thought from Washington to Marshall.* New York: Columbia University Press, 1962.

Wiebe, Robert. *The Search for Order, 1877–1920.* New York: Hill and Wang, 1967.

Williams, T. Harry. *Lincoln and His Generals.* 1952. Reprint, New York: Vintage Books, 2011.

Winton, Harold R. "Scorecards on Military Effectiveness." *Journal of Military History* 58 (October 1994): 719–34.

Wooster, Robert. *Nelson A. Miles and the Twilight of the Frontier Army.* Lincoln: University of Nebraska Press, 1993.

Young, Kenneth Ray. *The General's General: The Life and Times of Arthur MacArthur.* Boulder CO: Westview, 1994.

INDEX

Page locators with F indicate photographs.

Adams, Brooks, 40–41, 71
Addams, Jane, 111
Aero Club of America, 244
Aguinaldo, Emilio, 154
Ainsworth, Frederick, 215–16
the *Alabama* (commerce raider), 18
Aldrich, Nelson, 195
Aleshire, James B., 308–10
Alger, Russell, 74, 78–79, 87–88, 90–
   91, 168
all-big-gun battleships, 251–57, 279,
   287, 369
the Amazon, T.R.'s adventure in, 330–31
American Expeditionary Forces (AEF),
   309, 354–55
Ananias Club, 103–4
Andrews, Avery, 31, 37–38, 95, 306
anthracite coal strike of 1902, 128, 172,
   176, 232, 303
arbitration, 40, 68, 111
Army, U.S.: general staff of, 143, 158,
   162–63, 174, 184–85, 189–96, 196–216,
   309–10, 321, 367; gunnery skills of,
   143–44; infantry, 159, 185, 237–38, 297–
   98, 333; large-scale training maneuvers of, 178–87; and physical fitness
   of officers, 311–14; redesigning spurs,
   117, 236; redesigning uniforms, 116–18,
   236. *See also* cavalry
Army Aeronautical Board, 246
Army Appropriations Act of 1904, 171–72
Army Reorganization Act of 1901, 152

Army War College, 199, 210, 212, 214,
   308–10, 351
Asiatic Squadron, 54–55, 71–72, 124, 129
Austin, Elmore F., 92
Autobiography (T.R.), 15, 18, 90, 120
aviation, F8, 5, 64–65, 233–34, 243–47,
   303, 331–34, 369–70

Bacon, Alexander, 93–94
Bacon, Reginald, 257
Baker, Newton D., 177, 333–34, 347–53
Barry, Thomas, 160, 181, 214, 309
Bates, Arthur, 324
Bates, John C., 200–201
battle fleet, F11, F12; consolidation of,
   123–27; expansion and modernization of, 119–22, 247–60, 303, 367; world
   cruise of, 108, 277–82, 290, 292, 303,
   324–30, 370. *See also* battleships
Battle of San Juan Heights, F3, 1–4, 83–
   94, 159, 168, 237, 357
battleships, F9; all-big-gun, 251–57,
   279, 287, 369; design flaws in, 281–91;
   dreadnought-style, 252, 258, 279, 286–
   92, 300, 367; mixed-caliber, 252–56, 258,
   287; and Spanish-American War, 69. *See
   also* battle fleet; *names of specific battleships*
bayonets, 185, 205–8, 216, 236
Bell, James Franklin, 152–54, 181, 201–3,
   211–12, 214–16, 306
bicycles, 65, 314
Bishop, Joseph Bucklin, 263
black powder, 78, 90–91, 183
Blaine, James G., 29

Bliss, Tasker, 158–59, 309–10
Bonaparte, Charles, 118, 228, 241, 249–51, 296
Brands, H. W., 6, 329, 358
brass bearings, 250
Brodie, Alex, 28–29
Brooks, Sydney, 326
Brownson, Willard, 48, 282–83
Brownsville affair, 266–76, 300, 368
Bryan, William Jennings, 21, 105, 192, 336
Bryce, James, 358
Buencamino, Filipe, 114
Bugbee, Fred, 86
Bulloch, Annie, 19
Bulloch, Irvine, 18–19
Bulloch, James, 18–19
bully pulpit, 101–5, 181, 194. *See also* public relations
Bureau of Navigation, U.S. Navy, 34, 47, 124, 134, 138, 218–20, 255, 282, 325
Burton, David, 8
Burton, Theodore, 275, 319
Butler, Matthew C., 307
Butt, Archibald (Archie), 145–46, 294, 297, 314

Calhoun, John C., 195
Cannon, Joseph, 223–24, 259, 272
Capps, Washington, 285, 291–92
Carnegie, Andrew, 111
Carnegie Endowment for International Peace, 111
Carranza, Venustiano, 334
Carter, Jimmy, 144
Carter, William Harding, 158–59, 191, 309
Castro, Cipriano, 211
cavalry: in Cuba campaign of 1898, 72, 74, 78–79, 83, 90; and Cuban revolt of 1906, 212; and horsemanship training, 216, 312–13; and Mexican revolution, 332–33; and physical fitness test for officers, 313; redesigning spurs, 117, 236; and small-scale tactical exercises, 185; T.R.'s favoritism of, 162, 205, 332–33; weapons and equipment of, 205, 236–39. *See also* Rough Riders

Centennial Exhibition of 1876 (Philadelphia), 64
Chaffee, Adna R., 181, 184–85, 200, 204, 207–8, 237
Chandler, William, 54–55
Children's Aid Society, 17
Chilean Crisis of 1891–92, 54
Church, William Conant, 92
Churchill, Winston, 229
Citizens' Military Training Camps, 345
civic virtue, 7, 10, 42, 341
Civil Service Commission, 30, 37
Civil War: influence on T.R., 12, 17–19; sea warfare in, 22, 52, 69; and Theodore Roosevelt, Sr., 3, 17–18, 24; T.R.'s romantic notions of, 329; veterans of, 52, 85, 106, 151–53, 156–59, 163, 171–72, 186, 234, 310; volunteer formations of, 348
Clemenceau, Georges, 356
Cleveland, Grover, 29–30
coal miners' strike of 1902, 128, 172, 176, 232, 303
Cockrell, Francis, 167
Coffman, Edward M., 310
coinage design, 235
Colby, Bainbridge, 360
Committee on Department Methods (Keep Commission), 197
Connecticut (battleship), F12, 121, 328
Connolly, James Brendan, 109
conscription, 345–46, 349–51
Converse, George A., 285
Corbin, Henry C., 159, 191, 200–202
Council of National Defense, 309–10
Cowles, Anna Roosevelt, 35, 38, 43, 66, 101
Cowles, William Sheffield, 35–36, 48, 69, 134, 141–42
Craig, William, 98
Crawford, (Francis) Marion, 43
Croton Aqueduct workers' strike, 94–95
Crowninshield, Arent, 47, 128
Crozier, William, 150–51, 154–55, 158, 181, 309–10
Cuba campaign of 1898: action and field conditions of, 81–87; arming and pro-

visioning of troops, 78–79; cavalry in, 72, 74, 78–79, 83, 90; deployment of forces to, 76–81; and Guantánamo Bay, 295; hospital service during, 81; and Kettle Hill assault, 84; officer corps' incompetence during, 82–84; preparations for, 65–72; T.R.'s justification for, 71; T.R.'s maneuvering for command, 72–76; T.R.'s praise of McKinley's policy toward, 68; and T.R.'s romantic notion of war, 13, 84, 117; and USS *Maine*, 2, 68–69, 71, 123; weapons technology in, 84, 236–37; withdrawal of forces from, 87–88; and yellow fever, 87. *See also* Battle of San Juan Heights
Cuba expedition of 1906, 188–89, 211–16, 384n54
Czolgosz, Leon, 4

Dakota Territory, 27–29
Dalton, Kathleen, 6, 172
Dana, Paul, 62
Daniels, Josephus, 293, 336
Darling, Charles, 139, 226–27
Darwin, Charles, 9, 39
Davis, Cleland, 242
Davis, Richard Harding, 86
Davis torpedo, 242
Delafield Commission, 181
the *Delaware* (battleship), 255
Derby, Ethel Roosevelt, 217, 261, 358–60, 372
Derby, Richard, 355
Dewey, George, 54–55, 58, 70–71, 107, 110–11, 129, 219, 226, 319–20, 322
Díaz, Porfirio, 332
Dick, Charles, 174–76
Dick Act of 1903, 175
Diederichs, Otto von, 129
Dodge, Grenville, 193
Dodge Commission, 193
Dominican Republic. *See* Santo Domingo
draft, military, 345–46, 349–51
the *Dreadnought* (battleship), 251–52, 257–60, 279

dreadnought-style battleships, 252, 258, 279, 286–92, 300, 367
Dunne, Finley Peter, 85, 109, 153

Eisenhower, Dwight, 144
election of 1888, 29–30
election of 1896, 105
election of 1900, 153
election of 1904, 105, 170, 222, 231
election of 1908, 238, 246, 262, 274
election of 1912, 330
election of 1916, 335
election of 1918, 361–62
Eliot, Charles, 40
entrenching tools, 234, 236–37, 260, 369. *See also* trench warfare
Erben, Henry C., 35
European Squadron, 55, 127–28
Evans, Robley, 79
extraordinary promotions, 158–72, 202, 304–11

Farragut, David, 50, 54–55
favoritism in promotions, 154, 157, 162, 164–72, 306–8
First U.S. Volunteer Cavalry Regiment. *See* Rough Riders
Flint, Charles, 247
the *Florida* (battleship), 290
Flying Circus, 357
Folger, William, 48
Foraker, Joseph, 261–62, 270–76
Foss, George, 259, 299
Fourteen Points, 360
Frankfurter, Felix, 360
Fullam, William F., 295
Funston, Frederick, 152–54, 212

Garrison, Lindley, 342
Gatling guns, 237
General Board of the U.S. Navy, 49, 127, 190, 208, 219, 228, 254, 279, 317
General Staff, 188–230; of army, 143, 158, 162–63, 174, 184–85, 189–96, 196–216, 309–10, 321, 367; creation of, 190–96, 369; and Cuba expedition of 1906, 211–16; early staffing of, 196–205; of navy,

General Staff (*continued*)
138, 190, 216–30, 285–86, 293, 321, 395n66, 396n69; organization of, 198; as political clearing house, 206; and political patronage, 191–92, 223–25, 229, 275; poor initial management of, 204; and study of weapons, 205–7
General Staff Act, 198, 201
German High Seas Fleet, 124
Gladden, Washington, 111
Goodrich, Casper, 58–59
Grand Army of the Republic, 152
Grant, Frederick Dent, 152–53, 203
Grant, Ulysses S., 25
Grayson, Cary T., 314
Great War. *See* World War I
Great White Fleet, 108. *See also* battle fleet; battleships
Greene, Francis Vinton, 31–32
Gridiron Club, 272–73
Guantánamo Bay, 295, 318, 370
Guild, Curtis, Jr., 269
gunnery skills: of army, 143–44; of navy, 130–43, 326–27; reform of, 90–91, 130–44; in Spanish-American War, 131–32; T.R.'s interest in, 378n62

Hague International Peace Conference, 150
Hale, Eugene, 222–26, 279–80, 284–85, 292, 298
Hamilton, Alexander, 10, 23, 149, 173
Hanna, Marcus, 165–68
Haskell, Edwin, 103
Hawaii, 48–49, 57–58, 119, 309, 323–25, 370
Hay, John, 318
Herbert, Hilary, 34
Hoar, George Frisbie, 195
horsemanship, 216, 312–13
House Committee on Military Affairs, 194, 246
Howell, John Adams, 54–55, 377n35
Hoxsey, Archibald (Arch), 332
Huerta, Victoriano, 333
Hughes, Charles Evans, 365

Hull, John, 194
Humphrey, Charles F., 80, 308
Huntington, Robert W., 295

infantry, 159, 185, 237–38, 297–98, 333
The Influence of Sea Power upon History (Mahan), 23, 33
The Influence of Sea Power upon the French Revolution and Empire (Mahan), 34
international arbitration, 40, 68, 111
Isthmian Canal. *See* Panama Canal

Japan: and aircraft development, 331; battle fleet's visit to, 325–26; fear of war with, 57–58, 126, 133; and one-ship-per-year policy, 279; Pearl Harbor bombing by, 323–25; and segregation of Asian students in San Francsico, 125, 233, 277–78; and U.S. immigration policies, 210, 216. *See also* Russo-Japanese War
Jefferson, Thomas, 10, 23, 149, 173, 234, 335
jingoes and jingo doctrines, 2, 73, 278, 348
Joint Army-Navy Board, 319, 321
Joint Chiefs of Staff, 322
Jordan, David Starr, 111
Jusserand, Jean Jules, 347

Kearsarge (battleship), 18, 69
Keep, Charles, 197
Keep Commission (Committee on Department Methods), 197
Kentucky (battleship), 70
Kettle Hill, 84
Key, Albert L., 286–87, 291–92
Kipling, Rudyard, 365
Knickerbocker Club, 79
Knickerbocker Trust Company, 276
Koistinen, Paul, 310
Krag-Jørgensen rifle, 99

Lane, Ann, 275
Langley, Samuel, 64–65, 243–44
The Law of Civilization and Decay (Brooks), 40
League of Nations, 364–65
Lee, Arthur Hamilton, 326, 346
Lessons of the War With Spain (Mahan), 253
The Life of Nelson (Mahan), 34

Liliuokalani, Queen of Hawaii, 58

Lincoln, Abraham, 3, 19, 234, 304

Linn, Brian, 113

Lippmann, Walter, 360

Lodge, Henry Cabot: letters from T.R.,
3, 63, 79, 80–81, 84–85, 87, 91, 149–
50, 174, 278; and Philippine campaign
atrocities, 113–14; as sounding board
for T.R., 233; and Treaty of Versailles,
365; on T.R.'s appointment as assistant
secretary of navy, 43

Loeb, William, Jr., 103

Long, John D., 45, 69–70, 118, 218–20

Longworth, Alice Roosevelt, 102, 109,
240, 302, 372

the *Louisiana* (battleship), F9, 248–52

lubricating oils on naval vessels, 250

Luce, Stephen B., 33, 35, 124, 217

Ludlow, William, 152

the *Lusitania* (passenger liner), 341, 361

lynching, 267, 269

Lynn, I. H., 327

MacArthur, Arthur, 152, 202–3

machine guns, 237–39

Madero, Francisco, 333

Mahan, Alfred T., 23, 33–35, 48, 56–60,
110, 119, 123–27, 252–53, 256–57, 331

the *Maine* (battleship), 2, 57, 68–69, 71, 123

maneuvers, military, 178–87

Manila, 31, 54, 71, 319–20, 322; and war
plans, 57, 70–71

Manila Bay, 129, 131–32, 320

manliness, 3, 30, 41, 76–77, 100, 103, 355

manly virtue, 9–10, 26–27, 48, 54, 189,
311, 319

Marine Corps, U.S., 5–6, 46, 294–301, 368

Marshall, William L., 313

Maude, Frederick, 356

the *Mayflower* (presidential yacht), F12,
108–9, 140–41, 280, 289, 328

McCoy, Frank, 348

McKinley, William: appoints T.R. as assistant secretary of navy, 43, 45; assassination of, 4, 15, 98; and Dodge
Commission, 193; and election of

1896, 105; and election of 1900, 153;
and military reform, 151–54; and
National Guard of New York reform,
95–96; and Spanish-American War,
68–69, 71–72, 74, 83, 88

Medal of Honor, 86–88, 93, 153, 371

media relations. *See* public relations

merit-based promotions, 9, 50–55, 67,
150–57, 160–67, 170–71, 186, 201, 308

Merritt, Wesley, 179

Metcalf, Victor Howard, 118, 228, 245,
282, 284, 291, 321

Mexican border troubles (1880s), 28, 346

Mexican Revolution (1910s), 4, 177–78,
332–36, 346

Meyer, Adolph, 225

Meyer, George von Lengerke, 293

the *Michigan* (battleship), 258

Miles, Nelson, 153, 162–64, 169, 181,
194–96

military bases, overseas, 316–25

military promotions: extraordinary, 158–
72, 202, 304–11; merit-based, 9, 50–55,
67, 150–57, 160–67, 170–71, 186, 201,
304–11; and "Roosevelt hump", 310;
seniority-based, 51–53, 83, 151–57, 170–
71, 198–201, 307

military readiness, 55–64, 178–87, 338–
45, 407n4

military reform: redesigning uniforms,
116–18; of gunnery, 90–91, 130–44; and
merit-based promotions, 9, 50–55, 67,
150–57, 160–67, 170–71, 186, 201, 304–
11; of militia forces, 109–10, 172–78,
183; and mobilization of troops, 77–78;
of National Guard of New York, 95–
96; and overseas bases, 316–25; physical fitness of officers, 147–49, 311–16,
368–69; and readiness for war, 55–
64, 178–87, 303; redesigning spurs,
117; of retirement policy, 171–72; and
selection-out of officers, 52–53, 186;
and seniority-based promotions, 51–
53, 83, 151–57, 170–71, 198–201, 307; in
T.R.'s first term as president, 115–18.
See also general staff

military technology, 63–65, 233–39, 369, 378n62. *See also specific types of technology and weapons*

Militia Act of 1903, 175, 183

militia forces: in colonial America, 76; colorfulness of, 24–25; in other countries, 95; reform of, 109–10, 148, 172–78, 183. *See also* National Guard

Millett, Allan R., 210

Mills, Albert L., 85–86, 160, 168–71, 309–10

the *Missouri* (battleship), 141–42

mixed-caliber battleships, 252–56, 258, 287

Money, Hernando D., 101–2

Monroe Doctrine, 60, 121–22, 209–10, 263

Moody, William H., 110, 118, 124, 127, 140, 142, 220–21, 223–29, 293–94

Moody Commission, 293–94

Morgan, J. P., 172

Morison, Elting, 281, 287

Morris, Edmund, 3

Morton, Paul, 118, 228–29

muckraking, 282, 287, 289

National Defense Act of 1916, 216, 310, 343

National Guard: expansion of, 343; in Great War, 352; and Mexican revolution, 335; outdated weaponry of, 78; purpose of, 24; reform of, 13, 94–96, 110, 148–49, 172–78, 182–83, 343, 368; and selective service, 349; training maneuvers for, 183; T.R.'s contempt for, 6, 44, 89–96, 339, 352; T.R.'s service in, 23–26, 67–68, 174, 177. *See also* militia forces

National Guard Association, 177

National Guard of New York, 23–26, 67–68, 73–74, 89–96, 353

Naval War Board, 73, 193, 208

Naval War College, 33–35, 56, 58–59, 65, 138, 158, 208–9, 217–18, 254, 288

The Naval War of 1812 (T.R.), 21–23, 33, 119, 127

Navy, U.S.: Asiatic Squadron, 54–55, 71–72, 124, 129; consolidation of, 123–27; European Squadron, 55, 127–28; expansion and modernization of, 22,

115, 119–27; fleet exercises and maneuvers of, 127–29; gunnery skills of, 130–43, 326–27; North Atlantic Fleet, 124, 127; one-ship-per-year policy, 259, 279, 286; personnel reform of, 49–55; physical fitness of officers, 314–16; proposed general staff for, 138, 190, 216–30, 285–86, 293, 321, 395n66, 396n69; reform of, 217, 281–94, 303; South Atlantic Squadron, 127; two-ships-per year policy, 286; West Indies Squadron, 135. *See also* battle fleet; battleships; *The Naval War of 1812* (T.R.); *topics related to military*

Navy League, 110, 327

Newberry, Truman H., 118, 228, 293, 296, 327

Newberry Board (naval and Marine Corps personnel), 296

Newberry Plan (Navy Department reform), 293

the *New Hampshire* (battleship), 254–55

the *Newport* (gunboat), 47

Newport Conference, 288–91

Newsboys' Lodging House, 17

New York City Police Board, 30–31, 37–38, 50, 95, 102, 115, 203

New York state legislature, 24–25

Nobel Peace Prize, 264, 330

North Atlantic Fleet, 124, 127

the *North Dakota* (battleship), F10, 287, 290

Northern Securities Company, 172

Odell, Benjamin, 96

O'Donnell, W. J., 141

Office of Naval Intelligence, 56

O'Laughlin, John Callan, 345

O'Neil, Charles, 135, 137

Open Door Policy, 209

Oulahan, Richard, 62

overseas military bases, 316–25; Guantánamo Bay, 295, 318, 370; Pearl Harbor, 323–25, 370; Subic Bay, 221, 319–23, 370

Palma, Tomás Estrada, 188, 212

Panama Canal: and American foreign

policy, 300, 303; and battle fleet world cruise, 249, 278–79; and battleship fleet, division of, 125, 331; completion of, 323; funding for, 279; importance of, 327; and Panamanian revolutionaries, 165; planning of, 119, 121, 217; protection of, 317–18; T.R.'s pride in, 367

Panama Canal Treaty, 165–66, 172, 221

Panic of 1907, 276–77

Parker, Alton B., 231

Parker, Andrew, 38

Parker, James, 200

Parker, John Henry, 237–39

patronage, political, 30, 91, 128, 157, 159, 191–92, 223–25, 229, 275

peace movement, 111

Peace Society of New York City, 111

Pearl Harbor, 49, 323–24, 370

Penrose, Boies, 270

Perkins, George C., 233, 285

Pershing, Helen Frances (née Warren), 305

Pershing, John J., F5; in Cuba campaign, 159; friendship with T.R., 31, 366; and Great War, 354; as leader of AEF, 309, 354–55; in Mexican Revolution, 333–34; in Philippines campaign, 159–60; promotion to brigadier general, 161, 304–11; social connections of, 306; T.R.'s praise of, 366

Personnel Act of 1899, 53–54

Pettus, Edmund, 175

Philippines campaign: and Adna R. Chaffee, 200; American atrocities during, 4, 100, 111–15, 265; flare-ups after, 303; gunnery skills during, 131–32; importance of battleships in, 119, 124; and J. Frank Bell, 202, 212; and John J. Pershing, 159–60, 305–7; and Leonard Wood, 265–66; and Nelson Miles, 164; shifting public attitudes toward, 264; T.R.'s inheritance of, 4. *See also* Subic Bay

physical fitness: of military officers, 147–49, 311–16, 368–69; of T.R., 9, 27–29, 74, 103, 120, 145–46, 150, 302, 347

Pillsbury, John E., 325

Platt, Thomas Collier, 96, 128

Platt Amendment (Cuban Constitution), 188, 210

Plattsburg movement, 339–45, 354, 371

the *Plunger* (submarine), F7, 239–42, 246, 372

political patronage, 30, 91, 128, 157, 159, 191–92, 223–25, 229, 275

Poor, Henry Varnum, 395n66

populism, 36

Portsmouth Treaty (1905), 265

Poundstone, Homer, 254

Practical Peace League, 111

press relations. *See* public relations

Proctor, Redfield, 55, 167, 226–27

Progressivism, 8–11, 77, 292, 330, 332, 338–39, 345, 364

promotion reform, 51–55; merit-based, 9, 50–55, 67, 150–57, 160–67, 170–71, 186, 201, 304–5, 308; seniority-based, 51–53, 83, 151–57, 170–71, 198–201, 307. *See also* military promotions

public relations, 62–63, 86, 100–115. *See also* bully pulpit

Puerto Rico, 82, 90–91, 127, 249, 371

Quay, Matthew, 128

racism: and Brownsville affair, 266–76; toward Japanese, 125, 233, 277–78; and lynchings, 267, 268; T.R.'s attitude on, 16, 104, 266–76

Ramsay, Francis, 34

Rathbone, Estes G., 166

Reed, Thomas, 47

the *Relief* (hospital ship), 283

Reserve Officers Training Corps, 371

Reuterdahl, Henry, 281–85, 287–89

Richardson, James, 194

Richthofen, Manfred von, 357

rifles, 99, 162, 182, 185–86, 205–8, 233–36

Riis, Jacob, 62

Rivers, William C., 307

Rixey, John, 225–26

Rixey, Presley M., 283, 314–15

Robinson, Douglas, 68, 81

Rockefeller, John D., 276

Roosevelt, Alice (daughter). *See* Longworth, Alice Roosevelt

Roosevelt, Alice (née Lee) (first wife), 23, 27, 109

Roosevelt, Anna (sister). *See* Cowles, Anna Roosevelt

Roosevelt, Archibald (Archie) (son), 261, 342–44, 354–56, 359–60, 371–72

Roosevelt, Edith (née Carow) (second wife), 37, 66, 69, 233, 305, 347, 362

Roosevelt, Elliott (brother), 20, 38–39, 330

Roosevelt, Ethel (daughter). *See* Derby, Ethel Roosevelt

Roosevelt, Franklin (cousin), 49, 105, 144

Roosevelt, Kermit (son), 104, 216–17, 231, 249, 302, 330, 343–44, 355–59, 367, 371

Roosevelt, Martha (née Bulloch) (mother), 3, 18, 27

Roosevelt, Quentin (son), 66, 69, 247, 343, 355–60

Roosevelt, Theodore, Jr. (Ted) (son), 69, 343–44, 354–56, 359, 371

Roosevelt, Theodore, Sr. (father), 3, 15–18, 117, 366

Roosevelt, Theodore (T.R.), F1, F3, F6, F13, 3, 11; Amazon adventure of, 330–31; as assistant secretary of navy, 4–5, 45–66, 69–70, 73, 78–79; and aviation, 5, 64–65, 233–34, 243–47, 303, 331–34, 369–70; becoming his own man, 21–36; on benefits of war, 2; on civic virtue, 7, 10, 42, 341; and coinage design, 235; Dakota barroom fight of, 120; death of, 363; thoughts on America's future, 39–42; failed third-term bid of, 330; family background of, 7–8, 15–21; father's influence on, 3, 15–18, 117; favoritism, accusations of, 154, 162, 164–72, 306–8; first presidential term, 15; on foreign policy, 99–100; frontier years of, 9, 27–29, 120, 370; as governor of New York, 4, 88–97; health issues of, 20–21, 351, 358; and horseback riding, 101–2; legacy of, 1–13, 301–4, 364–72; on lobbying and influence peddling, 67; on manliness, 3, 30, 41, 76–77, 100, 103, 355; on manly virtue, 9–10, 26–27, 48, 54, 189, 311, 319; Medal of Honor nomination, 86–88, 93; on military command, 75–76; moral code of, 15–16, 48, 71–73, 147, 269, 300, 303, 316, 366, 370; mother's death, 27; mother's influence on, 18–19; and national crises of 1890s, 36–42; National Guard service, 23–26, 67–68, 174, 177; on New York City Police Board, 30–31, 37–38, 50, 95, 102, 115, 203; in New York state legislature, 24–25; and Nobel Peace Prize, 264, 330; personal appeal of, 102; personal finances of, 276; philosophy of government of, 23–24; and physical fitness, 9, 27–29, 74, 103, 120, 145–46, 150, 302, 312–16, 347; popularity of, 38, 88–89, 105, 115, 231–32, 240, 277; post-presidential life of, 330–36; public relations skills of, 62–63, 86, 100–115; and racism, 16, 104, 267; and romantic notion of war, 13, 85, 117, 329; second presidential term, 231–32, 261–66, 300–304; streetcar accident of, 98–99, 176, 181, 232, 331, 358; as war hero, 72, 88–89. *See also* Battle of San Juan Heights; Cuba campaign; Great War; Rough Riders

Roosevelt Board, 50–55

Root, Elihu: on army maneuver exercises, 178–79; background of, 117; and Carnegie Endowment for International Peace, 111; and general staff creation, 163, 190–98, 220, 227; and military reform, 151–53, 158, 160–62, 167–68, 171, 187; and National Guard of New York reform, 95; and National Guard reform, 174–76; and Philippine campaign atrocities, 113–14; as secretary of war, 32, 95, 109–10; as sounding board for T.R., 233

Rough Riders, F3, 1–4; deployment problems of, 80–81; deployment to Puerto Rico (proposed), 90–91; organizing and equipping of, 28–29, 78–79;

popular image of, 12; return to New York, 88–89; senior officers' failings, 82–83; and T.R.'s romantic notion of war, 13, 84, 117; and T.R.'s test of battle, 44. *See also* Battle of San Juan Heights; Cuba campaign of 1898

The Rough Riders (T.R.), 85, 168, 199

Round Robin Letter, 87, 91, 200

Russo-Japanese War, 31, 124–25, 205, 207, 209, 236, 256–57, 264, 325, 331

Sandburg, Carl, 8

Sanger, William Cary, 95–96, 116–18, 174

Sanger Report (militia systems), 96, 174

Santo Domingo (Dominican Republic), 13, 209, 263, 265

Schurz, Carl, 40, 111–12

Scott, Hugh, 353

Scott, Nathan B., 170

Secret Service, 98, 262

selection-out of officers, 52–53, 186

selective service, 349

Selfridge, Thomas, 51, 246

Senate Military Affairs Committee, 155, 163, 165, 168–69, 196, 305, 309

Senate Naval Affairs Committee, 222–25, 227, 279, 285

seniority-based promotions, 51–53, 83, 151–57, 170–71, 198–201, 307

Seventy-First Regiment, NY National Guard, 92–94

Shafter, William, F2, 82–83, 87, 146, 148, 186

Sheridan, Philip, 181

Sherman, Philemon, 68

Sicard, Montgomery, 131

"The Significance of the Frontier in American History" (Turner), 9

Sims, William S., F4, 49, 130–39, 141–43, 248, 254–57, 281–88, 291–92, 314

Smith, Clinton, 92–93

Smith, Jacob, 112–13

smokeless powder, 78, 116, 218

Social Darwinism, 9, 39

South Atlantic Squadron, 127

Spanish-American War: effect on T.R.'s thinking, 66, 75, 85, 89, 97; as launch of T.R.'s political career, 4; National Guard in, 174, 176; preparations for, 56–57; unfit officers in, 148, 151, 186. *See also* Cuba campaign of 1898; Philippines campaign; Rough Riders

Spector, Ronald, 395n66

spelling reform, 9, 105, 109, 235

Sperry, Charles, 325–26

Spooner, John, 195–96

Spring Rice, Cecil Arthur, 42, 46, 111

spurs, redesign of, 117, 236

Standard Oil Company, 250, 262, 275, 281

states' rights, 149

Steffens, Lincoln, 111

Sternberg, Hermann Speck von, 180, 236

Storer, Maria Longworth, 37, 43

Straus, Oscar, 245

Strong, William Lafayette, 37

Subic Bay, 221, 319–23, 370

submarines, F7, 4–5, 233–34, 239–43, 246–47, 260, 303, 347, 367, 369–70, 372

swords, 205–9, 233, 236

the *Sylph* (presidential yacht), 239

Taft, William Howard: on Adna R. Chaffee, 200; and army artillery improvements, 143; and army general staff, 197–98, 204; and Arthur MacArthur, 203; and battleships, 125, 329, 331; and Brownsville affair, 270, 274; and election of 1908, 238, 246, 262, 274–75; and half-brother Charles's run for Senate, 261; and Mexican revolution, 332–33; and Moody plan, 293; at Pershing-Warren wedding, 305; and physical fitness of military officers, 312, 314–15; and T.R., relationship with, 197, 330

Tarbell, Ida, 111

Taylor, Henry C., 124, 127, 134–39, 217–21, 225–29, 395n66, 396n69

technology, military, 63–65, 233–39, 369, 378n62. *See also specific types of technology*

Teller, Henry, 165–66

Tillinghast, C. Whitney, 66–67

Tillman, Benjamin, 233, 261
torpedo boat destroyers, 247, 327
torpedo boats, 60, 64, 69, 119, 125, 139, 251–52
torpedoes, 64, 240, 242–43
Trask, David, 70
trench warfare, 84, 202, 205, 236–37, 347, 354. *See also* entrenching tools
Trevelyan, George, 188, 213, 302, 304
Turk, Richard, 126
Turner, Frederick Jackson, 9
Turner, George Kibbe, 223
Twenty-Fifth U.S. Infantry, 267–76

uniforms, army, redesign of, 116–18, 236
universal military training, 339, 343, 350, 370–71
Upton, Emory, 191
U.S. Army. *See* Army, U.S.
U.S. Marine Corps. *See* Marine Corps, U.S.
U.S. Navy. *See* Navy, U.S.
the *Utah* (battleship), 290

Venezuela, 211–12, 384n54
veterans, Civil War, 52, 85, 106, 151–53, 156–59, 163, 171–72, 186, 234, 310
Villa, Francisco, 333–35
Villard, Oswald Garrison, 167
voluntary military service, 77–78

Wagner, Arthur, 182
War College Board, 199
War of 1812, 19, 21–22, 130. See also *The Naval War of 1812* (T.R.)
Warren, Francis, 298, 305–6
Washington, Booker T., 267
Washington Naval Conference: of 1909, 293; of 1921–22, 365
weapons. *See specific weapons*
Weaver, John, 275
West Indies Squadron, 135
Wheeler, Joseph, 83, 86, 152
White, Henry, 286

White, William, 255
Whitehead, Walter, 249
Whitman, Charles, 353
Wilhelm II (Emperor of Germany), 331, 337
Williams, John Sharp, 266
Wilson, Woodrow: and election of 1912, 330; and Fourteen Points, 360; and Great War, 338, 341–43, 345–46, 348–53, 360–64, 366; and League of Nations, 364–65; and Mexican revolution, 333–36; on sinking of *Lusitania*, 341; T.R.'s criticism and dislike of, 4–5, 20–21, 177, 330, 334–36, 338, 341–42, 345–46, 348, 353, 360–62, 366
Winton, Harold, 256
Wood, Leonard, F13; background of, 74–76; as chief of staff under Wilson, 215; considered for chief of staff, 203; and Cuba campaign, 32, 74–76, 80, 83; and German army maneuvers, 180; as governor of Cuba, 101, 154; and Marine Corps, 298; in Philippines campaign, 265–66; and Plattsburg movement, 339–44; political and social connections of, 74–75; promotion to brigadier general, 152–54; promotion to major general, 159, 164–71, 306; and Spanish-American War, 32, 75–76; and Subic Bay naval base, 319–20; and T.R., relationship with, 32, 74–76, 101–2, 145–47, 164–71, 232
"wooden thinking", 241, 305
world cruise of battle fleet, 277–82, 290, 292, 303, 324–30, 370
World's Columbian Exposition, 36, 64
World War I (Great War), 337–63, 407n4
Wotherspoon, William, 308–10, 331
Wright, Luke, 238, 245
Wright, Orville, F8, 65, 244–47
Wright, Wilbur, 65, 244–47

Young, Samuel B. M., 185, 199–200